Broadsides

Other Books by Nathan Miller

Star-Spangled Men: America's Ten Worst Presidents

War at Sea: A Naval History of World War II

Theodore Roosevelt: A Life

Stealing from America: Corruption in American Politics from Jamestown to Whitewater

The U.S. Navy: A History

Spying for America: The Hidden History of American Intelligence

F. D. R.: An Intimate History

The Naval Air War: 1939–1945

The Roosevelt Chronicles

The U.S. Navy: An Illustrated History

The Founding Finalgers: A History of Corruption in American Politics

Sea of Glory: A Naval History of the American Revolution

The Belarus Secret (with John Loftus)

Broadsides

The Age of Fighting Sail, 1775–1815

NATHAN MILLER

John Wiley & Sons, Inc.

New York • Chichester • Weinheim • Brisbane • Singapore • Toronto

Published by John Wiley & Sons, Inc.
Published simultaneously in Canada

This publication is designed to provide accurate and authoritative information in regard to the subject matter covered. It is sold with the understanding that the publisher is not engaged in rendering professional services. If professional advice or other expert assistance is required, the services of a competent professional person should be sought.

Library of Congress Cataloging-in-Publication Data:
Miller, Nathan
 Broadsides : the age of fighting sail, 1775–1815 / Nathan Miller.
  p. cm.
 Includes bibliographical references and index.
 ISBN 0-471-07835-2 (paper)
 1. Naval history, Modern—18th century.   2. Naval history, Modern—19th century.
 I. Title.
 D215.M55 2000
 359'.009'033—dc21   99-052346

Printed in the United States of America

10 9 8 7 6 5 4 3 2

To
Cassie and Pat Furgurson
For Reasons
Known to Us All

He that commands the sea is
at great liberty, and may take as much
and as little of the war as he will.

Francis Bacon

Contents

Preface   xi

Prologue   1

Chapter 1
"Attack, Take, or Destroy"   11

Chapter 2
Uncombined Operations   23

Chapter 3
Revolution Becomes World War   37

Chapter 4
Sea Fights—Classic Style   53

Chapter 5
"The World . . . Turned Upside Down"   69

Chapter 6
Sea Fight—New Style   87

Chapter 7
"Heart of Oak"   99

Chapter 8
"To Glory We Steer"   111

Chapter 9
"Engage the Enemy Closer"   123

Chapter 10
"Nelson's Patent Bridge"   139

Chapter 11
"A Breeze at Spithead"   161

Chapter 12
Proud New Frigates 181

Chapter 13
"A Band of Brothers" 195

Chapter 14
"Naples Is a Dangerous Place" 211

Chapter 15
Of Nelson and the North 221

Chapter 16
"To the Shores of Tripoli" 239

Chapter 17
". . . He Will Not Come by Water" 259

Chapter 18
The Long Watch 273

Chapter 19
"England Expects . . ." 289

Chapter 20
". . . The Beautiful Precision of Our Fire" 301

Chapter 21
Free Trade and Sailors' Rights 329

Chapter 22
Tattered Ensigns 345

Epilogue 359

Appendix I
The Composition of the Royal Navy, 1793–1816 363

Appendix II
Nelson's Trafalgar Memorandum 364

Maps 367

Bibliography 371

Index 381

Preface

FEW ERAS OF the past hold more fascination for us than the Age of Fighting Sail, as is clear from the popularity of the novels of Patrick O'Brian, C. S. Forester, and Alexander Kent, among others. Yet, in spite of popular interest in the long-vanished world of wooden men-of-war and pigtailed sailors, there is no readily available history of this period for a general audience. Ever since I began reading the Hornblower novels more than a half century ago, I have looked for such an account without success. I hope this book will fill that gap. It is intended to provide the historical background to the fictional works that have such a devoted readership.

This is a work of imagination and history—with the imagination limited by history. Fortunately, despite the hazards of time there is no shortage of documentation about the era. Logbooks, official reports, letters, and memoirs have been preserved—and they have served as the foundation of my book. Inasmuch as this book is intended for the general reader, I have not weighted it with an array of footnotes. But he or she is assured that each quotation or statement of fact is based on documentary evidence. I take full responsibility for the interpretations drawn from them.

My designation of the Age of Fighting Sail as the years between 1775 and 1815 is arbitrary. Usually it is given to the period beginning with the Anglo-Dutch Wars in 1650, when sea power became a dominant factor in geopolitics, and ending with the fall of Napoleon in 1815. But I have limited the period covered here to the final forty years, which most fascinate modern readers—the naval side of the American Revolution; the twenty-two-year struggle between Britain and Revolutionary and then Napoleonic France, which began in 1793; the organization of the U.S. Navy in 1797; the forgotten undeclared naval war between the United States and France; the American struggle against the Barbary pirates; and finally the useless War of 1812 between the British and the United States. One man, Horatio Nelson, epitomizes this era, and I have used his life as a framework for the narrative but have continued it on for the decade following his death at Trafalgar in 1805.

This book is not a mere account of disconnected battles or campaigns, however. I have tried to place the battles within the strategic, political, and social contexts of the time. The question might well be asked whether the era of sailing ships and muzzle-loading guns has anything to teach us in the age of the nuclear submarine and the cruise missile. The answer is yes. Tenacity, steadfastness, and resolution in adversity—qualities that were valuable for a nation two centuries ago—are just as important at the start of a new century. No ship sails alone. There is a unity between the past and the vessels of the present and future—and the men and women who sail in them.

As in all my naval books, full attention has been given to ordinary seamen who served in these ships and fought the battles. For the most part, they did not keep journals or write memoirs, and this book is intended to help keep their memory alive. Although they endured conditions that are savage by today's standards, the sailors of the Age of Fighting Sail—French, British, Dutch, Portuguese, Danish, Spanish, Russian, Swedish, and American—usually went willingly into battle, shouting defiance and proud of their moment of glory.

It only remains for me to express my gratitude to those who helped in the preparation of this book: Hana Umlauf Lane, my editor, who patiently waited for the completion of a long-delayed manuscript, and her assistant, Michael Thompson; David Black, my agent, who was generous with his time and efforts; Dr. Kenneth Hagan, professor of history and museum director emeritus at the U.S. Naval Academy, who read the manuscript and suggested numerous changes that improved it; Sigrid Trumpy, curator of the Beverley R. Robinson Collection at the Naval Academy, and her assistant, Laura Hubicsak; James W. Cheevers, curator of the Naval Academy Museum; and the staffs of the Nimitz Library at the Naval Academy and the National Archives in Washington.

And above all to my wife, Jeanette, who stood with me during a trying period in our lives.

Prologue

FRESH GALES BRINGING squally weather and snow blustered up the River Medway in March 1771, and even in these sheltered waters the ships lying offshore swung uneasily at their anchors. Huddled against the chill wind, a small boy in the uniform of a Royal Navy midshipman trudged along the streets of Chatham. Tavern signs creaked overhead, and the slick cobblestones shone like metal. Uncertainty gnawed at the lad's spirit. He had arrived earlier in the day by coach from London, but there had been no one to meet him. Anxiously, he inquired about the location of *Raisonnable*, a sixty-four-gun man-of-war, which he was to join as his first ship, but no one knew where she lay.

Eventually he found a sailor who did. The seaman pointed out into the river, where *Raisonnable* rode to anchor in the choppy swell along with several other ships that were being recommissioned in the wake of a war scare with Spain over the Falkland Islands. But there was no boat to take the boy to the ship, and she was too far out in the stream for him to attract the attention of anyone on board. A passing naval officer noticed the forlorn child. Upon hearing his tale, he took him home for tea and arranged for a boat to carry him out to *Raisonnable*. The officer forgot the boy's name but years later had good reason to recall it: Horatio Nelson.

The twelve-year-old Nelson was the fifth son of a widowed Church of England parson who had eight children and limited financial means but good family connections. With so many mouths to feed, opportunities had to be provided for some of the children. Horace, as he was known to his family, made his own choice of career. Captain Maurice Suckling, his maternal uncle, was a welcome visitor to the parsonage at Burnham Thorpe in Norfolk, and his tales of savage sea fights in the various wars against the French fired the boy's imagination. Born not far from the North Sea, he lived amid men who spoke of ships and their qualities as men elsewhere gossiped of horses, and even though small and delicate for his age, he chose a career in the Royal Navy.

Reading in a newspaper that Captain Suckling had been appointed to

1

the command of *Raisonnable,* the boy urged his father to write him of his wish to go to sea as a midshipman. Captains were allowed to choose the "young gentlemen" serving in their ships, and these appointments were doled out as a form of patronage—or "interest," as it was known—to oblige a relative or friend, win the support of an influential family, or settle a tradesman's debt. Some were designated midshipmen. Others awaiting an opening as midshipman were designated as captain's servants or able seamen, but all were aspiring officers.

"What has poor Horace done, who is so weak, that he, above all the rest, should be sent to rough it out at sea?" Suckling wryly asked. "But let him come and the first time we go into action a cannon-ball may knock off his head and provide for him at once." Young Nelson's name was entered on *Raisonnable's* muster book as of January 1, 1771, so his seniority would date from that time. But with the ship still in the preliminary stages of fitting out, there was no immediate need for his presence, so Suckling suggested he appear when she was more habitable.

As the boat approached *Raisonnable,* Nelson sat in the stern sheets, examining her closely. The wooden man-of-war of the Age of Fighting Sail was a thing of malevolent beauty. Timber, cordage, and canvas were combined into a majestic and technologically complex instrument—the largest and most intricate movable object of the day. Two rows of cannons poked from the vessel's high buff sides like stubby black fingers, her three masts reached heavenward, and her rigging was a maze of spars and ropes engraved against a lowering, slate-gray sky. A hail from the deck broke the boy's reverie, and the steerman replied "Aye aye"—which meant the boat carried an officer, but of low rank.

The craft bumped to a stop against *Raisonnable's* starboard side with a hollow thud, and a waterman caught the main chains with a hook, holding it steady alongside. Hand over hand, young Nelson clambered uncertainly up a ladder of battens nailed to the vessel's high, inwardly curving side to the deck just abaft—to the rear—of the mainmast. His chest was hoisted up behind him and unceremoniously dumped there. Nelson's mounting sense of dread was confirmed when he was told that Captain Suckling was ashore and it was uncertain when he would return. No one expected the new midshipman or seemed to care about him.

Raisonnable's decks were a bedlam as seamen passed casks of salt beef and pork, cheese, ship's biscuit, beer and rum, cannon shot, and powder into the hold from boats alongside amid the shouted commands of the officers and knotted ropes' ends wielded by the boatswain's mates. Yards and fresh sails were being sent aloft. Tar-stained riggers and ropemakers moved briskly about. Nelson waited miserably for someone to tell him what to do or where to go. Eventually an officer ordered a sailor to take him and his dunnage to the cockpit, or midshipmen's berth.

The boy followed his guide down three decks to the orlop, below the waterline. There were fewer than five feet of headroom, and even a lad as slight as he had to be careful to keep from hitting his head on one of the thick wooden knees that supported the overhead deck. Shipbuilders compressed the decks of a man-of-war to lower the center of gravity so the heavy weight of the upper gun decks would not overturn the vessel in a heavy sea. The only light came from a few candles that sputtered in the fetid air, and the smells that assailed Nelson's nostrils were as strange as the noises that assailed his ears. *Raisonnable* reeked of bilgewater, unwashed bodies, and long-dead rats. Someone introduced him to his fellows, gave him a hammock, and showed him how to sling it from ring bolts in the overhead.

Following Captain Suckling's return—amid salutes and the squealing of boatswains' pipes—Nelson was undoubtedly invited to his cabin for a brief welcome and an explanation of the complexities of a naval career. In his blue, gold-trimmed uniform, Suckling was more imposing than the avuncular figure the boy had known at Burnham Thorpe. At sea, he was told, he would be instructed every morning in navigation, nautical astronomy, and trigonometry. He would be required to take the sun at noon every day with his quadrant, and would not be allowed to eat until he had worked out the ship's position.

When school hours were over, midshipmen were assigned to one of the watches. They commanded small boats and went aloft with the topsmen to learn how to set, reef, and furl a sail. Midshipmen mustered the men at night and commanded watering parties ashore. Above all, they were at the beck and call of the captain and the lieutenants. If a midshipmen misbehaved, he would be sent to the masthead, to remain there without food or drink to repent of his sins. Sometimes he would be unceremoniously bent over a gun—the "gunner's daughter"—and whipped on his buttocks.

To be "made" or commissioned a lieutenant, a midshipman had to be recommended by his captain and survive a verbal examination by a board of three captains. He had to have attained the age of twenty and had six years of sea service, although the age requirement was often ignored. The next step—promotion to captain—depended, however, on "interest" or having performed some deed that brought an officer to the attention of his superiors rather than energy and competence. Lieutenants who were promoted to sloops of war—under twenty guns—were named master and commander. In 1794 the rank was simplified to commander.

Once having been designated a post captain, an officer could count on hoisting his flag as an admiral if he lived long enough and avoided serious mishaps.* Only rarely did a man rise to captain from the ranks. The great explorer James Cook, who had held a warrant as master, or navigator, was one of the exceptions. On the other hand, luckless junior officers lacking "interest" lived in terror of being unable to obtain billets, with only their totally inadequate half pay to fall back on. For midshipmen there was not even the solace of half pay. Nevertheless, the Royal Navy was a meritocracy compared to the army. Naval officers had to prove their competency, there was no purchase of commissions, and there were few aristocrats. Most officers were either the sons of naval officers or middle-class professionals—lawyers, doctors, or Anglican parsons—like young Nelson. For now his task was to obey orders and learn the art of seamanship.

Nelson was a bright and curious lad, and he tried to make sense of the strange new wooden world in which he would spend the remainder of his life—and where he was to win undying renown. *Raisonnable,* herself, had been captured from the French in 1758, the year of his birth. French warship design and construction were substantially superior to British vessels—which, it was said, were built by the mile and hacked off to fit the need—and she was taken into the Royal Navy as a third-rate ship of the line.

Beginning in the 1750s, warships were classified, or rated, by the number of guns they carried. Sea battles were fought by opposing lines of warships sailing parallel to each other, and those powerful enough to take their place in the battle line were designated ships of the line. A first-rate ship of the line, such as *Victory,* Nelson's flagship at Trafalgar, carried a hundred or more guns on three decks; a second-rate, ninety to ninety-eight; a third rate sixty-four to eighty on two gun decks; and a fourth-rate, fifty. Fifth and sixth rates, or frigates, carried from twenty to forty-four guns on a single gun deck, and as scouting vessels—the "eyes of the fleet"—had no place in the fighting line. There were also numerous unrated vessels—sloops, schooners, cutters, and bomb ketches—that mounted a variety of small guns.

Ships' cannons were cast-iron, smoothbore muzzleloaders and were classified by the weight of the solid round shot they fired. The most com-

*For purposes of organization, the Royal Navy was divided into three divisions: the Red, White, and Blue squadrons. Flag officers—admirals, vice admirals, and rear admirals—were ranked in order of seniority in these squadrons. A captain newly promoted to flag rank would be a rear admiral of the Blue. Then he would become a rear admiral of the White and finally a rear admiral of the Red. His next promotion would be to vice admiral of the Blue, and so on. Until 1805, there was no admiral of the Red: the admiral of the fleet took its place. A captain promoted to rear admiral without a command was said to be assigned to the "Yellow Squadron" and was known as a "yellow admiral."

mon were nine-, twelve-, and eighteen-pounders, with twenty-four and thirty-two-pounders being carried by the largest vessels. Solid shot was used to smash an enemy's hull or bring down his masts; grapeshot, or masses of musket balls, was intended for use against boarding parties, and chain and double-ended bar shot were fired to rip up an enemy's sails and rigging. The guns were mounted on four-wheeled wooden carriages, or trucks, and were secured against the rolling and pitching of the ship, or recoil when in action, by heavy breeching ropes.

With her sixty-four guns, *Raisonnable* was small in comparison to other ships of the line. Approximately 160 feet in length and about 45 feet in beam, she was about twice as long as a standard lawn tennis court but only a few feet wider. Some five hundred officers and men were cooped up in this space, cheek by jowl, for months on end. *Victory*, in contrast, was 226 feet from figurehead to sternpost and 51 feet in beam. The side planking of a sixty-four was at least 6 inches thick, impervious to musket balls but not against heavy shot, which could smash through her sides, scattering huge splinters that were as deadly as shot itself.

Nelson was soon skylarking in the rigging with the other midshipmen. He learned the names of the sails and the various parts of the heavily tarred standing rigging that supported the masts, and about the halyards, lifts, sheets, and braces used to manage the yards and sails. *Raisonnable* was ship-rigged, meaning that she was fitted with three masts—fore, main, and mizzen—of Baltic or North American fir. A mast had three overlapping sections: the mast itself, the topmast, and the topgallant mast. At the head of the lower mast was a platform known as a top; at the head of the topmast were the crosstrees. Both served as bases for the men working aloft and as posts for lookouts. In battle, marines manned the tops and tried to pick off the enemy crew on the deck below. Nelson, himself, fell victim to such a sharpshooter at the moment of his greatest triumph.

Courses, topsails, and topgallants were spread on yards on the foremast and mainmast, while there was only a topsail and topgallant on the mizzenmast, along with the driver or spanker, a large, gaff-rigged fore-and-aft sail. To make and reef sail, topmen, the younger and most agile sailors, swarmed up the shrouds, or rope ladders on the sides of the masts, to the tops, sometimes more than two hundred feet above the deck. From there they edged out onto the swaying yardarms, with their only support the footropes hanging below the yard.

Laying across the yard, topmen used one hand to claw at the lines holding the sail furled to the spar, or fighting the salt-stiffened canvas while hanging on with the other. Each roll of the ship whirled them about in a dizzying circle—up, forward, sideways, down—and then around again. If a man lost his grip, he fell to almost certain death. Topmen worked with the captain's eye on them, because a ship's smartness was judged by how quickly sail was set or taken in. Some captains had the last man off the yards flogged to emphasize the need for speed.

The more experienced sailors were stationed on the forecastle to work the anchors and foresails, the triangular-shaped jib and staysails set on the jibboom and bowsprit, which jutted out from the bow at about a thirty-degree angle. Additional fore-and-aft sails known as staysails were set between the masts. If more sail was needed, royals were set atop the masts, and studding sails were set on extensions to the topsail and topgallant yards. The afterguard handled the halyards, sheets, and braces, pulling the big square sails around to either fill or spill the wind so the topmen could furl them. The waisters—the inexperienced landsmen and less bright sailors—performed similar duties amidships or worked as pumpers and sewermen, scavengers, and pigsty keepers. With all sail set, a sixty-four-gun ship spread several acres of canvas, and under the best conditions of wind and sea, might make seven knots.

Nelson learned that the raised area at the vessel's stern was called the poop and the area just forward of it was the quarterdeck, the ship's command center. Ranged on both sides of the poop and the quarterdeck were the after guns, usually nine-pounders on a sixty-four, six to a side, snugged down in their breechings with wooden tompions in their mouths to keep out seawater. The large double steering wheel and binnacle, the housing of the compass, lay slightly forward of the mizzenmast. Rope nettings ran along the top of the bulwarks, or rail, where the crew's rolled-up hammocks were stowed when not in use. In battle they provided protection against small-arms fire and splinters.

The ship's waist, which lay just forward of the quarterdeck, was undecked, and ladders led down into the interior of the vessel. Spare booms and spars were lashed in place between the mainmast and the foremast, resting amidships on crossbeams. The ship's boats—the longboat, the launch, the cutter, and the captain's gig—rested atop the spars, with their sails and oars stowed inside. The decks flanking the open space on both sides were called gangways and connected the quarterdeck and the forecastle, the area from the foremast to the bow.

A few guns, including a pair of twelve-pounders sighted to fire directly ahead, called bow chasers and used when pursuing enemy vessels, were mounted on the forecastle. There was also a carved wooden belfry, from which the ship's bell hung. The iron galley funnel, the chimney of the ship's stove, which was on the deck below, thrusted upward through the forecastle deck.

The captain's quarters were in the afterpart of the ship under the poop and led out to the quarterdeck. A red-jacketed marine sentry with a drawn sword was permanently posted at the entry. A captain enjoyed a great cabin that extended across the stern of the ship and which led out onto a balconylike open gallery, a sleeping cabin, and a day cabin or office. These quarters usually contained a settee built in under the stern windows, a large fixed table, some heavy chairs, a shelf of books, a swinging cot, a washstand, and a pair of guns. The deck was covered with checkered canvas. One of the quarter galleries—the glassed-in balconies that protruded from the sides of the stern—served as the captain's private lavatory.

When a captain appeared on the quarterdeck, the windward side was instantly cleared for his solitary promenade. No one dared speak to him— except on a matter pertaining to the operation of the ship—without being spoken to first and never without removing his hat. One uncovered to one's captain as to one's God. Few men had as much power over their subordinates as the captain of a man-of-war in the Age of Fighting Sail. He could have a man flogged senseless, make and break officers, and order the ship's company into harm's way.

Sixty-four-gun ships usually had three or four lieutenants and two marine officers plus several midshipmen. The first lieutenant, the most senior of these officers, commanded in the absence of the captain, and was responsible for the day-to-day operation of the ship. He stood no watches but was on call during the night. Junior lieutenants stood watches and made certain that the ship's business was smartly carried on. In action, lieutenants and senior midshipmen commanded batteries of guns.

Once or twice a week, the captain might ask some of the officers to dine with him. One of the "young gentlemen" might also be invited, to expose him to the company of his betters. Such dinners were formal affairs, but even though the food was prepared with more style, it was similar to that in the rest of the ship, especially after the private stock of luxuries laid in by the captain for his own use had been consumed.

Raisonnable's upper gun deck, the next down, was unobstructed from end to end except for the masts and a pair of capstans used in raising the anchors. The sides were painted red to lessen the shock of the sight of blood, which was often liberally splattered around when the ship was in action. Twenty-six eighteen-pounders, thirteen to each side, were mounted on this deck, and an equal number of twenty-four-pounders on the gun deck below. In contrast, the standard field piece of the land armies of the time was a horse-drawn six-pound gun, and owing to the difficulties of transport, even these were few. Thus a single sixty-four had far more firepower than all but the largest armies—and under favorable sailing conditions could cover nearly two hundred miles in a single day, in contrast to the few miles traveled by troops on the march.

The officers were quartered aft on the upper gun deck in closet-size cabins that lined the sides of the ship. Like the captain, they had a quarter gallery for sanitary purposes. They took their meals in a partitioned-off space between cabins called the wardroom, which was sparely furnished with a long table and a few chairs. All partitions were light and removable, and when the ship was cleared for action, the cabins and their few furnishings were unceremoniously cast below, into the hold. The master, the surgeon, and the chaplain, if any, had use of the wardroom, although they were warrant, not commissioned officers. Up in the bow, forward of the galley stove, was a manger for pigs, poultry, goats, and sheep purchased by the officers for their own use.

Cabins for the warrant officers, the master, boatswain, gunner, captain's clerk, and carpenter were one deck down, in the stern of the lower gun deck, in an area called the gun room. Forward of these cabins, the men slung their hammocks fore and aft from hooks in the overhead beams in a continuous carpet of bodies. The regulation distance between hammocks was fourteen inches, but this sounds worse than it was in practice because half the crew was on watch at any given time. This was a two-edged sword, however. In a watch-and-watch system, a sailor could never count on more than four hours of uninterrupted sleep. And he never knew when he might be jolted awake by a drummer calling him to fight or for another drill.

Sailors seldom bathed, and they slept in their clothes. With the ports closed because of a high sea and 250 dirty and wet men of the watch below crowded together in the darkness, the lower deck was a damp and noisome place. To relieve themselves, the men went up to the bow, where there were several seats under the figurehead with wooden pipes to carry the waste into the sea. In bad weather they could not always be used, and in a rough sea the lower deck was described as "no better than a cesspool."

The orlop, the next deck down, housed the midshipmen's berth and the surgeon's cabin and dispensary; the storerooms of the boatswain, the gunner, and the carpenter; and racks for the seabags of the men. The sail locker, with its extra suits of sails, was amidships. Up forward were the cable tiers, where the anchor cables were stowed after being hoisted in. The hold, the lowest level of the vessel, housed the fore and after magazines, where the ship's powder was stored. These were sealed-off, copper-lined compartments, with no surface contact with the ship's sides or bottom to avoid water seepage. No one was allowed to enter a magazine without putting on thick felt slippers to prevent striking a chance spark that could destroy the vessel. Casks of provisions and water sufficient for six months were stowed between magazines. Regulations required that older provisions be stowed on top so they could be eaten first.

Young Horatio Nelson saw no action in *Raisonnable* because the Falklands affair was settled by diplomacy. But Captain Suckling, who later served in the prestigious post of comptroller of the Navy Board, kept a benign eye out for the interests of his nephew. Over the next few years and in a variety of ships and climates, the youth absorbed the rudiments of his profession and made his way in it. He served in the Caribbean and in an Arctic expedition in which his ship was frozen in the ice. He survived an attack by a polar bear by clubbing the snarling beast about the head with a musket butt. During extended service in the East Indies he came under fire for the first time when his ship captured an armed vessel belonging to Hyder Ali, the ruler of Mysore, who was in revolt against the British East India Company. Nelson also came down with malaria and nearly died.

When appointments were scarce in the peacetime navy, he went to sea in a merchantman, a period in which he saw at firsthand the resentment merchant seamen felt toward the Royal Navy and gained a respect for them unique among naval officers. He met men who had been pressed into service and still feared the very sight of a naval officer's uniform. "I returned a practical seaman, with a horror of the Royal Navy," Nelson wrote, "and with a saying constant with the seamen, 'Aft the most honour, forward the better man.'"

Soon after the beginning of the American War of Independence, the nineteen-year-old Nelson was promoted to lieutenant in a frigate. With a wide variety of experience at sea and ashore, he was now ready for whatever fortune might offer.

CHAPTER 1

"Attack, Take, or Destroy"

BLASTED DOWN BY the hammer of the sea, the handful of ships buried themselves to their hawseholes in the long Atlantic swells, only to rise again, white foam exploding over their bows. Under the stress of wind and waves, they creaked, groaned, and heaved like living things. The day before, February 18, 1776, the Continental Navy's first fleet had slipped past the loose British blockade of the Delaware capes to the open sea. Heavy weather had struck the ships almost immediately, and black squalls swept across their decks. With the coming of daylight, the swaths of rain parted long enough for Commodore Esek Hopkins to discover that two of his ships, the sloop *Hornet* and the schooner *Fly*, had drifted off during the night. He ordered lookouts to the mastheads of his six remaining vessels with the hope of sighting the stragglers.

Now, even though the sea had moderated, the pitching horizon was empty except for a ragged edge of steely gray clouds. Hopkins studied the logboard of his flagship, a bluff-bowed ex-merchantmen named *Alfred*, now rated as a frigate and armed with thirty guns. He made a rough calculation, and once it was completed, signaled his remaining ships to proceed to a previously arranged rendezvous off Grand Abaco Island in the Bahamas to await the missing craft.

Ten months had passed since the news of the fighting at Lexington and Concord raced through the American colonies like fire in a ship's rigging. The rebellious colonists had immediately organized an army to besiege the British army in Boston, with George Washington named as its chief. But more time was needed to get a makeshift navy to sea because the insurgents were reluctant to challenge the might of the Royal Navy. Hopkins, a fifty-seven-year-old Rhode Island merchant skipper and onetime privateersman, was chosen by the Continental Congress to command its first fleet more as a tribute to the political influence of his elder brother, Stephen Hopkins, a member of the body, than to his fighting skills. Events were to

11

prove that he lacked the strategic sense and qualities of leadership for a naval commander.

In addition to *Alfred*, Hopkins' ships consisted of *Columbus*, also rated as a frigate and armed with twenty-eight guns; the brigantines *Andrew Doria*, sixteen, and *Cabot*, fourteen; the sloop *Providence*, twelve; and the schooner *Wasp*, eight. A new flag that combined the British Union Jack with alternating red and white stripes flew over them—the emblem of the United Colonies—but the ships looked like the stolid merchantmen they had been until transformed into a semblance of men-of-war.

Hopkins had been instructed to take his ships to Chesapeake Bay, where he was to "attack, take, or destroy" a small armada amassed by Lord Dunmore, the deposed royal governor of Virginia, that was harassing the area. If adverse weather conditions prevented this mission from being carried out, the commodore was to use his own discretion. Having received word that the British had stockpiled a large amount of gunpowder and arms at New Providence (now Nassau) in the Bahamas, Hopkins targeted that island rather than the Chesapeake, without informing Congress of his decision.

While lying in the lee of Grand Abaco, vainly awaiting the missing *Fly*, of eight guns, and *Hornet*, ten, Hopkins learned that New Providence was heavily fortified, so he decided to capture it by surprise.* Two Bahama sloops were seized, crammed with marines and sailors and sent into the harbor while the remainder of the ships were to keep below the horizon until the initial advantage had been gained. But the plan miscarried because the Americans showed their hand too soon. Instead of keeping out of sight, the fleet went bowling along in the wake of the sloops. Suddenly a puff of smoke blossomed from a fort. This was followed by the thud of a heavy gun and the nearby splash of a round shot.

Surprise lost, Hopkins diverted his ships to the opposite side of the island. Under cover of the guns of *Wasp* and *Providence*, about two hundred marines and fifty sailors landed on an empty beach on March 3, 1776, for the first amphibious landing ever made by American forces. Marching overland, they took the defenders from the rear and compelled their surrender after a parley. Eighty-eight cannons, fifteen mortars, and other military equipment sorely needed by Washington's army were captured, but there was little gunpowder. The island's governor, forewarned by Hopkins' blundering approach and failure to blockade Nassau, had managed to spirit most of it away. Nevertheless, the booty was so great that it took two weeks to load it on the American ships, and the raid was the Continental Navy's most successful operation.

Fly rejoined the fleet at New Providence, while *Hornet* made her way back to Delaware Bay after being severely knocked about by the storm.

As the heavily laden vessels wallowed homeward, smallpox and fever raced from ship to ship, devastating their crews. With the epidemic unchecked, the daily routine of seakeeping was broken by the grim business of burials at sea. Two small British ships were taken, however. *Wasp,* whose crew was badly ravaged by sickness, disappeared during a three-day blow and made her way back to Philadelphia only with difficulty.

Early on the morning of April 6, 1776, the remaining ships encountered the twenty-gun British frigate *Glasgow* off Block Island. The Yankee vessels cleared for action as they gave chase. Guns were cast loose, loaded, and run out. Additional powder and shot were brought up from below. Matches were lit. Sand was spread on the decks to keep them from becoming slippery with blood, and galley fires were doused. The courses were brailed up to keep them from catching fire from a chance spark. The men cast off all their clothing except their trousers to keep any wounds clean. They worked with zeal, and Hopkins undoubtedly hoped that the few weeks of training they had undergone would have some effect.

Glasgow should have been easy prey, but she escaped after badly cutting up her opponents in a four-hour melee and chase. Hopkins did not issue a single order except to recall his ships at the end of the affair. "Away we went Helter, Skelter, one flying here, another there," observed Nicholas Biddle, the disgusted captain of the *Andrew Doria* and a onetime midshipman in the Royal Navy. Although the depletion of the American crews by sickness and their inexperience in battle were extenuating factors, this inept action made all too clear that patriotism was not enough to create a navy. Experience, training, and a tradition of victory were all required.

GEORGE WASHINGTON put it best: "Whatever efforts are made by the land armies, the navy must have the casting vote in the present contest," he declared. These remarks were made following the timely arrival of a French fleet off the Chesapeake Capes that sealed the fate of the British army at Yorktown in 1781, a combined operation long sought by Washington. But he understood from the very beginning that the American War of Independence would be a maritime war. Both the Americans and the British relied on supplies shipped from across the oceans to support their armies in the field, and command of the sea was a determining factor in the outcome of the struggle.

The failure of the Royal Navy to stem the flow of arms from France, Spain, and Holland and their Caribbean colonies to the Americans was fatal to Britain's efforts to suppress the rebellion. Without these weapons, the American cause would have foundered early on. Ninety percent of the gunpowder available to the colonists before the end of 1777—about 1.5 million pounds—was brought in by sea. On the other side, the British army was dependent on supplies of food, fuel, and forage from Canada and the West Indies or from Britain. Enjoying undisputed control of American waters and their approaches, the Royal Navy should have had no difficulty in snuffing out the rebellion by choking off the flow of munitions to the rebels from abroad and supporting the army's efforts to pacify the country.

But the navy failed to halt the arms trade because of political partisanship, muddled planning, a shortage of ships and crews, indecision at times of crisis, and the courage and skill of Yankee seamen. Britain never used her naval superiority intelligently. The mobility provided by sea power was often dissipated in raids and diversonary attacks. The army was committed in "penny packets," and little use was made of the fleet to effect surprise. These lapses provided Britain's old enemies France and Spain with the opportunity to humble her. "The opening conflict between Great Britain and the North American Colonies teaches clearly the necessity, too little recognized in practice, that when a State has decided to use force, the force provided should be adequate from the first," wrote Admiral Alfred Thayer Mahan, the philosopher of sea power.

Obtaining adequate men was a problem throughout the Age of Fighting Sail because warships needed large crews to man their guns and to serve as prize crews in captured vessels. Although dashing frigate captains who had won vast amounts of prize money could always attract crews by sending a recruiting party drumming through the port towns, most captains found it difficult to obtain men. Life in the Royal Navy was harsh and dangerous, and the pay was inadequate and sometimes years in arrears. "No man will be a sailor who has contrivance enough to get himself into jail . . ." observed Dr. Samuel Johnson. "A man in jail has more room, better food, and commonly better company."

To make up for the shortage of recruits, the Impress Service and individual ships sent out armed men to sweep the streets and back alleys and to board fishing and merchant vessels as they entered harbor. Legally, only seamen could be pressed, but any likely looking fellow might to be kidnapped and deposited on a man-of-war's deck, especially during a "hot press" or emergency. The pressed men deserted in droves, despite severe penalties if caught, leading to even greater brutality to stem the hemorrhage of manpower. Ship's logs of the day repeat a refrain of "swam away 4 men" or "5 sailors ran off with the whaleboat."

But as N. A. M. Rodger points out in *The Wooden World*, life at sea, while no bed of roses, was no more harsh than on land. And the lot of the merchant seaman, who worked for shipowners trying to trim costs, was sometimes worse than that of his counterpart in the navy. The conventional view presented in films and novels is that the wooden fighting ship was a living hell in which crews were the refuse of society and terrorized by cruel officers, cowed by the lash, and solaced only by rum. If so, how did the Royal Navy and the U.S. Navy achieve brilliant fighting records and reputations for efficiency? In truth, brutal captains were the exception, and the cadres of the lower deck of both services were professional seamen whose job required fitness and sobriety.

BRITISH NAVAL OPERATIONS were controlled from the Admiralty in Whitehall, a building whose main distinction was a screen wall designed by Robert Adam to protect it from rioters. The nerve center was the gracefully proportioned Board Room on the second floor where John Montagu, fourth earl of Sandwich, presided for most of the Revolution as first lord of the Admiralty, the navy's civilian head. The lords commissioners of the Admiralty, or the Admiralty Board, was composed of civilians and naval officers, and met each weekday at noon. With a secretary, a deputy, and a handful of clerks, their lordships conducted the bulk of the navy's administrative business. They ordered fleets to assemble or to sail, assigned officers to their duties, and told the dockyards which ships to repair. Independent agencies—the Navy Board, the Victualing Board, and the Sick and Hurt Board, among others—handled specific parts of the navy's administration and sometimes were at odds with the Admiralty Board and with each other.

Few historical figures have had a worse press than Sandwich. Along with Lord George Germain, the secretary of state for the American Department who conducted the land war, he stands accused of sloth and corruption that eventually caused the loss of the colonies. In reality, judged by the standards of his own day, Sandwich was an efficient administrator. Recent research has disposed of the legend that his regime at the Admiralty was a carnival of corruption and incompetence. He had been first lord twice before being appointed to the post in 1771, and few men knew more about the navy's administrative side. Sandwich could take credit for dispatching James Cook on his second and third voyages of discovery—Cook named what are now the Hawaiian Islands the Sandwich Islands in his honor—and Sandwich promised immediate answer to communications limited to a single sheet of paper.

Sandwich was very much an eighteenth-century man. An inveterate gambler, he is credited with inventing the sandwich so he could spend more time at the gaming table. He also kept his mistress, by whom he had several illegitimate children, at the Admiralty, and was a member of the

Hellfire Club, whose members were said to dress as monks and take part in bizarre religious and sexual rites with prostitutes. Yet Sandwich was not without humor. Answering a letter from a critic, he replied: "Sir, your letter is now before me, and will presently be behind." Much of the blame for the shortcomings of the Royal Navy attached to his name really belongs to the prime minister, Lord North. Even as France was rebuilding its armed forces, North believed a strong navy was an unnecessary luxury, and low taxes ensured his hold on power.

⌒

BRITISH POLICY IN North America in the dozen years between Britain's victory over France in 1763 and the outbreak of the Revolution in 1775 led the colonists to wage war against Britain at sea as well as on land. Financially exhausted by the conflict, successive ministries hoped to ease monetary burden by collecting taxes and duties long ignored in the American colonies. The Royal Navy was ordered to collect these levies, and the aggressive measures adopted by the navy to put an end to smuggling, combined with the widespread use of impressment to man its always shorthanded vessels, turned the service from a welcome symbol of imperial defense into a hated symbol of oppression.

New England was at the storm center of the colonists' struggle because Britain's restrictive policies threatened the region's substantial commercial and maritime interests. Yankees became sailors, fishermen, whalers, and slavers because the thin, boulder-strewn soil of the northern colonies was inhospitable to farming. Soon their vessels dominated the coastal trade that, in the absence of good roads, was the natural link among the colonies. Enjoying the protection of the British flag, they also had a brisk commerce with the sugar islands of the Caribbean, the African slave coast, and the Mediterranean. "No sea is but vexed with their fisheries," observed the English statesman Edmund Burke. "No climate but what is witness to their toils."

This maritime tradition was not limited to peaceful pursuits. During the century of wars between the British and the Dutch, Spaniards, and French, hundreds of American privateers—small, swift, privately owned commerce raiders licensed by the Crown—had slipped out to sea in search of prizes. Colonial-manned ships had taken part in the British campaigns against Québec, Louisburg, and Havana, and thousands of American sailors had experience in the man-of-war's trade. Lamenting the conflict brewing with the Yankees, a member of the House of Lords described America as "a great nursery where seamen are raised, trained, and maintained in time of peace to serve their country in time of war." American shipyards had also shown considerable skill and craftsmanship in building armed vessels and had been turning out ships of up to forty-four guns since 1690.

The outbreak of war with the American colonists occurred at a difficult time for the Royal Navy. On paper, Britain had 131 ships of the line and 139 smaller vessels in 1775, but these figures were deceiving. Large sums voted for repair and refitting of ships had disappeared into the pockets of corrupt politicians and contractors, and the Admiralty's official lists bore little relation to the actual strength of the navy. Wooden ships usually had an average life span of about a dozen years unless they were well maintained, and many of the vessels laid up in "Rotten Row" were mere stacks of decayed timber in the shape of men-of-war. No fewer than 66 British warships were to founder at sea during the American War because they were in poor condition.

Moreover, the massive building programs of the Seven Years' War had sharply reduced the supply of seasoned English oak. Some twenty-five hundred trees, as many as could be grown on sixty acres over a century, were felled to provide the frame timbers and stout sides of a three-decker such as *Victory*. An assured supply of seasoned timber was as vital to the defense of Britain's island realm during this period as was oil in World War II. The break with the colonies had also deprived Britain of one of its primary sources of masts, the forests of New Hampshire. In fact, the last shipment of masts from America reached British ports not long after the news of the Battle of Bunker Hill. As a result of the shortage of "great sticks," which now had to come from the Baltic, many of the king's ships were unable to get to sea at critical junctures during the war.

Some officials believed it would be futile to try to subjugate the colonies with troops because of the vast area involved. America was not Ireland or Scotland, which were terrorized into submission by relatively small forces. Lord Barrington, the secretary at war, proposed instead that the Royal Navy impose a blockade that would cost little in blood or treasure and would cut the rebellious colonies off from the outside world. Just such an operation was feared by the wisest of American leaders, but the navy was too weak to impose it. One official estimated that at least fifty ships would be required to support the royal governors in America, blockade the American coast to prevent supplies from reaching the rebels, and assist the British army in suppressing the rebellion.

Vice Admiral Samuel Graves, the commander of the North American Squadron, had only twenty-nine ships—mostly small vessels short of men and/or in disrepair—to patrol the eighteen hundred miles of coast from Nova Scotia to Florida. Moreover, Boston, where the British army was besieged by the Americans, was a strategic liability. It was dominated by heights held by the Yankees and the British position would be untenable if the Americans managed to emplace heavy artillery on the high ground. Thus, even though Graves is usually assailed for failing to stamp out the rebellion, he was merely a scapegoat for the failure of the Admiralty to provide him with proper direction and enough ships to carry out a hard-hitting policy.

Even so, Graves failed to make the best use of the force he had. With his bluff manner and rough exterior, he seemed just the type of old sea dog to teach the Americans a lesson. But at sixty-two he was in poor health, had never achieved a record as a fighter or administrator, had strained relations with the army, and seemed more interested in advancing the careers of several young relations serving under him than in stamping out the rebellion. And it did it not take the Yankees long to discover that Graves was not even supreme in the waters surrounding Boston.

All through the summer of 1775, fast-darting whaleboats manned by willing oarsmen swarmed out of hidden creeks and coves to harass British ships riding at anchor in Boston Harbor, sweep forage and cattle from the inshore islands, burn lighthouses, and remove navigational aids from the channels. Soon Graves feared for the safety of even his larger ships. The rebels also interfered with British efforts to secure provisions and fuel for the besieged army from the surrounding area, and the first seaborne clashes of the war grew out of these efforts.

On June 12, 1775, a group of Maine woodsmen captured the Royal Navy schooner *Margaretta* in a brisk, bloody battle off Machias while she was trying to obtain a cargo of timber for fortifications and firewood. Three days later, two small vessels commissioned by Rhode Island and placed under the command of Abraham Whipple, a former privateersman, captured a tender, or auxiliary vessel, serving the twenty-gun frigate *Rose,* which was marauding Yankee trade in Narragansett Bay. It was the first authorized capture by an American vessel of a British ship at sea. Captain James Wallace, *Rose's* skipper, thundered he would hang Whipple from a yardarm; Whipple blandly replied, "Sir, Always catch a man before you hang him."

Having authorized the first armed vessels operated by any colony, the Rhode Island Assembly followed up by passing, on August 26, 1775, a resolution that led to the organization of the Continental Navy. It instructed its delegates to the Continental Congress to introduce legislation calling "for building at the Continental expense a fleet of sufficient force, for the protection of these colonies, and for employing them in such a manner and places as will effectively annoy our enemies. . . ."

This resolution was introduced into Congress on October 3, 1775, but was brushed aside. Sectional jealousies made it difficult for the northern and southern colonies to cooperate with each other. Southerners were convinced that a navy was a venture that would profit only New England. Moderates also regarded the creation of such a force as a radical step. Many of the delegates still regarded themselves as loyal British subjects fighting the tyranny of a corrupt ministry and did not view the break with Britain as final. Sending a navy to sea would denote sovereignty—and independence. Widespread fears were also expressed that should any Yankee sailor be so bold as to fire a pop gun from his deck, the Royal Navy would visit a terrible vengeance on defenseless ports from Maine to Georgia.

～

UNKNOWN TO CONGRESS, George Washington had already taken steps to begin the war at sea to obtain powder and arms for his army. The troops besieging the British at Boston were so short of weapons and powder that he had issued orders that guns were not to be fired at sunset out of fear of provoking a British bombardment that could not be answered. Benjamin Franklin suggested that the shortage of muskets be remedied by arming sentries guarding the roads around Boston with bows and arrows. Besides, he said, a man could fire four arrows in the time it took to load and fire a musket just once.

With mounting desperation, Washington watched the unchallenged passage of British transports and supply ships into Boston Harbor—and decided to do something about it. Noting that British storeships were all but unarmed and rarely traveled in convoy, he observed that "A fortunate Capture of an Ordnance Ship would give new life to our camp." Acting upon his authority as commander in chief, he launched a fleet of his own with the hope of making such "a fortunate Capture."

The first vessel commissioned by Washington, the stubby seventy-eight-ton schooner *Hannah*, put to sea on September 5, 1775. She was under the command of Captain Nicholson Broughton and manned by a crew recruited from a regiment of Marblehead sailors and fishermen who had joined the army. Although the first ship of what became known as "George Washington's Navy" failed to capture any significant prizes, the general pressed ahead with the project. Over the next twenty-six months he commissioned seven more lightly armed vessels, which took fifty-five enemy craft, including four troop transports carrying a total of 320 soldiers.

John Manley, a rough-and-ready Boston shipmaster, was the most successful of Washington's captains. On November 27, 1775, sailing in the six-gun schooner *Lee*, he seized the British ordnance brig *Nancy*, inbound to Boston. She proved to be a floating arsenal. Manley's eyes probably bulged when he read her manifest: two thousand muskets with bayonets, thirty-one tons of musket balls, thirty thousand round shot of various weights, a hundred thousand musket flints, and—most imposing of all—a huge thirteen-inch mortar that would be invaluable to the Continental Army's siege of Boston. A delighted Washington observed that the loot from the *Nancy* gave "new Life to our camp." In the meantime, the Continental Congress was making the first effort to launch a navy.

~

THE FOUNDING OF an American navy is difficult to follow because the process proceeded on a number of tracks. On October 5, 1775, Congress, still unaware of General Washington's naval efforts, was informed that two unarmed and unescorted transports carrying equipment and supplies for the British army in Québec had sailed from Britain. If they could be captured, their cargoes would be priceless to Washington's army. A motion was introduced calling for a special committee to prepare a plan for intercepting these storeships, but the proposal met with robust objections.

"The opposition . . . was very loud and Vehement," reported John Adams, a pronavy delegate from Massachusetts. "It was represented as the most wild, visionary, mad project that has ever been imagined. It was an Infant, taking mad Bull by the horns." Nevertheless, by a narrow margin, Congress appointed a committee to draft a plan to intercept the transports. It quickly recommended the purchase and fitting out of two armed vessels to deal with the transports. In the meantime, heated debate took place on the Rhode Island proposal for the establishment of a Continental Navy. The walls of the Pennsylvania State House resounded to attacks on the proposal. But George Wythe of Virginia asked, "Why should not America have a navy? . . . We abound with firs, iron ore, tar, pitch, turpentine; we have all the materials for the construction of a navy."

Realizing that the time was not yet ripe for a full-scale fleet, the pronavy forces shifted position. The Rhode Island plan was temporarily shelved, and the special committee's more limited proposal for two armed vessels was brought forward. On October 13, 1775, the Continental Congress took the step that the U.S. Navy regards as marking its official birth. It adopted a recommendation that two armed vessels be purchased and sent out to capture the Canadian-bound transports. The larger of the two vessels became *Andrew Doria;* the smaller, *Cabot.* Having cleared this first obstacle, the navy's supporters moved ahead with greater assurance. Two larger ships, which became *Alfred* and *Cabot,* were authorized on October 30. Significantly, the mission of these last two vessels was not limited to intercepting the transports. They were "to be employed . . . for the protection and defense of the united Colonies."

A seven-member Navy Committee—forerunner of the Navy Department—laid the administrative foundation for the service. Each evening after the regular session was over, its members met at a waterfront tavern, where they accomplished a considerable amount of business in a remarkably short time. Merchant vessels were purchased and refitted; their sides were strengthened, gunports were cut, and cannon put in place. Officers were chosen, sailors and marines were recruited. Rules and regulations governing the new navy were drafted, primarily by John Adams. Although based on existing British naval regulations, they provided for more humane treatment of enlisted men.

Congress, in selecting the ranking officers of the Continental Navy, followed the same principles of patronage and nepotism that were the bane of politics. The Hopkins clan dominated the Navy List. Besides Esek Hopkins, it included Abraham Whipple, who had married into the Hopkins clan, and John Burroughs Hopkins, the commodore's son. The senior captain, Dudley Saltonstall of Connecticut, was the brother-in-law of Silas Deane, a member of Congress. Nicholas Biddle's brother, Edward, represented Pennsylvania in Congress. John Paul Jones, a somewhat mysterious Scots sea captain, was named senior lieutenant through the influence of Joseph Hewes of North Carolina.

Next, Congress turned its attention to the long-delayed Rhode Island resolution. Southern reluctance to approve a Continental navy had been overcome by Lord Dunmore's raids along the shores of the Chesapeake. On December 13, 1775, Congress authorized the building of thirteen frigates at a cost of $66,666.66 each, or a total of $866,666.58—a considerable sum for the period. Five ships of thirty-two guns, five of twenty-eight, and three of twenty-four were authorized. Showing more regard for political influence than the shipbuilding capacities of the individual colonies, Congress ordered two of these ships to be built in Rhode Island, two in Massachusetts, two in New York, four in Pennsylvania, and one each in New Hampshire, Connecticut, and Maryland. No one expected these ships to oppose Royal Navy warships, but they could interdict supplies for the British army in North America, disrupt trade, and provide coastal defense.

⟃

FOLLOWING THE New Providence raid, the Continental Navy's first fleet swung uselessly to anchor in Narragansett Bay, unable to get to sea because of sickness and a shortage of experienced seamen. Sailors found it more profitable to ship out in privateers than to accept the rigors of the Continental Navy. The outcry in Congress over Esek Hopkins' inept performance against Glasgow despite the overwhelming strength of his fleet, plus southern unhappiness with his failure to rid the Chesapeake of Lord Dunmore's raiders, added to the navy's problems. Following considerable political maneuvering, he was suspended from command in 1777 and formally dismissed the following year.

From time to time, however, some of the vessels—Andrew Doria, under Nicholas Biddle; Columbus, under Abraham Whipple; and Providence and Alfred, successively commanded by John Paul Jones, who had been promoted to captain—made successful cruises on their own. Among other captures, Jones took the armed transport *Mellish* off Cape Breton with a cargo that included ten thousand winter uniforms, which were dyed and issued to Washington's ragged men. The success of the American war effort depended on such lucky captures and the ability of fast-sailing Yankee ships to elude the still-porous British blockade and return from Europe and the Caribbean with vital cargoes. Yankee privateersmen who captured British supply ships sometimes complained about the poor quality of the provisions they found on enemy ships.

Powder and artillery captured at sea and at Fort Ticonderoga, on Lake George, made the worst nightmare of the British come true. Under the cover of a heavy rainstorm on the night of March 4–5, 1776, the Americans fortified Dorchester Heights, which dominated Boston and its harbor. Unwilling to repeat the bloody fiasco of Bunker Hill the year before, in which they took heavy casualties in capturing a Yankee position, the British evacuated Boston. Some nine thousand troops and about a thousand dejected Loyalists sailed away to Halifax in Nova Scotia on March 17, 1776. Washington wasted little time celebrating this victory, however. He quickly moved his army to New York City, where he expected the British to strike next. The successful British withdrawal provided Washington with another lesson in the importance of command of the sea. As long as what he called the Royal Navy's "canvas wings" gave the British control of the sea, he was helpless to prevent them from evacuating beaten armies or making new seaborne attacks on the American coast.

CHAPTER 2

Uncombined Operations

LORD GEORGE GERMAIN, the director of the land war in America, smarted from the defeat at Boston and lost no time in planning a counteroffensive. Against all odds, the Yankees had at least survived the opening phase of the war. They had forced the British to evacuate Boston, were harassing the army's communications and line of supply along the Atlantic coast, and were laying siege to Québec. The rebellion had to be crushed before France and Spain were tempted to take advantage of Britain's difficulties and intervene in the struggle. "One decisive blow by land is absolutely necessary," Germain declared. "After that, the whole will depend upon the diligence and activity of the officers of the Navy."

Germain planned to accomplish his goal in 1776 in a single campaign: a three-pronged operation designed to chop up and then annihilate American forces. But this plan was based on a fallacy. Even though he had never visited America, he had, like many British aristocrats, a low opinion of the fighting capabilities of what he called the American "peasants." Moreover, Germain was viewed with suspicion by his own commanders because he had been cashiered from the army and declared unfit to serve in any military capacity. But he had won royal favor as a result of his fire-eating attacks on the Americans. Haughty and reserved, he was unpopular, was rarely asked to dine out, and was rumored to be a homosexual.

The first phase of Germain's plan called for the relief of Québec. The previous year American troops had invaded Canada, with the hope that the restive, predominantly French inhabitants would join them in throwing off British rule. General Richard Montgomery captured Montréal, while troops led by Colonel Benedict Arnold placed Québec under siege. On New Year's Eve 1776 the Americans, in a blinding snowstorm, launched an assault on the walled city that was beaten off with heavy casualties. Montgomery was killed and Arnold wounded, but the siege of Québec continued.

Once the Yankees were driven from Montréal and Québec, the British intended to drive down the Lake Champlain–Hudson line and separate New England, the focal point of the rebellion, from the rest of the colonies. The second phase of the plan called for the destruction of Washington's army at New York City. The third involved an invasion of the Carolinas, to provide a rallying place for southern Loyalists as well as a base for operations in the South. On its face, the launching of three powerful strikes against the Yankees at widely separated points was an appealing strategy, but in reality it was a prescription for disaster. The plan violated the principle of concentration of force because the available troops and ships were divided into uncorrelated units. The southern operation was particularly ill-conceived. The British had convinced themselves that the vast majority of Southerners were loyal and would flock to the royal standard once British ships and troops appeared in the area. Events were to prove this a fallacy.

Nevertheless, the first part of the British plan was crowned with success. A squadron under the command of Captain Charles Douglas broke through the thick ice blocking the St. Lawrence River in April 1776 and relieved Québec. Decimated by hunger, cold, and smallpox, Arnold's tattered army hastily retreated when the sails of the ships were sighted off Cape Diamond. Reinforcements and supplies for the next stage of the British offensive, the strike along the Lake Champlain–Hudson line, began pouring into Canada, but the major focus was on the southern enterprise.

This expedition exhibited in microcosm all the logistical problems facing the British during the war in America. With some fifteen hundred men, General Sir Henry Clinton arrived off the Cape Fear River in North Carolina on March 12, 1776, to rendezvous with a squadron under the command of Commodore Sir Peter Parker and twenty-five hundred troops from Ireland. But the convoy was delayed in departing by a shortage of supplies and then scattered by violent Atlantic storms. Conditions on the transports were bad even by the standards of the time. "The men were packed like herrings," states one account. "A tall man could not stand upright between decks, nor sit up straight in his berth. To each such berth six men were allotted, but as there was only room for four, the last two had to squeeze in as best they could." To add to the misery, the men suffered from cold and seasickness.

Parker did not join Clinton until May 3—well after the reason for the expedition had vanished. Weeks before, an uprising by southern Loyalists, mostly Highland Scots who hated the Lowlanders and Ulstermen prominent in the rebel cause, had been crushed, and they were driven into the Carolina back country, to be hunted down like wild game. The southern operation should have been canceled, but the strong-willed Parker now browbeat Clinton into a combined land-sea assault on Charleston, the South's largest city, said to be ill-prepared to meet an attack.

Charleston was better defended than the British knew, however. Putting the window of opportunity afforded by enemy fumbling to good use, the South Carolinians had fortified the barrier islands commanding the entrance to the harbor, which with its sandbars and shallows was tricky for large ships. The main redoubt was a crude palmetto-log bastion on Sullivan's Island known as Fort Moultrie after its builder and commander, Colonel William Moultrie. Parker's ships arrived off the city on June 1 but were unable to run past Fort Moultrie's guns. Clinton put his troops ashore on nearby Long Island (now the Isle of Palms), with the intention of crossing to Sullivan's Island and taking the uncompleted fort from the rear. But British intelligence was faulty; the channel between the two islands was not eighteen inches at low water as expected, but pocked with holes seven feet deep. Before boats could be gathered for a crossing, the Americans emplaced two field pieces at the tip of Sullivan's Island, blocking a British landing.

Parker now despaired of cooperation from the army, and on June 28 launched a naval attack designed to silence Fort Moultrie. The assault began as the bomb ketch *Thunder* hurled a ten-inch mortar shell into the bastion, but much to the chagrin of the British, it was swallowed up by the loose sand. Shot after shot struck the fort's ramparts, only to be absorbed by the spongy palmetto logs. On the other side, the garrison had but twenty-eight rounds of powder for each gun, so Colonel Moultrie ordered his men to aim carefully and make every shot count. Several British ships grounded on the shoals under the American guns and were badly damaged. A frigate was set ablaze and abandoned. Parker's flagship, the fifty-gun *Bristol,* was hit repeatedly, and forty-six of her crew were killed. The commodore ignominiously lost his britches and was wounded in the thigh.

With ammunition supplies running down and darkness falling, Parker called off the attack, never to renew it. Clinton's troops spent another uncomfortable three weeks among the mosquitoes of Long Island without accomplishing anything. At the end of July they reembarked, and the fleet sailed away to join Sir William Howe's army as it prepared for an attack on New York. The assault on Charleston was a humiliating defeat for the British, a boost to rebel morale, and a classic study in how not to conduct combined operations. Had Clinton and Parker speedily launched an assault rather than allowing the Americans to prepare their defenses, they might have been successful. Britain suffered worse defeats in the war, but no more egregious fiasco.

⌐

ON JULY 4, 1776, while Congress was proclaiming the independence of the British colonies in America, George Washington warned of an impending enemy attack on New York. By day, the sails of 52 warships and 427 transports testified to British command of the waters around the city. By night, the campfires of some 35,000 troops—the largest British expeditionary force of the eighteenth century—twinkled on Staten Island. Against them, Washington could muster barely 20,000 men, most of them poorly trained militia. Immediately after his arrival in New York, he had put his soldiers to work with pick and shovel to prepare the city's defenses, but his position was weak.

The British fleet had free play to maneuver and envelop the exposed American flanks with amphibious attacks in the waters around New York. To counter the enemy, Washington built forts on both sides of the Hudson to prevent British ships from outflanking Manhattan and dug in on Brooklyn Heights, across the East River from the city. Although Brooklyn Heights dominated lower Manhattan just as Dorchester Heights had dominated Boston, he was in danger of being squeezed between British troops in his rear on Long Island and the Royal Navy in the East River.

Yet General Howe and his older brother, Vice Admiral Richard Lord Howe, who now commanded the British fleet in American waters, refrained from launching an all-out attack. They waited until the last reinforcements filtered in, including the battered squadron returning from the Charleston misadventure. Except for a foray past the Hudson forts by a pair of frigates that sailed up the river to the Tappan Zee, there were no lightning strikes against the vulnerable American positions, nor was there a naval bombardment to soften up the fortifications.

The Howe brothers wished to make peace, not war. Admiral Howe was one of Britain's most respected fighting seamen—known to his sailors as "Black Dick" because of a swarthy complexion and "the Sailor's Friend" because of a rare compassion for the ordinary seaman. Both he and Sir William viewed the war as a personal as well as a national tragedy because of family ties to America.* As early as 1774, the admiral had volunteered to mediate the crisis between Lord North's government and the colonists, but the ministry rejected his offers in favor of coercion.

When the iron fist failed to bring the rebels to heel, North sent Admiral Howe to America as both naval commander and peace commissioner. But the admiral and his brother could only offer terms that were obnoxious to the Americans. They were empowered to grant pardons for traitorous acts and remove troublesome restrictions on trade that angered the Yankees—

---

*Another brother, George Augustus Howe, had been one of the most popular British officers in the colonies, and after his death at Ticonderoga in 1758, the Massachusetts authorities erected a memorial in his honor in Westminster Abbey. The mother of the Howe brothers was supposedly the illegitimate daughter of King George I, so they were, in effect, cousins of King George III.

Admiral Richard Lord Howe, by John Singleton Copley. (U.S. Naval Academy Museum)

but only after receiving assurances that the rebellion would be ended and the royal governors restored to their posts. Nevertheless, Admiral Howe was optimistic about the possibility of success, and not even the Declaration of Independence dimmed his determination to make peace.

Repeated rejections of his offers convinced Howe that the rebels would have to be taught a military lesson before they would seriously consider his offers of an olive branch. The amphibious operation that followed was conducted with great skill. On August 22, 1776, General Howe put fifteen thousand men ashore at Gravesend Bay on Long Island with their cannons and equipment, while a feint was made up the Hudson. Five days later, the British crushed Washington's army, which fell back upon Brooklyn Heights. But Howe did not press the attack, apparently convinced that the smashing defeat inflicted on the rebels had persuaded them that they had no option but to give up.

Washington desperately looked for a way out. Much to his surprise, the British had failed to block his obvious line of retreat to lower Manhattan by stationing ships in the East River. Once again, he called on the regiment of Marblehead fishermen who had provided the crew for the first ship of his navy. Under cover of a rolling fog, the remnants of his army were silently ferried across the East River in small boats, and the surprised British did not realize the Yankees had escaped until morning.* In all, some nine thousand men were saved to fight another day. The evacuation underscores Washington's reliance on amphibious operations. Both his most desperate defensive move, the retreat from Long Island, and his boldest offensive stroke, the attacks on Trenton and Princeton later that year, made excellent use of this tactic.

Rather than finishing off Washington's army, as might have been expected, the Howe brothers renewed their peace initiative. Over the next two weeks Lord Howe engaged in a round of fruitless negotiations with a delegation from Congress while the Americans used the respite to improve their defenses on Manhattan. Frustrated by the lack of progress at the negotiating table, the admiral decided to escalate pressure on the rebels. Under cover of a bombardment laid down by the fleet, General Howe landed a picked force at Kip's Bay, about midway between lower Manhattan and Harlem, for another textbook operation. The Yankees fled for their lives. A leisurely chase followed, in which the British drove the Americans from Manhattan with frontal assaults and flanking maneuvers but were unable to completely destroy Washington's badly bruised army, which retreated into New Jersey. The task of simultaneously acting as military officers and peacemakers proved to be beyond the capacity of the Howe brothers.

WHILE THESE EVENTS were unfolding around New York City, the other side of the British pincers designed to close about New England was stalled

---

*The evacuation of Washington's troops from Long Island is often compared to Dunkirk in 1940, but the comparison is poorly chosen. The Americans were not under fire while the operation was under way, and the number of troops involved was only about one-fortieth of the total lifted from France. See my book *War at Sea: A Naval History of World War II,* chapter III.

on the shores of Lake Champlain. Stretching some 125 miles from north to south, the lake was, in the absence of roads through the wilderness, the vital link in the strategic waterway between the St. Lawrence and the Hudson. Whoever controlled Lake Champlain and the choke points at Crown Point and Fort Ticonderoga controlled the invasion route from Canada. As a result of the foresight of Benedict Arnold, the Americans held a tenuous naval supremacy on the lake, which blocked a British advance on General Washington's rear.

The previous year, Arnold had captured three small lake schooners, and although armed with only an assortment of small guns, they were enough to prevent the British from smashing their way up the lake.* Both sides settled down to a small-scale naval race in which the British had the advantage. They could draw on their fleet in the St. Lawrence for the resources and skilled manpower to build and man a flotilla more powerful than anything that could be built by Arnold, whose own source of supplies was 250 miles away, on the Atlantic coast. Nevertheless, he accepted the challenge without hesitation.

At thirty-five, Arnold was at the height of his remarkable powers and still four years away from the treason that was to forever blacken his name. He was a member of a prominent Connecticut family and had begun his career as a New Haven druggist and bookseller. Having become a successful merchant, he sailed his own ships to the Mediterranean and the Caribbean—experience that was to prove invaluable on Lake Champlain. Proud and ambitious, he was a man of intelligence, tremendous energy, and stamina but was also sharp-tongued, sensitive to criticism, and unable to control a volcanic temper.

Arnold both designed and built the Champlain fleet. The capital ships of his battle line were four two-masted row galleys that carried a variety of guns and were fitted with high-pointed lateen sails, a type of rig he had seen on his voyages to the Mediterranean. With a minimum of sails and rigging, these craft could easily be handled by lubberly crews. Nine gondolas—each armed with three guns and propelled by a pair of square sails set on a single mast as well as oarsmen—plus three schooners and a sloop constituted the remainder of his fleet. Most of these vessels were hastily built of oak and pine growing beside the lake. They were manned by some 750 volunteers from the army—"a wretched motley crew," in Arnold's words—mostly attracted by a bonus of eight shillings a month.

As soon as General Sir Guy Carleton, the British commander, realized that he would have to fight for control of Lake Champlain, he set about

---

*Because Lake Champlain drains northward into the Richelieu River, south is considered up the lake.

building a fleet that would overawe anything the Yankees could put in the water. The mainstays of his force were the eighteen-gun sloop *Inflexible*, built in Québec, dismantled, and hauled overland to the lake shore, where she was reassembled, and a two-masted, scowlike floating battery built on the lake. This craft, alone, mounted enough firepower to deal with Arnold's entire fleet all by itself. Carleton also had several small sailing vessels and a score of oar-powered gunboats, each mounting a single heavy gun in the bow.

Sails bellying taut in a chill wind that stripped the lakeside trees of the last of their leaves, the British began their move southward on October 11, 1776. Undaunted by this superior force, Arnold anchored his vessels in a narrow bay between Valcour Island and the New York shore. As expected, the British sailed by without spotting his fleet. When they did, they had difficulty beating back against the wind to give battle. As the enemy struggled to bring their guns to bear, the Americans poured a heavy fire into them. Arnold, who flew his flag in the galley *Congress*, moved from gun to gun, training and elevating her cannon for maximum effect. One of the British gunboats blew up, leaving only a pillar of smoke and fire where it had been moments before. Bits of human figures floundered among the floating timbers. The schooner *Carleton* was roughly handled and maneuvered out of danger by Midshipman Edward Pellew, later one of the Royal Navy's greatest frigate captains.*

Slowly, the British clawed into position, and the results were devastating as their guns came to bear. The light wooden sides of the Yankee craft were shattered by heavy shot, their cannon dismounted, and their crews badly cut up. The cliffs and tall trees surrounding the lake magnified the thunder of gunfire to frightful proportions. It was as if a tremendous glass bowl had been pressed down on the scene. By nightfall, most of Arnold's fleet was severely damaged, and some of his vessels were sinking. But Arnold was at his best in adversity. Fog settled in, and with *Congress* acting as a rear guard, the darkened vessels slipped through the British line and headed south, toward Crown Point.

The British, who had intended to mop up the Americans the next morning, were amazed to find that the Yankees had escaped. A three-day chase ensued. Arnold ordered his most severely damaged vessels to be sunk or set ablaze and pressed ahead with the rest. What followed must have been a nightmare for his men. Bucking contrary winds and currents, pelted by sleet and rain, they bent and tugged at their oars as the pumps thumped

---

*Midshipman Pellew's previous claim to fame was his ability to stand on his head on a yardarm without holding on to the rigging.

and clanked in their ears. At any moment they expected the British to loom out of the thick mist and unleash their fire.

The wind shifted around, but it provided the wretched Yankees little comfort. Blowing in from the north, it filled the sails of the British first, and the gap between the two forces was reduced to little more than a mile before its gusts reached the tattered sails of Arnold's vessels. With a pair of cannon firing from the windows of her stern cabin, *Congress* tried to hold off the British, but one by one the rebel vessels were overhauled and shot to pieces. With no other option left, Arnold signaled his captains to run the remaining craft ashore and burn them. He personally set his flagship afire and was the last to leap from the stranded hulk. Along with his surviving crewmen, he escaped overland to Crown Point.

The British now controlled Lake Champlain and the invasion route to the south. But the four weeks required to build a fleet to match that of Arnold had delayed them so long that they had to call off their advance because the approach of winter marked the end of the campaigning season for European armies. The following year General John Burgoyne launched a new invasion from Canada, but this time the Americans were ready. Burgoyne was forced to surrender at Saratoga in upstate New York—a victory that brought France into the war and ensured American independence. Valcour Island is merely a skirmish in the roll call of naval battles, but its consequences were immeasurable. "That the Americans were strong enough to impose the capitulation of Saratoga," said Admiral Mahan, "was due to the invaluable year of delay secured to them by their little navy on Lake Champlain, created by the indomitable energy, and handled with the indomitable courage of the traitor, Benedict Arnold."

WORK ON THE thirteen frigates authorized by Congress took place with agonizing slowness throughout 1776 at shipyards from Portsmouth in New Hampshire to Baltimore. Politics, poor planning, and shortages of labor and materials had much to do with the delays. Just as seamen found it more profitable to go privateering than to serve in the Continental Navy, shipyard workers earned premium wages building private commerce raiders. Because of the delay, only seven of the frigates ever got to sea—all to be eventually captured or sunk—while the other six were destroyed to keep them from falling into British hands.

Seasoned timber was the key to the construction of a wooden man-of-war. English shipwrights swore by Sussex oak, saying it was the finest shipbuilding material in the world. "Heart of oak are our ships, heart of oak are our men," patriotic Britons lustily sang in the Age of Fighting Sail—

and the song had a strong basis in fact. As if to ensure that Britain would always have a supply of oak for her "wooden walls," Vice Admiral Cuthbert Lord Collingwood, Lord Nelson's second in command at Trafalgar, never ventured from his home at Morpeth in Northumberland without a handful of acorns in his pocket. As he wandered over the moors and rugged hills with his dog Bunce frolicking at his side, he would frequently stop and press an acorn into the soil wherever he saw a good place for an oak tree to grow. Some of the oaks planted by Collingwood still flourish nearly two centuries later, in the era of the nuclear submarine.

Trees with natural curves, or "compass timber," were much sought after for the shaped parts of the hull. Most ships built in America were constructed of white oak, which was found in abundance in the northern colonies, but it was thought inferior to the best English timber. The North American live oak that grew in the South was later discovered to be superior to English oak, but shipbuilders made little use of it until a later era.

Shipyards, in both Britain and America, were the largest and most complex industrial enterprises of the day. Most were without much machinery, and the bulk of the work was done by hand. Shipyards echoed to the rhythmic thud of the shipwright's adze, the clatter of hammers, and the hoarse cough of long ripsaws as they shaped great balks of oak and spruce into frames and planking. The first stage in the construction of a wooden warship took place in a large shed called a mould-loft. Master shipwrights laid out the lines of the vessel in full scale on the floor and chalked out the side elevation on the walls. The timbers were cut and shaped to these designs and dimensions.

The keel, or backbone of the vessel, was laid down first upon oak blocks set four or five feet apart on ground that sloped gently down to the water. Several thick timbers, measuring as much as two feet square, were joined together by overlapping joints, or scarfs, to produce a keel of the required length. These joints were held together with copper bolts, which were more resistant to underwater corrosion than iron. Two upright members, the stempost and the sternpost, were raised at the front and rear of the keel. They were followed by the frames, or structural ribs, which were built in sections and bolted together on the ground before being hoisted into place at right angles to the keel. Pear-shaped with the greatest width at the waterline, they sloped inward with a pronounced "tumble home" or curve. The ribs were placed close together, nearly touching each other, and when all were erected, the structure was almost solid. Knees and beams to support the decks were added, and then the vessel was ready for planking, which was applied in two layers.

Little metalwork was used in ships constructed in the colonies because iron and copper were expensive. Planking was fastened to the frames with treenails, or wooden pegs, driven into holes already prepared for them.

Treenails had the disadvantage of rotting, and allowing the sea to pour in. This was probably the cause of the loss of many wooden ships that disappeared without a trace, but custom and thrift prescribed the continued use of treenails. The hull was caulked with oakum and tar, and the part below the waterline was sometimes painted with white lead in a vain attempt to hinder the accumulation of marine growth on the vessel's bottom. Before 1778, when the Royal Navy began an extensive program of sheathing the bottoms of its vessels with copper, ships, especially those in service in tropical waters, had to be careened, or hove down on their sides, every year or so, so their bottoms could be cleaned.

Once launched, the ship was brought alongside a sheer hulk, an old vessel that had been cut down and fitted with a single sturdy mast and block and tackle for stepping, or lowering, masts into ships. Following installation of the masts and bowsprit, the vessel received her rigging, which was set up by master riggers working with her officers. Yards and sails were next. With the addition of guns, ballast, and provisions, the ship was now ready for sea in a bravery of new paint and canvas.

In the first flush of revolutionary fervor, recruiting men for the ships of the Continental Navy was comparatively easy. Usually a junior officer, perhaps a lieutenant or a midshipman. set up a rendezvous at a popular tavern, printed broadsheets presenting a glowing account of his vessel, and then, with the hope of attracting volunteers, sent out a detail of sailors and marines to march through the town behind merrily rattling drums.

Later, patriotism had little appeal, and experienced seamen were wary of the navy. They were reluctant to join a service in which discipline was strict, the share of prize money only a fraction of that offered on privateers, and pay was low—only $6.67 a month for an able seaman, paid in depreciated Continental currency. John Trevitt, a marine lieutenant serving in *Columbus,* noted that several months' salary "would pay for 2 pair of shoes." And despite the new regulations specifying humane treatment in the new navy, there were complaints of mistreatment. "We are used like dogs," protested the crew of *Providence* to Esek Hopkins. "We hope you will find us a new Captain or a new Vessel." John Hazard, the ship's skipper, was court-martialed and dismissed from the service.

Some captains tried to outbid the privateers for crews by offering bonuses and advances on wages. As often as not, the volunteers took the money and deserted at the first opportunity. To make up for the shortage of experienced hands, large numbers of landsmen were signed on. One captain reported that most of his crew of "green country lads" were seasick as their ship went into action and had to be led to their stations. The army sometimes got rid of its hard cases by sending them to the navy, and criminals were offered the choice between prison and naval service. In emergencies, captured British seamen were hustled on board Continental ships in irons and put to work. One such group conspired to seize the frigate *Alliance,* murder her officers, and sail her to a British port. Luckily, the plot was thwarted.

Upon several occasions, the recruiting of seamen for privateers was embargoed until Continental ships could be manned. On others, exasperated naval officers seized men who had deserted their ships from the decks of privateers to which they had fled. In a few extreme cases. they resorted to impressment, much to the anger of the civilian authorities ashore. All these efforts were of little avail, however. Continental Navy ships were often unable to get to sea because they lacked crews.

⌒

JUST HOW EFFECTIVE were the privateers that consumed so much of the infant nation's maritime resources? Congressional records list 1,697 vessels with Continental letters of marque, or commissions to go privateering. Several states and American agents in the Caribbean and Europe also issued commissions. Taking duplications into account, the best estimate is that more than 2,000 commissions were issued by the various authorities. Lloyd's of London estimated that, not counting those ransomed or recaptured, 2,208 British ships were taken by Yankee privateers. Placing an average value of $30,000 on these prizes, as suggested by one authority, the loss to Britain amounted to more than $66 million, no small sum at the time. To a nation suffering from depleted finances, engaged after 1778 in mortal combat with France and Spain, and with a large part of its population unsympathetic to the war, these losses, while by no means fatal, were strong arguments for ending the struggle.

The Gulf of St. Lawrence was most favored hunting ground for smaller privateers. Protected by intermittent fogs and storms, they targeted fishing sloops and trading vessels almost without risk. If pickings were slim, they ran into helpless fishing villages and plundered them. To extend the blockade as widely as possible, Admiral Howe had to deploy his vessels singly, risking their destruction or capture. On June 7, 1777, *Fox,* twenty-eight, was captured on the Grand Banks by the Continental frigates *Hancock,* thirty-two, under the command of Captain John Manley, and *Boston,* twenty-four.*

Larger privateers swarmed over the Caribbean, where they refitted, resupplied, and sold their prizes in the neutral French, Dutch, and Danish

---

*A month later, *Hancock* was seized by a British squadron, which also recaptured *Fox. Hancock* was taken into the Royal Navy and renamed *Iris.* In 1781 *Iris* captured *Trumbull,* twenty-eight, the last of the thirteen original frigates in American hands.

islands. The most successful Yankee raider was the speedy sixteen-gun Philadelphia brig *Holker,* which became known as "the millionaire-maker." On her first cruise, she captured six rich prizes, including a vessel carrying eighty cannon for the British army. The captain retired from the sea on his prize money. On another voyage, she captured prizes worth more than a million pounds, and during one six-week period *Holker* bagged sixteen prizes. But her luck finally ran out on March 2, 1783. She was scudding along the channel between St. Lucia and Martinique under stormy skies when a British frigate gave chase. The privateer was drawing away when she was suddenly struck by a line squall that kicked her over on her beam ends. Fewer than half of the *Holker*'s crew of a hundred men were saved.

British trade with the West Indies was especially hard hit by Yankee privateers. As early as 1777, a resident of Grenada reported that only twenty-five ships of a convoy of sixty vessels carrying provisions to Britain's Caribbean possessions arrived safely. "God knows, if this American war continues much longer we shall all die from hunger," he lamented. More than three hundred British trading vessels were captured by the Americans that year, and only a handful of the raiders were taken. Insurance rates soared, and the Admiralty was bombarded with demands from the West India merchants for protection. The Royal Navy organized convoys and dispatched independent cruisers to foil the raiders. Among these cruisers was the frigate *Lowestoft,* thirty-two, in which Horatio Nelson was serving as a lieutenant.

Nelson participated in the capture of several prizes while on the Jamaica station. He achieved his first command when he was named captain of the schooner *Little Lucy,* one of these captured vessels, which was pressed into service as an armed auxiliary to the frigate. A typical entry in *Lowestoft*'s log reads:

> Fresh breezes and fair. At 10 p.m. saw two sail to windward and gave chase. Fired one 12 pdr. shot at Ditto, she returning the same. Fired two 12 pdrs with round and grape shot with a volley of small arms, upon which they brought to and proved to be from Philadelphia bound to Jamaica, three weeks out. . . .

In the final analysis, although the trade war had little effect upon Britain's ability to continue the conflict, it had a major influence on strategy. The demands of the merchants for escorts had to be met. Plans for action on both land and sea had to include organizing, routing, and protecting convoys, all of which placed an even greater burden on the already stretched Royal Navy. In view of the limited resources available to the Americans, John Adams was correct when he stated that privateering was "a short, easy, and infallible method of humbling the English."

CHAPTER 3

Revolution Becomes World War

"LET OLD ENGLAND see how they like to have an active Enemy at their door, they have sent Fire and Sword to Ours." With this exhortation, the Continental Congress dispatched Captain Lambert Wickes and the aptly named eighteen-gun sloop-of-war *Reprisal* on one of the most momentous missions of the American Revolution. Wickes, a native of the Eastern Shore of Maryland, was in late 1776 ordered to carry Benjamin Franklin to France, where he was to serve as the new nation's diplomatic representative. Once the old man had been safely deposited ashore, Wickes was to mount a raid on enemy commerce in the seas around Britain.

With his usual craftiness, Franklin saw an attack on British trade in home waters as just as much an instrument of diplomacy as it was a blow at her commerce. If it could be arranged so there was an appearance of French collusion in these raids, an outraged Britain might be tumbled into war with her traditional enemy—much to be benefit of the United States. Franklin lived long before the age of psychological warfare, but he well understood its principles. Behind his benevolent smile lurked a master intriguer, skillfully maneuvering the vacillating powers of Europe to his own ends.

Lying low in the water with her tall masts rising from a rakish hull, *Reprisal* looked more like a privateer than a man-of-war. Wickes used the long voyage across the Atlantic to whip his largely inexperienced crew into a disciplined band of fighting seamen. To force his green hands to over-come their fear of working aloft, Wickes resorted to a familiar device: a cask of drinking water and a cup were placed in the maintop. If a man wanted a drink, he had to climb for it. Wickes did his job so well that Franklin observed that discipline on *Reprisal* was "equal to anything of the kind in the best ships of the King's fleet."

Storms do not occur at sea as often as landsmen might surmise, and the ship's crew quickly fell into the routine of a man-of-war, with the regime patterned on that of the Royal Navy, which had been refined over two centuries. Life at sea was marked by the sounding of the ship's bell and the changing of the watches.* The men stood four-hour watches with four hours off. To keep them from always standing the same watch, there were two two-hour "dog" watches—from 4:00 P.M. to 6:00 P.M. and from 6:00 P.M. to 8:00 P.M.

The day began at midnight or at four in the morning, depending on the watch to which a man had been assigned. If he had the middle watch, between midnight and 4:00 A.M., the work was easy in fair weather. The duty men had but to trim the sails and be on call to make any change. Lookouts were posted forward and in the tops. The officer of the watch, the helmsman, a midshipman, and a marine sentry had stations on the quarterdeck. The only sound was the rhythmic creaking of the ship and the gurgling of the waves as they bubbled past the hull in the blackness.

At eight bells of the first watch, the boatswain's mates took their pipes to the fore and main hatchways and made the prolonged, shrill call "All hands." This was followed by a shouted "Starboard [or Larboard] watch. Ahoy! Rouse out there, you sleepers! Lash and carry!" The watch below tumbled out of their hammocks and had twelve minutes to lash and stow them in the nettings. Laggards were enlivened by the "starters" wielded by the boatswain's mates. Lookouts and the helmsman were relieved. The log was heaved and the ship's speed recorded. The watch that had been on duty since midnight was allowed to go below.

The cook lit the fires in the galley stove, and the watch on duty were put to work. Rolling up their loose trousers, they rigged the pumps, got out swabs, buckets, and holystones, and scrubbed and washed down the deck in their bare feet. Sailors seldom wore shoes except in the coldest climes. The deck was flogged dry with the swabs, brightwork was polished, and lines were flemished into place. At seven o'clock the crew was piped to a simple breakfast of "burgoo," or coarse oatmeal and water, washed down by "Scotch coffee" made from burned bread boiled in water sweetened with a little sugar.

Sick call was held after breakfast. Traumatic wounds in battle accounted for only a fraction of the business of a naval surgeon. Seasickness afflicted many of the men at the outset of a voyage, for which "a draught or two" of salt water was recommended. The surgeon spent much of his time dealing with fevers, which, according to the medical doctrine of the day, stemmed from an imbalance of "humors" or fluids within the body. These were blood, phlegm, cholor, and melancholy or black choler. Treatment,

---

*The first half hour of a four-hour watch was marked by a single stoke and those succeeding were signaled by an additional stroke until the watch was relieved with the sounding of eight bells, when the process started again for the next watch.

therefore, consisted of restoring the balance of humors. Castor oil and ipecac were administered to purge the body of bad humors. Amputation was the operation most frequently performed, and in the absence of anesthetics, the surgeon had to work with speed and decisiveness. Shock and infection killed many of these patients.

Most mornings were taken up by gunnery drills; putting on and taking off sail; and practicing evolutions such as tacking, which permitted a ship to sail against the wind and showed the level of skill of her officers and crew.*

"Ready ho!" called a voice from the quarterdeck when the ship was to be placed on a new tack. "Put the helm down!"

The wheel would be eased over so the vessel's bow began to swing across the wind. "Helm's a'lee!"

Up forward, the men working the foresails would let go of the headsail sheets so these sails lost the wind and did not interfere with the ship's swing. In a few moments she would swing so far over that the wind, instead of hitting the square sails at right angles, would blow along their edges, making the canvas noisily flutter and flap.

"Off tacks and sheets!"

Sailors now threw some of these lines off their cleats and hauled on others as they prepared to trim the sails. By now the ship's bow was almost pointing into the wind.

"Mainsail haul!"

Quickly the men would haul sheets and tacks so the sails, now hanging loose from the yards, would be ready to receive the wind as the bow swung across it to the other side.

"Let go and haul!"

The yards were braced smartly around, sails filled, and the ship heeled over slightly, with her canvas taut and billowing as she settled in on her new tack.

There was also a constant round of cleaning, painting, and polishing to keep the vessel shipshape. Several men were assigned to the pumps that wheezed away as they sucked out the accumulation of bilgewater. Twice a week the men washed their clothes in seawater. Those who had the watch below could do as they wished—sleep if they could find space on deck not being used by the carpenter, the cooper, or the sailmaker, chat with their mates, or mend their clothes.

Common seamen did not wear uniforms, although some captains clothed the crews of their gigs in costumes they designed. Most men wore what they had on their backs when they joined the ship until it fell apart and

*The following section is based on Dudley Pope, *Decision at Trafalgar,* pp. 192–193.

then resorted to the purser's slop chest, for replacements for which their pay was docked. Check shirts were common in all navies, as were white trousers instead of the breeches and stockings worn by landsmen. Sailors also favored a short blue jacket, a small-brimmed hat to minimize that chance of it blowing off, and a handkerchief knotted around the neck to protect the jacket from the grease of a man's pigtail. In battle, the wearer wrapped it around his head to protect his eardrums against the pounding of the guns.

At eleven o'clock the captain made his appearance on the quarterdeck. He had breakfasted alone in his cabin, scanned the midshipmen's journals, examined the accounts of the various departments of the ship, and had a talk with his first lieutenant. Sometimes the captain carried a blacklist of malefactors. "All hands witness punishment!" bawled the boatswain's mates as the master at arms, or ship's policeman, brought up the prisoners who were to be flogged. The captain and his officers took their places on the poop, the marines fell in with loaded muskets on the quarterdeck, and the ship's company gathered in the waist.

Continental naval regulations provided that no captain could order more than a dozen lashes without a court-martial, but some captains circumvented this prohibition by awarding twelve lashes for each violation contained in a single crime. The amount of flogging on a ship depended almost entirely on her captain. In some vessels, punishment was administered almost daily; in others, it was rare. Most floggings were for drunkenness or the myriad crimes covered by the bland term "neglect of duty."

It might be well at this point to discuss the question of homosexuality during the Age of Fighting Sail. Winston Churchill once defined the traditions of the Royal Navy as "rum, sodomy, and the lash" but most accounts are tight-lipped in discussing the degree of homosexuality among officers and men. The penalty for "the unnatural and detestable sin" of buggery and sodomy specified in the Articles of War was death by hanging. In many cases the accused was charged with lesser offenses such as indecent behavior, indecent liberties, or uncleanliness because of the embarrassing nature of the crime. Some were given a hundred lashes for the crime of "going to another man's hammock."

Michael A. Lewis, in his *A Social History of the Navy, 1793–1815,* states that "The Courts martial of the period include a good many cases of sodomy on the Lower Deck, in spite of the ferocious punishment of death inflicted upon those found guilty." In 1797 two men were hanged on *St. George,* seventy-four, for participating in homosexual acts. Officers were not immune; Captain Henry Allen of the sloop *Rattler* was hanged that same year for sodomy. And in 1807 the first lieutenant of the frigate *Hazard* was executed after being found guilty of unnatural practices. Continental Navy records are silent on the subject.

Upon being ordered to rig the gratings, the carpenter and his mates laid one of the wooden gratings that covered the hatches flat on the deck and placed another against the bulwarks. The offender, having been ordered to strip to the waist, was tied to the upright grating. Removing the cat-o'-nine-tails from its traditional red baize bag, a boatswain's mate laid the whip on the man's bare back with all his strength. The impact would have knocked him down if he were not supported by the grating. One blow was enough to produce a welt. Six turned his back raw. Twelve lashes—the usual dose—made it a bloody mess. After each stroke, the mate drew the tails of the cat through his fingers to wipe off the clotted flesh and gore that might cause them to stick together and prevent each from having the maximum effect. Once the sentence had been carried out, the victim was cut down and taken below by his mates, who treated his raw back.

Punishment administered, the officers broke out their sextants and quadrants and fixed the ship's position. Eight bells was struck, and dinner, the main meal of the day, piped. The crew took their meals at tables and benches suspended from the deckhead between the guns. Utensils were simple: work knives, wooden bowls, and tar-stained fingers. The men were divided into messes of four to eight men each, presided over by a mess cook appointed by his messmates for the week. He received the provisions allotted for the mess from the purser; tagged and delivered them to the cook, who boiled them in one of the two large "kettles"; and then brought the meal to his companions.

Food was usually adequate in quantity although not of high quality. Naval literature is filled with stories of rotten meat and biscuits tunneled by weevils, but it was better than many sailors would have received ashore. The basic diet consisted of salt pork or beef, ship's biscuit, pease pudding, beer, and dollops of butter and cheese until they turned rancid or the supply gave out. One day a week, the ship's company received—in place of beef—flour, suet, and currants or raisins with which to make a duff, a stiff pudding boiled in a bag or steamed. The cooks whistled while they worked to prove to their mates that they were not eating the raisins. Beer was the drink of preference in the Royal Navy because water, after a few weeks at sea, had a coating of slime. When a butt was opened, it was left sitting in the open air until the noxious smell had dissipated.

This meal was followed by the cheeriest part of the ship's routine: the first issue of grog.* Fifers tootled a merry tune as the men received a mixture of a gill of high-proof rum and three gills of water. A gill was not enough to turn an old sailor's head, but if he managed to save the noon

---

*The rum ration, first introduced into the Royal Navy in 1731, was abolished as of August 1, 1970. The U.S Navy, which substituted whiskey for rum in 1806, ended the grog ration in 1862 and closed the officers' shipboard wine mess in 1914.

issue until supper, when another ration was doled out, and took both together, he might feel like an admiral. Hence the word "groggy."

At one o'clock the crew returned to their duties, which lasted until 4:00 P.M., at which time the routine ship's work was secured for the day. A light supper of cheese and butter and biscuits was served along with another tot of grog. Just before sunset, the drummer beat to quarters and the men scampered to their battle stations. The guns were cast loose and the officers inspected the ship, keeping a weather eye out to see if any of the men were drunk, particularly those who had combined their noon and supper grog rations. A little thickness of speech, a little too much gaiety, a little unsteadiness of gait could win a date with the cat. The smoking lamp was lit, but smoking was allowed only in the vicinity of the galley.

Once the guns were secured, the hammocks were piped down from the nettings and slung into place. The first night watch was set and the watch below were allowed to crawl into their hammocks until midnight. Lights were extinguished or covered so they would not show from a distance. Quiet settled over the ship except for the periodic striking of the ship's bell and an occasional "All's well" from the sentries.

UPON HIS ARRIVAL in Paris, Franklin found the French cautious about revealing their hand, although they thirsted for revenge against the British. Comte de Vergennes, foreign minister to the young King Louis XVI, was sympathetic to the colonists but had no wish to provoke a war with Britain except on French terms and until he was certain the Yankees were capable of a sustained fight for their independence. But to keep the fires of revolution burning, large quantities of arms and other equipment were declared surplus, and secretly funneled to the Americans from the French arsenals through a dummy private trading company, Hortalez & Co.* Thus, if the British complained, Vergennes could plausibly deny that his government had anything to do with this transatlantic gun-running operation.

The arrival of *Reprisal* at Nantes marked a fresh turn of events. She was the first Continental warship to appear in European waters, and brought with her two British vessels that Wickes had captured on the passage across the Atlantic—the first American prizes brought into a French port. Lord Stormont, the British ambassador, lost no time in pointing out to Vergennes that this was a violation of French neutrality and demanded that the prizes be released. But of course, Vergennes quickly assured him, the

---

*This sham company was the brainchild of the adventurer, spy, and playwright Pierre Augustin Caron de Beaumarchais, who was, among other things, author of *The Marriage of Figaro*.

vessels would indeed be returned to their rightful owners. Wickes was forewarned and surreptitiously sold the ships to French agents, who had them painted and given new figureheads and names. French red tape made it all but impossible for their original owners to trace them, and Stormont could only fume at these machinations.

Following a refit, *Reprisal* put to sea shortly after the beginning of 1777, for the Continental Navy's first raid in European waters. She had a French pilot and several Frenchmen among her crew, which deepened British suspicions of French collusion in Wickes' operations. Wickes captured five prizes, including the Falmouth–Lisbon packet, which put up a fight, and took the captured ships into Lorient. Stormont demanded that the Yankee vessel be immediately expelled from her haven; Vergennes formally acquiesced but used various subterfuges to keep from forcing *Reprisal* out to sea, where several British frigates awaited her. To avoid embarrassing the French, Franklin assured Vergennes that Wickes had been forbidden to send prizes into French ports.

On May 28, 1777, Wickes again sailed, this time in command of a small squadron that consisted of *Reprisal*; the fourteen-gun brigantine *Lexington*; and the cutter *Dolphin*, which was armed with ten three-pounders. Sailing into the heretofore sacrosanct Irish Sea, Wickes captured eighteen ships in a month, creating frantic demands from British merchants that the Royal Navy institute convoys in home waters. "The sea is overspread with privateers," grumbled Lord Sandwich, "and the demand for convoys and cruisers so great we know not how to handle them."

Elated by his success but running low on supplies, Wickes set a course for the French coast. Before he could make port, however, *Reprisal* was pursued for a full day by the seventy-four-gun *Burford*. The Americans escaped only after Wickes ordered *Reprisal*'s guns heaved over the side to lighten her. She put into St.- Malo to become the centerpiece in a diplomatic ballet, which was eventually concluded by a British ultimatum that the French expel the American vessels without delay or face the consequences. No longer able to resist British pressure, Vergennes complied. But Wickes stretched out his stay at St.-Malo as long as he could, making excuses that the winds were contrary, his ships were in poor repair, and that he did not have sufficient provisions for an ocean voyage.

Reprisal and *Lexington* finally sailed for home in September 1777, while *Dolphin*, which was considered unseaworthy, was left behind. *Lexington* was captured by the British off the French coast, and months later it was learned that *Reprisal* had foundered in a storm off Newfoundland. Wickes and all but 1 of her crew of 130 men were lost. The survivor was picked up by a passing ship. "This loss is to be extremely lamented," observed Benjamin Franklin, as Lambert Wickes "was a gallant officer and a worthy man."

In the meantime, Gustavus Conyngham, a Philadelphia shipmaster stranded in Europe by the outbreak of the war, had been given a captain's commission in the Continental Navy and command of a lugger, a type of small vessel much favored by the French for privateering. On May 1, 1777, Conyngham took his craft, named *Surprise,* out of Dunkirk and captured a British mail packet carrying important dispatches, which were tuned over to Franklin. The British outcry against the "Dunkirk pirate" was so violent that Vergennes felt it necessary to seize the lugger and place Conyngham under arrest. He refused, however, to turn the Yankee skipper over to the British for trial.

A few months later, Franklin procured Conyngham's release and a four-teen-gun cutter for him, which he named *Revenge.* Ranging off the coasts of England, France, and Spain, he took nearly sixty prizes over the next eighteen months, striking terror into the hearts of British merchants and shipowners. When the French no longer allowed him to use their ports, Conyngham moved his base of operation to Spain, where the authorities pretended he didn't exist. Wickes and Conyngham did little real damage to British trade, but they helped upset the delicate balance that kept Britain and France and Spain at peace. Soon the American victory at Saratoga opened a new phase of the struggle.

↬

FOR SOME SUPERSTITIOUS folk, 1777 was the "Year of the Hangman." They saw in its last three digits a portent of the gibbets awaiting the leading rebels, and gallows jokes were freely exchanged in the State House in Philadelphia, where Congress met. But the humor faded in midyear as reports filtered in of the stately advance down from Canada of seven thousand British troops led by General John Burgoyne, who had resumed the previous year's campaign. Fort Ticonderoga, keystone to the American defense, fell to the British without a fight, and the country lay open to the invaders. To add to the peril, Sir William Howe's even larger force in New York City was expected to march up the Hudson to unite with Burgoyne at Albany and sever New England from the rest of the colonies.

But Howe had plans of his own. He decided to reserve the final triumph in America for himself by capturing Philadelphia, the largest city in the colonies, and to crush Washington's army in the bargain, before cooperating with Burgoyne. Howe ignored critics who pointed out that he lacked the time and sufficient troops to carry out both objectives. Lord Germain reluctantly agreed to the plan, with the expectation that Howe would launch a quick overland campaign, capture Philadelphia, and then return to New York for an advance up the Hudson.

But Howe had decided to take the much longer sea route to Philadelphia, rather than risk another disastrous attack on his line of communications, such as had occurred at Trenton when Washington had crossed the Delaware River on Christmas Eve 1776, and caught his troops unaware. On July 23, 1777, a fleet of some 280 sail under the command of Admiral Lord Howe, with 15,000 men on board, left New York and disappeared into the Atlantic. Frigates and sloops of war that might have been better used to blockade American ports and suppress Yankee commerce raiders were tied up guarding the convoy.

Even the elements conspired against the British. The prevailing winds were adverse, slowing the fleet to a snail's pace. Twenty-four days were required to cover the 350 miles to the Delaware capes. Originally the Howe brothers had intended to sail up the Delaware to Philadelphia, but were warned by the commander of the blockading squadron that the Americans had constructed fortifications and placed obstructions farther upriver. Instead of landing the troops on the lower river and bypassing these defenses, the Howes diverted the fleet to Chesapeake Bay—condemning the troops to another three weeks on their transports. Food and water for men and animals ran short; many of the troops and most of the horses sickened and died in the sultry heat.

To the north, Burgoyne was committing blunders that sealed the fate of his army. Once he had captured Ticonderoga, the easiest way south was by Lake George, but Burgoyne chose to march overland—a decision made for reasons that had nothing to do with tactics or strategy. To go by water meant doubling back a short distance, but Burgoyne could not bring himself to turn his back on the rebels for any reason, and ordered an advance through the forest. As his soldiers laboriously hacked out a road for their artillery and wagons, the Yankees felled trees across their path, made hit-and-run guerrilla raids, and scorched the surrounding territory. On July 29, Burgoyne's worn-out troops stumbled into Fort Edward, only twenty miles from Albany, but they were too exhausted to push on.

Burgoyne vainly looked for signs of Howe's advancing force, but it was still wallowing down the Atlantic coast, oblivious to the perils threatening the northern force. The nightmare voyage finally ended on August 25, 1777, when the troops landed at the head of the Chesapeake near Elkton, Maryland. Howe outmaneuvered and defeated Washington's army at the Battle of Brandywine, and a month after the landing, the British entered Philadelphia. Congress fled, first to York, Pennsylvania, and then to Baltimore. Only part of the British operation had been completed, however. The Yankee fortifications on the Delaware still obstructed the free passage of ships to Philadelphia.

By early October, Admiral Howe had moved most of his ships from the Chesapeake to the Delaware capes and began clearing the lower river, which was accomplished largely without incident. Moving farther upstream, the British ran into more obstructions, these defended by rebel vessels and batteries. Flaming rafts were sent downriver to harass the British as they worked at removing obstructions, and the Delaware forts tenaciously held out despite repeated assaults. The sixty-four-gun *Augusta* ran aground on the mud flats and caught fire, blowing up with such force that the shock "felt like an earthquake in Philadelphia." She was the largest vessel lost by the British in action with the Americans both in the Revolution and in the War of 1812.

Another month of fighting followed, and it was not until November 23, 1777, that the Delaware was open to British shipping. The sky was lit by the flames licking up the masts of *Andrew Doria, Hornet,* and *Wasp,* of the Continental Navy's first fleet, set ablaze to prevent them from falling into enemy hands. Forty-five ships in all, including *Washington* and *Effingham,* two of the original thirteen frigates, were lost. The British victory was a hollow one, however. Washington's army escaped, and Philadelphia was captured at the expense of the blockade and efforts to suppress the Yankee cruisers. Even more damaging was the news from the north. Burgoyne had been run to ground at Saratoga and had surrendered on October 17, 1777. Until the last moment, his men had looked vainly down the Hudson for a sign of Howe's army.

⌐

EAGER TO GET the news of Burgoyne's surrender off to Paris, where it would have tremendous impact, Congress sent two sets of dispatches to Benjamin Franklin—the originals by the French merchantman *Penet,* and duplicates with the sloop-of-war *Ranger,* eighteen, under the command of John Paul Jones. *Penet* arrived first by a two-day margin, setting off wild celebrations in Paris at the humbling of Perfidious Albion. Now convinced that the Americans were indeed in the war for the long haul, Vergennes informed Franklin on December 17, 1777, that France would recognize the independence of the United States.* War with Britain did not formally begin until the next summer, however, because the French Navy needed the time to prepare for a conflict.

France's decision to intervene, followed by that of Spain a year later, transformed what had been a minor struggle between Britain and its North

---

*Baron Turgot, the controller general of finance, warned against supporting the Americans and engaging in a war with Britain because it would lead to the bankruptcy of France, but his warnings were ignored. Events were to prove him correct. France's precarious financial condition after the war contributed to the outbreak of the French Revolution in 1789.

American colonies into a world war that spanned continents, hemispheres, and thousands of miles of open sea, from the English Channel to the Indian Ocean. The nightmare of French and Spanish entry in the war, which had haunted British statesmen, became a grim reality. Lord Sandwich pleaded with Lord North to put the Royal Navy into a state of readiness, but the prime minister resisted because of the cost and that a mobilization might alarm the French.

In previous wars, Britain had dealt with similar strategic problems by imposing a close naval blockade on the French fleet while using financial subsidies* to other European nations to distract the French with land campaigns in Continental Europe. Now, although Sandwich assured Parliament that "our navy is a match for the whole House of Bourbon," she not only lacked enough ships to blockade French ports because of late mobilization and the deterioration of the reserve fleet, but also had no allies. Prussia, Britain's traditional ally on the Continent, was estranged, while Austria, Spain, and Holland had all gone over to the French camp. Moreover, Russia and the Baltic States, angered by British efforts to restrict their trade with France, organized an Armed Neutrality to protect their commerce. With the rejuvenated French Navy enjoying almost complete freedom of movement, the British army in America was in danger of being isolated if the Royal Navy lost command of the sea.

Under the able direction of the Duc de Choiseul and his successors as minister of marine, the French Navy had made a spectacular recovery since the end of the Seven Years' War. Popular support for the navy was aroused, discipline restored, and a new building program begun. The French naval revival was accompanied by a similar resurgence in Spain. French ships, markedly superior in design and quality to those of the Royal Navy, were better proportioned, faster, stronger and mounted more powerful batteries than anything built in British yards in this period. Captured French vessels were highly prized and usually taken into the Royal Navy. But British designers seemed to learn nothing from them. British warships were badly designed and badly proportioned, often carrying more guns than they could fight.† And unlike the Royal Navy's battered ships, the French had not suffered the wear and tear of two years of wartime operations.

The Royal Navy had the advantage in practical seamanship, but the French were more advanced in gunnery, tactics, and signaling. The French corps of seaman gunners was made up of the most skilled marksmen of the age, especially at long range. French officers received training in special

*Known as the "cavalry of St. George" from the image on the gold sovereigns with which these troops were paid.

†For example, *Victory* sometimes carried so much ballast to hold her steady that her lower gun ports rode only four feet above the water.

"evolutionary" squadrons established to teach the art of fleet handling in combat. Young cadets at the Académie de Marine were instructed in mathematics, hydrography, astronomy, naval architecture, and instrument construction, while British midshipmen learned the rudiments of their profession on the quarterdeck and amid the brutalities of the cockpit.

To ensure an adequate supply of seamen for the French Navy, a system of classes was established in which all seafarers were registered. Each year a separate class was mobilized for service in the navy if needed. This was far more efficient than the Royal Navy's haphazard reliance on the press gang and the sweepings of the jails and gutters. Yet the French Navy had one great failing: it lacked a tradition of victory. French admirals were accustomed to playing a defensive role, and a century of inferiority to the Royal Navy had left an indelible mark on the French naval mind.

Having lost its gamble to subdue the Americans before the French entered the war, the North ministry reappraised British strategy in March 1778 and decided that the European conflict would take precedence over the struggle in North America. Sir Henry Clinton, who had replaced General Howe as overall British commander, was instructed to evacuate Philadelphia and return to New York. Efforts to blockade the American coast all but ceased, allowing Yankee raiders free play. With the exception of plans to capture St. Lucia to provide a base near Martinique, the principal French stronghold in the Caribbean, military operations were to be limited to hit-and-run amphibious raids on American coastal towns. "The object of the war now being changed and the contest in America being of secondary consideration, our principal object must be distressing France and . . . defending His Majesty's possessions," Sandwich declared.

British naval strategy depended on forcing her enemies to keep their fleets divided between their bases in the Atlantic and the Mediterranean— most importantly Brest, Rochefort, Cádiz, Cartagena, and Toulon. The French also had to be denied access to the vital naval stores of the Baltic. Of most immediate concern to the British were two powerful French fleets: one, at Brest on the Bay of Biscay, was commanded by the Comte d'Orvilliers and consisted of twenty-one ships of the line and thirty-five frigates; the other, twelve of the line and thirteen frigates, was at Toulon, in the Mediterranean, and flew the flag of Comte d'Estaing. The Toulon fleet represented the most immediate threat to Britain because it was nearly ready to sail. Would d'Estaing head for America? A rendezvous with d'Orvilliers at Brest? With the Spaniards at Cádiz?

On April 25, 1778, British intelligence reported that d'Estaing had sailed from Toulon thirteen days before with eleven ships of the line, one of fifty guns, and five frigates plus four thousand troops. Lord Germain, who bore major responsibility for the war in America, was convinced the French were headed across the Atlantic. He demanded that ships be immediately dispatched to Gibraltar to prevent the fleet from passing through the strait. If d'Estaing reached America, warned Germain, Lord Howe's fleet, which had only five of the line and three fifty-gun ships, would be destroyed. Halifax, Québec, and New York would fall into enemy hands, and the British army in America would be caught between the hammer of the French fleet and the anvil of Washington's army.

Sandwich, who saw the defense of the realm as his primary duty, adamantly refused to weaken the Channel fleet. If a squadron were sent to Gibraltar, he declared, d'Orvilliers might sortie from Brest and overwhelm the weakened fleet, which would raise the specter of an invasion of Britain. Under pressure, the first lord cobbled together a fleet of thirteen of the line under the command of Vice Admiral John Byron, the poet's grandfather, which was to be sent in pursuit of d'Estaing once the French admiral's intentions were determined. But men-of-war that had been stripped, dismantled, and laid up for years could not be quickly manned, equipped, and made ready for sea. Several anxious weeks followed. On May 16 d'Estaing's ships were sighted by a British frigate as it passed Gibraltar. From the fleet's course and the great press of sail, her captain reckoned the French were bound for America. Byron attempted to put to sea forthwith, but contrary winds held him back, and he did not sail until June 9. D'Estaing had more than a three-week head start on him.

⌒

BYRON WAS KNOWN AS "Foul Weather Jack," and the name was apt. From the moment his fleet sailed, it was battered by gales and scattered across the ocean like confetti. Under the stress of wind and waves, the ships creaked, groaned, and heaved like living things. For those on board, life was a nightmare of stinging spray and violent, swooping thrusts as the ships smashed their way through troughs and roaring crests. Byron's passage provides a most striking example of the influence of the timber problem on naval operations. As a result of the shortage of masts and the haste to get the fleet off to reinforce Howe, many of the ships put to sea with old masts and secondhand rigging.

Masts, yards, booms, and rigging, deprived of their elasticity by age, cracked or shredded in the storms. Repairs were made at sea, but some masts were so weak that Byron's captains refused to run before the wind except under reduced sail. "The mainmast was sprung close to the gundeck, so much that it was expected to go with every roll," reported the captain of *Invincible*, seventy-four. "The foremast went in three pieces.... The bowsprit being sprung ... we had to cut part of that away."

Luckily for the British, d'Estaing, a former army brigadier who, ironi-cally, had once proclaimed that "speed is the foremost of military virtues," took an astonishingly slow seven weeks to cross the Atlantic, and did not reach the Delaware until July 8. Critics blamed the long voyage on his insis-tence on holding tactical drills during the passage. The admiral attributed it to the poor sailing qualities of some his ships and the need to keep them together. Whatever the reason, d'Estaing missed the opportunity to bottle up Lord Howe's fleet in the Delaware and later destroy it, for Howe had sailed for New York ten days before.

War-weary and frustrated by the refusal of the Americans to take up his peace overture, Lord Howe had resolved to haul down his flag on his arrival in New York. But as the British ships dropped anchor, he received news of the sailing of the Toulon fleet and the dispatch of reinforcements under Byron. Realizing that it was too soon to expect support from Byron, Howe prepared for an attack by the French while d'Estaing leisurely cruised up the American coast. Howe, the Royal Navy's premier tactician, decided to make a stand at Sandy Hook, at the entrance to New York Har-bor. The shallow bar there was hazardous to ships of the line, so Howe placed his ships broadside across the entrance to the harbor, in a position to rake d'Estaing's vessels while they gingerly sounded their way over the shoals.

For eleven days the two fleets eyed each other across the bar while d'Es-taing awaited favorable winds and currents to carry him into the harbor. General Washington enthusiastically welcomed the French fleet, sent aides to promise full cooperation for an attack on New York, and provided the French with experienced pilots. Early on the morning of July 22, d'Es-taing's ships weighed anchor, and borne along by a flood tide and a strong following wind, made for the bar. Lord Howe ordered his men to their guns and prepared to rake the French vessels as they bore in. "We . . . expected the hottest day that had ever been fought between the two nations," said one British seaman.

Suddenly the French fleet turned away and stood out to sea as the British gaped in surprise. The American pilots were said to have flatly refused to take the ships across the shoals because there were only twenty feet of water—not enough for such heavy vessels. Only a perfunctory attempt appears to have been made to check on the accuracy of these state-ments by taking soundings. Also, the British reported that a combination of flood tide and a brisk northeast wind actually provided a depth of thirty feet at the bar. D'Estaing's decision to call off the attack because of the pilots' warnings appears to have been a cover for his doubts about the operation. Mahan states that he "probably reasoned that the French had nothing to gain by the fall of New York, which might have led to peace between America and England, and left the latter free to turn all her power against his own country."

The French sailed north to Rhode Island to join the Americans in a previously agreed-upon joint land-sea attack on Newport, one of the finest harbors on the Atlantic coast, and under British occupation since the end of 1776. But the Americans had not yet completely organized their forces, and there was little d'Estaing could do except anchor in Narragansett Bay until the Yankees were ready. A combined attack on the beleaguered British was about to begin on August 8, when Admiral Howe's fleet, reinforced by one of Byron's battered seventy-fours and several smaller vessels, arrived offshore. Despite enemy superiority, Howe intended to buy time by harassing d'Estaing while hoping more of Byron's ships would join him. To the distress of his American allies, d'Estaing abandoned the land attack and headed for the open sea to fight the British despite warnings of an approaching "August gale"—a hurricane racing out of the Caribbean.

For the better part of two days the fleets maneuvered within sight of each other, each trying for an advantage, with the superior sailing qualities of the French ships clearly evident. Toward evening on August 11, the predicted hurricane struck. All thoughts of battle vanished as both sides struggled to survive the storm's fury. Badly battered—the ninety-gun *Languedoc*, d'Estaing's flagship, was dismasted and without a rudder—the fleets limped off to their bases, the British to New York and the French to Boston. In the meantime the Americans, deprived of their naval support, abandoned their siege of Newport.

Working at a furious pace, Lord Howe repaired his damaged ships and within eight days was back at sea. He pursued the French to Boston and then relieved the British garrison at Newport. Six more of Byron's ships joined him, and the British again held naval superiority in North American waters. With imagination, boldness, and skill, Howe had saved New York and Newport for the British with an inferior fleet. Yet his accomplishments were in no small measure linked to d'Estaing's failures. If the French admiral had made a speedier passage across the Atlantic, if he had crossed the bar at Sandy Hook, and if he had held his station at Newport, significant defeats would have been inflicted on the British. As 1778 drew to a close, d'Estaing, ignoring Yankee pleas that his fleet should clear the Atlantic coast of British men-of-war or attack Halifax or Québec, left Boston for the West Indies. The promise of the Franco-American alliance remained to be fulfilled.

CHAPTER 4

Sea Fights—Classic Style

WITH THE UNRUFFLED majesty of a flock of swans, the Channel fleet of thirty ships of the line cruised off the French coast on the foggy afternoon of July 23, 1778. Even though naval operations were already under way in North American waters, war between France and Britain had been formally declared only thirteen days before. Admiral Augustus Keppel, flying his flag in *Victory*, was searching for Comte d'Orvilliers and the Brest fleet of thirty-two of the line, which had put to sea the previous day. The two fleets sighted each other about seventy miles from Ushant, a rocky island off the Brittany coast.

Keppel had distinguished himself in the previous war at the siege and capture of Havana, but like numerous senior officers, he had refused to serve at sea against the Americans until France entered the conflict. By seniority and by reputation he was the obvious choice to command the Channel fleet, but he did not trust Sandwich because of political differences and accepted the post only after an audience with King George. Even so, friends warned Keppel not to trust the first lord for so much as "a piece of rope yarn." Having an inferior fleet and fully realizing the danger to Britain should his ships be shattered, Keppel had sought advice from the Admiralty as to whether or not he should give battle, but it was not forthcoming. This was not a sign of timidity, as his political enemies were to charge, but a judgment that such a decision should be made at the highest level of government.

For the first time, *Victory* cleared for action in the face of a fight as Keppel signaled his ships to form a line of battle. Throughout the fleet, the marine drummers received the shouted command "Beat to Quarters!" and thumped out a short, quick, and determined roll that summoned the men to their battle stations. Galley fires were extinguished, cabin walls were raised, all movables were thrust into the hold, the decks were sanded to prevent the gun crews from slipping in blood, and marines were sent aloft to the fighting tops. Tubs of water for drinking and extinguishing fires were placed between the guns, and battle lanterns were hung above each gun, for the fighting decks would soon grow dark with smoke. Extra (preventer) rigging was set up as well as additional slings for the yards, while nets were spread over the upper deck to protect the men stationed there from wreckage falling from aloft. In the midshipmen's berth on the orlop, the surgeon and his assistants, looking like butchers in their long aprons, laid out their instruments, and the mess table at which the "young gentlemen" made merry became the operating table. Freshly scrubbed tubs for the amputated arms and legs were a grim reminder of what was to come.

To load the guns its crew cast loose the heavy breechings securing the gun truck, or wooden carriage, to the ship's side and pulled the weapon inboard as far as it would go for loading. Powder monkeys scurried up from the magazines with powder bags. A bag of powder and a wad were rammed down the gun barrel, followed by a shot and another wad. It was then hauled up against the ship's side until the muzzle poked through a gun port. As soon as it was in place, the gun captain took out his priming iron—an instrument resembling a needle with a corkscrew tip—and thrust it down through the touchhole into the powder bag and pulled it out. From a box strapped about his waist he took a priming tube made of goose quill and placed it in the touchhole so the sharp end entered the powder bag. If there were no priming tubes, he primed the gun with fine-milled powder from his powderhorn. Sights were crude, if available at all; the gun was aimed by elevating a quoin, or wedge, beneath the breech, while the truck was manhandled to left or right with handspikes, or wooden levers.

To fire the weapon, the gun captain, who had been blowing on a lighted match, a twisted cotton wick soaked in lye that rested on the edge of the water tub until needed, applied the red-hot end to the touchhole and smartly drew it back to avoid the "huff" of flame from the vent at the moment the gun fired. Beginning in 1780, the British replaced matches with the more efficient flintlock, which was triggered by jerking a lanyard.

Once the gun had fired, recoil sent it flying back with tremendous velocity to the limit of the breeching. Its path was unpredictable, and men were killed or injured by misjudging the recoil of their own weapons. If the gun had fired successfully, it recoiled into position to be reloaded. The barrel was swiftly swabbed out with a long-handled sponge dipped into the tub of water to prevent flaming scraps of the previous powder bag from prematurely igniting the new one. Then a fresh powder bag and shot were thrust down its muzzle, and the gun was hauled into position to be fired again. A well-trained gun crew could get off three shots in two minutes. In training exercises the guns were loaded and fired by command; when the ship was in action, the crews were expected to perform their tasks automatically even in the hellish fury of battle.

Sea battles were fought during this period in a manner as rigidly formal as a minuet. To prevent ships of the same fleet from getting into each other's way, from blanketing the fire of their consorts, or worse still, firing into them during the confusion of battle, ships were brought into action in line ahead. The vessels of a fleet trailed their leader in a single column, following the flagship's movements and signals. Each ship placed itself abeam of its opposite number in the enemy line—ships in the van, or lead division, against the enemy van, the center against his center, and the rear against his rear. French gunners fired on the upward roll to cripple the rigging and masts of the enemy ships so they could break off the battle whenever they wanted, while the British fired on the downward roll, aiming at the hulls of the opposing ships and the crews at the guns to sink them.

Signals were primitive, often obscured by the smoke of battle, and the various vessels of a fleet had different sailing qualities, with some forging ahead while others lagged. Because of the difficulty in controlling a large number of ships in an action, admirals issued written instructions before a battle for the guidance of their captains. Over the years the corpus of British tactical doctrine was codified in the *Permanent Fighting Instructions,* which had become so formalized that they were not an aid in fighting a battle but an end in themselves. The *Fighting Instructions* pressed down on fleet commanders with a dead hand, inhibiting originality and making a decisive engagement all but impossible. An admiral who obeyed them could not lose a battle, it was said. But neither could he win it.*

As Keppel's fleet went into battle, it was handicapped by the corrosion of the professional skills of many of its officers by fifteen years of peace and a lack of coordination among its hastily assembled elements. Moreover, there had been considerable difficulty in manning the ships, so the gap was filled with products of the press gangs and the prisons. On the other side, d'Orvilliers had orders to avoid battle unless he was certain of victory.

Keppel was between the French and their base at Brest, but the French held the weather gage—the position closest to the wind—with the advantage of choosing to fight or to avoid battle, while the British fleet had to claw its way to windward to mount an attack. For the next three days Keppel maneuvered to overcome the disadvantage of the downward or leeward position, while d'Orvilliers, more interested in returning to Brest unscathed than in fighting, avoided battle. Two of the French ships lost touch and were

---

*Lord Howe had developed a numerical signaling system that for the first time allowed ships to converse and thereby provide for better command and control of a fleet in battle. Unfortunately its use was limited only to his own ships in American waters, and an improved version was not adopted for the entire navy until after the war, when Howe was first lord of the Admiralty.

not seen again, so each fleet now numbered thirty vessels. Eager to be at the enemy, Keppel had ordered a general chase on the morning of July 27, enabling him to close with them, but his vessels were in disorder.

As a result, some of his ships failed to engage as the two fleets slowly passed each other under easy sail on parallel but opposite tacks, while exchanging broadside after broadside. Guns slammed to the limits of their breechings, and the crews jumped instantly to sponge out their steaming weapons and reload. The wind drove acrid banks of smoke down on Keppel's vessels, blinding the gunners. Some ships had to hold their fire in the choking darkness because they were unable to tell friend from foe. Several of the British ships, particularly those in the rear division, were badly cut up aloft by the French high-angle fire. The ninety-gun *Formidable,* flagship of Vice Admiral Sir Hugh Palliser, commander of this division, was racked by an internal explosion and suffered the heaviest causalties of the day.

After two hours of pounding, most of the British fleet was clear of the French line, trailed by a flotsam of broken spars and other debris. Keppel, with the intention of attacking again, ordered his fleet to wear, or reverse direction. But the battered rear division failed to comply with his repeated signals to form up on *Victory.* Instead the ships lay to, repairing damage. Darkness was falling by the time Keppel had collected a sufficiently powerful line of battle—too late to renew the action. He expected to bring the French to bay the next day, but during the night d'Orvilliers slipped away to the safety of Brest. The first major sea fight between French and the English fleets since the Seven Years' War had ended in a drawn battle. But for the Royal Navy, used to victories, such an outcome was almost as unwelcome as a defeat.

The indecisive battle off Ushant raged on in British politics long after the guns had fallen silent. Keppel claimed he had been denied a triumph by the failure of Palliser's rear division to support him; Palliser charged that Keppel had violated the *Fighting Instructions* by not reforming his line before attacking the enemy. Palliser was a supporter of the ministry, while Keppel had links to the Whig Opposition, so the ensuing official inquiries had more to do with a search for scapegoats than naval tactics. Both men were eventually acquitted of the charges brought by the other, but the affair constituted a massive, self-inflicted wound on the Royal Navy.* Nevertheless, it had a beneficial aspect. Keppel's acquittal was a clear sign that rigid and slavish conformity to the *Fighting Instructions* was no longer mandatory. An admiral could hope to conduct a battle according to his own best judgment and the circumstances in which he found himself.

*With the feuding families in Shakespeare's *Romeo and Juliet* in mind, wits dubbed the two factions the Montagues (Lord Sandwich's family name was Montagu) and the Capulets, a play on Keppel's supporters, the Keppelites.

FOLLOWING THE ENCOUNTER off Ushant, there was a lull in European waters, and the West Indies became a magnet for the major navies. Today it is difficult to appreciate the strategic significance of this string of tiny islands. Some changed hands several times over during the course of the war. Sugar was then as important to the economies of the western European nations as oil is in our own time, and the West Indies was the principal wealth-producing area of the eighteenth-century world. "Our [West Indian] Islands must be defended even at the risk of an invasion of this island," King George declared. "If we lose our Sugar Islands, it will be impossible to raise money to continue the war. . . ."

The aura of wealth surrounding the Sugar Islands was responsible for a fatal flaw in French naval strategy. In their eagerness to win control of the islands, French admirals regarded territorial conquest as their primary goal and the destruction of the enemy fleet as secondary. In reality, the conquest of the West Indies would have been easy once the British fleet was destroyed. Weather also had much to do with the emphasis on the Caribbean. Storms made winter campaigning risky off the North Atlantic coast, so both sides shifted their fleets to the warm waters of the West Indies as soon as the hurricane season had blown itself out. But campaigning in the Caribbean presented special problems because of malaria and yellow fever. Half a newly arrived force from Europe could expect to be disabled or dead by the end of the first summer.

The French drew first blood. On September 7, 1778, a makeshift force from Martinique surprised the weak British garrison on Dominica, which lay just to the north-northwest, and easily captured it. Britain's turn came soon afterward. Reinforcements from New York, including five ships of the line and five thousand troops, joined Rear Admiral Samuel Barrington's two ships at Barbados near the end of the year and he immediately sailed for St. Lucia, long a British objective because of its proximity to the main French base at Martinique. The French garrison had just surrendered to Barrington when, late on the afternoon of December 14, 1778, a frigate approached the British anchorage in the Grand Cul de Sac under a cloud of canvas and flying the signal "Enemy in sight."

The ships belonged to Comte d'Estaing's fleet of twelve of the line that had sailed from Boston at almost the same time as the British squadron had left New York. After touching at Martinique, d'Estaing had immediately sailed to the relief of St. Lucia. Unable to get out of the harbor in the face of a fleet almost double his strength, Barrington herded his transports into the harbor and, repeating the tactics used by Lord Howe at Sandy Hook, placed his ships across its entrance, with his guns sighted on the approaching French. D'Estaing made two attempts to break the British line, but both failed. Frustrated at sea, he put his experience as a soldier to use and launched a land attack on the British positions. It was repulsed with heavy losses, and the chagrined French admiral sailed away to Martinique, leaving St. Lucia in British hands.

With the coming of 1779, both the British and the French reinforced their fleets in the Caribbean. "Foul Weather Jack" Byron arrived in January to bring the number of British ships of the line to twenty-one and to take over command of the Leeward Islands station. As a result of the British failure to blockade Brest and French ports, d'Estaing received a steady stream of reinforcements. By the end of June 1779 his fleet totaled twenty-five of the line. Byron kept a watch on the French fleet, but early the following month d'Estaing evaded the British, because their crews had been decimated by fever. Without too much trouble he pocketed Grenada, the richest island of the Lesser Antilles. Thirty rich merchantmen in St. George's harbor, as well as the nearby island of St. Vincent, also fell into d'Estaing's bag.

Byron, with twenty-one of the line in which two regiments of army troops were detailed to fill out his crews, hastened to Grenada and appeared off the island on July 6. Unaware that the French fleet was superior to his own and wishing to attack before d'Estaing could form a line of battle, Byron signaled a general chase, and as at Ushant, the British fleet entered battle in disarray. Rushing pell-mell on the French, the speedier of the British ships plunged ahead but were badly knocked around by the enemy van and shore batteries. A freshening wind permitted the entire French fleet to emerge from St. George's Bay, and Byron now realized he faced a superior force.

Only after some difficulty he formed a line almost parallel to that of the French, but the rigging of several of his ships was severely cut up, and three had drifted out of action. Rather than pounce on them, d'Estaing, whose main preoccupation was—correctly—the defense of newly captured Grenada, tacked and returned to harbor. He merely cannonaded the stragglers as he passed, much to the surprise of Byron, who had expected the enemy to snap them up. French casualties were higher than those of the British, but d'Estaing had won a tactical victory—even if he had failed to take full advantage of it.

⌐∿

THE ONSET OF THE hurricane season in August all but cleared the board in the West Indies. Byron returned to England with his ships, while d'Estaing turned westward. Following a feint at Jamaica, he steered for the American coast with twenty-two ships of the line and four thousand soldiers to join the Americans in repelling British attacks on South Carolina and Georgia. Following the collapse of the Franco-American attempt to capture

Newport from the British, the war in the North had fallen into a stalemate, and the scene of action had shifted to the South, where the British had captured Savannah at the turn of the year.

The arrival of d'Estaing's fleet off Savannah on September 1, 1779, was so unexpected that *Experiment,* a fifty-gun ship carrying the payroll for the British army, fell into the hands of the French along with several other vessels. The city was surrounded by marsh and creeks, and the British had blocked the channel to prevent the French warships from getting in close enough for an effective bombardment, so the French and the Americans settled in for a siege. Both George Washington and General Clinton were surprised by the return of the French. Washington immediately suggested that d'Estaing come north for an attack on New York, where Vice Admiral Marriot Arbuthnot had but five ships of the line. Worried about the possibility of just such an attack, Clinton ordered Newport evacuated so he could concentrate all available troops and ships at New York.

The French were masters of the art of siege warfare, but such operations took time—and this was the one element d'Estaing lacked. He was under pressure from his captains to withdraw from the American coast because of the approach of the hurricane season, the dire need of the fleet for a refit, and the poor condition of the men, who were dying from fever and disease at a rate of thirty-five a day. With the siege making little progress, d'Estaing ordered an assault on the British defenses of Savannah on October 9. Still a soldier at heart, he personally led the attack. The Franco-American force was repulsed with heavy losses in savage hand-to-hand combat in which d'Estaing was severely wounded.

Over the vigorous protests of the Americans, who urged him to continue the siege, d'Estaing, nerves undoubtedly shaken by the casualties, his wounds, and the pleas of his officers to be gone, reembarked his troops and sailed away to France, leaving bitterness and disappointment in his wake. The Americans withdrew into South Carolina. Once again, they had seen the great strategic promise of French sea power dangled before their eyes, only to be preemptively withdrawn.

⌐

FOR BRITAIN, THE WORST crisis of the war was brewing nearer home. She was confronted in mid-1779 by the possible loss of control of the English Channel to the combined fleets of France and Spain and faced the specter of invasion. Spain had declared war on Britain on July 16 of that year, but in a vain attempt to insulate her own colonies from the virus of revolution, not as an ally of the American rebels but as a partner of her sister Bourbon kingdom of France. The French agreed to aid Spain in recovering Gibraltar, Minorca, Jamaica, and the coast of Honduras from Britain as the price of

Spanish support. Thus the United States, bound by treaty not to make peace without the approval of France, found itself obligated—without being consulted—to remain at war until Spain captured Gibraltar, even though Spain was not an ally.

The Royal Navy was unable to maintain a blockade of Brest because of a shortage of ships and trained crews. The lack of seasoned timber was responsible for the long delays in fitting out the necessary ships. Admirals and captains cried out for men so they could get the available vessels to sea, but American sailors who had filled the gap in the navy's manpower needs were no longer available. Sickness and desertion had a crippling effect on operations—particularly in the Channel fleet, which received the largest proportion of the unseasoned men and where weather conditions were most severe.

From 1774 to 1780 the Royal Navy took in 175,990 new recruits, an enormous number considering that Britain's total population was only about 10 million people. Of these, 1,243 were killed in action or died of wounds, 18,541 died of disease, and 42,069 deserted—marked "run" on the muster books. The number killed in battle was small compared to land engagements; losses by sickness were inevitable, considering the state of medical knowledge at the time.* The loss by desertion provides a basic reason for Britain's failure at sea in the American war. Brutality and poor living conditions were accepted—after all, such conditions existed both onshore and in merchant ships. What sailors did object to was poor and irregular pay and lack of leave—and made their views known by deserting in droves, leaving the navy so short of men it could not carry out its duties.

IN AUGUST 1779 an armada of sixty-six ships of the line—thirty French and thirty-six Spanish—sailed into the Channel to prepare the way for a landing by some forty thousand troops on the Isle of Wight and the destruction of the nearby British naval base at Portsmouth as a preliminary to a full-scale invasion of England. Not since the Anglo-Dutch wars of a century before had an enemy fleet thrown down such a challenge. The French fleet was under the command of the Comte d'Orvilliers, and Admi-

---

*Scurvy, although not fatal in itself, was the curse of life at sea because it weakened sailors and made them susceptible to other illnesses. Although Dr. James Lind had as early as 1747 linked scurvy to a diet lacking in fresh vegetables and prescribed oranges and lemons as an antiscorbutic, the Admiralty believed that these were too expensive. British seamen did not receive a daily serving of lemon juice until 1795, when it was mixed with the grog ration to make certain the men drank it.

ral Don Luis de Cordoba was in charge of the Spanish fleet. The seventy-year-old d'Orvilliers was ailing, while Cordoba, another septuagenarian, had seen little service at sea and was distinguished only for his piety.

The two fleets were to have rendezvoused off the Spanish port of Corruna in early May so they would have adequate time to coordinate their movements and good weather to carry out their mission. But the French did not get to sea until early June, and the tardy Spaniards failed to put in an appearance for six more weeks, leaving d'Orvilliers nothing to do except sail aimlessly and consume his provisions. By the time the Spanish fleet came in sight on July 23, the French had eaten half their supplies, and fever and smallpox stalked the decks of their ships.

To face this "Second Armada," the Admiralty could muster only thirty-nine ships of the line, some barely able to float or carry guns. Moreover, the Keppel-Palliser affair had so bitterly divided the Royal Navy's flag officers that no admiral of stature was willing to accept command of the Channel fleet. By default it devolved on sixty-three-year-old admiral Sir Charles Hardy, who had a fairly distinguished record but was ailing; his most recent post was governor of Greenwich Hospital for old and infirm seamen. To lend some sense of competence to the direction of operations, Richard Kempenfelt, an officer of considerable ability, was assigned as Hardy's captain of the fleet, or chief of staff.

Kempenfelt was appalled by what he saw when he reported to *Victory.* "There is a fund of good nature in the man, but not one grain of the Commander-in-Chief," he wrote of Hardy to the Admiralty. "My God, what have you great people done by such an appointment?" The fleet's discipline was poor and its level of efficiency low. On one occasion Hardy ordered the fleet to form a line of battle and was amazed to see his ships promptly heave to and lower boats. The signal hoisted had ordered the captains to send their weekly reports to the admiral. This fiasco spurred Kempenfelt to hurry work on an improved version of Lord Howe's signal book, which he produced the following year.*

Additionally, Hardy's strategy was defective. His fleet was superior to the French fleet, and had he stationed his vessels off Brest while the French were preparing for sea, he could have prevented them from sailing. After

---

*Tragically, Kempenfelt, who had been promoted to rear admiral, lost his life in 1782 when *Royal George,* his flagship, sank at the naval anchorage at Spithead while being careened for repairs, with the loss of eight hundred to nine hundred officers, men, women, and children. Legend has it that the rotten bottom fell out of the ship, but this does not appear to have been the cause of her loss. Instead, she appears to have been tipped over too far, and water came into her gun ports. For many years after, the tip of the vessel's topmast marked her resting place. See R. F. Johnson, *The Royal George.*

allowing the French and Spanish fleets to unite, Hardy did nothing except sail up and down the Channel, waiting for the Combined Fleet to appear. He was off the Scilly Islands with an easterly wind driving his ships out into the Western Approaches when on August 16 he heard the appalling news that the enemy fleet had slipped past him and was riding unchallenged within sight of Plymouth. Panic spread across England's southern coast: business ceased, shops closed, and many residents fled inland. Fear mounted as the thud of gunfire was heard. The sixty-four-gun *Ardent,* on her way up the Channel to join Hardy, had blundered into the enemy fleet and hauled down its flag after a brief exchange of fire.

Had the populace known what was taking place on *Bretagne,* the French admiral's flagship, they would have breathed easier. The shortage of food and water was now desperate, and the epidemic was making such headway that many of his ships were little more than floating pesthouses. D'Orvilliers' son, a young lieutenant, was among those carried off by fever. And the admiral had no idea of the position of the British fleet. As he juggled these problems, d'Orvilliers received new instructions. The landing was to be made at Falmouth on the Cornish coast rather on the Isle of Wight, and his beachhead was to be held throughout the winter.

For d'Orvilliers this was the last straw. He begged his superiors to recall the expedition in view of the sickness rampant in the Combined Fleet. When they refused, he decided to bring the British to battle and defeat them before supplies ran out. In the meantime, the wind had shifted, and Hardy had sailed back up the Channel from the Atlantic. On August 31 the two fleets caught intermittent sight of each other amid patches of fog and mist. While Hardy was outnumbered, the enemy fleet was so spread out that had he forced a battle it is doubtful that many of its ships could have joined in the action. But Hardy was aware only of his own inferiority, and avoiding action, slipped away to Spithead. D'Orvilliers made a half-hearted effort to chase the British, but his fleet was straggling so badly— especially the Spaniards—that he was unable to close with the enemy.

Hardy's officers and men felt humiliated by his refusal to give battle, which, correctly or not, they regarded as running away from the enemy. Captain Adam Duncan of *Monarch* railed against the "indignation and shame." *Victory*'s crew hung hammocks before the eyes of her figurehead so it could not see a British fleet chased from the Channel. Nevertheless, Hardy was now between the opposing fleet and Britain's southern ports, and thus they were now secure from invasion—not due to his own skill, but to the incompetence of his enemies. Supplies exhausted, d'Orvilliers returned to Brest with his ships and part of the Spanish fleet, with the rest going to Gibraltar to tighten a land and sea siege established the previous

June. Neither Hardy nor d'Orvilliers was ever employed at sea again. Queen Marie Antoinette best summed up the affair, saying it "cost a great deal of money to do nothing."

꙳

WHILE THE GREAT FLEETS were futilely maneuvering in the Channel, John Paul Jones was at sea on a raiding voyage in the Continental sloop-of-war *Ranger*, of eighteen guns, intended to strike at Britain's all-important trade in essential naval stores with the Baltic. "I wish to have no Connection with any Ship that does not sail *fast*, for I intend to go in harm's way," he declared—and it was the guiding principle of Jones's naval career. Born John Paul, Jr., the son of a gardener on an estate near the border between Scotland and England, he went to sea in 1761 as a lad of thirteen. Years of voyaging to the West Indies and American followed, and by age twenty-one he was a captain in the merchant service, no small accomplishment for a young man without influence.

In 1773 the course of the youthful Captain Paul's life was forever changed. According to his own account, a mutinous seaman attacked him while his vessel was at Tobago, and in self-defense he struck and killed the man. Fearing retribution from friends of the dead sailor, he fled. What he did for the next two years is a mystery—there were rumors that he spent the time in the slave trade—and when he reappeared in America he called himself John Paul Jones.

Upon his arrival in France at the end of 1777, Jones was determined to strike at an unsuspecting English port so the enemy might feel the lash of war. Before departing on this mission he wished to have the honor of being the first Continental Navy officer to exchange salutes with a French admiral. On February 14, 1778, *Ranger* sailed into Quiberon Bay, where a French fleet was anchored, and a thirteen-gun salute boomed out from her sides as she passed the French flagship. The latter answered with nine guns—the first salute rendered to the Stars and Stripes by a foreign warship.

Like Horatio Nelson, Paul Jones was short and slight, brave, reckless, and eager for fame. But unlike Nelson, Jones neither inspired complete loyalty nor attracted abiding friendships. While no seagoing tyrant, he was an exceedingly quarrelsome man and a perfectionist who was always criticizing and nagging subordinates, damning them in fits of temper for which he was later apologetic. Like many self-made men, Jones was extremely self-centered. He took good care of his men, but not out of sympathy or consideration. To him, they were like his cannons and ships—merely means to an end.

John Paul Jones. From a drawing done in May 1780 by Jean Michel Moreau *le jeune,* which, along with a bust by Houdon, is the best likeness of Jones. (U.S. Naval Academy Museum)

Although burdened with jealous officers and a crew restive under strict discipline, Jones captured several prizes in the Irish Sea and attempted to burn the shipping in the harbor of Whitehaven, from which he had sailed as a youthful apprentice. No one had launched such an attack since 1667, when the Dutch burned Sheerness. With the help of a rainstorm, the inhabitants extinguished the blaze before much damage was done. Jones also attempted to seize the earl of Selkirk, the local laird, with the hope of exchanging him for American seamen being held in English prisons. Upon learning that Selkirk was not home, Jones wanted to abandon the expedition, but his men insisted on taking the family silver. Jones, who considered himself a gentleman, not a brigand, was appalled by the suggestion but thought it prudent to give in to the demands of his unruly men. To satisfy his honor, he purchased the silver from the crew and returned it to the Selkirk family, who were less than grateful.

Next, Jones crossed the Irish Sea to deal with *Drake*, a twenty-gun sloop-of-war, previously sighted in Belfast Lough. Shortly before sunset on April 24 the two ships cleared for action. Although they were almost equal in firepower, *Drake* was manned by raw volunteers and was several officers short. "The action was warm, close, and obstinate," Jones reported. *Ranger* stood off with the intention of crippling but not sinking her opponent so she could be taken as a prize. With most of her officers dead, her masts splintered, and her sails hanging in tatters, *Drake* surrendered an hour after the first broadsides.

Returning to France after a cruise that included a raid on an English seaport and the capture of the first British warship taken in European waters by an American vessel, Jones expected to be rewarded with a more powerful ship. Instead, after considerable delay, he was given command of *Duc de Duras*, a tired old East Indiaman armed with a mixed bag of forty-two guns, some of questionable reliability. To compliment his patron, Benjamin Franklin, whose almanacs, translated into French as *Les Maximes du Bonhomme Richard*, were popular in Paris, Jones rechristened the vessel *Bonhomme Richard*.

Jones put to sea from Lorient on August 14, 1779, with the Baltic convoy as his target. *Richard* was accompanied by *Alliance*, a fine new American frigate of thirty-two guns under the command of a strange and erratic Frenchman named Pierre Landais, three ships of the French Navy, and two French privateers. The privateers quickly disappeared, and none of the other captains took Jones's authority as commodore very seriously—least of all Landais. Several rich prizes were captured on a cruise around the British Isles, and panic spread in the wake of the "Yankee pirate," but a planned attack on Leith, the port of Edinburgh, had to be abandoned because of a lack of support by Jones's officers.

But as evening fell on September 23, 1779, Jones hit the jackpot. The squadron was off Flamborough Head, a chalk outcropping on the eastern coast of England, when a convoy of forty-one ships inbound from the Baltic was sighted. They were shepherded by the powerful new frigate *Serapis*, of forty-four guns, and the sloop-of-war *Countess of Scarborough*, twenty. Jones ordered an immediate attack on the escort that had interposed themselves between the merchantmen and his squadron. As the ships closed, Captain Richard Pearson of *Serapis* called out:

"What ship is that?"

"*Princess Royal!*" replied Jones. The creak of yards and masts and the squeak of ropes in the blocks sounded louder than usual as the two ships ran side by side through the darkness. Jones stood by with a speaking trumpet in his hand but remained silent.

"Where from?" asked Pearson with growing irritation. "Answer directly or I'll fire into you!"

Instead of replying, Jones struck the British ensign being flown by *Richard* and raised a flag with red, white, and blue stripes. Broadsides erupted from both *Richard* and *Serapis,* raising the curtain on one of the most desperate single-ship actions in the history of naval warfare. "The battle being just begun, was continued with unremitting fury," Jones reported. Much to his anger, his consorts shied away, leaving him to take on *Serapis* alone. Later, however, the French frigate *Pallas,* twenty-six, engaged *Countess of Scarborough* and, after a sharp fight, captured her.

At the first or second broadside, there was a burst of flame on the *Richard*'s gun deck, and she shook from stem to stern. Agonized screams and the smell of scorched flesh filled the night. Two of the old eighteen-pounders that were the mainstays of her armament had exploded, wiping out their

The nighttime battle between *Bonhomme Richard* and *Serapis* off Flamborough Head on September 22, 1779. *Alliance* is shown firing into *Richard.* (Beverly Robinson Collection, U.S. Naval Academy Museum)

crews and blowing a gaping hole in the deck above. Their shrieks were soon lost in the uproar. In an instant, the weight of the old vessel's broadside had been reduced to 195 pounds, as compared to 300 for her opponent.

Realizing that his ponderous ship was no match for *Serapis,* Jones tried to lay *Richard* alongside the enemy vessel and carry her by boarding. But every attempt to accomplish this was thwarted by the speed and maneuverability of the British frigate and Pearson's skill. At one point Jones had the sickening experience of seeing the bow of his ship jammed into the stern of *Serapis* and was unable to bring a single gun to bear to answer the murderous British fire. Having clearly demonstrated the superior firepower and handling of his ship, Captain Pearson hailed: "Was your ship struck?"

"I have not yet begun to fight!" replied the indomitable Jones.*

A full moon had risen, and hundreds of Yorkshiremen gathered on Flamborough Head to watch the battle. As the two ships maneuvered to rake, *Serapis'* bowsprit rode up on *Richard*'s poop deck like a lance and became entangled in her mizzen rigging. Jones called for grappling hooks, and the vessels were locked together in a dance of death, bow to stern, the muzzles of their guns grinding against each other's side. Fires broke out on both ships, and periodically it was necessary to break off combat to subdue the flames before they reached the magazines. The British prisoners previously taken by Jones were put to work under guard manning the pumps.

The murderous pounding continued, and *Serapis'* cannons were doing tremendous damage. *Richard*'s hull was riddled, and only a few stanchions supported the upper deck. "My prospects became gloomy indeed," Jones said, and his vessel was "mangled beyond my power of description." Within two hours of the start of the struggle, all of *Richard*'s broadsides with the exception of a pair of nine-pounders on her quarterdeck had been knocked out of commission, and her gun crews decimated. Jones had guns from the unengaged port side hauled over, and sighting one himself, concentrated on bringing down the enemy's mainmast.

Unexpectedly, *Alliance* loomed out of the darkness. The ragged cheer from *Richard* that greeted her appearance was drowned out by the roar of the frigate's guns. "To my utter astonishment he discharged a broadside full into the stern of the *Bonhomme Richard,*" Jones reported. "Every tongue cried out that he was firing into the wrong ship." But Landais put about and unleashed another broadside into the stricken vessel. Although it may have been difficult to distinguish the two ships from each other in the moonlight and Landais did cease firing after Jones raised recognition signals, Jones

*The first account that includes this statement was given in 1825 by Richard Dale, Jones's aged first lieutenant, to an early biographer of John Paul Jones. Jones did not mention having said these words in his report on the battle.

regarded the Frenchman's actions as deliberate—apparently inspired by a desire to get rid of Jones and take credit for the victory. Once ashore, Jones brought charges against the addled Landais, who was ultimately dismissed from the navy.

The British also were having problems. Pearson's frantic efforts to get free of *Richard*'s deadly embrace so he could bring his superior firepower into play came to naught. French marines stationed in *Richard*'s tops swept the enemy vessel's upper deck clear of men, and sharpshooters stationed below picked off the British gunners through shot holes and gun ports. Powder monkeys were bringing cartridges up from the magazines faster than they could be used. The frightened boys simply dumped them on the deck near the guns and raced below for more. One of Jones's men carried a basket of hand grenades out to the end of a yard that hung directly over *Serapis'* open hatches. He lobbed one onto the gundeck and it exploded among a pile of loose cartridges with a searing flash. Twenty British sailors were killed and more were horribly burned.

Not long after, Jones succeed in bringing down *Serapis'* mainmast. For Captain Pearson, this was the final blow and he decided to surrender. *Countess of Scarborough* had already struck to *Pallas,* so he could expect no help from that quarter; *Alliance* was undamaged and might return at any moment to attack him; his ship was on fire and only four of his eighteen-pounders were still firing. "I found it in vain and in short impracticable from the situation we were in to stand out any longer with the least prospect of success," he later reported to the Admiralty. With his own hand, he hauled down his colors three and a half hours after the start of the battle.

Casualties were high on both sides, with one of Jones's officers saying the blood was "over one's shoes." *Richard* was so severely battered that Jones was unable to attack the Baltic convoy, which reached port without the loss of a single ship. Two days later he watched "with inexpressible grief" from the deck of the captured *Serapis* as *Bonhomme Richard* plunged bow first into the dark waters of the North Sea. Although not much of a man-of-war, she had given him undying fame.

Jones returned home to be given command of *America,* the Continental Navy's only seventy-four-gun ship, but she was presented to the French, and he never again commanded an American vessel. He served for a time as a rear admiral in the Russian Navy under Catherine the Great and returned to Paris, where "like a wine-skin from which the wine has been withdrawn," he died in obscurity in 1792. In 1905 his body was brought to the United States and buried in the crypt of the chapel of the Naval Academy at Annapolis, as a symbol of America's emerging naval power.

CHAPTER 5

"The World . . . Turned Upside Down"

FEW ROYAL NAVY officers have aroused more admiration and antipathy than Admiral Sir George Bridges Rodney.* While regarded as one of Britain's more masterful and enterprising seamen, he was also vain, avaricious, and heartily disliked by many of his fellows for his unbending Toryism and cold haughtiness. Yet as the Admiralty desperately cast about for a capable but politically reliable officer to carry the war at sea to the enemy after Keppel's failure at Ushant, Byron's mishaps in the Caribbean, and Hardy's near-fatal hesitations in the Channel, the eye of Lord Sandwich fell on Rodney's aging figure.

In early 1780 there were signs that the war was turning in Britain's favor. The island kingdom no longer faced the threat of invasion. In America, Washington's army was freezing in its camp at Morristown, New Jersey, under conditions worse than at Valley Forge. Sir Henry Clinton, taking advantage of the mobility conferred by command of the sea, was planning to move south from New York to capture Charleston, where he had been ignominiously repulsed four years before. With the dispersal of the combined fleet to its ports, the Admiralty thought it safe to transfer ships from the Channel fleet to relieve besieged Gibraltar, which was running short of supplies. Once this was accomplished, some of these vessels were to proceed to the West Indies to restore British control of the disputed area. With no one else to turn to, Sandwich entrusted Rodney with command of this vital expedition despite the fact that the two men disliked each other, the admiral had not commanded a fleet in wartime in seventeen years, and he suffered from gout and kidney complaints.

Having entered the navy as a lad of fourteen under direct royal patronage, which assured him of a quick rise in his profession, Rodney was sixty-

---

*Although Rodney's middle name is usually given as "Brydges," he spelled it with an "i."

Admiral George Lord Rodney. An engraving based on a portrait by Thomas Gainsborough. (U.S. Naval Academy Museum)

one at the time of his appointment to the Leeward Islands station.* Politics and gambling were his passions—and would be his undoing. He lost large sums at the gaming table and went heavily into debt buying himself a seat in Parliament. Fleeing from his creditors, he sat out the early years of the American War in Paris. Once France entered the conflict, however, the old sea dog expressed a willingness to serve—with an eye on the possibility of restoring his fortunes with prize money. To keep his greed in check, a special commissioner was placed at the admiral's elbow during the purchase of stores and equipment for his fleet.

Rodney was the beneficiary of a technological breakthrough of immense importance. By the time his fleet was ready to sail, most of the bottoms of his ships had been coppered. This prevented marine growth from fouling their bottoms, increasing speed and allowing them to remain longer at sea. Experiments in coppering the bottoms of ships began toward the end of the Seven Years' War, but because of corrosion of the iron bolts binding the hulls together as a result of the galvanic action of the copper, interest in the project lapsed. In 1775 the corrosion problem was solved by insulating the hull from the copper by inserting a sheet of tarred paper between the wood and the sheathing. Much of the credit for coppering should go to Vice Admiral Sir Charles Middleton, who succeeded Maurice Suckling, Nelson's uncle, as comptroller of the navy, and who insisted on it despite the cost.

Rodney sailed for Gibraltar with twenty-two ships of the line shortly before New Year's Day along with a massive convoy of merchantmen bound for the Mediterranean and the Caribbean. Within a week the armada was past the danger zone off the French coast, and the trading vessels destined for the West Indies were sorted out and dispatched on the long voyage west. The remainder plowed on toward Gibraltar with Rodney. Shortly after daybreak on January 8, 1780, a Spanish convoy of twenty-two ships came into view and was quickly snapped up. They included a sixty-four-gun two-decker and three frigates, which were added to Rodney's force, while the merchantmen were sent home under prize crews—where they were undoubtedly greeted with delight by the admiral's creditors.

Eight days later, on the afternoon of January 16, part of the Spanish fleet blockading Gibraltar, nine of the line and two frigates, was sighted off Cape St. Vincent, at the tip of Portugal. As night fell, the Spanish commander, Don Juan de Langara, ordered his ships to flee from the superior British force. But Rodney, who was in bed with an attack of gout, had already signaled for a general chase, beginning what became known as the

---

*Rodney took an imperious view of nepotism, promoting his sixteen-year-old son to captain. He, himself, had not reached that rank until age twenty-four.

"Moonlight Battle." Although the British had double the number of Spanish ships, the encounter was fought in a near gale, with seas so high that the
British three-deckers were unable to open their lower gun ports, and they
ran close to a lee shore to prevent the Spaniards from escaping into port.

The newly coppered bottoms of Rodney's ships allowed them to overhaul
the fleeing Spanish squadron, and one by one, the Spaniards were caught
and battered into submission. The seventy-gun *Santo Domingo* blew up with
a tremendous roar while engaged with three British ships. It was "a most
shocking and dreadful sight," Prince William Henry (later King William IV),
the third son of King George, serving as a midshipman in *Sandwich*, Rodney's flagship, wrote his father. Five enemy ships were captured, including
the flagship. Because of the disparity of the forces involved, the battle could
have had only one outcome, but the victory was welcomed by a nation
starved for good news. Public buildings were illuminated, and Rodney was
awarded a two-thousand-pound annual pension, then a significant sum.

Gibraltar was successfully relieved amid cheers from the beleaguered
garrison. After detaching those ships that were to return to the Channel
Fleet,* Rodney sailed for the West Indies in mid-February with four of the
line. Unknown to the British, a French fleet of sixteen ships of the line—
half the Brest fleet—and a large convoy of merchant vessels and transports
under the command of the Comte de Guichin had sailed for the Caribbean
on a course almost parallel to their own. Both fleets arrived at their destinations within days of each other.

Since the departure of Comte d'Estaing's fleet the previous year, the
Royal Navy had controlled the area, but de Guichin's arrival at Martinique
tipped the balance in favor of the French—twenty-three ships of the line to
twenty-one. Moreover, most of the French vessels were fresh from home,
completely refitted and with clean bottoms. On the other side, the bulk of
the British ships had been in the West Indies for some time and had been
battered by storms, their seams opened by the heat of the tropical sun and
their crews decimated by sickness.

Rodney and de Guichin were two of the most skillful naval tacticians of
the day—in fact, the Frenchman was a former commander of the Squadron
of Evolution. But like his predecessors, he was handcuffed by orders not
to hazard his ships, while Rodney was eager to give battle. In his Parisian
exile Rodney had thought much about the deficiencies of the *Fighting
Instructions* and had worked out new tactics that he was confident would
produce a decisive victory. To overcome an enemy's numerical advantage,
he intended to concentrate his entire force on the French rear division and

*On their way home these ships fell in with a French convoy bound for Mau-
ritius in the Indian Ocean and captured several transports and a sixty-four-gun
ship carrying sixty thousand pounds sterling.

defeat it before the rest of the enemy fleet could come to the rescue. Unhappily, the admiral had only a limited time to communicate his ideas to his captains, and some were confused about the exact details of his plan.

Rodney got his chance to put these tactics into effect during an encounter on April 17 a few miles south of Dominica. The French ships carried three thousand troops for the planned capture of Barbados. Shortly before noon, following considerable maneuvering, the two fleets were sailing on parallel courses, with the French line somewhat more advanced. Rodney, who held the weather gage, ordered his ships to close with and engage the vessels opposite them, thereby massing his heaviest force against the enemy's rear. To his utter amazement, *Stirling Castle,* seventy-four, which was in the British van, did not engage the French ship opposite her. Instead, in slavery to the *Fighting Instructions,* her captain slanted down along the enemy line to open fire on the leading French ship. The other ships of the van division followed her example, and to Rodney's disgust the battle was fought in the orthodox line ahead. At one point *Sandwich* fought her way through the French line, but there was no signal for breaking the line, and none of the other ships joined her in attacking the enemy's unengaged side. Neither side lost a ship, but the French were forced to abandon their attempt to capture Barbados.

De Guichin came out again early in May, this time with the intention of retaking St. Lucia. Over the next twelve days the fleets engaged in another two indecisive battles. Holding the weather gage and confident of their strength, the French danced around the plodding British vessels, threatening but always staying out of reach of the enemy's guns. Rodney used this frustrating period to drill and instill discipline into his fleet.

On May 15 he succeeded in luring the French closer by simulating a withdrawal. De Guichin swallowed the bait, and Rodney, aided by a fortuitous shift in the wind, moved to cut off part of the French line. But the wind shifted again in favor of the French, who bore away after a brief clash that left both sides unscathed. Four days later there was another passing encounter, in which the French got the worse of it. De Guichin broke off the action and returned to Martinique, a victim of the fatal French doctrine of trying to achieve strategic results without accepting tactical risks. As for Rodney, he had fought three battles, held his own with ships inferior in numbers and quality to the French, and had not lost an island.

Early in June 1780, the naval balance tipped farther against the British with the arrival of a dozen Spanish ships of the line and nearly twelve thousand troops under Don José Solano. The French and Spaniards now had thirty-six battleships to only seventeen British, and they might well have swept the Union Jack from the Caribbean. But the Spanish fleet was devastated by scurvy, and Solano refused to cooperate in French plans for joint operations against the British islands. Tempers flared among the proud Spanish and

French officers, and there were several fatal duels. In July the Spanish fleet sailed for Havana to defend Cuba and Puerto Rico against a possible British attack without having engaged in any offensive action.

Under orders to leave the Caribbean before the hurricane season, de Guichin accompanied the Spaniards as far as Cap François, a major French base on the northern coast of Haiti. There he found letters from the ardent young Marquis de Lafayette, who was serving on Washington's staff, as well as from the French minister in Philadelphia, imploring him to come north. Not long before, Lafayette had returned from a quick visit to France in which he was told that troops under the command of the Comte de Rochambeau were soon to be sent to America, and he wished de Guichin to cooperate with this force. But the admiral, worn out from his exertions and mourning the loss of a son in battle, left these pleas unanswered and sailed for France in mid-August.

Rodney, facing bad weather and suspecting the French had indeed gone to America, prepared to follow. His fears were confirmed when he received the disquieting news that a French fleet and transports filled with soldiers had arrived in Newport. However, it was not de Guichin but a new force, led by the Chevalier de Terney with seven ships of the line and Rochambeau's fifty-five hundred troops. This was more than enough to deal with the only large British ships in American waters—Admiral Arbuthnot's four of the line, which were with Clinton at Charleston. Rodney divided his fleet, sending the ships in the poorest condition to Jamaica to escort the September convoy home while keeping the ten ships in best repair with him as "without a moment's hesitation" he sailed for New York.

WHILE THE GREAT FLEETS were conducting operations in European waters and in the Caribbean, the remaining ships of the Continental Navy were being lost through capture at sea, blockaded by the British, or unable to sail because of a shortage of crews and supplies. The one bright event was the seizure in early 1778 of New Providence by Captain John Rathbun—this time with but a single ship and a handful of sailors and marines. Several valuable prizes were taken, the fortifications were dismantled, and some American prisoners were released. This success was marred, however, by the loss within a ninety-day period of the new frigates *Randolph* and *Virginia* as well as the veterans *Alfred* and *Columbus*.

The loss of *Randolph*, commanded by Nicholas Biddle, was especially tragic. Having achieved some success as a commerce raider, the frigate was sailing off Barbados on March 17, 1778, when a large British vessel was sighted. Biddle unhesitatingly gave battle even though the opponent proved to be the sixty-four-gun *Yarmouth*, which carried double the number of guns mounted by *Randolph*. The Yankee frigate was holding her own, and an eyewitness reported that she "appeared to fire four or five broadsides to *Yarmouth's* one." Suddenly there was an explosion, and *Randolph* vanished in a tower of flame and smoke. Nicholas Biddle and all but 4 of his crew of 305 were lost.

Two weeks later, on the night of March 31, Captain James Nicholson, the Continental Navy's senior officer following the dismissal of Esek Hopkins, tried to run the twenty-eight-gun *Virginia* through a blockade that had kept her bottled up in Chesapeake Bay. In the darkness the pilot put her aground on a shoal at the mouth of the bay under the guns of a British squadron. When daylight came, Nicholson had himself rowed ashore, leaving *Virginia* and her crew to be captured. Awaiting a British boarding party, some men broke into the rum stores and got drunk. "It was "All Fools' Day," Joshua Barney, the frigate's first lieutenant, caustically observed.

Two of the largest naval expeditions launched by the Americans during the war also ended in disaster. The first, mounted in July 1779, was aimed at driving the British from a base at Castine on the Penobscot River in Maine. The Massachusetts authorities recruited a force of a thousand men, who were transported to the Penobscot by a sizable flotilla of ships, some belonging to the Continental Navy and others to the state. Captain Dudley Saltonstall, skipper of the thirty-two-gun frigate *Warren*, was named commodore of the naval force of seventeen armed ships, among them the old sloop *Providence*, sole survivor of the navy's first fleet. Cooperation between the naval and land forces quickly broke down, and an operation that should have been conducted with rapidity settled into a wearying siege of the British outpost.

As the Yankee commanders squabbled, a powerful British relief force under Commodore Sir George Collier, an experienced and pugnacious officer who flew his flag in the sixty-four-gun *Raisonnable*, which had been Horatio Nelson's first ship, arrived on August 12. Panic seized the Americans. Instead of attempting to make a stand, they made a mad rush for safety, with every man for himself. Ships were run aground and set afire while terrified soldiers and sailors fled into the woods. Nearly five hundred men were killed or captured by the British, nineteen armed vessels were lost, and nearly seven million dollars was squandered.

Nine months later, a second disaster struck the Continental Navy. As soon as word was received of the British attack on Charleston, the frigates *Boston, Providence,* and *Queen of France*, as well as *Ranger*, John Paul Jones's old ship, were dispatched to assist in the defense of the city. In the four years since the failed British attack of 1776, Charleston's defenses had been allowed to deteriorate. This time, following a month-long siege during which British land and naval artillery pounded the city to pieces, the Americans surrendered on May 12, 1780. Some five thousand prisoners were taken, along with the Continental Navy's last squadron. It was the most severe defeat suffered by American forces until Pearl Harbor in 1941. Except for a handful of commerce raiders, the Continental Navy had, for all practical purposes, been eliminated as an effective fighting force.

↬

UPON RECEIVING NEWS of the arrival of the French at Newport and fearing they would attempt to cut his communications with New York City, General Clinton hurried back from Charleston with four thousand troops and Arbuthnot's four ships of the line. The remainder of the British army, about eight thousand men, were left behind in the South under the command of General Earl Cornwallis, who had instructions to maintain control of South Carolina and avoid risky operations. As soon as he learned of the arrival of the French, Washington sent Lafayette to see Rochambeau with a plan for a combined land-sea attack on New York. "In any operation, and under all circumstances, a decisive naval superiority is to be considered as a fundamental principle, and the basis upon which every hope of success must ultimately depend," he told Rochambeau.

Clinton and Arbuthnot, now reinforced by six of the line flying the flag of Rear Admiral Thomas Graves, produced a plan for a lightning attack on Newport before the French had time to dig in. Speed was of the essence if the expedition was to succeed, but relations between Clinton and Arbuthnot, which had been stormy all along, collapsed under these new pressures. Rodney's arrival from the Caribbean added to the dissension when he and Arbuthnot fell out over the distribution of prize money for Yankee merchantmen and privateers taken by the fleet.

Washington finally put an end to the proposed operation by making a feint toward New York from his base in the Hudson highlands. Realizing that the opportunity to attack Newport had been lost despite the presence of a superior British fleet, Rodney sailed for the West Indies on November 16, 1780. Gloom also shrouded the American cause, for the hopes built upon the arrival of the French had crumbled. The squadron rocked uselessly at anchor off Newport under blockade by Arbuthnot while Rochambeau's troops went into winter quarters.

↬

RODNEY ARRIVED AT Barbados to find his base leveled by a ferocious hurricane. As his ships moved silently into their anchorage in Carlisle Bay, the admiral was shocked by the sights that greeted his eyes. The dockyard facilities lay in ruins, warehouses full of supplies had been destroyed, and nearly every building in nearby Bridgetown had lost its roof or been flattened by the fury of the storm. Two ships of the line that had been left

Admiral Samuel Viscount Hood. (U.S. Naval Academy Museum)

behind, as well as a forty-four and three frigates, were lost, and more than a dozen other vessels had been dismasted or severely damaged. One seventy-four was blown clear across the Atlantic, eventually making a landfall on the coast of Wales. The British fleet in the Caribbean had been more effectively crippled by the hurricane than by anything the French had done in two years of war.

In January 1781 Rodney received welcome reinforcements in the form of eight ships of the line under the command of Rear Admiral Sir Samuel Hood, who was designated by the Admiralty as his second in command. Hood was an old friend of Rodney's, and in contrast to many British admirals of the day, was at fifty-seven a prime fighting seaman. But Hood had a sulfurous temper and was a merciless critic of the conduct of others, although very touchy when criticized himself. On the other hand, he went out of his way to be kind to younger officers who did their duty—and Horatio Nelson was to become his prime pupil. With fresh stores and matériel brought in by Hood, Rodney's ships were refitted for battle. By the end of January the fleet consisted of twenty-one of the line ready for sea—once again giving the British command of West Indian waters.

At this point a sloop raced in from England with the news that war had been declared with Holland. Rodney's avaricious eye immediately focused on the Dutch island of St. Eustatius. The hitherto neutral—and therefore untouchable—island was the center of a thriving trade in contraband with the Americans, and even some British merchants were suspected of trading with the enemy. Rodney captured the "Golden Rock," as it was known, on February 3, without difficulty, and it lived up to its name. "The riches of St. Eustatius are beyond all comprehension," he chortled in a letter to his wife. The plunder included at least 130 ships in the roadstead, 12 flying the British flag—proof positive that the merchants were indeed engaged in illegal trade. A convoy of 30 ships that had sailed a few days before was bagged by the British along with its escort without a fight.

The splendor of the "Aladdin's Cave" into which Rodney had stumbled blinded him to the tactical realities. He was so engrossed in preparing his booty, valued at no less than three million pounds, for shipment to England, that he failed to take adequate precautions to deal with a French fleet of 20 ships of the line and a large convoy of storeships, on its way from Brest under the command of the Comte de Grasse. Topping six feet in height, de Grasse was a striking figure who had fought the British since boyhood and was credited with being a good seaman and a brave fighting man. He flew his flag in *Ville de Paris,* which carried 110 guns and was the most powerful warship in the world.

With a French fleet expected momentarily, Rodney sent Hood with 11 of the line to join the 4 ships already blockading the French base at Fort Royal on Martinique and to cruise to leeward, or west of the island. Hood, with mounting anger at the admiral's fixation on the loot of St. Eustatius, protested, pleaded, and argued against his orders. An incoming French fleet could not be intercepted from leeward, he declared. Rodney's real reason for this disposition was to prevent the French squadron at Martinique from getting at the St. Eustatius convoy when it eventually sailed.* Beat-

---

*This was to little avail, however, because more than half the convoy carrying the plunder of St. Eustatius was taken by the French off the Scilly Islands. Moreover, the West India merchants brought legal action against Rodney, and he was enmeshed in the toils of the law for the remainder of his life.

Admiral Comte de Grasse. From a portrait in the French embassy in Washington. (U.S. Naval Academy Museum)

ing back and forth against wind and current, Hood cursed Rodney for his greed and obtuseness. Hood was unable to send his ships to St. Lucia for fresh provisions, and scurvy broke out among his exhausted crews. "There never was a squadron so unmeaningly stationed as the one under my command," Hood angrily declared.

Toward midday on May 3, a battered two-decker limped into the St. Eustatius roadstead with her pumps working to keep her afloat. She was the seventy-four-gun *Russell,* of Hood's squadron, and she brought grim news. Five days before, de Grasse's fleet, after a relatively swift Atlantic crossing of thirty-six days, had brushed past Hood's poorly placed ships after doing heavy damage to *Russell*, among others, and anchored at Fort Royal. The balance of naval power in the Caribbean had again swung to the French. No British fleet pursued de Grasse because the entire Channel fleet was escorting another relief convoy to Gibraltar, and as a result there were no ships left to reinforce Rodney. In the long run, the price of Gibraltar was to be the loss of the American colonies.

As soon as Rodney learned of de Grasse's arrival, he hurried to sea, but there was nothing to be done but gather up the scattered pieces of Hood's command. Having taken on water and provisions at Antigua, Rodney sailed for Barbados, which he believed was the main French target. In the meantime, de Grasse made an attempt to surprise the British base at St. Lucia. The French were repulsed and de Grasse moved on to Tobago, which was easily taken. By the time Rodney came to the rescue, it was already too late, and he returned to Barbados. The two fleets came in sight of each other on June 5, but much to the chagrin of Hood, Rodney declined to attack the French on grounds that he did not wish to leave Barbados, the most important British base in the eastern Caribbean, undefended.

For the next several weeks the British and French fleets lay idle—the French at Martinique and the British at Barbados. But the time for a decision on future operations was approaching rapidly. The hurricane season was drawing near, and Rodney's health was deteriorating. The problem was resolved on July 5 when de Grasse put to sea with twenty-seven ships of the line and a convoy of nearly two hundred merchantmen. Rodney surmised that he was bound for Cap François, where the convoy would be detached for the voyage to France while the fleet would go on to reinforce French forces in America. Fast-sailing ships were sent to warn the British commanders at Jamaica and New York of these developments. Rodney's own fleet would follow, but without the admiral; he had decided that his health would not permit it.

Hood was instructed to take fourteen ships of the line, several in poor condition after long service in the tropics, to convoy some British ships to Jamaica, and then go on to New York. Rodney believed that these vessels, plus those already in North American waters, would be sufficient to deal with de Grasse because the Frenchman would probably detach some of his ships as an escort for the valuable West India convoy and leave others behind to defend the islands. Having made these dispositions, Rodney sailed for home on August 1, needlessly taking three ships of the line with him. Hood departed for New York ten days later.

On the other side, de Grasse had arrived at Cap François on July 16, to find dispatches from Rochambeau urging him to come north immediately, preferably to the Chesapeake Bay area, where British raiders were active. Twenty-five pilots familiar with the American coast were on hand to bring him in safely. With the imposing *Ville de Paris* leading the French van, de Grasse sailed for America on August 5 with twenty-six of the line and three thousand troops—every ship and soldier on which he could lay his hands. Rather than leaving some vessels behind to escort merchant convoys or protect the islands, as Rodney had expected, he brought all his ships with him.

⤳

THE JOINT FRANCO-AMERICAN land and sea operations that led to the surrender of Lord Cornwallis' army at Yorktown meshed so smoothly that they appear to have been planned, but in reality the victory was a matter of luck and circumstances. The groundwork for the final British disaster in America was laid the previous year, when General Clinton hastily left Charleston to defend New York against Rochambeau's newly arrived troops. Clinton had urged Lord Cornwallis to pacify the South Carolina back country so the Loyalists could be coaxed out into the open, and only then to expand British control into North Carolina and Virginia. Moreover, Clinton, with his eye always on the sea link that bound the British armies in the North and South together, cautioned that once the invasion of North Carolina began, it should follow along the coast, where the army would always be able to receive support from the Royal Navy.

Restless and ambitious, Cornwallis had more dashing ideas. After soundly defeating the Americans at Camden, South Carolina, he struck out northward. But the Yankees had not lost the will to fight and continued to harass the British. Brushing off Clinton's counsel to remain close to the coast, Cornwallis marched into the rugged North Carolina Piedmont, saying the coastal area was too unhealthy for major military operations—and putting his army out of reach of the navy and supplies and reinforcements from that quarter. He won a series of bloody but strategically meaningless victories that sapped the strength of his army. Unwilling to retreat to Charleston, he headed for the seaboard. On August 1, 1781, Cornwallis and his tattered force of some seven thousand men straggled into Yorktown, Virginia, a sleepy village on the York River, where they intended to hold out until evacuated by the Royal Navy.

Reporting to General Washington on the arrival of the British, Marquis de Lafayette, who had been shadowing Cornwallis, said: "If we should have a great fleet arrive at this moment, our affairs would take a happy turn." Fortuitously, de Grasse's fleet arrived on the scene at this very moment. Having sailed through the Old Bahama Channel between the northern coast of Cuba and the Bahama banks, a route usually avoided because of treacherous reefs and unpredictable storms, he made a fast passage and was not sighted by British cruisers as he neared the mainland. Learning of the approach of the French fleet, Washington abandoned a planned attack on New York and ordered a quick march to the south. Clinton, however, dismissed the movements of the French and American armies as a feint and remained in New York, ignoring the trap closing around Cornwallis.

Hood was also moving toward the American coast, although handicapped by the poor condition of some of his fleet. He intended to join Rear Admiral Thomas Graves, the newly appointed naval commander at New York, and give battle to either the French squadron at Newport, now commanded by Comte de Barras, or to de Grasse before they combined forces. On August 25 Hood sent a frigate to look into the Chesapeake, and when she reported no trace of the enemy, he hurried on to New York. What he found appalled him.

Ignoring Cornwallis' worsening plight, Clinton and Graves, who probably owed his place to the fact that was Lord North's brother-in-law, were leisurely planning to deal with the eight French ships at Newport. "You have no time to lose," Hood angrily told them. "Every moment is precious." He insisted that Graves immediately launch an attack on Newport or sail in search of de Grasse. Even as these discussions were taking place, de Barras, taking advantage of a storm that had driven off the British blockaders, had sailed for Virginia with Rochambeau's siege artillery. While Hood fretted about the delay, Graves took three days to prepare his ships for sea and fill out his crews.

About four hundred men were taken in a "hot" press, some of them snatched from their homes. Lieutenant Bartholomew James provides a vivid picture of the press gang in action: "The business . . . furnished us with droll yet distressing scenes—taking the husband from the arms of his wife in bed, the searching for them when hid beneath the warm clothes, and, the better to prevent delay taking them naked, while the frantic partner of his bed, forgetting the delicacy of her sex, pursued us to the doors with shrieks and imprecations, and exposing their naked persons to the rude view of an unfeeling press gang." Vessels manned through such desperate measures, Graves put to sea on August 31 with nineteen ships of the line and headed toward Chesapeake Bay. But he had lost the race, for de Grasse was already there—snapping the door shut on Cornwallis' army.

EARLY ON THE MORNING of September 5, twenty-four French ships of the line rode easily at anchor in Lynnhaven Bay behind Cape Henry, smoke curling from the breakfast fires in their galleys. Working parties were already ashore gathering wood and water and assisting the newly landed troops. Shortly before 8:00 A.M. the frigate *Aigritte*, on patrol at the entrance to Chesapeake Bay, sighted a cloud of sails coming down from the north. There were three . . . five . . . then eight ships. Apparently de Barras's squadron had arrived from Newport. There were laughing and cheering in the French fleet. Ominously, however, the distant sails continued to appear—until they reached nineteen ships. It could only be the British. Taken by surprise, the French hoisted urgent signals and fired guns to summon the working parties. Galley fires were doused, and men were sent forward with axes to cut the anchor cables in case the ships had to get out in a hurry.

Plodding along at little more than three knots—the best speed that could be coaxed out of some of Hood's ships—Graves needed nearly four days to sail down from New York. *Terrible*, seventy-four, was in the worst condition, with five pumps working. Other vessels were leaky, had their masts sprung, or were short of provisions and water. From ten miles out, a lookout on the frigate *Soleby* reported a forest of masts within Chesapeake Bay. At first Graves thought they were de Barras's ships. But as the count mounted, the admiral, unable to conceive that de Grasse would bring his entire fleet up from the Caribbean, surmised that a junction of the two French fleets had taken place. Although outnumbered, he cleared for action and bore down upon the enemy with a brisk northeast wind at his back. The curtain had risen on the Battle of the Chesapeake Capes—in which the fate of a continent was to be decided.

De Grasse had more ships and guns than Graves, but faced several tactical problems. The French fleet, which had been completely surprised, was held fast by the tide, and when the tide turned, the wind would be against it. The mouth of Chesapeake Bay is ten miles wide, but the channel between Cape Henry and Middle Ground, the shoal where James Nicholson had ignominiously lost the Continental frigate *Virginia* in 1778, is only three miles wide, leaving little room for maneuver. Rather than chance an encounter at sea, de Grasse could place his ships across the mouth of the bay and await a British attack. On the other hand, by venturing to sea he assumed a double risk—of being defeated, or having Graves slip into the Chesapeake behind his back. And what if the British picked off his ships one by one as they came out? But if he remained in the bay, de Barras's squadron, which was somewhere between Newport and Virginia, would almost certainly be lost, along with the army's siege artillery. Besides, he did not need to win a victory, but only to maintain control of the Chesapeake, which would result from even an indecisive battle. Having weighed his options, de Grasse decided to engage the enemy at sea.

As soon as the tide began to turn, at about noon, the admiral ordered his ships to cut their anchor cables. Signal flags shot up to the masthead of the *Ville de Paris* instructing the fleet to form a line of battle in the order of getting out to sea without regard to their usual fighting stations. First out was Commodore Louis-Antoine de Bougainville in the eighty-gun *Auguste;* he assumed command of the van. The first four ships got out in good order, but the rest straggled in their wake. De Grasse's flagship was twelfth in line, and the last French ship was more than three miles astern.

The British swept down on the French from the windward in a tight line ahead, the ships a cable length (approximately two hundred yards) apart. Hood, in *Barfleur*, ninety, commanded the van; Graves was in the center in his flagship, *London*, ninety-eight, and the rear was under Rear Admiral Francis Drake, a descendant of the Elizabethan sea dog, in *Princessa*, seventy. Graves was in an enviable position: he had only to fall on the French van with his entire fleet, and the day would be his. Hood urged him to do so, but Graves was an unimaginative formalist, and determined to maintain the regular line of battle, ignored the once-in-a-lifetime opportunity given him. As his fleet neared the French van, he gradually altered course to the west. This maneuver placed the two fleets on approximately parallel but opposite tacks—preliminary to the standard ship-to-ship, van-to-rear action. "The British fleet had a rich and most plentiful harvest of glory in view, but the means to gather it were omitted," Hood bitterly observed.

Shortly after 2:00 P.M. Graves noticed that his ships were perilously close to the Middle Ground shoals. A signal was hoisted instructing the fleet to wear together, or pivot 180 degrees, until the line was heading east to the open sea and in the same direction as the French. The order of the British line was now reversed. Hood's division, which had been in the van, was now in the rear, and Drake's vessels, which had been in the rear, were now in the van. As a result, Graves was now leading from weakness, because *Terrible* and several of the ships in poor condition would make the first contact with the strong French van.

While these maneuvers were occurring, de Grasse was working furiously to get all his ships out to sea, but he was saved from disaster by Graves. Instead of pinching off the leading French vessels with a determined attack, Graves waited with the topsails of his ships aback, while the enemy's center and rear divisions formed up. At about 2:30 P.M. Graves ordered his ships to edge down to starboard toward the French line, approaching at an angle from the north. But he signaled them to attack in line ahead, which meant that they would come against the enemy in piecemeal fashion. In doing so Graves violated a cardinal rule of naval tactics for an attack by an inferior fleet on a superior one: all elements must strike together for maximum effect. He waited until the opposing vans and centers were roughly parallel before signaling close action—while keeping the signal for line ahead still flying. The vans were within pistol shot of each other, the centers were a greater distance off, and the rear divisions were still miles apart when the first broadsides were exchanged. Eight hours had elapsed since *Aigrette* had first sighted the British fleet.

Heavy fighting raged between the vanguards of the two fleets, with the British getting the worse of it. *Shrewsbury*, seventy-four, which led the

British line, was soundly hammered. The sixty-four-gun *Intrepid* tried to cover her and sustained sixty-five shot holes in her starboard side. *Terrible*, the weakest ship in the British line, was so badly battered that she was taking on water at a rate of two feet every twenty minutes, and it was doubtful she could be kept afloat. After the first hour, the fighting extended down into the center divisions of the two fleets. In contrast, the seven ships of Hood's rear division had scarcely fired a shot.

Had the British ships massed their firepower against the disorganized French van, de Grasse would have suffered significant losses. Weaknesses in the Royal Navy's system of signals and Graves's lack of time to convey his intentions to his captains all contributed to the debacle. Hood claimed that Graves flew contradictory signals during the action—line of battle and close action. The line-of-battle signal took precedence, and as long as it was flying, no vessel could deviate from its position in the battle line. For the ships in the van, the dual signals caused no confusion because they were already closely engaged with the enemy. For the ships in the rear, it was an altogether different matter. Because of the angle at which the fleet attacked the French, these vessels were at such a distance from the enemy that they couldn't close without at least temporarily veering out of line.

Graves contended that the line-ahead signal was flown only intermittently after the signal for close action was hoisted—and then merely to call some ships back into line after they had bunched up. Hood, on the other hand, claimed that the two signals were flown simultaneously until 5:25 P.M., when the line-of-battle signal was lowered.* At this point he tried to bring the rear division into action, but it was too late. With the crews on both sides exhausted, firing was dying out. Graves had maintained his battle line, but as the British naval historian Michael Lewis has remarked, "He had merely lost America."

Over the next several days, the opposing fleets cruised off the Chesapeake Capes within sight of each other without offering battle. The British fleet was too knocked about to fight, while the French, although suffering far less, felt no urgency to give battle. Graves seemed to have forgotten his primary mission—the relief of Cornwallis—and made no effort to bar the entrance to the Chesapeake to the French. On the night of September 9, four days after battle, de Grasse, fearful that the British might do exactly that, broke off contact and returned to the Chesapeake. Hood urged Graves to clap on all sail to beat the French to the mouth of the bay, and after some delay during which the sinking *Terrible* was set ablaze, the admiral set a course for Cape Henry while the frigate *Medusa* was sent on ahead to scout out the situation.

*The logbook of *London,* Graves's flagship, confirms his account, while some witnesses support Hood's version.

Three days later, she returned to report that the French were in the bay.
Unknown to the British, Barras's fleet had joined de Grasse, and the French
now had an overwhelming thirty-two ships of the line on hand. Any chance
of relieving Cornwallis had faded. Uncertain about what to do next, a puzzled Graves turned to Hood. "Admiral Graves presents his compliments to
Sir Samuel Hood," he wrote, "and begs leave to acquaint him that the
Medusa has made signal to inform him that the French fleet . . . are at anchor
in the Chesapeake and desires his opinion what to do with the fleet. . . ."
Hood's reply was cutting. "Sir Samuel would be very glad to send an opinion, but he really knows not what to say in the truly lamentable state we
have brought ourselves." Not long after, the fleet returned to New York for
repairs and provisions, leaving Cornwallis besieged by eight thousand
French troops and an equally strong American force.

Over the next several weeks the British hatched various schemes to save
Cornwallis, but all came to naught. There was talk of diversionary
attacks—perhaps on Philadelphia—to lure de Grasse away from the
Chesapeake. Graves was promised fresh ships, but few reinforcements
arrived. The dockyards were cursed for delaying repairs and Graves complained that the supplies given him were rotten. But the fundamental reason for the lack of action was that no one wished to face the fact that a
rescue fleet would have to battle its way through a superior French fleet,
embark the troops, and fight its way out again. Everyone now realized the
significance of the few hours of indecisive cannonading off the Chesapeake
Capes. "All depended on a fleet," Clinton declared. "Sir Henry Clinton was
promised one, Washington had one."

On October 19, 1781, a rescue fleet of twenty-three of the line carrying
seven thousand troops shook out its sails and set a course for the Chesapeake. Clinton, who was on board *London* with Admiral Graves, wrote
George Germain to assure him that the fleet would arrive in time to rescue
Cornwallis. It was to no avail. Shortly before 2:00 P.M. that same day, Cornwallis surrendered. Some seven thousand Redcoats marched out of their
redoubts and passed between a long line of white-coated French troops
and an opposite rank of tattered Continentals. As the British trudged
along, a band struck up a melancholy tune that went:

If buttercups buzzed after the bee,
If boats were on land, churches on sea . . .
Summer were spring and the t'other way round.
Then all the world would be turned upside down.

CHAPTER 6

Sea Fight—New Style

"OH, GOD! It's all over!" cried Lord North upon learning of Cornwallis' capitulation at Yorktown. The news arrived about midday on November 25, 1781, and came first to Lord Germain. He immediately dispatched a messenger to King George and went himself to Downing Street to inform the prime minister of the disaster. The Sunday stillness of Whitehall was broken only by the random clip-clop of horses' hooves. Distant church bells tolled the hour. North received the news "as if he would have taken a ball in the breast," said Germain. He flung up his arms and paced the room, exclaiming over and over again that all was lost.

George Washington would have been greatly surprised by the prime minister's distress. To him, Cornwallis' surrender was merely "an interesting event that may be productive of much good if properly improved." Washington had plenty of reasons to believe the war in America would continue despite the British defeat at Yorktown. British troops still occupied New York; Wilmington, North Carolina; Charleston; Savannah; and St. Augustine. True, Britain had lost a quarter of its army at Yorktown, but her remaining forces in America were several times larger than Washington's own army. The French had won momentary naval superiority on the American coast, but Admiral de Grasse was already sniffing the breezes in preparation for a return to the West Indies. Under these circumstances it was inconceivable to most Americans that a dogged Britain would summarily end the long struggle to retain her colonies.

The last British prisoner had barely stacked arms when Washington tried to persuade de Grasse to follow up his victory with a joint expedition against one of the remaining British garrisons. The great strategic lesson of Yorktown, as far as the general was concerned, was that "no land force can act decisively unless it is accompanied by a maritime superiority." Now that he possessed this long-sought maritime superiority, Washington was eager to keep the pressure on the British. He proposed an immediate attack on Charleston, but de Grasse ruled it out on grounds that he had promised the Spaniards to return to the Caribbean after the hurricane season to attack Jamaica. Washington then suggested an attack on Wilmington, which could be taken more speedily. Again, the Frenchman declined.

Taking de Barras's squadron with him, de Grasse sailed for the West Indies on November 5, 1781, with thirty-three ships of the line. Six days later, Hood departed New York with eighteen of the line, also bound for the Caribbean. Only a few French frigates remained to protect Rochambeau's troops as they went into winter quarters at Williamsburg. The American army returned to the Hudson highlands to keep an eye on Clinton in New York. No one yet realized it, but the land campaign in America was over.

In the meantime, defeat after defeat rolled in on the British like a relentless tide in the closing months of 1781. West Florida was captured by the Spaniards; Tobago was taken by the French; and Jamaica, the largest and most important of the islands, was ripe for plucking. Minorca in the Mediterranean was about to fall after a seven-month siege, and Gibraltar was still beleaguered. At home, a combined French and Spanish fleet paraded unchallenged at the entrance to the English Channel.

In March 1780 there had been an ill-conceived British attempt to cut Spain's American Empire in two by sending an expedition up the San Juan River to the farther shore of Lake Nicaragua, where it would be only ten miles from the Pacific. Through the efforts of Horatio Nelson, who had been promoted to captain of a frigate the year before, at age twenty, the main Spanish fort on the river was captured. But the expedition foundered as many of the troops came down with fever and dysentery. Cuthbert Collingwood reported that all but twenty of his two hundred men died. Nelson himself was invalided home nearly at the point of death.

On the other side of the world, in the Indian Ocean, the redoubtable French admiral Pierre-André de Suffren de Saint-Tropez won control of the surrounding seas. Without a base and lacking adequate supplies and ships, Suffren fought a fleet commanded by Vice Admiral Edward Hughes to a standstill in a series of savage naval battles. Unhappily for the French admiral, he was given only indifferent support by his officers and was never able to win a knockout victory. Suffren was unique among French naval officers in believing that the object of a fleet should be to sink the enemy fleet and gain control of the sea rather than to husband its ships. Napoleon later said that "had he been alive in my time, he would have been my Nelson."

With her empire crumbling, with the national debt nearly doubled by the war, and with the army and the navy undermanned, Britain seemed to have little choice except to abandon the struggle. Only King George retained a crusader's unshaken faith in eventual victory, and he clung to Lord North because any other prime minister would have followed the logic of events and made peace.

Once more, the ministry turned in desperation to George Rodney for salvation. "The fate of the empire is in your hands," an anguished Sandwich told the old sailor, who was in Bath recovering from bladder surgery. By early December Rodney was at Plymouth on board his flagship, the ninety-gun *Formidable,* nursing an attack of gout while straining to sail with twelve ships of the line. Gales, heavy seas, and the usual dockyard inefficiencies prevented him from sailing until January 14, 1782.

The delay had a fortunate outcome, however: Rodney was able to obtain the services of Sir Charles Douglas as his captain of the fleet. Douglas was a noted gunnery expert and commander of the squadron that had punched through the St. Lawrence ice to relieve Québec in 1776. He immediately made a number of technical changes that improved the fleet's gunnery. The rate of fire was speeded up by installing flintlocks on the guns of some ships in place of the matches heretofore used. Douglas also devised a system of block and tackle that allowed broadside guns to be trained forty-five degrees fore and aft, which permitted them to remain on target longer. And most of the ships were fitted for the first time with carronades. These were short-barreled, close-range "smashers" produced at the Carron foundry in Scotland that were light for the weight of shot they fired. Now thirty-two-pounders could be mounted on quarterdecks and forecastles, thereby increasing the weight of a ship's broadside. The French had no such weapons.

French plans to reinforce de Grasse's fleet were upset by the same contrary winds that held Rodney in port. On December 12 Admiral Guichin got to sea with nineteen of the line and a large convoy of troops and stores that was sighted about 150 miles southwest of Ushant by twelve ships under the command of Richard Kempenfelt. The escort was caught to the leeward of the convoy, and with nothing to stop them, the British swooped up fifteen of the merchant vessels. A few days later a storm completed the work begun by Kempenfelt. Guichin's vessels were scattered and crippled, and only two ships of the line and five transports limped across the Atlantic to join de Grasse.

As Rodney ventured out into the Atlantic, the North ministry was breathing its last. Public opinion had turned against the war, and efforts to prolong the life of the government by jettisoning Germain and Sandwich, its most unpopular members, were not enough to save it. On February 27 Parliament approved a motion against continuation of the war by nineteen votes. A month later, over the resistance of the king, a new Whig ministry was formed by the marquis of Rockingham, who had long opposed coercive policies in America. The new prime minister dispatched Robert Oswald, a British merchant with considerable experience in America, to Paris to initiate talks with Benjamin Franklin and the other American commissioners. Oswald arrived on April 12, 1782—the same day Rodney won the most smashing naval victory of the war.

⤳

RODNEY HAD ARRIVED at Barbados two months earlier after a fast but stormy crossing—"the sea [was] mountains high," he reported—to find British bastions falling on all sides. St. Eustatius had been captured by the French along with the payroll of the British army, the settlements of Demerara and Essquibo (now part of Guyana) on the mainland of South America had fallen without a fight, and St. Kitts was in the process of being taken, despite a valiant effort by Hood,* to be followed by the loss of Montserrat. Only adverse winds and currents had prevented a French attack on Barbados. Moreover, intelligence reports indicated that as soon as de Grasse received reinforcements, he intended to rendezvous with the Spanish fleet at Havana or Cap François and add Jamaica to his bag.

Hood and Rodney rejoined forces off Antigua on February 25, bringing the total number of British ships to thirty-four of the line, while de Grasse had thirty-three. But many of Hood's vessels were in dilapidated condition. The captain of *Alcide*, seventy-four, painted a vivid picture of the situation in his vessel: "We cannot wash the Lower Deck, the seams are so open over the Bread Room, Sail Room and Store Rooms. . . . While we wash the Main Deck the people cannot lay in the Hammocks." Provisions were so short that yams were issued to crews in place of bread. Having placed frigates to watch the French anchorage at Fort Royal in Martinique, Rodney dropped down to St. Lucia to refit Hood's ships.

The French were also short of supplies, so they awaited the arrival of a convoy with reinforcements and provisions before embarking on the Jamaica operation. Rodney and Hood agreed that the convoy must be intercepted before its arrival, but once again they quarreled—as they had the previous year, in a similar situation—over where to meet the threat. Hood argued that the British fleet, now up to thirty-six ships of the line, be divided into two squadrons. One should patrol to the north and windward of Dominica, the island immediately to the north-northwest of Martinique, in case the convoy sailed in from the north. The other should guard the traditional southern approach between Martinique and St. Lucia. Rodney flatly refused to divide the fleet, arguing that this would allow de Grasse

*Hood arrived off St. Kitts to find the British garrison under siege. He lured de Grasse out of his anchorage and through a masterly set of maneuvers slipped in behind him—as he had suggested could have been done to relieve Cornwallis at Yorktown. But it was all wasted effort because the garrison had already surrendered.

to escape from Fort Royal. He insisted that the entire fleet cruise between St. Lucia and Martinique.

Hood turned out to be right. Shepherded by two ships of the line that had survived Kempenfelt's attack and the Atlantic storms, the convoy sailed in from the north at the end of March without hindrance, much to Hood's anger, and anchored safely at Fort Royal. The chastened Rodney now established a chain of frigates to patrol the waters off the French base day and night and to sound the alarm when the fleet sailed.

Rejuvenated by the prospect of decisive battle, the old man put aside his various ailments and acted with vigor. Hood, on the other hand, was taken sick with a liver complaint compounded by anxiety and worry over the capricious conduct of his chief. In what was an unusual move for him, Rodney had himself rowed over to *Barfleur,* Hood's flagship, and explained his plans. "I never found him more rational and he gave me very great pleasure by his manner of receiving what I said respecting future operations," Hood said. The British commanders were still enjoying this unusual state of harmony where the frigate *Endymion* arrived at Gros Islet Bay on the night of April 7, to report that the French fleet was at sea.

⌒

IN ADDITION TO HIS thirty-five ships of the line, de Grasse had a convoy of a hundred merchantmen with him, which were to head for France once they were out of range of British cruisers. With the intention of avoiding battle, he planned to skirt the edge of a chain of friendly islands where the convoy could take refuge in case of need. French ships were usually better sailers than British vessels because they were longer on the waterline, which, all else being equal, made them faster, a factor that even coppering had not been able to overcome entirely. With his head start, de Grasse expected to outdistance the enemy fleet, but the clumsiness of his armada wrecked his plan. Shortly before nightfall, the French fleet was made out from the mastheads of Rodney's ships.

Straining to catch any cat's-paw of a breeze, more than a hundred ships, British and French, maneuvered in the lee of Dominica. Shortly after daybreak on April 9, eight ships of Hood's van drew away from the rest of the fleet. Realizing that the British were gaining on him, de Grasse sent the convoy into the nearby harbor of Basse-Terre on Guadeloupe. Taking advantage of an opportunity to crush part of the enemy force, he ordered fifteen of his ships to come about and deal with Hood's vessels. For all their stateliness under sail, the fleets were hunting packs. To be isolated meant mortal danger.

Four of the British ships were damaged aloft in the brief encounter that followed, with the captain of *Alfred,* seventy-four, being cut in two by chain shot. On the other side, the sixty-four-gun *Caton* was so damaged that she had to be sent into Guadeloupe for refit. While the British lay to, repairing their ships, de Grasse ordered the convoy to proceed independently to Cap François under escort of a pair of fifty-gun ships. The merchantmen were soon safely out of sight.

Over the next two days both fleets pressed on to westward as the French continued to outdistance their pursuers. But an accident during the night of April 10 caused confusion in the French fleet. *Zele,* seventy-four, collided with the sixty-four-gun *Jason*—Zele's thirteenth collision in as many months—and the smaller vessel was forced to put into Basse-Terre to make repairs. The next morning, the crippled *Zele* and an escort vessel were seen by the British to have dropped away to leeward of the main body of the French fleet. Rodney ordered a general chase with the hope of snapping up the stragglers, but de Grasse, unwilling to lose any more ships, sent several vessels to protect them. Upon seeing that his leading ships were greatly outnumbered, Rodney broke off the chase. Nevertheless, the French had lost much of the lead they had gained over the past few days.

During the night the hapless *Zele* rammed de Grasse's flagship *Ville de Paris,* testimony to the declining standards of seamanship in the French Navy. The dawn of April 12 presented Rodney with a thrilling sight: the bulk of the French fleet was spread out on the sea only a few miles away to the windward, while off to leeward *Zele,* foremast gone and bowsprit snapped short, was under tow by a frigate in the direction of Guadeloupe. This left de Grasse with thirty of the line to face Rodney's thirty-six. The fleets were now in a basin of blue tropic water between the northern tip of Dominica and a clutch of islets known as the Îles des Saintes. The scene was now set for the major naval action of the war in the Caribbean.

Shortly before 6:00 A.M. Rodney ordered four of Hood's ships to attack the stricken *Zele* and her consort in an attempt to entice de Grasse to abandon his position to windward and come to their rescue. As the admiral had hoped, the French accepted the challenge and turned to assist the crippled vessel. With a battle likely, Rodney ordered his men to breakfast, for it was a tradition in the Royal Navy to send sailors into battle with full stomachs. On the quarterdeck of *Formidable,* Captain of the Fleet Douglas watched the slow unfolding of these preliminary maneuvers in the scant early morning breeze. Suddenly he snapped his long glass shut and went below to Rodney's cabin, where the admiral was resting from the rigors of four sleepless nights. "I give you joy, Sir George," he said with a theatrical sweep of his gold-laced hat. "Providence has given you your enemy broad on the lee bow." Douglas's estimate was premature, but Rodney had at last brought the enemy to bay.

Signals were broken out on the British flagship at about 7:00 A.M. to recall the four ships from their chase of *Zele* and to order a line of battle one cable—or two hundred yards—apart. Hood's damaged ships were shifted to the rear of the British fleet, and the van came under the command of Francis Drake in *Princessa*. For the first time during the war, a British fleet was going into battle against the French with more ships and guns than its opponent.

The two fleets approached each on different tacks: the French were heading south, the British north. De Grasse hoped to pass along the British line at a safe distance and avoid a serious action, but Rodney urged his van ahead in a desperate effort to cross the head of the French line and seize the weather gage. The silent fleets drew near each other, with the British in a well-ordered and compact line while the French straggled into position with sizable gaps between their ships. Gun captains, stooped like old men, peered through the ports, taking aim at the enemy ships. As the heads of the two lines crept toward each other, it became clear that Drake would be unable to cross the enemy line in time and the French would hold the weather gage.

At about 7:30 A.M. the leading French ships passed across the bows of Drake's vessels, firing ineffectually at long range. *Marlborough*, seventy-four, pressed on, and shortly before eight o'clock she reached the French line at the ninth ship from the van, the seventy-four-gun *Brave*. Turning parallel to the enemy, *Marlborough* unleashed the first broadside of the battle. The remainder of Drake's division followed in stately succession, their sides exploding in a thunder of gunfire. The center division came next, with the flagship *Formidable* unleashing her first broadside at 8:08 A.M. Recoiling thirty-two-pounders on her lower gundeck made her timbers quiver. The fleets moved slowly along on a parallel course, periodically hidden in clouds of smoke and flame.

To prevent the action from turning into another indecisive battle like Ushant or the Chesapeake Capes, Rodney kept the signal for close action flying and reinforced it with another to alter course to starboard—closer to the French. Captain Henry Savage of *Hercules* typified the fighting spirit of the fleet. Slightly wounded, he sat in a chair on the quarterdeck of his seventy-four-gun ships, shaking a fist at each enemy vessel as it passed and urging his sweating gunners to "sink the French rascals!"

The French, whose ships were crowded not only with their crews but also with fifty-five hundred soldiers for the invasion of Jamaica, suffered far more seriously than the British. The effect of the British carronades was murderous at the short range maintained by Rodney. Douglas's modifications to the fleet's guns also had their effect. The rule of classical naval warfare was "two or three quick broadsides in passing," but the special tackle enabled the British gunners to train their weapons well ahead or astern of their vessels, and they fired two or three extra broadsides before and after a French vessel could bring her guns to bear. The British also fired more rapidly because of the flintlocks fitted to their guns at Douglas's orders. So many bodies were cast overboard from the French ships that the sea boiled with the thrashings of schools of sharks.

Nevertheless, even though the French fleet was absorbing severe punishment, de Grasse was unworried. As long as he held the windward gage, he was committed to no more than a passing engagement. Within a hour or so his crews would be free to make repairs and press on to Cap François. Yet there was cause for alarm. De Grasse saw that his course was taking him into the still waters off Dominica, where there was little wind and where he would be unable to thwart Rodney's determined effort to close the range. He tried to break off the action and twice signaled his fleet to wear—change to the opposite tack by turning their stern to the wind—so his ships could head back in the direction from which they had come. But with the foe little more than a pistol shot to leeward, there was simply no room to wear without colliding with the British ships, so the French captains ignored their admiral's frantic signals.

Fate now played into Rodney's hands. Just after 9:00 A.M. a battered French seventy-four-gun ship, *Glorieux*, drifted alongside *Formidable*. *Glorieux* shuddered under the full fury of the British three-decker's broadsides, and her rigging and masts hung in a crazy tangle. Suddenly there was a shift in the wind that caused great confusion among the French. Some vessels were taken aback, or were pushed astern; others were forced to turn toward the British line to maintain headway. Ships fouled each other and fell away to leeward, opening a wide gap in the French line.

Here was the chance of a lifetime—and Rodney grasped it. Altering the flagship's course to starboard, he thrust her into the breach looming before him. The French line had been broken. Unlike the Battle of Martinique, where Rodney fought his way through the French line but was not supported by his captains, five British ships followed *Formidable* in among the French. Raking the enemy vessels on both sides as they forged into the gap, the British ships quickly reduced them to shattered wrecks. *Glorieux* lost all her masts and was transformed into a mere hulk filled with the dead and the dying. *Formidable*'s journal reported that "not a single shot missed and dreadful must have been the slaughter" aboard her. *Diademe*, to the port of the British ships, also suffered severely.

As soon as his ships had seized the weather gage, Rodney took stock of the situation. Captain Alan Gardner, of the ninety-eight-gun *Duke*, had followed the admiral's example and crashed through the enemy line at another point. And in the rear, Commodore Edmund Affleck had led Hood's entire division into the French line and to the windward. The French fleet was cut into three separate divisions and never re-formed. In the melee that followed, the superior firepower of the British ships quickly asserted itself. Several French vessels were almost torn apart by the volume of fire poured into them from both windward and leeward.

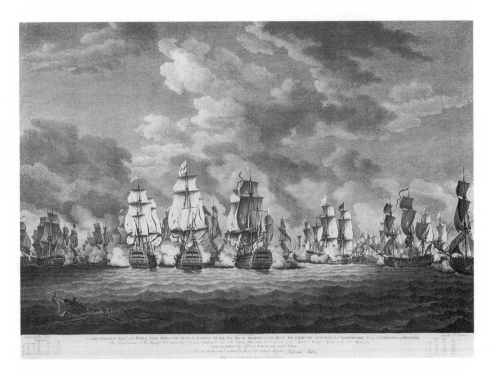

Rodney breaks the French line at the Saintes on April 12, 1782. (Beverley Robinson Collection, U.S. Naval Academy Museum)

Yet the French had suffered less aloft than the British, and even though some of their ships were battered wrecks, they managed to drift clear of the British. The dismasted *Glorieux,* her decks a shambles yet with her flag defiantly nailed to the stump of a mast, lay motionless between the two fleets, a mute witness to the effectiveness of British gunnery. So ended the first phase of the Battle of the Saintes—an action in which Rodney had broken his own line, the enemy line, and the whole formal system of fighting naval battles.*

The fruits of victory were yet to be harvested, however. By 1:00 P.M. the

*Following the battle, there was considerable debate over whether the breaking of the French line was deliberately planned by Rodney or whether it was accidental. Some writers say Rodney, while dining out in London, had stated his intention of breaking the enemy line the next time he met the French and demonstrated with cherrystones how it could be done. Others say he was influenced by a book on naval tactics written by John Clerk, laird of Eldin. And there are others who say he was persuaded to break the line by Sir Charles Douglas. In all probability the maneuver was unpremeditated, but what really matters is that Rodney took advantage of the situation, and inasmuch as he would have borne the blame had it failed, he is entitled to the credit.

smoke of battle had drifted away to reveal the French making off to leeward in several disorganized groups, with *Glorieux* under tow by a frigate. The British ships were moving in for the kill, with Hood having put his boats into the water to pull *Barfleur* into the wind. All that afternoon the British followed at the heels of the French due to Rodney's cautious decision that the fleet should conduct the pursuit as a unit. This provoked the usual muttering from Hood, who wanted to clap on all sail for a general chase. *Glorieux* was the first French ship taken; next a pair of seventy-fours, and then *Ardent*, a sixty-four-gun ship that had been captured by the French off Plymouth in 1779 and carried most of the French siege artillery.

The greatest prize was yet to be captured. Limping away under a few ragged scraps of sail, de Grasse's flagship, the great *Ville de Paris*, lagged behind the rest of the retreating French fleet. Abandoned by his officers, almost out of ammunition, his scuppers running with blood, de Grasse tried to fight his way out of a ring of hostile ships surrounding his flagship. But she no longer answered her helm, and shortly before sunset the admiral, one of only three men left standing on her upper deck, surrendered to *Barfleur.*

Elated by the capture of the French commander in chief and the world's greatest battleship, Rodney made the signal to break off action and lay to in the gathering darkness. An angry Hood groused that the disorganized French fleet should have been pursued during the night so it could be finished off the following morning. Had he commanded the fleet, Hood later claimed, he would have bagged twenty ships of the line, not the five captured by Rodney. On the other hand, the British were much cut up aloft, there was a shortage of ammunition, and there was always the danger that they might fire into each other in the dark. Moreover, the French may not have been as disorganized as Hood contended. Commodore Affleck, who had not seen the signal to break off action and pursued the enemy, found at daylight that they had outdistanced him. In his cabin Rodney was dictating to his clerk the opening words of his dispatch: "It has pleased God, out of His Divine Providence to grant His Majesty's arms a most complete victory over the fleet of the enemy. . . ."

There was a grim aftermath to the battle. Sir Gilbert Blane, physician of the fleet, reported, "The *Ville de Paris* had nearly three hundred men killed and wounded . . . *Glorieux* when boarded, presented a scene of complete horror . . . the decks were covered with the blood and mangled limbs of the dead, as well as the wounded and dying." The crew of one of the captured seventy-fours broke into the spirits room and got roaring drunk. Someone upset a candle, and within a few minutes the ship was ablaze from stem to stern. Everyone on board—400 Frenchmen and a 60-man British prize crew—died when her magazine exploded or met death among the sharks. Total French casualties for the day were estimated at more than 3,000 sailors and soldiers, while the "butcher's bill" for the British was 243 men killed and another 816 wounded.

For several days the British fleet lay to, repairing damage. Rodney entertained de Grasse on his flagship and was favorably impressed with his equanimity and bearing in the face of adversity. On April 17 the admiral ordered the fleet to set sail for Jamaica. Hood, who had been champing at the bit, was allowed to sweep ahead with ten of the line. Two days later, in the Mona Passage between Puerto Rico and Santo Domingo, he captured *Caton* and *Jason,* the two French sixty-fours that had put into Guadeloupe for repairs after the first brush between the fleets. From the prizes* he learned the disappointing news that the rest of the French fleet, now under the command of the Marquis de Vaudreuil, had passed through the passage the day before on their way to Cap François. The French had had enough, however, and although there was considerable maneuvering by both fleets, there were no more large-scale engagements in the Caribbean.

For the British people, Rodney's victory at the Saintes was a sudden burst of sunshine amid the gloom of defeat. The guns of the Tower of London roared out salutes, and Rodney and his commanders harvested a rich assortment of rewards. The admiral was given an English peerage, an additional pension of two thousand pounds a year, and the thanks of Parliament. Hood received an Irish peerage, and Drake and Affleck were knighted. The victory was followed by a third successful relief of Gibraltar, in September 1782, this time by Lord Howe, recalled to duty by the new ministry. Together these defensive victories restored Britain's confidence and enabled her to negotiate peace from a position of strength and equality.

In the peace treaty signed at Versailles on January 20, 1783, Britain formally recognized the independence of the United States but otherwise got off lightly, primarily because of Rodney's victory. Nearly all her lost West Indian islands were returned, while she staved off France's claims to Canada. The French reaped only Tobago and Sénégal from their generous—and ultimately bankrupting—expenditure of men and money on the American cause. Spain received Florida and Minorca in place of long-promised Gibraltar.

For France and Spain, the war was a story of lost opportunities. They had numerous opportunities to inflict crushing defeats on Britain but failed because they had divergent goals and consistently dissipated their strength upon secondary objectives. In the case of the French it was the capture of the British West Indian islands; for the Spaniards it was their fixation with

---

*Most of the prizes taken in the Battle of the Saintes, including *Ville de Paris,* were lost during a storm on the way home, along with as many as thirty-five hundred men.

Gibraltar. The French and Spanish should have concentrated on destroying the enemy's fighting fleets. Had this been accomplished, the Caribbean sugar islands and Gibraltar would have easily fallen into their hands. With the brilliant exception of Suffren in the Indian Ocean, the allied naval commanders were unaggressive and usually avoided action, or accepted it only on their own terms. They never tried to imposed their will on the British.

Although the loss of the American colonies temporarily weakened the British Empire, the Royal Navy had reestablished control of the oceans of the world. And its officers and administrators were to put the brutally instructive lessons they had learned in the American War to good use in the next one. Two decades later, just before leaving England to seek out and destroy the combined fleets of France and Spain at Trafalgar, Horatio Nelson remarked to a friend that "Rodney broke the line in one place; I will break it in two."

CHAPTER 7

"Heart of Oak"

BOWLING ALONG UNDER a full press of canvas, green sea surging about her hull, the frigate *Nymphe* prowled along the southern coast of England in the early dawn of June 19, 1793. Thirty-six guns poked menacingly from the open gun ports that lined her black and buff sides. Well-stowed hammocks filled the nettings from the ornate taffrail at the stern to the catheads. Aloft, sails bellied in the wind, and shrouds and backstays were strained taut as the strings of a violin. From *Nymphe's* gaff, the red cross of St. George snapped out like a flickering flame.

As the eastern sky lightened, a lookout at the frigate's masthead sighted a strange sail off Prawle Point. War with revolutionary France had broken out just after the turn of the year, and Captain Edward Pellew* carefully examined the approaching vessel with a long glass. She was a frigate flying the new tricolor flag of the French Republic and was identified as the forty-gun *Cleopatre*. The two ships were almost evenly matched in firepower—in fact, *Nymphe* had been taken from the French in the previous war—but the French crew was one-third larger. Snapping the glass shut, Pellew ordered his ship cleared for action and undoubtedly hoped the eighty Cornish tin miners recently recruited at Falmouth to help fill out her company would do their duty.

Pellew ordered his men into the shrouds as the two vessels ran alongside each other, and called out "Long live King George the Third!," for whom the crew gave three cheers. Not to be outdone, the French captain, Jean Mullon, manned the side of his vessel and shouted *"Vive la Nation!,"* at which his crew also gave three cheers. He also ordered a liberty cap placed atop *Cleopatre's* main truck. On hailing the French ship, Pellew had doffed his hat to her captain. Replacing it on his head was the signal to his gunners to unleash a broadside into the enemy craft. So began the first

---

*As a midshipman, Pellew had won notice for his bravery at the Battle of Valcour Island in 1776. He figures in C. S. Forester's Hornblower novels as the hero's early mentor.

Captain Edward Pellew in *Nymphe* makes short work of the French revolutionary frigate *Cleopatre* on July 19, 1793. (Beverley Robinson Collection, U.S. Naval Academy Museum)

action between naval vessels in a titanic struggle—first against revolutionary France and then against Napoleon and the French Empire—that, with one brief interval, engulfed the globe for more than two decades.

Within fifty minutes, *Nymphe*'s steady fire turned her opponent into a battered wreck. Lieutenant Israel Pellew, the captain's younger brother who was serving in the ship as a volunteer because he had no billet of his own, sighted in one of the guns. His first shots killed the helmsman, and succeeding rounds swept away three replacements, then shattered the wheel itself, and brought down *Cleopatre*'s mizzenmast. Out of control, she collided bows on with the side of her antagonist and was raked with broadside after broadside.

Fearing that the desperate French were about to board, Pellew sent his own men swarming onto *Cleopatre*. They found few unwounded Frenchmen still on deck, most having fled below, and hauled down her flag. The mortally wounded Captain Mullon was trying in his death throes to eat what he thought was his private list of coast signals, but was actually his commission. Sixty French officers and men had been killed or wounded; British casualties totaled fifty-two. Two days later, *Nymphe* brought her prize into Portsmouth amid cheers from every ship in the harbor. When the news reached London, the king announced it from his box at the Opera. Edward Pellew was knighted, and Israel Pellew was promoted to captain. *Cleopatre* was taken into the Royal Navy, so the victors capped their triumph with a tidy bit of prize money. She was renamed *Oiseau*, since the navy already had a *Cleopatra*.

The significance of this almost ritualistic encounter lay in the fact that the French crew, despite the gallantry of Captain Mullon, refused to fight after the tide of battle had turned against them. The fervor and élan of the revolutionary armies that carried them to victory over the professional armies of Europe had not been transmitted to the navy. If *Cleopatre* was a typical ship—and she was said to be above average—the poor showing of her crew indicated that naval discipline had more or less collapsed. The action proved that despite concern that the radical appeal of liberty, equality, and fraternity might find a ready response among the abused and neglected sailors of the Royal Navy, British seamen were apparently unaffected by the French revolutionary example.

FOLLOWING THE END OF the war in America, French officials regarded the cessation of hostilities as little more than a truce in a century-long struggle with Britain. This was particularly true of the Ministry of Marine, where successive chiefs began to prepare for the next war no sooner than the previous one was over. New ships were laid down to replace those lost, efforts were made to stamp out the insubordination among junior officers that had handicapped de Grasse and Suffren, and the lot of the ordinary seaman was improved. Work was also begun on a naval base on the Channel, at Cherbourg, the lack of which had thwarted attempts to invade Britain during previous wars, and on improving the naval facilities at Dunkirk, just across from the Thames Estuary; Dunkirk was an ideal place from which to harass British trade. But these costly projects contributed to the insolvency of the French treasury, which had been on shaky grounds for years, and helped bring on a revolution in 1789—and as an unintended consequence, mutiny and disorder in the French Navy.

From the security of their island, Englishmen followed the kaleidoscopic turn of events in France with interest. Radicals applauded the downfall of a frivolous and extravagant court and hailed the proclamation of the egalitarian ideals of the Revolution. "Bliss was it in that dawn to be alive," wrote William Wordsworth. Ordinary Britons believed the French were doing what they had done during their own Glorious Revolution of 1688 and hoped that a constitutional monarchy would emerge from the upheaval. Others, thinking in geopolitical terms, welcomed the disorder because Britain's chief rival would be weakened.

The government took a wait-and-see attitude. William Pitt, second son of the earl of Chatham, the architect of victory in the Seven Years' War, who had become Tory prime minister in 1784 at age twenty-four, regarded the revolution as purely an internal problem for France. Pitt's goal was to restore prosperity to Britain after the loss of the American colonies, and his mathematical mind and eloquence were devoted to convincing the nation that a victory over the national debt was as glorious as the taking of Québec in his father's day. Peace and retrenchment were the keynotes of his policy. Reductions were made in both the army and the navy, although the navy, with the respected Lord Howe at the Admiralty and Sir Charles Middleton still serving as comptroller, fared better at Pitt's hand than the army.

Among the varied tasks assigned the Royal Navy during the interwar years was the dispatch in 1787 of the armed transport *Bounty* to Tahiti to gather breadfruit trees for transplanting in the West Indies, where they were to provide a cheap and healthful food for the slaves. Lieutenant William Bligh, who was handpicked for this command, had served as master of *Resolution* during Captain James Cook's last voyage of Pacific exploration and was considered one of the navy's most skilled navigators. Bligh was not the sadistic tyrant portrayed in numerous novels and films. By the standards of the day, he was not at all a harsh captain and was sparing of the lash. His worst failings were a volcanic temper and an inability to acknowledge responsibility for mistakes, which he tried to deflect on others. Unable to control himself, he was unable to control his men.

On April 28, 1789, a segment of the crew led by Fletcher Christian, a master's mate befriended by Bligh and named acting lieutenant, seized control of the ship. Bligh and eighteen men were cast adrift in *Bounty*'s launch and eventually reached safety at Timor in the Dutch East Indies after an epic open-boat voyage of thirty-six hundred miles. Another ship later brought the breadfruit to the Caribbean islands, where the plant flourished, but paradoxically, the slaves refused to eat it. Christian and eight of the mutineers plus some Tahitian men and women took shelter on Pitcairn Island in the South Pacific. In 1808, an American vessel found their refuge. Only one mutineer and a sizable number of women and children were alive.

Opinions differ as to the cause of the *Bounty* mutiny, but the most likely was that Christian and the other mutineers had fallen under the spell of the South Seas and were reluctant to return to the grim reality of life in the Royal Navy. Others believe the uprising resulted from the breakup of a homosexual relationship between Bligh and Christian.

Some of the navy's smaller elements were pressed into service by the thrifty Pitt to bring in revenue by pursuing smugglers, collecting duties, and enforcing the Navigation Acts designed to keep the newly independent Americans out of the lucrative West India trade. Captain Horatio Nelson was among those employed in this service. He spent a brief period at war's end on half pay—an interlude in France during which he intended to learn the language but spent much of his time pursuing an English girl named Elizabeth Andrews, who refused his marriage proposal. In 1784 Nelson took command of the twenty-eight-gun frigate *Boreas*, on the Leeward Islands station. In addition to her regular complement, she carried thirty midshipmen assigned to the station. When Nelson learned that some were afraid of going aloft, he encouraged them by racing them to the masthead. Nelson performed his duties well—all too well for the Caribbean traders, the governor, and his own admiral. They all profited from the illegal trade and were furious at the blow to their pocketbooks. Nelson also uncovered finagling at the Antigua dockyard, which robbed the nation of two million pounds.

For relief from his cares, the young captain sought solace ashore, and after an unrequited affair with an older married woman at Antigua, found it with Frances Nisbet, a doctor's widow of his own age (twenty-seven) and niece of the president of the Council of the island of Nevis. She was quiet and grave and said to have a way with difficult people; Nelson took her silence for sympathy. But *Boreas* was at sea for a good part of the year, "always on the wing . . . always exercising, chasing, etc.," and the courtship went slowly. Nevertheless, it prospered, and Nelson and Fanny were married on Nevis in March 1787. Prince William Henry, now a captain in the Royal Navy whose frigate was visiting the island and who had been Nelson's friend during the American War, gave the bride away.*

Not long after, *Boreas* was ordered home, and Nelson had the ignominy of spending the next five years at half pay on the beach at Burnham Thorpe—a period of genteel poverty for himself, Fanny, and Josiah, her son by her previous marriage. He was racked by old fevers, pinched for money, and harassed by a prodigious damage suit brought by the Caribbean traders. Unrelenting in his efforts to secure a ship, Nelson was well known in the anterooms of the Admiralty: a small and wiry figure with a lined face under an unruly shock of sun-bleached hair, quick in his movements, and

*In 1782, the Prince described Nelson as "the youngest and shortest captain I had ever seen; he had a full-laced uniform, his lank unpowdered hair was tied in a stiff Hessian tale of extraordinary length; the old-fashioned flaps of his waistcoat added to the General quaintness of his figure. Altogther he was a somewhat eccentric figure. I had never in my life seen anything like it."

dressed in clothes that bagged about his slight body. "If your Lordships should be pleased to appoint me to a *cockle-boat*, I shall feel grateful," he declared at one point.

Obviously the West India merchants were successful in exacting revenge for Nelson's attempts to do his duty in the Leewards. His friendship with William Henry was also a liability, because the prince was always quarreling with his father, which prejudiced the king against his son's friends. Not even successive embroilments with France, Russia, and Spain provided Nelson with a command at sea—and there seemed little prospect of obtaining one, for Pitt had no intention of going to war. "There never was a time in the history of this country, when, from the situation in Europe, we might more reasonably expect fifteen years of peace, than we may now at the present moment," he declared in February 1792.

Yet, fewer than six weeks later, much of Europe was plunged into war. France, anticipating an attack by Prussia and Austria, the birthplace of Queen Marie Antoinette, declared war on these states. Every man not crippled by age or infirmity was pressed into the revolutionary armies. Led by young and able officers—Ney, Murat, Bernadotte, Soult, and others who were to win legendary glory for France—these ragged peasant battalions triumphed over the professional armies of the *ancien régime* in a fog at Valmy in the Argonne and flung them back over the Rhine. A major reason for this victory was the adherence to the Revolution of the French Army's artillery officers, who were drawn to a large extent from the middle class. Among them was an ambitious young Corsican-born captain named Napoleon Bonaparte.

The radical Jacobins, who had seized control of the governing National Convention, immediately abolished the monarchy, proclaimed a republic, and executed King Louis XVI. "Allied kings threaten us, and we hurl at their feet as a gage of battle, the head of a king!" proclaimed Georges-Jacques Danton. Revolutionary armies swept into the Austrian Netherlands (now Belgium), captured the port of Antwerp, and announced the annexation of the area to France. Britain was alarmed by these moves, and by decrees promulgated by the Convention offering assistance to all who wished to rid them themselves of tyrannical monarchies. Britons saw the Revolution's militance as a threat to their security, their trade, and the legitimacy of the Hanoverian dynasty.

French occupation of the Flemish coast and the threat that Antwerp would become a commercial rival to London were unacceptable.* But with

*In 1914 Britain sent troops to the Continent for the first time in a century to defend Belgium against an invasion by Imperial Germany as a result of her fear of having an enemy on the nearby shore.

the nation suffering from a poor harvest, and with riots flaring in the newly industrialized Midlands in protest against the skyrocketing price of bread, Pitt was even more reluctant than ever to go to war. In an effort at appeasement, he offered to recognize the republic if the French withdrew from the occupied territory and renounced the revolutionary decrees. France's reply was not long in coming. On February 1, 1792, she declared war on Spain, Holland, and Britain, the latter in the mistaken belief that a revolution was imminent in England.

POST NUBLIA PHOEBIUS . . . After clouds come sunshine," a euphoric Nelson wrote Fanny from London as the Royal Navy mobilized for war. "The Admiralty so smile upon me that really I am as much surprised as when they frowned." Inspired by the crisis, Lord Chatham—the prime minister's affable elder brother who had succeeded Lord Howe as first lord in 1788—offered Nelson command of a sixty-four-gun ship of the line. Other able naval officers, among them Collingwood, Pellew, Thomas Troubridge, and James Saumarez, also chafing on half pay, were summoned to active duty.

Within a few weeks Nelson was striding the quarterdeck of a man-of-war for the first time in five years: the veteran third-rate *Agamemnon,* which had been in the thick of the fighting at the Saintes. Josiah Nisbet, now twelve, joined his stepfather as a midshipman. Although the "Eggs and Bacon," as she was affectionately known to her crew, had been laid up at Chatham for about ten years, Nelson was delighted with her. "My ship sails very well indeed," he declared. "We think better than any ship in the fleet." To fill out her complement, he sent a lieutenant and four midshipmen to recruit men at the drumhead in his home county of Norfolk, where he was known and respected, and they attracted numerous volunteers.

British policy for the coming struggle was made by three men: Pitt; his diffident cousin Lord Grenville, the foreign secretary; and Henry Dundas, for whom he created the post of secretary of state for war and colonies. Dundas was the bachelor prime minister's best friend and boon companion in his one human failing: love of the port bottle. Pitt was master of the House of Commons—he demolished an opposition orator by merely crumpling and throwing away, with a contemptuous smile, the paper on which he had been making notes of the man's speech. But as he told Grenville, "I distrust extremely any ideas of my own on military strategy"—and left strategic planning to Dundas. Beefy and jovial, Dundas was a first-rate politician, a past master of compromise and the doling out of the loaves and fishes of patronage, but he, too, knew nothing about the art of war. Unhappily, he thought he did. The result was a policy of drift, delay, and the dissipation of resources on numerous unrelated enterprises.

What Pitt and Dundas wanted was a brief, cheap, and glorious war in which France's richest colonies were captured while Britain's own commerce was protected. They failed to understand that they were dealing with a new kind of conflict, an ideological war in which the capture of enemy colonies was not the key to victory, as it was in Pitt's father's day. Underrating the latent power of a nation in arms, they were convinced France would be unable to resist the powers of Europe very long. Contrary to the expectations of Pitt and Dundas, the Revolution, rather than being speedily suppressed, overleaped the frontiers of France and swept through the adjacent countries. The bankrupt French treasury was amply replenished by the loot of lands overrun by her armies and the proceeds of the war against Britain's trade.

Like his father, Pitt realized that Britain needed allies on the Continent, and Britain joined Austria, Prussia, Russia, Spain, Holland, Sardinia, and the Kingdom of the Two Sicilies* in what became known as the First Coalition, the earliest of a series of alliances directed against revolutionary France and then the French Empire. Britain's major contribution to the alliance was the Royal Navy, and cash subsidies to keep the armies of her allies in the field. In essence, Pitt hoped to strangle the French Republic with the strings of a moneybag.

As a result of the efforts of Howe and Middleton, the fleet was better prepared than at the beginning of any previous war of the century. The long rows of stripped-down hulks laid up in "ordinary" in the backwaters of coastal England in the wake of the American War had been well maintained, and there were ample reserves of naval stores, some earmarked for specific ships for when they were recalled to service. Twenty-one ships of the line were in commission at the beginning of the conflict; by the end of 1793 the number had grown to eighty-five. Several 110-gun ships had been built in the interwar years, including *Ville de Paris*, named after Admiral de Grasse's flagship, which had been captured at the Saintes and then lost in a storm. Other new British warships were larger than comparable vessels of the earlier period and were more seaworthy and better able to fight their guns. Nevertheless, the navy was still below the standard deemed necessary throughout the eighteenth century—a fleet equal to the combined strength of France and Spain. And because of the concentration on ships of the line, the navy was deficient in frigates, the workhorses of the fleet. "Were I to die at this moment," Nelson later lamented while in command

*All of Italy south of Rome plus Sicily, with the capital at Naples.

of naval forces in the Mediterranean, "'want of frigates' would be found engraved upon my heart."*

Coppering was now standard in the British fleet, and almost all vessels mounted carronades as well as the usual long guns. The Royal Navy had also taken great strides in improving its signaling. Lord Howe, while in charge of the Admiralty, had made his numerical system, as modified by Richard Kempenfelt, standard for the entire navy in an effort to overcome the sterility of naval tactics. Instead of following rigid rules, his *Signal Book for the Ships of War* allowed admirals to make decisions in the heat of battle and transmit their intentions to their fleets. The new signals system was based on multicolored flags numbered from one to nine,[†] preceded by the flag designating the recipient—the fleet, its frigates, or individual ships, which had their own numbers. The numbers of the these flags corresponded to numbers in the signal book which stood for a specific message.

Manning the fleet, as always, was a problem. The navy mustered only 16,000 men in 1793 compared to the 110,000 on the books at the end of the previous war. Parliament immediately voted funds for 45,000 men. Within four years the number tripled to 120,000 men. Bounties attracted some volunteers, and press gangs took up the slack. One man recalled such an encounter: The officer in charge "gave a whistle and in a moment I was in the hands of six or eight ruffians who I immediately dreaded and soon found to be a press gang. They dragged me hurriedly along through several streets amid bitter excretions bestowed upon them, [and] expression of sympathy bestowed upon me."

As Britain's great merchant fleets arrived in the Thames and other ports, press gangs boarded the vessels and stripped them of most of their hands before they could get ashore. Trading vessels were embargoed from sailing until the navy's needs were met. Merchants were soon complaining that sailors were in such short supply that sixty ships bound for the Caribbean and other destinations could not sail. In 1795 Parliament enacted a Quota Act, which required each parish to provide a certain number of men for the Royal Navy. This gave the local authorities the opportunity to rid themselves

---

*Both Britain and the United States committed a similar blunder in the years leading up to World War II when they failed to build an adequate number of destroyers and similar vessels for convoy escort duty, which gave the German U-boats an almost free hand in the Atlantic until 1943.

[†]For example:
General no. 1: Enemy in sight.
Frigates no. 9: Leave off chase.
General no. 78: Tack in succession.
This last signal was made by hoisting flags 7 and 8.

of undesirables and petty criminals—much to the unhappiness of professional seamen.* Large bounties, sometimes as much as 70 pounds, were also offered, which attracted bounty jumpers, who deserted at the first opportunity. Among the "quota men" were tradesmen, teachers, and clerks who had been jailed for debt. Better educated and more politically sophisticated than the ordinary sailor, they were not as easy to handle. They included numerous Irishmen, whose natural antipathy toward Britain was magnified by the brutalities of sea service and the subversive appeal of French revolutionary doctrine.

France began the war with a powerful fleet of eighty-five ships of the line, including three of 120 guns, five 100-gun ships, ten of 80 guns, and sixty-four of 74 guns. Because French ships were more heavily armed than British vessels, the British fleet had a superioriy in armament of only one-sixth rather then the 50 percent implied by the difference in size of the two forces. The Atlantic fleet was divided among three bases: thirty-nine of the line at Brest, ten 74-gun ships at Lorient, and another twelve at Rochefort. Two ships of 120 guns, three of 80, and nineteen of 74 were based in the Mediterranean at Toulon. These figures did not include the swarms of frigates, sloops, brigs, schooners and other small armed vessels engaged in a *guerre de course,* or war against British commerce. But supplies were short, and the ships were in varying states of disrepair and unreadiness.

France had the advantage of not being wholly dependent on overseas commerce and communications—although the West Indies trade accounted for about a third of her foreign commerce—which meant that unlike Britain, she did not have to maintain a navy at constant readiness. The French could select the moment for embarking on a maritime enterprise—a cruise against an expected British convoy, an invasion of restive Ireland, or an offensive in the East Indies or the Caribbean—rather than be prepared at all times to intercept enemy operations with at least equal strength. To be ready to deal with an enemy fleet of twelve sail of the line at anchor at Brest, the Royal Navy had not only to have an equal number of vessels on patrol but also a reserve of eight ships to replace those that were damaged by storms or replenishing stores.

The biggest problems confronting the *Marine de la République Français* were the shortage of experienced officers and the complete collapse of discipline. Mutinies were frequent, and the leveling effect of the Revolution

---

*Speaking of the "quota men," one petty officer complained: "Them was the chaps as played hell with the Fleet! Every finger was fairly a fish hook; neither chest nor bed nor blanket nor bag escaped their sleight of hand thievery. They pluck you—aye, clean as a poulterer, and bone your eyebrows, while staring you straight in the face."

deprived the navy of its best officers, reducing some crews to little more than unruly mobs without the skill and unquestioning obedience needed to successfully operate a man-of-war. The elite corps of seaman gunners had been abolished on grounds that it smacked of aristocracy. Officers who had served the Bourbon kings were driven from the service, arrested, or fled for their lives. For example, the comte d'Estaing, who was too loyal to emigrate and who favored moderate reform, was condemned to death for testifying in favor of Marie Antoinette at her trial. "Send my head to the English," he declared. "They will pay well for it."

The shortage of experienced naval officers due to the ruthless efficiency of the guillotine was so great that it was not uncommon for a lieutenant to be promoted to captain and then admiral in three years or less. Former petty and warrant officers became captains. A few were competent and skilled, but by and large the navy failed to throw up leaders of the same caliber as the revolutionary army. The ships were neglected and rarely went to sea. And when French fleet commanders fought, revolutionary zeal was no substitute for experience and training. Moreover, they operated under the baleful eye of what in our day were called political commissars, and faced loss of their heads for the crime of being unsuccessful. It was hardly the atmosphere for daring or imaginative use of a navy.

In fact, the French revolutionary leaders were aware that they would probably have little chance to contest Britain at sea and decided to concentrate their available strength on military operations on the Continent. With the flame of revolution emblazoned on their banners, they intended nothing less than to dragoon all of Europe and its resources into the republican system. Britain's contacts with the Continent and the outside world were to be cut off, and the British, isolated in their island fortress, would be forced in the end to either yield or face economic ruin. For her part, Britain adopted the classical maritime strategy used by the elder Pitt. Facing the French military jugernaut in Europe, the British financed a series of Continental allies but always maintained the ability to withdraw to the sea when these allies did poorly. As long as the French could not end British resistance, they could not win a final victory. In essence, the war between France and Britain became a struggle between land power and sea power—between the Elephant and the Whale.

⌐

FORMAL NAVAL OPERATIONS began with the appointment of two of the Royal Navy's most distinguished officers to the top commands: Lord Howe was given the Channel fleet, and Lord Hood received an independent command in the Mediterranean. Nearly seventy years old and reluctant to go on active service because of declining health, Howe hoisted his flag in the 100-gun *Queen Charlotte* only after he was personally urged to do so by his friend—and relation—King George. Unhappily, although the admiral had been responsible for numerous improvements in naval tactics and was known for fair treatment of the British seaman, his strategic judgment had become impaired in old age. Like many elderly sailors, he was more deeply concerned about the safety of his ships than strategic considerations.

The hinge of British naval strategy was the blockade of Brest, but Howe ignored this imperative. Rather than stationing his two dozen ships of the line off Brest to establish a close blockade of the Atlantic Fleet of the type that had proved so effective in the Seven Years' War, he held his fleet at Spithead and Torbay. There, he reasoned, they could be easily supplied, and be safe from the rough seas and gales of the turbulent Bay of Biscay. In the meantime, a picket line of frigates patrolled off Ushant and looked into Brest to see if the French were preparing to come out. Periodically he took his growing fleet to sea to cover convoys and to drill newly arrived vessels. But the American War had demonstrated that a distant blockade was ineffective. Spithead was too far down the English Channel from Brest for a British fleet based there to react quickly if enemy squadrons tried to get to sea. Moreover, keeping the fleet in port reduced efficiency and damaged the morale of the crews.

Trade protection was left to a few roving frigates, and Britain's maritime commerce suffered heavily from the depredations of French commerce raiders and privateers that had no difficulty getting to sea. Convoys were often exposed to attacks by forces far stronger than their escorts, and Howe was unable to do little more than skirmish with the French squadrons that appeared off the Brittany coast to prevent the British from supporting Royalist insurrections ashore in the adjoining Vendée. Critics suggested he might have brought them to bay had he spent more time on the French coast and less in port, and lampooned him as "Lord Torbay." In mid-December Howe ordered the battle fleet snugged down for winter, leaving only a few frigates on patrol.

CHAPTER 8

"To Glory We Steer"

LORD HOOD, WHO FLEW his flag in *Victory,* arrived off Toulon, France's premier naval port in the South, in August 1793 with twenty-one of the line, among them Nelson's *Agamemnon.* Although Hood was sixty-nine years old, he was impetuous as ever and described by Nelson as "active as a man of forty." He immediately imposed a blockade on Toulon and its fortified naval base where some twenty ships of the line, including the French flagship, the 120-gun *Commerce de Marseilles,* lay, along with several vessels being refitted or built. Over the next month the British fleet not only maintained station off Toulon in the face of a blowing mistral but also played a key role in preventing a French military thrust into Italy by disrupting coastal shipping that supplied the Army of the Alps. But the fleet was starved for fresh provisions after being so long at sea. "All we get is honour and salt beef," grumbled Nelson.

The Mediterranean was vital to Britain's strategy even though she had no colonies there and her trade with the area was limited. Until the opening of the Suez Canal, the Mediterranean was a dead end for shipping, and commerce with India was carried on around the Cape of Good Hope. Geopolitical considerations were more important than commerce, however. Ships operating in the Mediterranean had access to France's southern flank and could prevent the Toulon fleet from breaking out into the Atlantic. A naval presence also reassured Britain's allies of her continued support. Nevertheless, such a fleet could not operate without a secure base, and the British faced a chicken-or-egg situation. Which should come first—a base or a fleet?

In the meantime, to the north, in Flanders, affairs were taking a nasty turn. A force of ten thousand Redcoats had been sent there under the leadership of the duke of York, the King's twenty-nine-year-old second son who had been apprenticed to Frederick the Great, to cooperate with Austrians and Prussians and to seize Dunkirk, the French commerce raiders' haven. They laboriously advanced on Dunkirk through towns that figured not for the last time in British history—Ypres, Furnes, Nieuport—but when the army arrived in the outskirts of the city, there were no ships offshore bearing the siege artillery that had been promised by Lord Chatham, the first lord of the Admiralty.

Not only was there a breakdown in coordination between the army and the navy, but also a lack of cooperation among the Allies. Before they could organize their forces, the French struck. Using superior numbers to make up for lack of training and experience, they attacked in seemingly endless waves that overran the allied forces. The duke of York, threatened with encirclement between the marshes and the sea, ordered his troops to fall back through mud and rain into the Austrian Netherlands, abandoning his field artillery and stores. Some of the officers fled, leaving their troops behind.

The Dunkirk fiasco almost brought down the government, for the Admiralty had not only failed to send the promised naval assistance, it also had not even protected the hapless Redcoats from bombardment by French gunboats. But hard on the heels of this disaster, London received news that events in the Mediterranean had suddenly taken an extraordinary turn. Toulon was strongly Royalist, as was the Comte de Trogoff, commander of the French Mediterranean fleet. Terrified by the arrival of Jacobin commissioners with a portable guillotine, the populace overthrew the revolutionary regime, swore allegiance to King Louis XVII—the dauphin imprisoned in Paris—and Trogoff surrendered the base and the entire fleet to Lord Hood. The British were then unexpectedly joined at Toulon by twenty-four ships of the line flying the Spanish flag under the command of Don Juan de Langara.

Pitt and his ministers were beside themselves with joy. "I am much mistaken," said Lord Grenville, "if the business at Toulon is not decisive of the war." The prime minister was of a similar mind. Toulon might indeed have been decisive if Hood had possessed the men to exploit the windfall. But the town and anchorage were in a basin surrounded by rugged hills some eighteen hundred feet in height, with fortresses dominating the key points. Large numbers of troops were needed—perhaps as many as fifty thousand—to defend Toulon against the republican armies. Instead, the admiral had about fifteen hundred marines and sailors and a few thousand ill-disciplined Spanish soldiers whose main objective seemed to be to cut the throats of any prisoners unlucky enough to fall into their hands.

Unable to count on receiving a significant body of British reinforcements because Henry Dundas had dispersed most of the nation's minuscule army to the Caribbean, India, and Flanders, Hood appealed for troops and ammunition from Spain, Sardinia, and Naples, France's enemies in the Mediterranean. Captain Nelson was sent to Naples to urge King Ferdinand

IV, a Spanish Bourbon, to waste no time in dispatching troops to Toulon. Nelson was chosen because of his forceful personality and because his ship was fast.

Agamemnon anchored in the shimmering brilliance of the Bay of Naples on the evening of September 10, 1793. Vesuvius was in the midst of a spectacular eruption that portended volcanic future events. All hands spent the night on deck, upturned faces lit by the glare of flaming lava. The next morning Nelson, wearing his best uniform, made contact with Sir William Hamilton, for nearly thirty-five years the British envoy to the exotic Neapolitan court. Nelson probably regarded Sir William with curiosity, for he had heard much gossip about the ambassador and his strikingly beautiful wife, Lady Hamilton, because scandal swirled about them like a scented silk scarf.

At sixty-two, Sir William was a renowned connoisseur of classical antiquities, an amateur archaeologist, and an expert on volcanoes. Two years before he had married Emily Lyon, daughter of a West Country blacksmith, onetime artists' model, and mistress of a succession of young rakes, whom he had purchased for his bed from a bankrupt nephew, as if she were another art treasure. Lady Hamilton, who now called herself Emma, learned Italian and French and was a favorite of Queen Maria Carolina, sister of the soon-to-be-beheaded Marie Antoinette and said to be the real ruler of Naples.*

Sir William immediately secured an audience for Nelson with King Ferdinand—known to his subjects as *il Lazzarone* (the Rascal) because of his dissipated ways—who readily approved the dispatch of troops to Toulon after being promised a British subsidy. Local officials cautioned, however, that two weeks would be needed to gather provisions for the detachment. Sir William, once a soldier himself, forcefully pointed out that because of the urgency of the situation, it would be better to send two thousand men in three or four days rather than a larger force in several weeks. These arguments carried the day. "You do business in my own way," an approving Nelson told Sir William. For his part, the envoy developed an immediate liking and respect for the enterprising sailor.

While arranging for embarkation of the troops as well as provisions and water for his own ship, Nelson was the guest of the Hamiltons at their palatial villa, Palazzo Sessa, a treasure-house of Renaissance art and classical statuary. Sir William had also gathered a notable collection of paintings of his wife, including several by George Romney. Some of the midshipmen, including Josiah Nisbet, Nelson's rather awkward stepson, were invited ashore for sight-seeing. "Lady Hamilton has been wonderfully kind and good to Josiah," Nelson wrote Fanny. "She is a young woman of amiable

*Some gossips whispered that Emma was the queen's lesbian lover.

manners . . . who does honour to the station to which she has been raised."
Four days after *Agamemnon* arrived in Naples, she sailed—and five years
would pass before Nelson saw Sir William and Lady Hamilton again.

〜

TOULON WAS UNDER SIEGE by the French when Nelson returned to the
realities of war. "Shot and shells are throwing about us every hour," he
noted in his journal. "The enemy have many strong posts on the hills which
are daily augmented with men." Lord Hood's mixed bag of some twelve
thousand troops—Spaniards, Sardinians, Neapolitans, and French Royalists augmented by two thousand British regulars scraped up at Gibraltar—
was weakened by dissension. At one point, Admiral de Langara, who had
lost his squadron to Rodney in 1780 in the Moonlight Battle and who was
consequently a prodigious Anglophobe, quarreled with Hood and tried to
seize command from him. Redoubt and redoubt fell to the French, and
increasingly accurate fire was being brought to bear on the harbor by guns
sighted in by twenty-four-year-old Lieutenant Colonel Napoleon Bonaparte, the chief of the French artillery. Hood tried to answer the fire of the
enemy positions on the heights, but the ship's guns could not be elevated
enough.

The end came on the night of December 17, 1793. Bonaparte had turned
his brilliant mind to the intensive study of the allied position and quickly
pinpointed its place of major weakness. French infantry carried it in a
nighttime assault as the Spaniards and the Neapolitans panicked. With his
ships in danger of being shot to pieces by the French batteries, Hood had
no choice but to abandon Toulon. As many of the French men-of-war as
possible were to be brought out, while the arsenal and the rest of the ships
were to be burned. Hood was also convinced that he had a moral obliga-
tion to save as many French Royalists as possible from revolutionary
vengeance.

The evacuation of Toulon was a nightmare. French artillery pounded the
town without mercy. Flames and smoke leaped skyward from exploding
vessels and burning warehouses, making it difficult to breathe. Panicked
soldiers and civilians hacked and clawed at each other for a place on the
departing ships. People were injured and killed when the fires touched
off loaded guns on the burning craft. The smell of charred flesh hung in
the air. Although four French ships of the line and a dozen frigates were
brought out, only nine of the big ships that had to be left behind were
burned, largely due to the failure of Spanish incendiary parties to do their
jobs. De Langara later acknowledged that he saw no advantage to Spain in
helping the British augment their fleet. Because of this betrayal, eighteen

French ships of the line survived the holocaust and provided the French with the nucleus of a fleet to challenge the British in the Mediterranean.

Some fifteen thousand Royalists were saved, but there was not enough room for all those scrambling to leave on Hood's ships. Once the fleet sailed, those who could not find a place on the British ships tried to escape on whatever vessels remained. Several were swamped, pitching the screaming passengers into the sea. The conquering republican troops shot and bayoneted men, women, and children by the hundreds. Another six thousand Royalists paid on the guillotine for the sin of resisting the Revolution. Young Bonaparte was promoted to brigadier general in reward for his services, and the capture of Toulon marked the beginning of his ascent to fame. Years later, during his imprisonment on St. Helena, he entertained audiences with graphic accounts of the city's siege and fall.

⤚

FOLLOWING THE RETREAT from Toulon, Lord Hood withdrew his fleet to Hyères Bay, a short distance to the east, where a group of small islands offered shelter against the prevailing wind. But to keep an effective watch on the French fleet, he needed a base of operations nearer than Gibraltar where his ships could be sent to provision and water. Minorca was ruled out because Spain seemed likely to abandon the First Coalition at any moment. The obvious place was Corsica. There was a splendid anchorage on the northwestern coast, at San Fiorenzo Bay, that could shelter all of Hood's ships. The island was also the source of the French Mediterranean fleet's reserves of timber and naval stores, and vessels based there would fulfill the double purpose of severing enemy communications and protecting British trade.

Corsica had been sold by the Republic of Genoa to France in 1768 against the will of its people—just in time to make Napoleon, who was born a year later, a French citizen. The turbulent island submitted to its new rulers only after a desperate resistance led by Pasquale de Paoli was put down. In the spring of 1793 Paoli mounted another revolt against the hated French, and his partisans drove the republican garrison into the fortress-cities of Bastia and Calvi, where they were short of food. Napoleon's "traitor" pro-French family fled to Marseilles. Paoli offered to cede Corsica to the British if they assisted him in expelling the French, and Hood took up the task.

Nelson, now recognized by Hood as his outstanding subordinate, was assigned to blockade Corsica and prevent the French from sending in reinforcements. *Agamemnon* and her accompanying frigates worked close inshore, often under fire, making raids ashore, burning the island's only flour mill, and chasing and boarding blockade runners. "My ship's company behave most exceedingly well," Nelson wrote Fanny. "They really mind shot no more than peas." In early January 1794, British troops and a contingent of sailors and marines totaling four thousand men landed and captured San Fiorenzo. Two days of close-range naval bombardment were needed to subdue a squat, stone tower at Cape Mortella overlooking the anchorage.*

Heavily fortified Bastia, with four thousand French troops and Corsican loyalists and seventy cannon, was the next British target. But Major General Sir David Dundas, the army commander who undoubtedly received his post because he was the brother of Henry Dundas, refused to advance over the rugged mountains from San Fiorenzo until reinforcements arrived from Gibraltar. Nelson volunteered to take the fortress with only his sailors and marines and a handful of soldiers without delay—causing some army officers to sarcastically refer to him as "the Brigadier." Later Nelson was to say, "In my mind's eye, I ever saw a radiant orb suspended which beckoned me onward to renown."

On the night of April 3–4, 1794, a force of 1,248 men landed to the north of the town, and by noon eight twenty-four-pounders had been swayed out from *Agamemnon*'s lower gun deck and wrestled onto the heights above Bastia. Another six days were needed to emplace several large mortars that Nelson had asked Sir William Hamilton to obtain from King Ferdinand. Bastia refused Lord Hood's demand for surrender—the French commander said he had "hot shot for our ships and bayonets for our troops"—and on April 11 the British began shelling the citadel, which returned a steady fire. Not long after, Nelson had a close call. He had taken a friend, Captain Thomas Fremantle, to inspect a battery, and Fremantle related that "walking with Nelson from thence a shot knocked him down." Despite a bad cut on his back, Nelson directed the establishment of two more batteries only a thousand yards from the enemy bastion.

For the next thirty-seven days, bombardment and counterbombardment echoed and thudded among the mountains, burying everything—vegetation, fieldworks, guns, and men—under a cloud of dust. The French, on the verge of starvation and frightened of falling into the hands of Paoli's Corsican partisans, finally laid down their arms after being promised that they could surrender to the British. Nelson led the way into Bastia and was astonished at the size of the garrison: four thousand men had surrendered

---

*The British were impressed with the structure, which they misnamed a Martello Tower, and scores of them were built around the coast of Britain and in eastern Canada as a defense against invasion. The opening scene of James Joyce's novel *Ulysses* occurs in an abandoned Martello Tower overlooking the Irish coast near Dublin.

to fewer than a third their number. After this, in Nelson's view, one Englishman was a match for three Frenchmen. That evening, Dundas's troops plodded through the mountain passes from San Fiorenzo just in time to claim the glory.

By now an old amphibious hand, Nelson commanded the naval forces that attacked Calvi, on a headland in the northwestern corner of the island. Defended by three strong forts, the town was even more challenging than Bastia. Wild gales blew the ships out to sea and delayed the landing of cannon and supplies. Once again, the sailors dragged the guns over the intervening mountains, thought by the French to be impassable, to positions from which they commanded Calvi's outer fortifications. "By computation we may . . . have dragged one 24-pounder with its ammunition . . . upwards of 80 miles, 17 of which were up a very steep mountain," Nelson reported.

The siege of Calvi began on July 4 and continued for fifty-one days. Fighting the batteries was dangerous work because they were in range of the citadel's guns. Several of Nelson's cannon were dismounted by enemy fire and their crews killed or wounded. Nelson's own luck ran out on July 12, as he was watching the effects of the bombardment from a rock with a view of the entire battlefield. A round shot kicked up a shower of sand and stones about him, and blood poured from cuts on his face, the most severe over his right eye and which penetrated the eyeball.

The wound was painful, but Nelson tried to make light of it. In spite of a throbbing in his head and a bandage around his eye, he wrote Lord Hood: "I got a little hurt this morning; not much, as you may judge from my writing." The surgeons held out hope that the eye had not been damaged, but his vision faded over the next several weeks, finally leaving him able only to distinguish light from dark. To his wife, Nelson wrote his eye "as to all the purpose of use, it is gone." Nevertheless, he managed a little joke. "The blemish is nothing . . . so my *beauty* is saved."*

Though Nelson was now half blind, it was no bar to active service in those days, and he remained in command of his batteries. The time of what the Corsicans called the "lion sun" was now at hand. Exhaustion from hauling heavy loads in the summer heat, malaria, typhoid, and dysentery all took their toll of the besiegers, and more than a thousand men reported sick. Would the besieged run out of food and water before the besiegers

---

*Nelson did not wear a black eyepatch following the loss of his eye, even though some artists have erroneously depicted him with one, sometimes over his *left* eye. Instead, he wore a green eyeshade on his hat to protect the damaged eye from bright sunlight, which caused him pain. Later, growing concerned over the weakness of his good eye, he had the eyeshade extended to cover both eyes.

were laid low by fever and disease? By the time the French surrendered on August 10, 1794, fewer than four hundred British soldiers and sailors were fit for duty.* Much to Nelson's chagrin, the army commander hogged the credit for the victory, and Nelson was not even mentioned in dispatches. Nor was he listed among the wounded. "They hate us sailors; we are too active for them," he declared. "We accomplish our business sooner than they like."

Not long after the fall of Corsica, the aging Lord Hood hauled down his flag after a series of disagreements with the Admiralty and went home in *Victory,* leaving command to his deputy, Vice Admiral Sir William Hotham. Hood ended his career as governor of Greenwich Hospital, a home for superannuated sailors. "Oh, Miserable Board of Admiralty," wrote Nelson, "they have forced the best officer in our service away from his command." Under the lethargic watch of the new commander in chief, the blockade of Toulon went on, with the Mediterranean fleet standing out to sea under patched sails and with hulls battered by relentless winter storms.

⤸

THE BRITISH TROOPS WHO might have made a difference at Toulon had been dispatched to the Caribbean on an expedition that was the brainchild of Henry Dundas. Although he believed that the seizure of France's West Indian colonies would cripple the young republic by depriving it of badly needed revenue, Dundas's strategy was based as much on the hope for loot to pay for the war as it was on geopolitics. Oblivious to local conditions, he failed to realize that the all-consuming French Revolution had made campaigning in the Caribbean an even more hazardous prospect than ever before.

Besides the usual diseases, which carried away an estimated nineteen thousand British soldiers and sailors over the next two years and disabled an equal number, the islands were swept by slave revolts aroused by French revolutionary agents with promises of freedom and equality. Ironically, the British found themselves allied with the Royalist and British planters, even though Pitt and a significant body of English public opinion considered slavery not only a vile abomination but also economically wasteful.

*"Never," said Colonel John Moore, "was so much work done by so few men." Winston Churchill obviously had this statement in mind when during the Battle of Britain in 1940 he so famously said of the fighter pilots of the Royal Air Force: "Never in the field of human conflict was so much owed by so many to so few."

War had come to the West Indies in April 1793. Upon learning of the outbreak of hostilities, Vice Admiral Sir John Lafory sailed down from Barbados with a single fifty-gun ship plus a few smaller vessels and a handful of troops to recapture Tobago, which had been ceded to France after the last war. In Santo Domingo, the richest of the French West Indian islands, the planters, terrified by a slave revolt led by a black coachman named Toussaint L'Ouverture, invited the British to occupy the ports of Jérémie and Môle Saint Nicolas. But an attempt to take Martinique with the assistance of Royalist forces ended in fiasco.

The arrival of Vice Admiral Sir John Jervis at Barbados in January 1794 with seven thousand troops under the command of Lieutenant General Sir Charles Grey ushered in a more vigorous phase of the war in the Caribbean. The fifty-eight-year-old Jervis was one of the most remarkable figures of the Age of Fighting Sail. With his long nose, heavy brows, and a head set low on bulky shoulders, he had a bull-like quality and a blunt way of speech. Without family influence, he had risen in the navy solely through his abilities, and lived on his pay.* Jervis was knighted in 1782 when his ship captured a French eighty-gun vessel in an hour-long gun duel without the loss of a single man. Known as "Old Jarvie," he was a stern taskmaster and harsh disciplinarian, but was respected for his efforts to care for his crews.

Unlike most British military and naval officers of the period, Jervis and Grey meshed their operations without friction and even became personal friends. Within three months they captured almost all the French islands in the Caribbean, with only light casualties, through a masterly use of amphibious operations. Martinique was their first target. Troops were landed there on February 5 at three widely separated locations to prevent the defenders from concentrating, while Jervis's ships kept the coastal fortifications busy. It was done "in the good old-fashioned way, within pistol shot," the admiral observed. To ensure swift lodgment, the assaulting troops did not fire their muskets but took the defenses by bayonet.

By March 16, little more than a month after the original landings, the island had fallen into British hands except for two forts defending the capital of Fort de France. Guns were lightered in from the ships and manhandled into position, and a bombardment was began. Six days later, the forts

---

*Jervis ran away to sea in 1747 at age thirteen. When he was caught and brought home, his father, a struggling barrister, obtained an appointment for him as a midshipman. He gave the boy twenty pounds and told him he could expect no further help from the family. Jervis's first uniform coat hung down to his knees because he could afford only a secondhand one.

Admiral John Jervis, Earl St. Vincent. (U.S. Naval Academy Museum)

surrendered. St. Lucia was taken on April 4 after only three days of fighting. Guadeloupe, the Saintes, and its other dependencies fell on April 20. Shortly afterward, the British forces on Santo Domingo captured Port-au-Prince, along with considerable spoils.

The British triumph was short-lived, however, primarily because reinforcements promised by the lackadaisical Lord Chatham failed to arrive. While the troops on hand were sufficient to garrison the islands, yellow fever took its deadly toll, and soon the number of men fit for duty was not enough to defend them against a force of even moderate strength. Jervis also lacked enough ships to maintain patrols to intercept vessels sent from France. Early in June, while he was watering his fleet at St. Kitts, the admiral received news he had been dreading: nine enemy ships of the line had slipped out of Rochfort, evaded Lord Howe's lax blockade of the French coast, and arrived off Guadeloupe, where they landed about six thousand men.

With them was Victor Hugues, a mulatto who had been a ruthless public prosecutor in Rochfort—and who was soon to be known as the "colonial Robespierre." He brought from Paris a decree of the National Convention giving freedom and the franchise to everyone in the Antilles, regardless of race. Unlike at Santo Domingo, no black army existed in the Windwards, so Hugues armed the liberated slaves and sent them into battle under the colors of the Republic. By denouncing slavery—the gap in Britain's moral armor—the French made the slaves into a formidable ally in the struggle for the Caribbean. On the other side, Pitt, knuckling under to the political clout of the West India planters, forbade the enlistment of blacks.

Guadeloupe's small garrison put up a stout defense as Jervis hurried to the rescue. But he was stricken with yellow fever, like so many of his men, and was unable to accomplish much against an enemy who outnumbered his own force and who were largely inured to tropical pestilences. Time was also on Hugues's side. With the approach of the hurricane season, the British ships would soon have to abandon their stations. The surviving defenders of Guadeloupe, most reduced to trembling, fever-racked skeletons, were finally evacuated from the island in October.

Having driven the British out of the captured French islands, Hugues's agents moved on to the British colonies, spreading the gospel of liberty and plunder and offering arms to all who would join the revolt. Old brutalities were repaid with new savagery. On St. Lucia, British captives asked for food and had bayonets jammed down their throats. On Grenada, the governor and forty-seven guests were slaughtered as they sat down to dinner. On St. Vincent, the planters and their families were butchered and their hearts ripped out and eaten.

By drawing on the islands for troops and supplies, the French cut themselves loose from Europe, and with no external lines of communication to be severed, could ignore the Royal Navy. Promised reinforcements for the fever-stricken British garrisons never appeared, or when they did come were under strength and without clothing suitable for campaigning in the tropics. French commerce raiders slipped through the area's numerous passages to cut British trade to pieces. Sick and disgusted, Jervis and Grey finally resigned when false charges of corruption were brought against them by the West Indies merchants.

Except for Barbados and Dominica, the British were driven out of the Lesser Antilles. It was the most complete defeat inflicted on a British expeditionary force until Gallipoli in World War I. Pitt and Dundas "poured . . . troops into these pestilent islands, in the expectation that thereby they would destroy the power of France," writes one historian,* "only to discover, when it was too late, that they had practically destroyed the British army."

*John W. Fortescue, *History of the British Army,* vol. IV, p. 385.

CHAPTER 9

"Engage the Enemy Closer"

FROM A HILL ABOVE Cowes on the Isle of Wight a young Rhinelander in the diplomatic service of Austria watched on May 2, 1794, as the Channel fleet escorted two large convoys of merchantmen to sea. Years later, when Prince Metternich was the first statesman of Europe, he described it as "the most beautiful [sight] human eyes have ever beheld."* At a signal from Lord Howe's flagship, *Queen Charlotte*, the vessels shook out their sails. Those bound for the East Indies passed to the east of the island, and those going to the Caribbean to the west. The great ships of war, having emerged from a winter-long hibernation, followed each other over the horizon like ghosts. Off the Lizard at the tip of Cornwall, Howe detached escorts to accompany the convoys out of harm's way, and then sent a pair of frigates to look into Brest to check on the French fleet.

With France threatened by famine due to the failure of the harvest and the anarchy accompanying the Revolution, the government had purchased a large supply of grain in the United States, which was sympathetic to its onetime ally. British intelligence reported that a mammoth convoy of 130 merchantmen had left Hampton Roads in Chesapeake Bay in April, and Howe expected the French fleet to sortie to protect it. Easing up to the dark cliffs guarding the entrance to Brest, the British frigates reported a large number of ships in the roadstead that appeared ready to sail. Howe, as eager to fight the French fleet as to intercept the grain convoy, made no attempt to prevent it from escaping. Without putting a watch on Brest, he sailed off with twenty-six of the line to sweep the seas to the west of

*Memories are fickle, however. Metternich claimed that he was visiting Lord Howe on his flagship on May 30, 1794, when the news reached the admiral that the French were at sea. He said he begged Howe to be allowed to remain for the battle that was obviously brewing. This hardly seems likely, for Howe already knew the French were at sea by then, and the Channel fleet was not in Portsmouth on that day but fogbound in Atlantic waters. See Alan Palmer, *Metternich*, p. 24.

Ushant, convinced that he had placed himself between the convoy and the course likely to be taken by the French fleet commander, Rear Admiral Louis Thomas Villaret-Joyeuse, when he sailed.

Rear Admiral George Montagu, with six seventy-four-gun ships that had escorted the outbound East India convoy past Cape Finisterre on the northwestern coast of Spain, was assigned to search for the enemy between Finisterre and Belle Isle in the Bay of Biscay. Howe, himself, sailed out into the Atlantic. Strangely, no effort was made to intercept the convoy off the Chesapeake Capes while it was still unorganized and weakly defended. The concept of total war in which famine was a weapon lay in the future.

To ensure the safe arrival of the grain ships, the French mobilized the full power of their navy. Two seventy-fours, two frigates, and a brig commanded by Rear Admiral Pierre Jean Vanstebel had already been sent to the Chesapeake as a close escort. A squadron of five seventy-fours and an eighty under Rear Admiral Joseph Marie Nielly departed Rochefort on May 6 to cruise three hundred miles to the west of Belle Isle to add its weight to the escort as soon as the convoy was sighted. The bulk of the fleet, twenty-six of the line under the command of Admiral Villaret, who flew his flag in *Montagne,* of 120 guns, remained at Brest in readiness to reinforce the ships sent out earlier.

Having found nothing in the wastes of the Atlantic, Howe took another look into Brest on May 19 and discovered the roadstead empty. With nothing to stop him, Villaret had sailed three days before. In the interval, the opposing fleets had passed so close to each other in an all-enveloping fog that the French had heard drums beating on the decks of the British ships. Having failed to prevent the enemy's departure, Howe had no clear idea of his whereabouts or that of the inbound convoy. All he knew was that the grain ships and Villaret's fleet were somewhere out in the Atlantic. Hoping to come upon one or the other, he again headed west.

Several other developments occurred that same day. Nielly captured a large part of a Newfoundland-bound convoy, including its sole escort, the thirty-two-gun frigate *Castor.* Villaret also fell in with a Lisbon convoy and seized numerous prizes, mostly of Dutch origin. On the other side, Howe learned for the first time that Nielly's ships were out, and he was now concerned about the safety of Montagu's squadron. He altered course to southwest to join Montagu and on May 21 overhauled and recaptured some of the Dutchmen that had been previously taken by Villaret.

From the captured logs kept by the prize crews, Howe determined that the French fleet was sailing in a westerly direction, away from Montagu's squadron. Now certain that Montagu was safe, he steered west with the hope of finding Villaret, who would lead him to the convoy. Montagu was ordered to conduct a search for the convoy, and if it was unsuccessful, to rejoin Howe's fleet. But he disobeyed orders for reasons of his own, and on May 30 anchored at Plymouth. Had he continued the search or been with the Channel fleet when Howe brought Villaret to bay, his ships might well have made a difference in the outcome of events.

As the British and the French fleets drew together, the two commanders in chief had different objectives. Lord Howe was seeking a fight; Villaret wished to draw the British away from the grain ships and to fight only if he had to. "It is not naval action that we need at this moment, but our convoy," he had been told. Villaret had learned his trade under the great Suffren, but apparently without influence; he was an aging lieutenant with a bleak future when the Revolution came. Under the republic, his rise had been rapid. Nevertheless, the Terror was at its height, and Villaret was warned that if he failed to bring in the convoy he would lose his head. To keep his mind focused on this fact, André Jeanbon Saint-André, the National Convention's naval "expert," sailed with him.

For a week, Howe vainly searched the Atlantic for the convoy and Villaret's fleet. A straggling brig and sloop from the latter were snatched up and then burned because the British fleet was too shorthanded to spare prize crews. A seventy-four headed for Nielly's squadron was chased but got away. Early on the morning of May 28, some four hundred miles to the west of Ushant, a frigate signaled *Queen Charlotte* that there was a body of ships steering to the northwest about fifteen miles ahead. Howe, who was running eastward, dispatched four fast seventy-fours under the command of Rear Admiral Thomas Pasley in *Bellerophon* to examine the strangers. They proved to be Villaret's twenty-six ships of the line, sailing in three columns in a rolling sea. As the Channel fleet cleared for action, a woman named Geneva Annie, a sailor's sweetheart in *Royal George,* requested the captain to enter her name on the muster roll so she could serve a gun and qualify for prize money.*

The French held the advantage of the weather gage, which permitted them to give battle or refuse it, and they were between the British and the

---

*The presence of women in Royal Navy ships in port is well known, but sometimes there were significant numbers of women on board ships at sea as well. Some were legitimate wives of warrant and petty officers; others were prostitutes clandestinely plying their trade. The former often earned money by washing clothes and sewing for the officers. Captains grumbled about the presence of women on the lower deck but accepted it as an inevitable fact of life and carried on as if the women did not exist. See Suzanne J. Stark, *Female Tars: Women Aboard Ship in the Age of Sail.*

grain fleet. At first Villaret held his course under topsails, a sign that he intended to give battle. As he later explained, he had decided to fight because the convoy was probably near at hand, and the only way to prevent it from falling prey to the British was to disable Howe's fleet. Once Villaret determined that the opposing armada was a match for his own, he hauled to the wind, or changed course to the west. But the former pilots and promoted lieutenants who captained his ships were inexperienced and had trouble forming even a ragged battle line. Some of the French vessels had to heave to, with yards backed, to keep from ramming the next ahead.

Villaret was trailing his coat, hoping that the British would follow him away from the approaching convoy. Howe swallowed the bait. By noon, when he sent his crews to dinner while he took his own off a tray on the flagship's quarterdeck, the British fleet was also steering westward. Because of poor handling, four of the French ships dropped astern of the main fleet, and Villaret, fearing that they would be picked off by the British, tacked in succession—or turned his ships one after the other to again head east—to allow the laggards to fall back into formation. Lord Howe followed suit. Throughout this stately minuet, which was conducted at a speed of three or four knots, his sailors offered critical comment to each other as to how this or that ship answered her helm or how well her topmen did their work.

The French lost some ground in putting about, and at approximately 2:30 P.M. Howe signaled a general chase. Pounding after the enemy in rain squalls and heavy seas that poured into their lower gunports, Pasley's flying squadron of 74s peppered the rearmost ships at long range. The 110-gun *Revolutionnaire*,* which had lost a spar to the whipping wind, dropped back to deal with them. *Bellerophon* raced ahead to engage the French giant alone, was badly cut up aloft, and drifted back to the British fleet.

Russell and *Marlborough* and then *Leviathan* and *Audacious* took up the gauntlet. In the fading twilight the gun flashes from the embattled ships were white-hot in the dark. By 10:00 P.M., when Howe recalled his ships, the French three-decker had lost her mizzenmast and most of her spars and was unmanageable. Some eyewitnesses reported that *Revolutionnaire* struck her flag, but it may merely have been shot away. In any case, she had sixty-three men killed and another eighty-six wounded, and her fourth lieutenant was her senior surviving officer. The British lost only a dozen or so men. Nevertheless, *Audacious* was too badly damaged to try to

*As *Bretagne* she had been the comte d'Orvilliers' flagship at another battle off Ushant sixteen years before.

take possession of the wallowing Frenchman. Fog settled in, and *Revolutionnaire* drifted away from the rest of the French fleet. She was found by one of Admiral Nielly's vessels and towed into Brest, while the British sent the battered *Audacious* into port. Thus the first day's skirmishing ended with each fleet having lost a ship.

⸏

TENSION RAN HIGH in all the ships during the short summer night as they continued to run on to the southeast about three miles apart and on parallel courses. Admiral Villaret and Jean-Bon Saint-André, the political commissar, argued over the best way to keep the enemy interested in them rather than the grain convoy. In *Queen Charlotte* Howe catnapped in a chair on her quarterdeck, awakening now and then to receive reports and discuss with his flag captain, Sir Roger Curtis, which ship should lead the van when action resumed in the morning. Curtis pressed for the honor to go to his friend Captain John Pye Molloy of the eighty-gun *Caesar.* Howe had his doubts about Molloy, but wearying of the discussion, he reluctantly agreed to give him the post of honor. Rear Admiral Alan Gardner repeatedly went onto the stern gallery of his ship, the ninety-eight-gun *Queen,* in his nightshirt and carrying a lantern, which he energetically waved at the ship astern to make certain she did not collide with his vessel.

The next day, May 29, dawned hazy and with a heavy sea still running as the rival fleets steered a westerly course about six miles apart, with the French running ahead. The British formed up in a line with *Caesar* in the van, as Howe had promised. With both fleets about equal in strength, the admiral realized that if the battle were fought in the conventional line ahead there would be no clear-cut decision. At 7:00 A.M. he signaled his ships to tack in succession toward the enemy to break through the French line and seize the weather gage. Not long after, the lead British vessels were pounding away at the French rear. In an effort to defend these ships, Villaret also tacked in succession, bringing his van into action against the British van. Both fleets were now heading east, about three miles apart.

Unfortunately, Howe's initial judgment of Molloy proved correct. *Caesar* failed to carry enough sail even though repeatedly signaled to do so, and the British line jammed up behind her. Howe again made the signal to tack in succession and pass through the enemy line, but Molloy, who should have begun the maneuver, failed to do so. As a group of *Queen Charlotte*'s lieutenants gathered together on the quarterdeck to loudly criticize Molloy's performance, Howe cautioned: "I desire you to hold your tongues, sirs. Not to close your eyes but hold your tongues."

Alan Gardner's *Queen*, the vessel immediately astern of *Caesar*, reached the French line but was unable to break through because the ships were too close together. As a result of the heavy smoke, Howe's signal to turn toward the enemy line was largely unseen, and *Queen* was unsupported. She passed along the leeward side of the French line, trading broadsides with each enemy ship until she reached the end, in no shape to either fight or maneuver. Villaret saw an opportunity to capture the disabled three-decker and ordered his ships to come around in succession and cut her off. But in doing so, his line was strung out and passed even closer to the British.

Howe saw his own opportunity and struck. Setting an example for the fleet, *Queen Charlotte* stood toward the French line under a full press of sail and broke through astern of *Eole*, seventy-four, the sixth ship from the enemy's rear. *Queen Charlotte* poured broadside after broadside into the French ships on either side as she passed through Villaret's line to windward. *Bellerophon* and *Leviathan* followed, the former passing across the bow and the latter the stern of the 110-gun *Terrible*, the third ship from the enemy's rear.

Once the flagship had cut her way through the enemy line, Howe signaled for a general melee, and along with the two accompanying ships severely battered the three rearmost French vessels. No other British ships broke through, but about a dozen were seriously engaged with vessels on the leeward side of the French line. Faced with the loss of the three rearmost vessels, Villaret put about to come to their rescue, which cost him the weather gage. After about an hour of cannonading, firing gradually died away, ending altogether shortly after 5:00 P.M.

Three French vessels had been so damaged that they had to return to Brest for repairs. The tide was running in favor of the British. So far the French had lost the services of four ships to Howe's one. In almost forty hours of almost continuing maneuver and fighting, he had reversed his initial mistake of allowing Villaret to get to sea and could look forward to going into action the next day with the weather gage and twenty-five ships of the line to Villaret's twenty-one. But Howe had failed to find the grain convoy—and that was what mattered the most.

Fog rolled in during the night, and for the next two days the fleets were hidden from each other. Villaret edged away to leeward to give his crippled ships time to get away and for the convoy to gain distance. Occasionally, lookouts at the mastheads of the British frigates clinging grimly to the flanks of the French fleet caught glimpses of the shadowy giants gliding along under towering peaks of white canvas. And then the mists would close in again. By chance Villaret encountered four ships of Nielly's squadron, so his fleet was up to its original strength when he met Howe again.

⁓

SUNDAY, JUNE 1, 1794—henceforth to be known to Britons as the Glorious First of June*—dawned fine and clear and with a moderate sea running. The two fleets, about four miles apart, were standing to the westward four hundred miles into the Atlantic from Ushant under single-reefed topsails. They were in the same area of the sea where nearly a century and a half later the Royal Navy sank the great German battleship *Bismarck.* True to tradition, Howe piped his men to breakfast and then sent them to quarters. He was seen to smile as he issued orders, and the news spread quickly through the flagship. "Black Dick" smiled only rarely—and when he did, it meant action was in the offing.

At 7:16 A.M. Howe signaled for the fleet to attack the enemy's center. Nine minutes later, signal 34 was run up *Queen Charlotte*'s yardarm—ordering his captains to break through the French line at all points, deliver a broadside, and turn in column parallel to the enemy to cut off any damaged French ships that tried to retreat to leeward. Howe's intention was to bring about a melee in which the superior gunnery of his ships would have the most effect. The fleet was to approach bows-on in a slanting line called a line of bearing. Such an attack was considered risky because the head-on approach allowed the enemy to rake the oncoming vessels while they would be unable to return fire. Having observed the low quality of French gunnery over the past several days, Howe thought the chance worth taking.

Two hours after his first signal, Howe told Sir Roger Curtis to prepare the signal for close action. There was no such signal, he was told. "No, sir," said the admiral, who was well aware of the fact, "but there is a signal for *closer* action"—no. 5 with a red pennant over it—and he ordered it hoisted and kept flying throughout the action. With that, Howe snapped his pocket signal book shut with an air of finality. "And now, gentlemen," he declared to his officers, "no more book, no more signals." For five days and nights the old man had been continuously on his flagship's poop, giving orders, taking his meals there, and snatching what sleep he could in a chair. He had done all he could; the final decision now rested in the hands of his captains and crews.

Noting the presence of one of the younger midshipmen on the quarterdeck, Howe told the child to go below. "You can be of no service here and you may be killed." "I am Captain Montagu's† son," piped up the

---

*A term first used by the playwright Richard Brinsley Sheridan in a musical extravaganza celebrating the victory.

†Captain John Montagu of *Montagu,* seventy-four, who was mortally wounded in the upcoming battle.

lad. "What would my father say if I left the deck during a battle?" On *Barfleur,* ninety-eight, Cuthbert Collingwood watched the distance between the two fleets narrow and observed to another officer that at home their wives were at that moment going to church. "The peal we should ring about the Frenchmen's ears will outdo all the parish bells in England," he added.

The French van opened a distant fire on the approaching British vessels at 9:24, but with little effect. Except for *Caesar,* which began firing at long range, the fleet pressed on in silence, with gunports shuttered. Howe tapped his flag captain on the shoulder and pointed to *Caesar.* "Look, Curtis, there goes your friend," he said. "Who is mistaken now?" Belowdeck, the gunners, stripped to the waist and with neckerchiefs knotted around their ears to muffle the roar of their weapons, waited for the command to fire with the easy discipline of professionals who knew their business. On *Brunswick,* seventy-four, the men joked in the darkness and sang "Rule Britannia." Midshipman William Dillon of *Defence,* seventy-four, reported that sailors aloft and on deck of the various ships cheered each other into battle.

Defence, which was carrying more sail than any of the other ships of the fleet, pressed ahead and was the first British vessel to reach the French line. "Look at *Defence!*" declared Lord Howe. "See how nobly she is going into action!" As she crashed through to leeward, the vessel was heavily engaged by several large enemy ships. "The lower deck was at times so completely filled with smoke that we could scarcely distinguish each other, and the guns were so heated that, when they fired, they nearly kicked the upper deckbeams," Dillon reported. *Defence* was dismasted and was drifting along the French line when *Royal Sovereign,* 100, came to her rescue. *Defence*'s captain, James Gambier, was a vigorous Bible thumper and known throughout the navy as "Gloomy Jemmy." As Gambier's mastless vessel drifted by, Captain Thomas Pakenham of *Invincible* hailed: "Never mind, Jemmy! Whom the Lord loveth, he chasteneth."

Queen Charlotte steered for the French flagship and shouldered her way between *Montagne*'s stern and the eighty-gun *Jacobin,* passing so close to Villaret's vessel that the French ensign brushed along her sides. Firing at point-blank range, *Queen Charlotte* sent two fifty-gun broadsides crashing into *Montagne,* wiping out three hundred of her crew and blowing a gap in her stern through which a coach could be driven. Jean-Bon Saint-André, who said he had an injured hand, found business belowdecks. Another broadside shattered the bow of *Jacobin.* The French fire also was heavy. "Our main topmast and main yard being carried away by the enemy's shot," recalled Midshipman William Parker, "the Frenchman gave three cheers, upon which our ship's company . . . returned them the three cheers and after that gave them a furious broadside."*

Bleeding bodies were heaved overboard to clear the way around the guns. For the wounded there were the horrors of the cockpit, where the surgeon performed amputations without anesthesia except for a tot of rum while his assistant held the writhing victim down by brute force. If the patient survived the shock of such primitive surgery, tetanus and gangrene were always threats because of the unsanitary conditions of the cockpit. Moreover, there was no system of triage: hopeless cases were often treated, while many savable wounded bled to death as they awaited treatment.

For a combination of reasons, only seven of Howe's ships cut through the French line—*Defence, Queen Charlotte, Royal George, Queen, Majestic, Marlborough,* and *Valiant.* Villaret had kept his ships massed together, and not all the British captains were certain of what was expected of them. Some vessels, such as *Orion,* of seventy-four guns, were so badly cut up aloft that they lacked the momentum to break through. Others, such as *Barfleur,* found it impossible to pass through without interfering with the fire of other ships. The captains of these vessels placed their ships against the windward side of the enemy line and blazed away. Only Molloy in *Caesar* fired at long range.† A general melee followed in which both fleets dissolved into scattered groups of vessels, smothered in smoke and furiously engaging their assailants. By 10:00 A.M. the battle had settled into a series of single-ship engagements.

Badly battered and dismasted, *Queen* drifted to leeward and at one point faced no less than eleven enemy ships. "Swayed a fore studding sail up," reported one of her officers. "They began a heavy fire on us, which was so faithfully returned, occasioned them to pass on, not wishing to have any more fire from a disabled British ship." *Marlborough* passed through the line astern of *Impetueux,* seventy-four, and ranged up alongside her, touching off a fierce action. Another French ship joined the fray, and there was

---

*Parker was only eleven but was not the youngest person present at the battle. A boy was born to a woman in *Tremendous,* seventy-four, just as the fighting was about to begin. A half century later he was awarded the Naval General Service Medal with a battle clasp for the First of June.

†Lord Howe, who wished to keep the glory of his victory unsullied, did not bring charges against Molloy after the battle. But with rumors of misconduct by him swirling about, Molloy demanded a court-martial. He claimed to have been unable to close with the enemy because of trouble with *Caesar*'s sails and rudder. Molloy was found guilty of failure to do his utmost, dismissed from his ship, and never again held a command at sea.

some talk in the British ship of striking their colors. But the vessel's senior surviving lieutenant declared: "I'll be damned I should ever surrender." At that moment a cock that had escaped from a broken coop suddenly perched on a stump of a mast and let out a rousing crow. The ship's crew gave three cheers and *Marlborough* fought on, dismasting both her opponents. *Bellerophon* fought off two French antagonists, and *Royal George* did the same despite severe damage to her masts and rigging.

The most memorable of these ship-to-ship duels was between the seventy-four-gun ships *Brunswick* and *Vengeur du Peuple*. Thwarted in her efforts to break through the French line, the British ship ran alongside *Vengeur* and her anchors fouled the Frenchman's forechains, locking the two ships together. One of *Brunswick*'s officers proposed to cut her loose, but Captain John Harvey replied, "No, as long as we've got her we'll keep her." Neither ship being able to maneuver, they had no option but to fight to the death. Unable to open their gunports, which were jammed against *Vengeur*'s side, *Brunswick*'s gunners fired through them. The muzzles of some of her guns were depressed to fire directly into the enemy vessel's decks. At such close range, the effect of the double-shotted British carronades created havoc. *Achille,* another French seventy-four, tried to interfere, but she drifted off after the British shot away her last remaining mast.

Vengeur managed to break the bonds that held her fast to her foe, but other British vessels came up and poured repeated broadsides into the stricken ship. With all masts gone and torrents of seawater pouring into her shattered hull, she finally hauled down her colors. Over the next several hours *Vengeur* sank slowly into the Atlantic with half her crew, some three hundred men, most wounded, still on board. *Brunswick* was in little better state. Twenty-three of her guns were dismounted, and she had been on fire three times and lost 43 killed and had 114 wounded, including Captain Harvey, who died of his wounds. *Vengeur*'s last stand became legend in France, where it was reported that she had gone down with the tricolor nailed to the stump of a mast, guns firing and her crew shouting *"Vive la République!"* Like most legends, this account was highly colored, but the truth was impressive enough.

Long before *Vengeur* met her fate, the battle had already been decided. Twelve French ships were badly cut up aloft or had lost masts, nine of them completely dismasted. Villaret gathered up three of the cripples as the battle drifted to an end, and in the late afternoon he withdrew to the northwest with the remnants of his fleet. The British captured six French ships—two of eighty guns and four of seventy-four—plus the foundering *Vengeur* without the loss of a single ship. Two more dismasted Frenchmen were about to fall into British hands when Howe, worn out by his exertions and satisfied with the results achieved, recalled his ships as darkness fell.

COMBAT DU VENGEUR.

A romanticized French version of the last stand of *Vengeur* at the Glorious First of June 1794. (Beverley Robinson Collection, U.S. Naval Academy Museum)

Exhausted by tension and physical strain, the old man collapsed and was carried below to his cabin. Some officers urged Flag Captain Curtis to continue the chase and send out frigates to search for the grain convoy, but he believed the Channel fleet had suffered too much damage and was in no condition to continue the search. Official British casualties for the three actions totaled 287 killed, and 811 wounded. The French losses in the six captured vessels alone were nearly 1,200 killed, and some authorities estimate their total casualties were 8,500 killed, wounded, or taken prisoner. British prize crews reported the captured ships resembled nothing so much as slaughterhouses. Piles of bodies and mangled limbs were strewn about their decks.

A wild welcome greeted the battle-scarred Channel fleet as it returned to Spithead on June 13 with its prizes under tow. This was the first opportunity Britons had to celebrate in a war of failed operations, defeats, and disappointments, and they made the most of it. Lord Howe landed to the strains of "See the Conquering Hero Comes," and the Royal Family visited him on his flagship; bonfires were lighted across the country, and every window in London and Portsmouth was illuminated in celebration of the Glorious First of June or smashed by patriotic mobs. Titles, knighthoods, gold chains, medals, promotions, and considerable prize money were showered on the victors. Howe, always the "sailors' friend," donated his share to the wounded.

"We have conquered the rascals!" young midshipman Parker wrote home to his mother in triumph. Others were not so sure. They claimed that Howe, or after the admiral left the quarterdeck, Sir Roger Curtis, should have pushed their advantage and taken more ships. Later, Nelson was to speak slightingly of a less than complete "Lord Howe victory." Louis Thomas Villaret-Joyeuse had the last word. The day before the British fleet returned, the long-awaited grain convoy had anchored safely in Brest roadstead. "What did I care for [the] half-dozen rotten old hulks which you took?" he later told a British officer. "I saved my convoy and my head."

⤿

IN SPITE OF HOWE'S victory, Britain's prospects were gloomy. Holland was occupied by the French in January 1795 and transformed into the satellite Batavian Republic, the duke of York's shattered forces were withdrawn from northern Europe, and to the grief of the Admiralty the Dutch fleet of fifteen ships of the line fell into enemy hands. A few small vessels escaped to English ports but, improbably, most of the Dutch warships were captured by a detachment of French cavalry and artillery as the ships lay frozen in the ice of the Zuider Zee. Spain was about to switch sides, and Prussia turned from fighting France to the more profitable business of partitioning Poland. The First Coalition was now reduced to merely two major partners: Britain and Austria.

The defeat of the allied armies in the Low Countries gave the French control of the entire Continental coastline facing Britain. French forces were now on the flank of her trade route with northern Europe and the Baltic—the lifeline over which she imported masts; naval stores; and in times of bad harvests, stocks of grain. Moreover, the work of the Royal Navy was doubled because the area to be blockaded now reached from Hamburg to Genoa. As if to underscore the danger, five ships were withdrawn from the Channel fleet on the day Amsterdam fell to the French to begin a watch on the Dutch ports.

In the East, Britain prevailed. To forestall a French attempt to seize the Dutch colony at the Cape of Good Hope and cut British communications with India, Vice Admiral Sir George Keith Elphinstone captured Cape Town. Dutch holdings in Ceylon were taken as well as those in the Moluccas. British forces in India had little difficulty in rolling up French outposts on the subcontinent. With the exception of Mauritius (then called Île de

France) and Réunion Island, which remained in French hands, the British flag soon flew unchallenged across the Indian Ocean.

But failure was legion, and there was some question whether the navy could stand the additional strain of its worldwide obligations. Sierra Leone, on the West African coast, was plundered by a French squadron. Rumors were rife in the summer of 1794 that King George, while visiting Weymouth, was in danger of being kidnapped by French smugglers who put nightly into the Dorset coves. British shipping losses over the year reached the alarming total of 949 vessels—more than 11 percent of the merchant marine. As a result of Lord Howe's policy of keeping his fleet in harbor during the winter, the seventy-four-gun *Alexander* was overwhelmed off Ushant by a French squadron after a bitter fight.*

Nor was the state of naval discipline satisfactory. The crew of the seventy-four-gun *Cullodon*, which had been ordered to the West Indies, claimed she was unfit for sea and mutinied at Spithead. The men were persuaded to return to duty, but five of their leaders were hanged from a yardarm of their own ship with all hands present. The executions were regarded by the lower deck as a breach of a promise of amnesty, and the incident was to cast a long shadow.

There were also ominous signs of war-weariness and unrest among the British people. Although patriotism was a stronger force than social discontent, the repeated depredations of the press gangs were met by riots. Inflation, high taxes, and food shortages led to considerable turbulence. There were demands for the reform of Parliament so the new industrial cities could have representation. Small farmers were being expelled from their land, which was used for more profitable sheep pasturage and the dispossessed left to starve. "Peace! Peace! No Pitt!" cried demonstrators. Cheap copies of Thomas Paine's revolutionary *Rights of Man* circulated everywhere. Someone took a shot at the king as he drove through the streets of London to open Parliament, and stones were hurled at his coach.

Pitt's embattled government, unable to distinguish between treason and legitimate dissent, launched a campaign of repression. A laborer who cried "No George! No war!" was jailed for five years. The London Corresponding Society, a reformist group whose goal was universal suffrage, was suppressed as a sinister arm of Jacobinism. Radicals were found guilty of "constructive treason" and imprisoned or transported to Australia. Habeas corpus was suspended, and meetings of more than fifty people were banned. A government spokesman justified the use of "French violence" to resist the contagion of French principles.

*She was one of only five of this class of ship lost by the British during the entire war.

Had it not been for the demoralization of the French Navy, Britain would have faced disaster. There were thirty-five ships of the line at Brest with another eight building, but a shortage of crews and provisions held them in port. In the dockyards the workers went on strike against hunger. The French decided to solve the problem by capturing provisions from the British. Shortly after Christmas 1794, Admiral Villaret was sent to sea on a raiding voyage. Five ships were lost, three foundering in a gale, but even this ill-organized expedition cost Britain seventy merchant vessels.

Faced with these difficulties, the Royal Navy was ripe for change. Pitt, who had broadened the base of his ministry by bringing in elements of the Whig Opposition, dropped his incompetent brother Lord Chatham from the Admiralty and named George Earl Spencer as first lord.* Spencer knew little of the sea and ships, but he was willing to learn. Besides, he did not keep naval officers waiting around the Admiralty until he rose at noon. Lord Howe, weary and ailing, went to Bath to take the waters, and active command of the Channel fleet passed to his deputy, Admiral Lord Bridport. Bald and hook-nosed, he was at sixty-eight the younger brother—by three years—of the turbulent Lord Hood.

Under Bridport the fleet spent more time at sea, especially in the summer, but there was little change in its strategic dispositions. No attempt was made to effectively blockade Brest, and the ships continued to be based at Spithead. As a result, French reinforcements escaped to the Mediterranean—after all available provisions were pooled from the rest of the fleet. Villaret also got out with twelve of the line to protect another grain convoy, this one due in from Spain. Food was so tight that he had supplies for only fifteen days.

On June 16, 1795, Villaret encountered a squadron of five of the line under Vice Admiral Sir William Cornwallis, younger brother of Lord Cornwallis, whose defeat at Yorktown had ended the American War. Cornwallis made a fighting retreat in the face of superior force even though some of his ships were notoriously slow sailers. *Mars,* seventy-four, the rearmost British ship, was crippled aloft by enemy fire but the flagship, *Royal Sovereign,* drove off several vessels that tried to capture her. Cornwallis' coolness under fire plus the efforts of the frigate *Phaeton,* thirty-eight, in convincing the French that she was signaling a large fleet over the horizon,

---

*Spencer, a direct ancestor of both Winston Spencer Churchill and Diana, princess of Wales, had been ambassador to Vienna. He was married to the beautiful Lavinia Bingham, the daughter of the earl of Lucan and a social lioness of the era. He was president of the Royal Institution, a trustee of the British Museum, and a dedicated bibliophile who made the library of his home, Althorp House, the site of one of the finest private collections in Europe.

caused Villaret to break off an action in which he should have snapped up the entire British squadron. "Cornwallis' Retreat," as it was called, was hailed by the Royal Navy with all the enthusiasm of a victory.

A week later the tables were turned as Admiral Villaret fled from a stronger British fleet. On June 22 Lord Bridport was providing distant cover with fourteen ships of the line for a landing by Royalist exiles at Quiberon Bay in Brittany. Villaret, who had nine of the line, ran into the British fleet, and realizing he was outnumbered, tried to make a getaway. Early the following morning, Bridport's leading vessels overtook the French rear off île de Groix. Not only were the French outgunned, but also Villaret's captains were so ill-trained and inept that he was unable even to form a line of battle. Bridport captured three seventy-four-gun ships against feeble resistance.* As in the case of Lord Howe, he was satisfied with a limited victory and discontinued the action. Lucky to escape without further loss, Villaret took refuge in Lorient and then slipped back to Brest. Had Bridport pursued him energetically, critics said, the French fleet could easily have been taken or run ashore.

"Corwallis' Retreat" and the botched action off île de Groix marked the temporary end of French efforts to challenge British naval supremacy in the Atlantic. These events clearly demonstrated that the republic's sailors were unequal to their better-trained and more experienced opponents. The Brest fleet remained in port as a latent threat to Britain—a "fleet in being," in the words of Admiral Mahan—while only small units were sent to sea as diversions and to prey on British commerce. As the ships rocked uselessly in the roadstead, morale plummeted, officers and men drifted away, the ships deteriorated, and the fleet ceased for a time to be an effective fighting force. Once again the main focus of naval action shifted to the Mediterranean.

---

*Including *Alexandre*, formerly the British *Alexander*.

CHAPTER 10

"Nelson's Patent Bridge"

VICE ADMIRAL SIR William Hotham, the successor to Lord Hood as commander in chief of the Mediterranean Fleet, is one of those uninspiring men who were never beaten by an enemy but whose reputation suffers when compared to more audacious and energetic commanders. Unhappily for him, he was sandwiched between Hood, a renowned fighting seaman, and Horatio Nelson, whose reputation was in the process of being made. Cautious and unwilling to accept risks, Hotham was regarded by Nelson with contempt and was unequal to the demands of his post. As a result of his failures, the British were driven from Corsica and the Mediterranean, Napolean conquered Italy, and a pair of opportunities to destroy the French fleet was thrown away.

Hotham had two tasks: to prevent the French from escaping Toulon and recapturing Corsica, and to support the Austrian army in Italy by harrying French operations on the Riviera. Throughout the winter of 1794–1795, the blockading ships plunged through heavy seas off Toulon, battened down and under staysails. "We have had the most tremendous weather, such as I have never experienced before in any seas; it blew a perfect hurricane," Nelson wrote Sir William Hamilton. Moreover, *Agamemnon*, like the rest of Hotham's fleet, was shorthanded and sorely in need of a complete refit from keel to main truck.

In Toulon itself, the French had set to work repairing the ships left behind by the British when they abandoned the base and completing those still on the stocks. Under the hand of André Jeanbon Saint-André, who came down to Toulon to take on the job, a sizable fleet, including the 120-gun *Sans-Culotte*, was being readied for sea under the command of Rear Admiral Pierre Martin. Only a lieutenant just two years before, Martin knew little of managing a fleet. Most of his ships were undermanned, and more than half of the twelve thousand men who made up their complements were landsmen who had never been to sea before.

The main British base for repair and refreshment was the Italian port of Livorno (called Leghorn by the British), on the Tuscan coast, and the watch on Toulon was no tighter than the one at Brest. Flocks of women were attracted to Livorno, who sold their favors to the British officers and sailors, and venereal disease was rampant. Like many naval officers, Nelson, now nearly two years away from the worried and lonely Fanny, accepted the sailor's adage that marriage vows did not extend past Gibraltar, and enjoyed a liaison with Adelaide Correglia, a singer at Livorno's rather seedy opera house. "Dined with Nelson and his dolly," noted Nelson's friend Captain Thomas Fremantle in his diary. "He makes himself ridiculous with that woman." In the meantime, Nelson was writing his wife, assuring her of his "constant love and affection." He was not alone. Admiral Hotham had an attachment to a woman jokingly called "the commander of the fleet."

On March 8, 1795, Hotham received word that Admiral Martin had sailed from Toulon two days before with fifteen of the line and was to provide cover for an invasion of Corsica by five thousand French troops. Flying his flag in the 100-gun *Britannia,* he put to sea with fourteen of his own ships of the line and a Neapolitan seventy-four-gun ship to search for the enemy armada. The passage of the French fleet was agonizingly slow because many of its captains were as inexperienced as their admiral, and they maintained only the raggedest of formations. By good luck they captured the disabled *Berwick,* seventy-four, which had lost her masts off Corsica and was struggling under a jury rig to join the fleet at Livorno.

Hotham sighted the French on March 10 in the Gulf of Genoa, but the Mediterranean was notoriously fickle at that time of year. Bedeviled by haze, a heavy swell, and shifting winds, the rival fleets did not come into range of each other until three days later. A French seventy-four-gun ship lost her topmast during the preliminary maneuvering and was towed into port by a frigate, equalizing the size of the two fleets. Hotham signaled a general chase, and as the British pressed ahead under full canvas in the early morning of March 13, the French put their helms over and fled in the direction of Toulon.

In the confusion, the eighty-gun *Ça Ira,* named for the revolutionary battle hymn, ran afoul of *Victoire,* also of eighty guns, and lost her fore and main-topmasts. She fell behind the rest of the fleet, and Captain Fremantle bravely raced up in the frigate *Inconstant,* of thirty-six guns, to engage her, but was outgunned. With equal daring, the French frigate *Vestale,* also of thirty-six guns, took the stricken vessel under tow even as the British van approached with *Agamemnon* in the lead.

Nelson pressed ahead of the British line even though the French ship seemed "absolutely large enough to have taken *Agamemnon* in her hold. . . . At a quarter before eleven a.m., being within one hundred yards of the *Ça Ira*'s stern, I ordered the helm to be put-a-starboard. . . . As the ship fell off, gave her our whole broadside, each gun double-shotted. Scarcely a shot appeared to miss." Then Nelson put about and fired a broadside from *Agamemnon*'s other battery into the French vessel. The towing frigate was unable to pull *Ça Ira* around so her guns could bear, and Nelson continued to tack back and forth across her stern, pouring broadsides into her. "This manoeuvre we practiced till one p.m., never allowing the *Ça Ira* to get a single gun from either side to fire on us," he said. "The *Ça Ira* was a perfect wreck. . . ."

But Hotham, fearing that the French would turn and try to rescue the crippled vessel, hoisted the recall signal instead of hurrying ships to *Agamemnon*'s support. The next morning the French fleet was sighted several miles ahead, trailed by *Ça Ira*, now under tow by *Censeur*, seventy-four. Two British seventy-four-gun ships, *Captain* and *Bedford*, were sent forward to intercept the isolated vessels. They were badly mauled and signaled for assistance. Several British ships came up, including *Agamemnon*, and they crowded in on the French vessels. *Ça Ira* was completely dismasted, and *Censeur* lost her mainmast. Martin abandoned the crippled ships and stood away under all sail for Toulon. *Agamemnon* was the closest British ship to the prizes, so Nelson sent a lieutenant over to take possession of them. Together, they had suffered some 750 killed and wounded.

Hot to pursue the fleeing French, Nelson had himself rowed to *Britannia*, which was astern of *Agamemnon*, and tried to persuade Hotham to leave the two captured ships behind and pursue the disorganized enemy. He was very excited by his first fleet action, for he later described the admiral as much "calmer than myself." Hotham's reaction to the suggestion to continue the chase hardly cooled him off. "We must be contented. We have done very well."

Nelson's own reaction was as might be expected. To Fanny he wrote: "Now had we taken ten sail and allowed the eleventh ship to escape when it had been possible to have got at her, I could never have called it well done. We should have had such a day as I believe the annals of England have never produced. Nothing can stop the courage of English seamen. . . ."* This affair was soon forgotten, but it showed that the basic elements of Nelson's tactical doctrine were already in place—ruthless determination, total fearlessness, an unerring eye for enemy weaknesses, and a conviction that respect for hierarchy was but a means to an end.

In the strictest sense, Hotham had indeed "done very well." Corsica was saved, and a pair of French ships of the line were taken. Even Nelson recognized that the wind was tricky, which made pursuit difficult. But he saw with extraordinary perception what Hotham did not see—the wider picture of the whole war. If the Toulon fleet was destroyed or disabled, the

---

*As a reward, Nelson was given the sinecure of a colonel of marines, which carried with it a salary but no duties.

Royal Navy could range the Riviera at will and help the Austrian Army blunt and then drive back the French thrust into Italy. "The British Fleet," he wrote five years later, "could have prevented the invasion of Italy: and if our friend Hotham had kept his fleet on that coast, no armies from France could have been furnished with stores and provisions; even men could not have marched."

Four months of inactivity followed, a period in which the fleet lay "skulking in port," according to Nelson, after which Hotham threw away another opportunity to destroy the French fleet. In this interim both sides had received reinforcements. The Mediterranean fleet was increased to twenty-two of the line, while the French now had seventeen. The fleets again encountered each other on July 13, 1795, off the Hyères Islands, near the dark, mountainous coast of Provence, but neither Hotham nor Pierre Martin, who had been promoted to vice admiral, seemed desirous of a decisive battle. Both were more concerned with avoiding losses than with inflicting them on the enemy.

This action came about when *Agamemnon* and four frigates of an inshore squadron commanded by Nelson that were assigned to harass the French army advancing along the coastal road to Italy unexpectedly encountered Martin's fleet. Fleeing before the French, Nelson raced toward San Fiorenzo Bay in Corsica, where Hotham's main force lay. The British had a significant edge over the French, but Hotham's ships got out in considerable disorder and were spread over a wide area of sea. Indeed, the slow-sailing *Britannia* trailed the leading ships by seven miles. Once the French sighted the fleet, they fled. Hotham ordered a general chase with the hope of cutting off the enemy from their base.

Despite shifting winds, *Agamemnon* and the five other ships of the British van got into action with the rearmost French vessels. The seventy-four-gun *Alcide* soon struck her colors, then caught fire and blew up, taking with her half her 615-man complement. Just as *Agamemnon* and the eighty-gun *Cumberland* were getting within range of the other French ships, Hotham ordered them to retire, in the belief that they were too close to the coast of France for safety. Both captains pretended not to see the unwelcome signal, but it was repeated along with *Cumberland*'s distinguishing number, and they were obliged to obey.

"Thus ended our second meeting with these gentry," said a disgusted Nelson. "We had every prospect of taking every Ship in the Fleet. . . ." An officer in *Victory* was more blunt. "Had the British fleet only put their heads the same way as the enemy's and stood inshore . . . the whole of the French line might have been cut off . . . taken or destroyed." The eventual consequences of what was later called "this miserable action" were the loss of Corsica, the retreat of the British fleet from the Mediterranean, and Napoleon's invasion of Egypt.

Not long after, Hotham allowed a French squadron to escape from Toulon into the Atlantic, where it captured the entire Levant convoy of thirty-one ships and ravaged the Newfoundland fisheries. This was followed by a raid on a Jamaica convoy by French frigates. These disasters created havoc in the City, London's financial district, and there was talk of ending the war, now that the Jacobins had fallen and power in France had been assumed by a seemingly more moderate board of five directors. But the new rulers of France wanted peace no more than the old, and the war went on.

ON NOVEMBER 30, 1795, the frigate *Lively*, thirty-two, entered San Fiorenzo Bay flying the flag of Admiral Sir John Jervis, the new commander in chief of the Mediterranean Fleet. Jervis arrived "to the great joy of some and the sorrow of others," said Nelson, who was among the former. In sharp contrast to Hotham, the new commander was an active and resolute fighting seaman. The smoke from the salutes to his flag had hardly blown away, said one observer, when Jervis shifted it to *Victory* and ordered the fleet to sail for Toulon. For the first time, the port was effectively blockaded as the main body of the British fleet stood off the town cruising in two long columns without a break for nearly 150 days, while a detached squadron under Nelson supported the Austrians in the Gulf of Genoa. Under Jervis there was to be no more lying peacefully at anchor at San Fiorenzo or enjoying the fleshpots of Livorno.

Further proof that the fleet was in different hands was the imposition of new standards of leadership and discipline. Jervis insisted on frequent gun drills and tactical exercises and soon each captain knew what to do when the flagship changed course. A careful eye was maintained on the way officers and men dressed, and formal ceremonies were conducted smartly and with snap. No sleeping ashore was allowed when the fleet was in port. Ceremonial observances now taken for granted in all the world's navies, such as the morning and evening hoisting and lowering of the ensign, were introduced by Jervis. "Mediterranean discipline" became a byword throughout the Royal Navy—to the horror of those in other commands.

Although grim and unyielding, Jervis was no mere martinet. To counterbalance his ruthlessness, he was capable of small acts of kindness.* He personally inspected each of his ships and accepted no excuse for untidiness or dirt on the mess deck. He ordered the crew's bedding aired out and clothing washed once a week. Jervis made certain the men had adequate

---

*Learning that a veteran seaman had lost his life savings of seventy pounds, Jervis made it up from his own pocket.

provisions. Every ship was directed to have a proper sick bay away from the lower deck that was well equipped and regularly inspected. Soap was issued for the first time. To keep from wearing the crews out with the usual watch-and-watch system, Jervis established a three-watch system so a sailor could usually count on a full night in his hammock two nights out of three. Men who were sick or worn out were sent home.

For Nelson, Jervis's arrival coincided with the beginning of the last decade of his life, the ten crowded, glorious years that were to render his name immortal. He admired his new commander from the start. "Of all the fleets I ever saw," he later wrote, "I never saw one in point of officers and men equal to Sir John Jervis's." For his part, the admiral found Nelson a source of knowledge about conditions in the Mediterranean. The admiral took him into his confidence and talked "more as an associate than a subordinate."[*]

Nelson was now high on the list of captains, and his promotion to rear admiral of the Blue was due, so Jervis offered him command of a three-decker. Nelson chose instead to remain with the old "Eggs and Bacon," which had served him so well. Recognizing his talent for independent command and sound judgment, Jervis made him a commodore[†] pending his promotion. Flying his broad pendant from the main truck of *Agamemnon*, Nelson harried the French army's communications with a squadron of four frigates and a brig. Among his prizes was a convoy of five transports carrying the enemy's siege train—the final success in his veteran flagship. *Agamemnon* was in such wretched condition that Jervis sent her home in June 1796 for a complete refit.

Nelson was to have gone with her, but the senior officer of the seventy-four-gun *Captain* was sick, and Nelson traded places with him. Three years had passed since he had first taken the "poor old *Agamemnon*" out of Spithead, and many of those who had sailed with him had been dispersed through death, wounds, or disease, or drafted to other ships. New York-born Ralph W. Miller, an American Loyalist, became his flag captain, relieving him of the burden of managing his own ship as well as the squadron.

The British position in the Mediterranean was a difficult one. Jervis had eighteen ships of the line to face fifteen French vessels plus three building at Toulon. The French squadron of seven of the line that had captured the Levant convoy had taken refuge at Cádiz, where the Spaniards had a large fleet, and there were another seven Spanish ships of the line at Cartagena.

---

[*]"You did just as you pleased in Lord Hood's time, the same in Admiral Hotham's and now again with Sir John Jervis," grumbled a jealous fellow captain. "It makes no difference to you who is commander in chief."

[†]With the welcome addition to his pay of ten shillings a day.

Although Spain did not declare war on Britain until later that year, the admiral had to keep all these ships under observation to prevent them from combining against him. Even though Jervis maintained a tenuous command of the sea, on land the war was undergoing a seismic change because of the intervention of one man: Napoleon Bonaparte.

The Directory had resolved to knock the last two opposing powers—Britain and Austria—out of the war. Louis Lazar Hoche, who at twenty-nine rivaled Bonaparte as France's most brilliant young general, was named to command the Army of England, which was to launch an amphibious attack against Britain. Bonaparte was appointed to the Army of Italy and ordered to drive across Lombardy to capture Vienna.

Briefly imprisoned after the fall of the Jacobins, Bonaparte had emerged as a supporter of a political opportunist named Paul François Barras. When a Paris mob threatened the Directory, of which Barras was a member, General Bonaparte dispersed it with "a whiff of grapeshot" and was rewarded with the Italian command and Josephine de Beauharnais, Barras's cast-off mistress, whom he married. Upon his arrival in Nice in March 1796, Bonaparte found his army starving, despondent, and in rags. His first move was to revitalize it with something of his own dazzling vitality: "Soldiers! You are naked, ill-nourished," he declared. "I will lead you into the most fertile plains in the world, where you shall find great towns, rich provinces, within your grasp."

The young general was as good as his word. Leading his troops through the passes of the Alps, he defeated the Austrians in a whirlwind series of battles that were won over six weeks at great odds. Bonaparte flouted all the conventional rules of war: marching at night, fighting in the rain and on Sundays, gambling boldly, and winning decisive victories. Milan, Venice, Genoa, Mantua, Livorno, the Papal States, Naples, Palermo—all fell to the French, proclaimed their neutrality, or bought peace with the conqueror. Corsica was soon expected to fall into the French bag, and with it the last major British base in the Mediterranean.

The evacuation of the English colony from Livorno led to a brief diversion for the officers of the Mediterranean fleet. Among the refugees was a well-to-do family named Wynne, who had been living in Florence along with their two daughters, Elizabeth, seventeen, and Eugenia, sixteen. They were brought out by Thomas Fremantle in *Inconstant* and were transferred to *Britannia*. Pretty and vivacious, Betsey and Jenny brought to the long-exiled younger officers a touch of beauty, grace, and home. Their presence inspired a round of social activities that included shipboard musicales, dances, and supper parties.

One after the other, the various captains of the fleet hastened to pay their respects to the Wynne girls, including "old Nelson," as Betsey described the thirty-eight-year-old commodore in her diary. Even crusty Admiral Jervis was susceptible to the charms of the Wynne girls, and he called them "the Amiables." "The old Gentleman is very fond of kisses," noted Betsey. Before long, she settled on the fiery, dark-eyed Fremantle. "How kind and amiable Captain Fremantle is," she wrote. "He pleases me more than any man I have yet seen." Betsey's parents frowned on the romance, but Jervis forwarded Fremantle's cause. Early the following year, Betsey married her sailor at the British embassy in Naples, where Lady Hamilton stage-managed the wedding.

The grim business of war was never very far out of mind, however, and the British position in the Mediterranean was crumbling. Bonaparte's victories increased the possibility of a French descent on Corsica. To prevent it, the British blockaded Livorno, where the French were gathering an amphibious force for the invasion of the island. Nelson, with the permission of the local authorities, brought troops from Bastia to occupy Elba, a small island off the coast of Tuscany that was considered a stepping-stone to Corsica. These moves saved the island at least temporarily, but in August 1796, long-wavering Spain signed an alliance with France, and in October declared war on Britain.

Lacking a secure major base within the Mediterranean and with Spain lying athwart his fleet's line of communications, Jervis's position was untenable. At any moment the French fleets at Toulon and Cádiz might combine with the main Spanish fleet, which was also at Cádiz, or with the Spanish squadron at Cartagena to bring overwhelming force against him. The Royal Navy had only contempt for Spain's capacity for war at sea— "the Dons may make fine ships, but they cannot make men," Nelson said with a sneer. But the British, as in 1779 and again in 1781, faced the threat of invasion if a Spanish fleet passed Gibraltar and combined with the Brest fleet to seize control of the Narrow Seas.

To add to Jervis's problems at this critical moment, he was unexpectedly deprived of a third of his ships. Rear Admiral Robert Man had been sent to Gibraltar with seven ships of the line to bring in a convoy of direly needed supply vessels. Following a chase by a Spanish fleet of nineteen of the line commanded by Don Juan de Langara, Man apparently suffered a nervous breakdown and precipitously scuttled off to England, leaving Jervis in the lurch. He must have had influential friends, for instead of facing a court-martial, Man was merely ordered to strike his flag and was not employed again at sea—a surprisingly mild punishment. Only forty years before, Admiral Sir John Byng had been shot for far less heinous conduct.*

*Even more incredibly, Man continued to advance on the Navy List while on half pay, and died a full admiral in 1813.

After chasing Man, de Langara put into Cartagena, where he was joined by seven more of the line, bringing his total force to twenty-six vessels, while Jervis had only sixteen. With this formidable fleet, the Spaniards cruised in the vicinity of Corsica, but rather than seeking action against their much weaker foe, made for Toulon, where twelve French ships of the line were added to de Langara's command. This brought the Franco-Spanish fleet to thirty-eight, more than double the size of Jervis's force.

Badly outnumbered in the Mediterranean and fearing that the French and the Spaniards might invade Ireland, where the population was ripe for rebellion, the Cabinet decided to concentrate all available forces for the defense of Britain itself. Jervis was ordered to withdraw the remnants of his fleet from the Mediterranean. With supreme irony, Nelson, who had labored so hard to capture Corsica, had the task of evacuating the troops from the island and from Elba. As 1796 drew to a close, Jervis held on at San Fiorenzo Bay to the last moment, in hope that the errant Man would return with the supply convoy, but the only sails on the horizon belonged to de Langara.

With his crews on half rations or even less, Jervis could wait no longer. He sailed for Gibraltar in mid-November, but the harbor was too open for a large number of ships to be stationed there, so at year's end the fleet moved on to Lisbon to strengthen Portugal, Britain's last and increasingly reluctant ally. Before Jervis was out of sight of the Corsican coast, the French landed on the island. For the first time in centuries, no British flag flew between the Pillars of Hercules and the Golden Horn—and a full year was to pass before the Royal Navy returned in force to those historic waters.

A BLIZZARD WAS HOWLING across Bantry Bay on the southwestern tip of Ireland on Christmas Eve 1796 as the seventy-four-gun *Monarch*, three months out of the Cape of Good Hope, made a landfall and put into a neighboring inlet. Vice Admiral Sir George Keith Elphinstone immediately sent in a boat in hope of obtaining lemons to treat the scurvy rampant among his crew and a batch of prisoners he had captured along with the Dutch colony at the cape. The officers who went ashore heard the confusing sounds of signal guns above the gale, and learned that a sizable number of French ships of the line plus some smaller vessels were also anchored in the wide roadstead. Besides the storm-battered *Monarch*, the only British force nearby was an old sixty-four-gun ship and the half dozen frigates of the Irish Guard at Cork, forty-three miles away, whose duty was to convoy merchantmen through the Channel when privateers were about. "What we are to do or what is to become of us God only knows," lamented the local squire.

Ever since the beginning of the war, the French had dreamed of "planting fifty thousand caps of liberty in England," but this was the first occasion on which an attempt had actually been made to accomplish that goal. The roots of rebellion in Ireland lay in the demand by the Catholic Irish for an end to restraints on their religion and for relief from the crippling taxes that made life miserable for the Irish peasantry. Pitt had persuaded the English-dominated Irish Parliament to relax most of the anti-Catholic penal laws, but Catholics were still barred from Parliament, and nothing had been done to reform the land system. For the disappointed Irish Catholics, revolution had become a serious option.

The inspiration for a French invasion came from Theobold Wolfe Tone, a thirty-three-year-old Protestant barrister and founder of a patriotic society called the United Irishmen, who hoped for a nonsectarian Irish republic. Tone convinced the Directory that Ireland was ripe for an uprising and that a half million Irish would rise the day the French landed. Moreover, there were next to no British military forces in the country to oppose a landing. By controlling Ireland, Tone declared, France would not only be able to invade England but also could strangle her commerce by closing the Western Approaches, the main trade route to her ports.

Admiral Villaret-Joyeuse, who had commanded at the Glorious First of June, was ordered to prepare fifteen ships of the line of the Brest fleet and embark General Hoche, commander of the Army of England, with the first division of an invading force of fifteen thousand men, including Tone, who now called himself "General Smith." Bantry Bay was chosen as a landing site because of its fine anchorage and because no garrison was nearby. The rest of the troops were to follow in seven ships of the line from Lorient and another five from Toulon. Once Villaret had landed the troops, he was to take his eight fastest two-deckers into the Indian Ocean to harass British trade and assist Tipu Sahib, the sultan of Mysore, who, like his father, Hyder Ali, had revolted against the East India Company. The Spanish fleet was also to make demonstrations aimed at forcing the British to draw ships away from the Channel fleet.

The flamboyant Hoche saw few hazards in such an expedition. "Dash and a love of liberty is all that is necessary to overthrow Pitt," he assured the Directory. Villaret knew better. Although the new navy minister, Vice Admiral Laurent Truguet, had improved the efficiency of the fleet, including the banishment of the political commissars, most of the ships had remained in port since bringing in the grain convoy two and a half years before. The fleet was in desperate need of supplies; ships were only half manned; and the men available lacked discipline, training, and experience.

Villaret said so, and was replaced by Vice Admiral Justin-Bonaventure Morard de Galles.

Morard, who did not at all relish the command, complained of poor health and said he could barely see. "No matter," replied Hoche, "we shall see for him." The original plan was changed, and the various naval units were to rendezvous at Brest and sail together with the entire army, which was increased to eighteen thousand men. While the expedition was originally scheduled to depart in early October, the chaos in the dockyards caused delay after delay. "Damn them! damn them! sempiternally [everlastingly] damn them!" Tone scribbled in his journal. No one obeyed orders; no one respected anyone; no one worked.

With a gale blowing up, the fleet finally got to sea on December 15, 1796. Morard had seventeen ships of the line* plus frigates and seven transports. With only a few weeks of supplies on hand, Hoche planned to capture the Royal Navy victualing depot at Cork immediately after landing, to feed his men. The British, aware that the French were planning some major operation, had increased the blockading squadron to fifteen of the line under the command of Vice Admiral Sir John Colpoys. But he had been blown off station. The remainder of the Channel fleet lay snugged in at Spithead, and Lord Bridport, the commander in chief, was living at home in Somerset.

The only British presence as the expedition sailed was three frigates of the Inshore Squadron cruising back and forth on the Atlantic horizon. Its commander, Captain Sir Edward Pellew, in *Indefatigable,* of forty-four guns, had been watching developments in Brest and had repeatedly sent warnings to Colpoys that the French were preparing to come out. Pellew had captured the French frigate *Cleopatra* in the early days of the war and *Virginie,* forty, in April 1796, and was one of the most highly regarded officers in the navy.

To create the impression that the Channel fleet lay just over the horizon, Pellew fired minute guns and rockets throughout the night. The ruse worked so well that the French thought they were under attack by the enemy fleet. In the confusion and panic, a seventy-four ran on a rock and sank in the pounding surf. Nearly seven hundred French sailors and soldiers were drowned. Two other ships collided with each other. When morning broke, the French fleet was dispersed into three widely separated groups and each plodded through heavy seas toward Ireland. Worst of all, the command ship, the frigate *Fraternité,* carrying Admiral Morard and General Hoche, had vanished altogether. Having done his best, Pellew

---

*Only two of the ships from the Lorient squadron were found to be seaworthy, and the Toulon squadron did not arrive on time.

decided to join Colpoys at a previously established rendezvous and hoped the admiral had received his warnings and prepared countermeasures.

But Colpoys was lost in the Atlantic somewhere west of Ushant, and was not only not to be found, but had not received Pellew's messages. All Pellew could do was send in a fast-sailing lugger with a dispatch to the Admiralty and, as the gale worsened, withdraw to Falmouth, where he anchored on December 20. Bridport learned the following day that the fleet he thought to be blockaded at Brest had been at sea for a week. Following a two-day delay in reaching Portsmouth, he told the Admiralty that the Channel fleet would be ready to sail by Christmas. But the sailing was canceled when, in attempting to get out, four of his ships ran aground. With his fleet reduced to fourteen of the line, Bridport did not sail down the Channel until January 3, 1797. For all that he accomplished, he might well have remained in Somerset.

In the meantime, the weather had for the moment moderated, and the French, more by accident than design, had reassembled off the Irish coast on December 21, and entered Bantry Bay the following day. *Fraternité*, with the expedition's commanders, was still missing, however. As the ships beat up to the head of the bay to land the troops, the wind suddenly freshened into an easterly gale. French seamanship was unequal to the task, and the overcrowded ships, manned by landsmen, were constantly forced to give way to prevent collisions. The struggle against the elements continued for three days. "We have made 300 tacks and not gained 100 yards in a straight line," noted the infuriated Tone. Snow began to fall, and the weather turned bitterly cold.

In the absence of Hoche, his deputy, General Emmanuel de Grouchy, proposed to land the first six thousand men on Christmas Day, but no boat could live in the howling wind and pounding sea. "I am now so near the shore that I can distinctly see two old castles," an increasingly frustrated Tone wrote, "yet I am utterly uncertain whether I shall ever set foot on it." Supplies were already running out, and the men were sickening in the wet and cold. After nearly a week in the bay—during which not a man was landed nor a gun fired—the French captains cut their anchor cables and ran with the wind for the open sea. The last vessel to return to France was *Fraternité*, carrying the expedition's commanders, whose only sight of their fleet during the entire fiasco was two of its ships off Ireland, one sinking and the other rescuing her crew. Lord Bridport arrived off Bantry Bay on January 9 to find the anchorage empty.

Just as Pellew was the only British captain to see the enemy leave Brest, so his ship, together with *Amazon*, of thirty-six guns, were the only vessels on station to see them return. Early on the blustery afternoon of January 13 he sighted a new French seventy-four-gun ship, *Droits de l'Homme*, carrying

Destruction of LE DROITS DE L'HOMME,

Shewing her Situation at .. day break, as forced on shore by the two frigates, in Hodierne Bay, near Brest, with the Indefatigable under a press of Sail, close hauled to clear the Land and throwing off Rockets as Signals to her Consort the Amazon which was unfortunately wrecked at some distance from the Enemys Ship.

Pellew in *Indefatigable* harries *Droits de l'Homme* onto the rocks off the French coast. (Beverley Robinson Collection, U.S. Naval Academy Museum)

about seven hundred troops, about 150 miles off Ushant. Noting that she had lost her fore-topmasts and main-topmasts to the gale and was unable to put up enough sail to steady her roll and use the guns on her lower deck, Pellew closed with the enemy vessel, although *Amazon* was seven miles astern. Under normal circumstances two frigates were no match for a two-decker, but *Indefatigable* was much more formidable than the standard frigate. She was, herself, a cut-down, or razeed, two-decker, stoutly built and armed with twenty-four-pounders rather than the standard eighteens, and mounted forty-two-pound carronades on her main deck.

Pellew attempted to rake *Droits de l'Homme*, but the French captain evaded the maneuver and tried to lay his vessel alongside *Indefatigable* so he could board and use his larger crew to carry her. But the British frigate surged ahead, firing a broadside into the enemy ship. *Amazon* joined the fight, and throughout the night the two frigates hung on to opposite sides of *Droits de l'Homme*'s bow like terriers harrying larger prey. Periodically they yawed to starboard or port to rake her, while she would occasionally yaw to reply. With the ships fighting at pistol-shot range, the French troops lined her sides and fired volleys from their muskets at the enemy ships. Twice both sides broke off action to make repairs, and then the drums beat to quarters for a renewal of the battle.

Conditions on the ships were horrendous as they pounded ahead through rough seas. One of *Droits de l'Homme*'s guns exploded, spewing hot metal among her crew, and the casualties from British gunfire were heavy. The sea poured into *Indefatigable*'s gun ports, and the gunners were often up to their waists in water. Several guns broke their breechings and threatened to crash through the sides of the ship. By 4:00 A.M. *Droits de l'Homme* was nearly out of ammunition and almost unrigged; the British frigates were in little better condition.

The vessels were also near the forbidding coast, although in the darkness, no one knew where they were with certainty. Pellew thought he was in the bay leading to Brest and turned north. *"Non, non, mon capitaine!"* shouted his Breton Royalist pilot. "De oder way!" *Indefatigable* altered course to the southward and hoisted signal lanterns warning *Amazon* to do the same. First light revealed the dismasted hulk of *Droits de l'Homme* piled up on the rocks about a mile away and already breaking up in the heavy sea. *Amazon* also was lost, but her crew survived and were taken prisoner. More than a thousand French sailors and soldiers were drowned with *Droits de l'Homme*.

Such might have been the fate of the entire Irish expedition had the British fleet been in more vigorous hands. In addition to *Droits de l'Homme*, the French lost about ten vessels, almost entirely to the weather. The invasion was probably doomed from the start—launched at the wrong time of the year and supported by an ill-equipped and worse-led fleet. But had the French been able to land in Ireland, they would have found little to oppose them, and the Irish might well have risen in arms. On the British side, Bridport's poor placement of the Channel fleet and his sluggish reaction to the escape of the French from Brest, combined with Colpoys' failure to keep his designated rendezvous, almost proved fatal. Only Pellew and the crew of *Indefatigable* emerged from the affair with any credit.

The Irish fiasco had a bizarre coda. In February 1797 the French landed some eighteen hundred men on the coast of Wales near Fishguard. This force, about half ex-convicts and galley slaves, and known as the Black Legion, was under the command of Colonel William Tate, an American adventurer with a bloodcurdling reputation. Before they could fulfill their orders to burn nearby Bristol, they were rounded up by the local militia, led by a fox-hunting squire.* Nevertheless, the "invasion" threatened to

---

*They mistook some Welsh women wearing their traditional tall hats and scarlet cloaks for Redcoats, it is said, and less savage than reputed, offered no resistance.

bring down Pitt and his ministry and created a financial panic. The Bank of England was forced to suspend payments in gold, and for the first time in history issued paper notes. Rumors were also circulating of unrest in the Channel fleet. Yet, in the midst of this trough of depression, news reached London of a smashing naval victory over Spain and the emergence of a new hero: Horatio Nelson.

FROM TIME IMMEMORIAL, sailing ships rounding Cape St. Vincent, at the southwestern tip of Portugal, saluted the headland, the most westerly point of continental Europe, by lowering their topsails. It was there that Prince Henry the Navigator had watched his tiny caravels disappear below the horizon as they began their voyages of discovery. On February 13, 1797, Sir John Jervis's fleet was cruising to the west of the cape as the frigate *Minerve*, of thirty-eight guns, raced toward them. No one needed to consult the signal books for the meaning of the scarlet flag flying from her masthead: "Enemy in sight!" A Spanish fleet of twenty-seven of the line lay just over the horizon, reported Nelson. Jervis had only fifteen big ships, but he did not hesitate to offer combat. "It is men, not ships, that win battles," he had once said.

Two weeks before, Nelson had taken *Minerve* and another frigate into the Mediterranean to complete the evacuation of Elba. On his way to the island he encountered a pair of Spanish frigates off Cartagena, one, the forty-gun *Sabina*, under the command of Don Jacobo Stuart, a direct descendant of Britain's exiled King James II.

"This is an English frigate," hailed Nelson through a speaking trumpet as the vessels plunged along through the sea, side by side. "If you do not surrender, I will open fire."

"This is a Spanish frigate," replied Stuart, "and you may begin as soon as you please."

"I have no idea of a closer or sharper battle," Nelson later reported. For nearly three hours the two evenly matched vessels maneuvered and pounded away at each other at close range, with superior British gunnery finally giving *Minerve* the edge. Nevertheless, Stuart refused to surrender until more than half his crew had been killed or wounded. *Minerve* lost only seven killed, although she sustained considerable damage. Nelson formally accepted Stuart's sword when he was brought on board his ship, and promptly returned it in recognition of his gallantry. While this courtly exchange was taking place, a number of Spanish ships were sighted, and Nelson was forced to abandon his prize and prize crew. Stuart was later sent back to Spain under a flag of truce, and *Minerve's* prize crew was exchanged for prisoners held by the British.

Upon completion of his mission, Nelson passed Cartagena on his way west and learned that the Spanish fleet, now flying the flag of Don Juan de Cordova, had sailed on February 1. Four days later it passed the Strait of Gibraltar (or the "Gut," as it was known) into the Atlantic. Nelson supposed the Spaniards were bound for the West Indies, but in reality Cordova was on his way to a planned concentration of the French, Spanish, and Dutch fleets to cover another attempt by Lazar Hoche to invade Britain. The Spanish convoy also included troops for Algeciras, near Gibraltar, and four large merchantmen, or *urcas*. The latter were carrying mercury from Málaga to Cádiz for shipment to the silver mines of the New World, where it was used in refining the ore on which the Spanish—and now the French—economies depended.

Nelson followed de Cordova's fleet through the "Gut," and two Spanish ships that had remained behind at Algeciras gave chase. The fast-sailing *Minerve* was drawing away from them when a man fell overboard and a boat was lowered to pick him up. The search took longer than expected, and the boat, carrying the frigate's first lieutenant, Thomas Hardy, was in danger of being captured. "By God, I'll not lose Hardy," Nelson declared and ordered his vessel's topsails backed until the boat caught up. Bewildered by their prey's strange conduct, the enemy backed sail, too, and Nelson hoisted in the boat and escaped. Hardy survived to become his good friend and flag captain at Trafalgar.

Pressing out into the Atlantic, Nelson ran into a night fog. When it lifted slightly, he found that *Minerve* had, by chance, sailed into the middle of the Spanish fleet. Fortunately, his luck held: visibility was so poor that the Spaniards did not detect the presence of a British frigate among them, and he sped off to warn Admiral Jervis of their presence.

Following Jervis's strategic retreat from the Mediterranean, the British fleet had been based in the Tagus River below Lisbon, where it suffered disasters almost as bad as in a lost battle. Because of gales and accidents, two seventy-gun ships were wrecked, and a seventy-four, eighty, and ninety-eight were so badly damaged that they were out of action until repaired, reducing the fleet to only nine sail of the line. Fortunately, six more big ships had joined Jervis a week before—and a half dozen of his vessels were three-deckers. Cordova had six three-deckers of 112 guns each, and his flagship, *Santissima Trinidada*, was the world's only four-decker and mounted 136 cannon. "*Victory* is nothing to her," observed Nelson, who had resumed command of *Captain*. But the Spanish fleet was ill-disciplined and short of competent officers and men; in fact, the flagship had only sixty to eighty prime seamen, the rest of its crew made up of landsmen and soldiers.

Throughout the night before the battle, the Spanish fleet was so close that the British heard the muffled sounds of its signal guns. Jervis gave a dinner, attended by several of his captains, in *Victory*'s great cabin. The toast was downed enthusiastically: "Victory over the Dons in the battle that they cannot escape tomorrow." After the departure of his guests, the admiral made out his will. Unable to sleep, he restlessly paced the quarterdeck as he awaited the coming of dawn of February 14, 1797—St. Valentine's Day. It came slowly, cold and foggy, but Jervis had a feeling of pride as it revealed his ships standing toward the enemy in two perfect columns. To those around him, Jervis murmured: "A victory to England is very essential at this moment."

Slowly the shapes of the Spanish ships loomed out of the thinning mist "like Beachy Head in fog," noted one officer. Sir Robert Calder, the captain of the fleet, counted them:

"There are eight sail of the line, Sir John."

"Very well, sir."

"There are twenty sail of the line, Sir John."

"Very well, sir."

"There are twenty-five sail of the line, Sir John."

"Very well, sir.

"There are twenty-seven of the line, Sir John."

"Enough, sir, no more of that; the die is cast, and if there are fifty sail I will go through them."

"That's right, Sir John!" boomed the Canadian-born Captain Benjamin Hallowell* as he enthusiastically slapped the admiral on the back. "That's right! And by God, we'll give them a damned good licking!"

BLOWING FROM THE EAST, a strong wind called a Levanter had pushed the Spanish fleet farther out into the Atlantic than Cordova wished, and he was about thirty miles off Cape St. Vincent and working his way back to Cádiz when the British came into view. Spanish frigates had sighted some of Jervis's ships the day before, but the admiral, thinking them part of a merchant convoy, was unalarmed. On the morning of the fourteenth his fleet was heading toward Cádiz in two groups, one consisting of the main fleet and the other a convoy of the *urcas* and their escort under command of Vice Admiral Joaquin Moreno. Unaware that Jervis had been reinforced, Cordova believed the enemy had no more than nine ships and would avoid battle.

Thus, the Spanish admiral was astonished to see the fifteen ships of Jervis's battle line coming down on him from the north when the winter sun

---

*Hallowell's ship *Courageux,* of seventy-four guns, had recently been lost in a gale, and he was a passenger in *Victory.*

had burned off the haze. Hastily he signaled his captains to form a line of battle, and to gain the weather gage he ordered them to reverse course. This double maneuver was beyond the ability of the unskilled Spanish officers and crews. Seventeen ships managed to form a straggling line, but the vessels were so badly handled that some were bunched three or four abreast. Worse yet, the *urca* convoy had shot ahead of the main body and was three miles away to the leeward. In the chaos, the numerical advantage held by the Spaniards had vanished.

At 11:00 A.M. Jervis ordered his ships into a single column, with the seventy-four-gun *Culloden* in the van, *Victory* in the center, and Nelson's *Captain* the third vessel from the end of the British line. Sailing close-hauled and with bowsprits and sterns almost touching, the British fleet made straight for the gap between the Spanish forces. As the two fleets neared, the British ships ran up their colors. Belatedly, Admiral Moreno tried to close the gap by falling back on the main body, but it was too late, for *Culloden* had already plunged into the opening.

Under the hand of Captain Thomas Troubridge, *Culloden* had been transformed from a problem ship riven by mutiny into one in which morale and fighting spirit were unmatched in the fleet. As she drew near the enemy, the vessel's first lieutenant warned Troubridge that this course would bring her down on a Spanish three-decker, but the captain was unfazed. "Can't help that, Griffiths," he said. "Let the weakest fend off." This proved to be the Spaniard, who, fearful of a collision, gave way. Sweeping through the gap, *Culloden* poured two double-shotted broadsides into the enemy ship, "fired as if by a seconds-watch," said an observer. She visibly shuddered under the impact.

Troubridge was followed by the rest of the British van. At 12:08 P.M. Jervis signaled his ships to tack one after the other rather than together— as if they were making a U-turn—and come around on a course parallel to the Spanish line, with both fleets heading north, which gave the British the weather gage.

Having anticipated the order, Troubridge had the acknowledging signal ready to be broken even as the flags were being hoisted by *Victory*, and he put down his helm and came around. Such quick action was not lost on Jervis. "Look at Troubridge!" he declared. "He tacks his ship to battle as if the eyes of all England were upon him, and would to God they were." *Blenheim* and *Prince George*, both of ninety-eight guns, and *Orion*, seventy-four, were close behind *Cullodon* as she struck the rear of Cordova's battle line from the leeward. The fighting now became general, and the ships on both sides were hotly engaged. "We gave them their Valentines in style," declared a gunner in *Goliath*, seventy-four. In *Orion* Nancy Perriman, a gunner's wife who normally washed clothes and sewed for Captain Sir

James Saumarez, divided her time between helping her husband dole out powder in the magazine and assisting the surgeon in the cockpit.

Unexpectedly, the Spanish leeward division now made a desperate attempt to join the main force by cutting across the British line of advance. For some moments it appeared that Moreno's flagship, the 112-gun *Principe d'Asturias,* would collide with *Victory,* which had yet to make her turn. The Spanish three-decker backed off, presenting Jervis with the opportunity to pour a raking broadside into her. On the British flagship's gundecks the men stood to their cannon with the confidence of experience. Suddenly her ports snapped open, the guns were run out, and their crews broke into three tremendous cheers that were almost as daunting to the enemy as the thunder of her broadsides. *Principe d'Asturias* was turned into a shambles. Steering wheel shot away and rudder jammed, she drifted out of action. *Victory* led the remainder of the fleet to an attack on the enemy from the windward, thus enveloping the Spanish rear from both sides.

An enemy shot took the head off a marine, splattering Jervis with his blood and brains. Fearing the admiral was wounded, an officer ran up. "I am not at all hurt," Jervis coolly replied, wiping the gore off his face. "But do, George, try if you can to get me an orange." And he ordered the signal to "engage more closely" run up.

The climax of the battle came at about one o'clock. Cordova was now attempting to pass across the tail of the British line and join Moreno's leeward division, thereby confronting Jervis with a reunited Spanish fleet. Although some were battered, the Spaniards had not yet lost a ship, and the chance for a decisive British victory hung in the balance. This gave Nelson, whose ship had not yet made the U-turn, his golden moment. Ignoring the cardinal rule of British naval tactics that captains were to maintain their allotted stations in the battle line unless otherwise ordered, he told Captain Miller to wear, or reverse course 180 degrees. *Captain* passed between the two ships astern of her and headed straight for the Spanish flagship, the four-decked *Santissima Trinadada,* and four other large vessels.

Seeing *Captain* disappear into a billowing cloud of gunsmoke, Jervis immediately signaled the last ship in line, *Excellent,* seventy-four, commanded by Cuthbert Collingwood, to also swing out of line and come to Nelson's support. For about ten minutes it looked as if *Captain,* her sails and rigging slashed to pieces and her foremast and wheel shot away by the hurricane of fire, would be blown out of the water. Had the Spanish fleet been well trained, Nelson's daring act would have been suicidal. But he fully realized that the enemy crews were so raw they could not match his vessel's rapidity of fire—three broadsides in two minutes—and it turned out to be a decisive tactical stroke. When the smoke cleared, *Captain* was firing methodically into the enemy vessels, and Collingwood had come to her aid. Some of the Spanish gunners had fled their posts after firing only a single broadside.

Cullodon, Blenheim, Orion, and other ships of the British van, having fought their way up through the Spanish fleet, also joined in the attack. Calder, Jervis's fleet captain, fearful of the safety of these vessels, suggested they be recalled. "No," said the admiral. "I will not have them recalled. I put my faith in those ships. It is a disgrace they are not supported." Support was not long in coming, however, and all hope for a junction of the two divisions of the Spanish fleet had been blocked.

With the crippled *Captain* having nearly lost steerage way, Nelson had her laid alongside the nearest enemy ship, the 80-gun *San Nicolas,* which was, herself, entangled with *San Josef,* of 112 guns. *Captain's* bow crashed into the stern of *San Nicolas,* and the three ships were now locked together by a jumble of spars and rigging. Sword in hand, Nelson called "Boarders away!" Sailors and soldiers of the Sixty-ninth Regiment, who were serving in the ship as marines, leaped from one ship to another armed with pistols, pikes, and cutlasses. Edward Berry, who had until recently been *Captain's* first lieutenant,* was the first man on *San Nicolas.* Captain Miller was in the act of following him when Nelson pulled him back, saying, "No, Miller, I must have that honor."

Helped by a soldier of the Sixty-ninth, Nelson scrambled through one of the enemy vessel's quarter-gallery windows, and after a scuffle with some Spanish officers, led his men through the officers' quarters to the quarterdeck. There he found Berry already in possession of the poop and in the act of hauling down the Spanish ensign. Hardly had the surrender been accomplished when there was a burst of pistol and musket fire from *San Josef.* Nelson called over to Miller for more men, and then, shouting, "Westminster Abbey or victory!," led them onto the deck of the towering three-decker. The British met even less resistance than on *San Nicolas,* and her captain quickly surrendered. Nelson received the swords of the officers of both ships on the quarterdeck of the vanquished *San Josef* and handed them to a sailor, who blithely stuck them under his arm, as if they were a bundle of sticks.

Following an hour-long fight, *Salvador del Mundo,* of 112 guns, struck to Saumarez in *Orion,* and *San Isidro,* 74, was taken by Collingwood. *Santissima Trinidada,* which had perhaps two hundred men killed, also surrendered to *Orion,* the last ship to engage her. But Saumarez had used all his boats to send a prize crew over to *Salvador del Mundo,* so he could not take possession of the four-decker, and the Spaniards soon rehoisted their colors, staggered out of the melee, and escaped with the remainder of the fleet

---

*Berry had been promoted to commander, and without a ship of his own, was a passenger on *Captain.*

to Cádiz. Cordova and Moreno were cashiered and stripped of their titles by the Spanish authorities, and a half dozen captains were dismissed.

Nelson was the hero of the day. As *Victory* passed his clump of ships, her crew lined bulwarks to cheer him. Everyone was soon joking about "Nelson's patent bridge for boarding first-rates." Following the battle, he was summoned to the flagship to report before he could change into a fresh uniform. Part of his cocked hat had been shot away, his coat was torn in several places, and his face was stained with sweat and powder. Except for some internal contusions that troubled him for the rest of his life, he was unhurt. Jervis received him on *Victory*'s quarterdeck, clasped him in his arms, and "said he could not sufficiently thank me," Nelson related. After he left, Captain Calder sourly noted that by hauling his ship out of line Nelson had defied the *Fighting Instructions*. "It certainly was so," snapped Jervis, "and if you ever commit such a breach of your orders I will forgive you also."

Four ships of the line, two of them first-rates, had been taken from a fleet almost double the size of Jervis's. While not overwhelming—the admiral, himself, thought two more enemy ships should have been captured—the victory was decisive, and for the British was like a flash of light and color against a dark sky. The first part of the grand design to invade Britain had been thwarted, the Royal Navy had regained the initiative, and the Mediterranean was once more open to British shipping. Shattered and demoralized, the Spanish fleet was placed under blockade at Cádiz and did not play an offensive role in the war for another two years.

Pitt, whose ministry was saved by Jervis's victory, was generous with rewards. The admiral became Earl St. Vincent, with a pension of three thousand pounds a year, his subordinate admirals became baronets, and every captain received a gold medal. Berry was promoted to captain. Horatio Nelson was created a knight of the Bath—an honor he preferred to a baronetcy because of the ribbon and star that went with it—and his promotion to rear admiral came through. At thirty-eight, the youngest admiral of modern times, he had already won a place in the public imagination from which he was never to be dislodged.

To his wife, now Lady Nelson, he wrote that "the Spanish War will give us a Cottage and a piece of ground, which is all I want. I shall come one day laughing back, when we will retire from the busy scenes of life." Poor Fanny was unable to share altogether in his high spirits. "What can I say to you about boarding?" she replied. "You have been most wonderfully protected. You have done desperate actions enough. I do beg, that you never board again. *Leave it for Captains*." But as Nelson was enjoying the recognition he so craved, the nation—and the Royal Navy—faced one of the gravest challenges in their history.

CHAPTER 11

"A Breeze at Spithead"

EASTER SUNDAY MORNING, April 16, 1797, was bright and sunny, with a southwest wind that dappled the waters at Spithead, where the Channel fleet rode at anchor. Now and then, pendants swirled out from the top-masts of the sixteen ships in a gleam of scarlet or blue. From Portsmouth Point, where generations of British sailors have embarked and landed, the wooden walls of England appeared as serenely powerful as ever. But unrest stalked the holystoned decks of the vessels, and mutterings of mutiny were in the air. Shortly before noon, Lord Bridport signaled Vice Admiral Sir Alan Gardner to weigh and take his squadron down to St. Helens, the usual starting point for putting to sea.

Multicolored flags fluttered out the message, and all eyes were fixed on *Royal Sovereign*, Gardner's ship. No move to obey the order could be seen. All that could be made out was the gesticulating figures of the officers haranguing the crew to do their duty. No one manned the capstan. No one went aloft. Suddenly the sailors of *Queen Charlotte*, Lord Howe's old flag-ship, raced up the shrouds of their ship, manned the yards, and broke the silence with three rousing cheers. Other ships took up the cheer, and it echoed over and over again from the throats of thousands of men in the rest of the fleet. Instantly a boat put out from her that was followed by other boats, which rowed through the fleet, crying to each vessel as they passed to send two delegates to a meeting to be held in *Queen Charlotte*'s great cabin that evening.

Within the hour, the arms of the semaphore "telegraph" atop the square tower of Church of St. Thomas à Becket in Portsmouth were flailing out the urgent message to the Admiralty in London: The Channel fleet had mutinied, and the crews had seized control of the ships!

The message traveled eastward from station to station until it was received by the stationkeeper on the Admiralty roof. It took about three minutes to cover the seventy-five miles from Portsmouth. The Admiralty Board was hurriedly called away from Easter dinners to deal with the worst crisis in the nation's history since the Spanish Armada. Following an anxious meeting, Lord Spencer, the first lord, two junior lords, and the secretary of the Admiralty set out for Portsmouth to investigate.*

Surprise, terror, and grief appeared on every face as the news of the "breeze at Spithead" became generally known. As Herman Melville wrote in *Billy Budd,* his novel about the mutiny, it was "what a strike in the fire brigade would be to London threatened by general arson." The Royal Navy, which only weeks before had defeated the Spaniards at St. Vincent and saved the country from invasion, seemed ready to betray it to its enemies. The hour could not have been more fatal. The Austrians had asked the victorious Bonaparte for a truce. Ireland was smoldering with rebellion, and the French were preparing a new army of invasion to embark under convoy of a Dutch battle fleet. And now the Channel fleet—on which all depended—was in the hands of mutineers. Even the marines, whose duty was to maintain order in the ships, had joined the rebellion. Some people hourly expected the arrival of the French and the guillotine.

Britons were especially shocked by the mutiny because the Royal Navy touched a mystic chord in the national pysche. As the *Articles of War* expressed it, "the wealth, safety, and strength" of the island realm depended on the sea service. The sight of the fleet in all its majesty passing in review in the Channel had the effect of a trumpet call on the British soul. The seaman, with his tarry pigtail and rolling gait, was portrayed in song and story as simple, jolly, and loyal, with a heart of oak.

Yet, though praised and feted, Jack Tar was treated as a child. He was undisciplined, so he must be ruled by the lash. He was improvident, so adequate pay only indulged his weaknesses. He was a drunkard, so he must not be allowed ashore. Thus the mutiny—with all its skillful planning, secrecy, and discipline—came as a shocking surprise. Most Britons believed it had to have been plotted by Jacobin agitators and radicals, not by docile, honest British tars. For those aware of conditions in the navy, the mutiny was less of a shock, however.

⌒

LORD HOWE WAS among them. Nominally the commander of the Channel fleet, he was in reality in semiretirement at Bath, where he was taking the waters for gout and other infirmities, when, on March 3, 1797, he received three petitions. To his surprise, they were from his men, who

*Prime Minister Pitt was undergoing a crisis of his own. At thirty-eight he was still unmarried but had become attracted to Lady Eleanor Eden, the pretty, twenty-year-old daughter of Lord Auckland. But early in 1797 he broke off the engagement, probably because of the desperate state of his finances, and fell into a deep depression.

"humbly intreated" the "sailors' friend" to lay before the Admiralty their complaints about the inadequacy of their wages. Pay rates for the navy had not changed since the reign of Charles II despite "the rise in the necessaries of life, which is now double," the petitions declared, while the army recently had a raise. One was signed by the crew of *Queen Charlotte;* the others came from two more battleships of the Channel fleet.

The handwriting on the petitions differed but the phrasing was similar, so Howe suspected a common author—probably some pettifogging lawyer's clerk who had been pressed into the navy or been conscripted as a quota man. Unable to reply to the petitions because they were anonymous, he later explained, he sent them to Rear Admiral Lord Hugh Seymour, a member of the Board of Admiralty, with the suggestion that someone should look into the matter. Seymour went down to Portsmouth—while the Channel fleet was at sea—and consulted with the port admiral and the lord mayor. Neither had noted any signs of unrest, and the inquiry was dropped.

But the flow of petitions continued. Eight or more dribbled from the fleet to "Black Dick" Howe over the following weeks. Like the earlier petitions, these contained similar turns of phrase, although each purported to come from a different ship. Although Lord Bridport was in actual command of the Channel fleet, Howe had not yet formally struck his flag. Worried, he went up to London, where on March 22 he presented the latest batch of petitions to Seymour. Both men knew that the sailors' complaints about pay were understatements.

Navy pay was scandalously low—an ordinary seaman received only nineteen shillings per month and an able seaman twenty-four—a third of what a sailor could earn in the merchant service.* As miserable as these wages were, they were docked to support the seamen's retirement home at Greenwich Hospital, for the upkeep of a chaplain if a ship had one, and for overpriced clothing from the purser's slop chest. Particularly galling to the men was the fact that pay was suspended during sickness, even if a man was recovering from wounds received in battle. Often pay was two or three years in arrears. And when payment was made, it was by a warrant that could be cashed at face value only at navy offices, so most sailors sold them at a considerable discount to bumboat men and prostitutes for ready cash. And if a deserving old salt was lucky enough to reach a final harbor at Greenwich, his pension was half that of an ex-soldier at Chelsea Hospital.

Protests over conditions in the navy were not new. Shortly after the Glorious First of June, Lord Howe had vaguely indicated that he would try to do something about his sailors' pay. Not long before, Rear Admiral

---

*In contrast, a post captain earned about a pound a day, more than ten times the wages of a governess such as the fictional Jane Eyre.

Philip Patton had sent the first lord a memorandum on the subject of the seamen's grievances. Horatio Nelson vividly denounced a system that left its seamen "finished at forty-five, double-ruptured, raw with scurvy, and wracked with agonizing pains after every meal." In December 1796 Captain Thomas Pakenham protested to the Admiralty on behalf of several of his fellow officers about "the underpaid condition of the thoroughbred seamen." The Admiralty brushed off these complaints. "In the present state of country," it replied, "it is not possible to enormously increase disbursements, which are already sufficiently burdensome." This remained the official position in the face of the new petitions.

On March 30 the Channel fleet returned to Spithead and the men found, to their anger, that their requests had met only silence. In port, boats moved freely from ship to ship, carrying visiting "liberty parties" in lieu of shore leave, and the leaders of the protest used these opportunities to meet clandestinely between decks. They drafted a new petition restating their grievances that was to be sent not only directly to the Admiralty but to Parliament as well. If the fleet was ordered to sea, it stated, the ships would refuse to sail unless the men received an increase in pay.

The hands that drafted these documents have never been identified, but the authors were probably better-educated quota men or radical Irishmen dragooned into the navy to meet the chronic shortage of manpower. Some had links to revolutionary groups such as the United Irishmen, and provided leadership on the lower deck that brought long-festering resentments to a head. Valentine Joyce, a quartermaster's mate in *Royal George,* Bridport's flagship, and a failed lawyer known only as Evans were prominent in the Spithead mutiny and may have been the authors. The twenty-six-year-old Joyce was a Belfast tobacconist who had been jailed for sedition and came to the fleet as a quota man.

Typical of the Admiralty's failure to grasp the gravity of the situation was the fact that Lord Bridport was not informed about the petitions. He was not aware of them until April 12, when an informant reported that there was a plot to seize the ships and hold them until the seamen's grievances were redressed. Once Bridport had vented his anger at the failure of the authorities to keep him informed, he asked the Admiralty how it intended to deal with the impending crisis. Instead of receiving a reply, he was ordered to take the fleet to sea. Failing to recognize the seriousness of the situation, the Admiralty tried to sidetrack it—and by complacency and inertia brought the crisis to a head.

⌐⌐

UPON HIS ARRIVAL in Portsmouth to treat with the mutineers, Lord Spencer found the fleet in surprisingly good order. Officers were respected, although some of the more unpopular and brutal were ordered out of their ships;* watches were being kept; drunkenness was punished by flogging; and hangmen's nooses dangled from fore yardarms as warnings to those who breached discipline. The prince of Württemberg, who was to marry the princess royal, came down to Portsmouth and was cheered through the fleet by the sailors as if nothing unusual were happening. It was all very strange—and very British. The fleet was in mutiny, but the men did not regard themselves as mutineers. They had no sympathy with revolutionary France and proclaimed their willingness to sail immediately if the French put to sea. Frigates and other escort vessels were ordered not to take part in the mutiny and to continue to protect the nation's trade.

New issues were now raised in addition to higher pay. The sailors wanted increased and better food rations that were not subject to the peculations of thieving pursers,† fresh vegetables and beef in port, a better distribution of prize money, humane treatment of the sick and the continuance of pay to the ailing and wounded, and above all, shore leave. Sailors, the new petition said with an untutored eloquence, should be regarded as men defending their country and deserving of "the grant of those sweets of Liberty on shore, when in any harbour."

Curiously, this list of grievances made no mention of the barbarous punishments under which the men suffered and that so repel modern sensibilities. They lived in a brutal age and saw no unfairness because the penal law on land was even more savage than the *Articles of War*. Moreover, ill treatment was not the general rule throughout the Royal Navy. Conditions varied from ship to ship depending on the humaneness of the officers. For example, Nelson, Collingwood, and Lord Cochrane, the most dashing frigate captain of the age, did not resort to brutality and were loved and respected by their men.

Everyone agreed that the sailors' demands were reasonable, and Bridport

---

*The captain and six other officers left the frigate *Hind* after receiving an anonymous note from the crew saying "we wish you to leave . . . peaceably or desperate measures will taken." Lieutenant William Compton of *Minotaur*, noted for having men flogged down to the bone, and a Lieutenant Fitzpatrick of *Glory*, who punished sailors for slowness by putting their heads in a bag and having them tarred and feathered all over, were rowed to the beach and left there with their baggage. On the other hand, Captain Talbot of the frigate *Eurydice* received a testimonial from his crew that they looked on him as their "tender shepherd."

†Traditionally, provisions were issued to the men at a weight of fourteen ounces to the pound, with the difference going into the pocket of the ship's purser in lieu of pay. There was an old saying in the navy that Judas Iscariot was the first purser.

and several of his admirals urged that they be accepted. Spencer declined, however, to yield unconditionally to save official face, and offered only a small raise—about five shillings a month. The other demands were ignored. In a meeting held in the great cabin of *Queen Charlotte* with the Admiralty's representatives the delegates gave seeming agreement, but then, growing suspicious because of the first lord's bumbling, said a final settlement would have to await a king's pardon for all. Losing his temper, Admiral Gardner denounced the delegates as "a damned mutinous black-guard set" who were afraid to go to sea to meet the French. In his fury, he grabbed one man by the collar, shook him, and threatened to have all the delegates hanged from the nearest yardarm. The meeting broke up in a melee. Gardner was hustled off the ship, the "red flag of defiance" was raised in place of Bridport's flag, and the remaining officers were confined to their cabins.

A shaken Spencer immediately returned to London to obtain the royal pardon and, after having it printed, came back to Portsmouth. By this time, tempers had cooled. The sailors apologized to Bridport for striking his flag and begged him "as father of the fleet" to resume command. On the morning of April 24, the admiral returned to his flagship to read the royal proclamation of pardon and to assure all hands that their demands would be met. The mutiny appeared to be over. Next morning, the bulk of the Channel fleet dropped down to St. Helens to await an east wind to return to the blockade of Brest. Everyone breathed a sigh of relief as the week of crisis ended without a disaster.

Unhappily, however, the fleet failed to catch a fair wind, and as it lay windbound, the men read in the newspapers of parliamentary delays and political logrolling that held up passage of the bill for supplementary naval pay. Unfamiliar with the ways of politics, it appeared to them as if the government was backtracking on its part of the agreement. The fate of the *Culloden* mutineers who had been guaranteed a pardon only to be hanged was recalled. On May 7, when the wind changed and Lord Bridport hoisted the signal to sail, the men again manned the shrouds, broke into cheers, and refused to put to sea. And once again, the red flag flew over the Channel fleet. The virus of mutiny also spread to the Nore, at the mouth of the Thames estuary, and the North Sea fleet, which was awaiting a fair wind at Great Yarmouth to return to the blockade of the Dutch invasion fleet.

Violence and bloodshed were touched off by Vice Admiral John Colpoys, already disliked by his men for his ineffectual role in the Bantry Bay fiasco. He refused to allow a boatload of delegates to board *London,* and in the ensuing tumult, the vessel's first lieutenant shot and killed a sailor. Immediately, the rest of the crew pressed toward the quarterdeck, screaming, "Blood for blood!" "Blood for blood!" Three more men were killed, several were wounded, and the officer was seized amid cries that he be summarily hanged. A rope was being rove to haul him up to the yardarm when Valentine Joyce intervened. Colpoys and several of his officers were placed under arrest to await trial for murder.

Britain was almost defenseless, and gloom lay heavy over the nation. Boats laden with officers dismissed from their ships and guarded by piratical-looking fellows armed with pistols and cutlasses drew up to the quays of Portsmouth. What would happen if the French chose this moment to launch an invasion? Rumors percolated through the town that the mutineers intended to turn the Channel fleet over to the enemy if their demands were unmet. These reports sufficiently galvanized the politicians in Westminster to give immediate approval to the naval pay bill.

But would the men, now suspicious of all authority, believe their demands had been met? "Black Dick" Howe was dispatched to Portsmouth to carry the news to the fleet. No better selection could have been made. Even though he had been lax in dealing with their earlier petitions, the men still regarded him with favor and affection. Arriving on May 11, he had himself rowed from ship to ship despite his infirmities and met with the crew of each. With infinite tact and patience, he convinced them that the official promises of improved conditions in the navy would be made good and that a general amnesty would soon be granted. A stumbling block to a settlement was the men's insistence that the officers sent ashore not be permitted to return to their ships. Howe cannily resolved the problem by suggesting that these officers be persuaded to seek transfers, which would be granted by the Admiralty.

On May 15 Howe went down to St. Helens for the final act of reconciliation. From the quarterdeck of *Royal George* he read the king's pardon to the assembled ship's company, and held it over his head so the men could see the royal seal. Even though he was as exhausted as he had been after the Glorious First of June, the admiral was rowed about the cheering fleet to the strains of "Rule Britannia." Ashore, he was carried on the shoulders of the sailors to Governor's House, where he and his lady presided over a grand dinner for the delegates. Two days later, discipline restored, the Channel fleet put to sea to seek the enemy. The mutiny at Spithead was over.*

∽

BUT THE UPHEAVALS at the Nore and Yarmouth remained to be settled. Originally, the Nore mutiny began in sympathy with the Spithead uprising,

---

*A mutiny in some ways comparable to the one at Spithead occurred at Invergordon in September 1931 in the Royal Navy's Home Fleet, this time against a pay cut resulting from the Great Depression. As at Spithead, the affair was orderly, and no violence was recorded.

but continued well after all the sailors' demands had been met. The same ceremonies were observed—the cheering, the expulsion of unpopular officers,* the hoisting of red flags, the selection of delegates, and the interminable meetings—but the Nore mutineers were men without a cause because they had no clear objective once the Spithead mutiny was resolved. The situation was ripe for a demagogue, and he soon appeared in the person of Richard Parker, a thirty-year-old former midshipman who had been dismissed from the navy for insubordination. After a checkered career in civilian life, he had returned to the service via debtors' prison.

Parker marked his reentry into the navy by stirring up trouble in the depot ship *Sandwich,* a superannuated old three-decker, once Rodney's flagship but now rife with discontent because of her foul and overcrowded condition. Proclaiming himself "President of the Floating Republic," Parker adopted the full panoply of an admiral. He showed none of the moderation of his fellows at Spithead and established contact with pro-French radical societies. The Pay Act, he told the men, was only a temporary Order in Council; challenged, he claimed it had no validity beyond the end of the year. When a frigate arrived from Portsmouth with the news that the Channel Fleet had returned to duty, Parker ordered a ship of the line to go alongside the vessel with her gun ports triced up, and the frigate's crew lost no time in joining the mutineers. Several other ships were forcibly converted to the cause by similar measures.

On May 24, emissaries were dispatched to Yarmouth to urge the men of the North Sea fleet to join them. There, they were confronted by the towering figure of Admiral Adam Duncan, a hot-tempered Scot who stood six feet, four inches tall and was still powerful at sixty-six.[†] Only a week before, he had dealt with unrest in *Adamant,* of fifty guns, by transferring his flag to her and asking if any of the crew disagreed with his authority. When one man dared do so, Duncan picked him up by the collar with one hand, dangled him over the side of the ship, and called out, "My lads, look at this fellow who dares to deprive me of the command of the fleet!" The incipient mutiny immediately collapsed into laughter.

But as Duncan's thirteen ships stood out to blockade the Dutch coast on May 29, only his flagship, *Venerable,* seventy-four, and *Adamant* maintained their course. The rest joined the "Floating Republic" at the Nore. Fortunately,

---

*Among them was Captain William Bligh of *Bounty* fame—or infamy—who was put ashore from *Director,* sixty-four. Once the mutiny was over, however, Bligh was welcomed back to his ship. He interceded for his men, and the number punished as mutineers was reduced.

[†]As a young officer, Duncan was considered one of the handsomest men in the Royal Navy, and it was said the women of the seaport towns used to stand in their windows to see him pass by.

Admiral Adam Viscount Duncan. (U.S. Naval Academy Museum)

the Dutch fleet was not fully shaken down, and for a week, Duncan block-aded it with his two ships by making signals to an imaginary fleet suppos-edly lying just over the horizon, until the Admiralty sent him reinforcements.

The Nore mutineers were offered an unconditional pardon if they would return to duty but it was rejected, along with an address from "the Seamen at Spithead" urging an end to the mutiny. With the mutineers hav-ing lost all public sympathy, the Admiralty cut off the fleet's provisions and water. Gunboats were readied for an attack, navigational buoys were removed from the Thames estuary, and the forts were told to ready their furnaces for heating hot shot. In reprisal, the rebels blocked the river and plundered merchant and fishing vessels entering or trying to leave port. Effigies of Pitt were hung from yardarms, and there was talk of handing the ships over to the Dutch. Nevertheless, on June 4 the birthday of King George was celebrated with a salute from all the ships except *Sandwich*.

As food and water grew short, the mutiny no longer seemed to the sailors like a permanent holiday. There was increasing discontent with "Admiral" Parker's airs and peremptory orders. His control was also undermined by an Admiralty announcement on June 6 that henceforth the mutineers would be treated as rebels, although the offer of a pardon to all who would submit except the ringleaders remained on the table. On June 9 the fifty-gun *Leopard* lowered the red flag and ran through the fleet to the safety of the forts at Sheerness despite being fired on. She was followed by *Repulse*, sixty-four, which ran aground under a brisk fire that riddled her sails. As *Leopard* floated clear with the tide, Parker shouted, "Damn her, she's off!" and urged the gunners to sink the escaping vessel. The following day *Ardent*, of sixty-four guns, also made a successful break for freedom.

For the next several days the fleet presented a curious spectacle as the red flag fluttered up and down masts as various factions contended for control of the ships. Fighting broke out in a number of the vessels, and there was considerable bloodshed. With the mutiny petering out, some of the ringleaders argued that the ships should be taken to America or Ireland rather than surrender. But by June 12, only two of the twenty-two ships still at the Nore were in a mutinous state. Three days later, the mutiny ended as the crew of *Sandwich* repudiated "Admiral" Parker and surrendered. Parker was arrested, court-martialed, and hanged from a yardarm of his own ship. Fifty-eight others were condemned to death, of whom twenty-eight were actually executed. Some three hundred men were flogged, sent to prison, or transported. Parker spent his last hours preparing a tirade against the men he had mislead.*

Spontaneous acts of mutiny also occurred at various foreign stations, with the bloodiest taking place in the frigate *Hermione*, of thirty-two guns, in the West Indies. The vessel's captain, Hugh Pigot, was a sadist who delighted in floggings. Unsatisfied with the speed at which his mizzen topmen were taking in sail, Pigot threatened to flog the last man off the

---

*"Remember, never to make yourself the busybody of the lower classes for they are cowardly, selfish and ungrateful," Parker wrote. "The least trifle will intimidate them, and him whom they have exalted one moment as their Demagogue, the next day they will not scruple to exalt upon the gallows."

yard. In their haste to complete their task, three sailors fell to their deaths on the deck below. "Throw the lubbers overboard," Pigot ordered as his men looked on in horror. The following night, September 21, 1797, the crew murdered Pigot and nine of his officers, sailed the ship to Venezuela, and turned her over to the Spaniards. The Admiralty launched a global manhunt for the mutineers, and over the next eight years thirty-three were captured, of whom twenty-four were hanged.*

          ↜

THROUGHOUT THE UPHEAVALS at Spithead and the Nore, Sir John Jervis, now Earl St. Vincent, maintained a close blockade of a Spanish fleet of twenty-eight ships of the line at Cádiz while warily watching for any signs of unrest among his crews. With his fleet now numbering twenty-one of the line, St. Vincent divided it into two divisions, with the inshore squadron of seven of his best ships, under the command of Rear Admiral Sir Horatio Nelson, operating directly off Cádiz. "Spain shall have no trade," the newly minted admiral proclaimed. "We are in advance day and night, prepared for battle; bulkheads down, ready to weigh, cut, or slip, as the occasion may require." Nelson bombarded Cádiz on two successive occasions and took part in several skirmishes between small boats that prowled Cádiz Harbor at night. Leading as always from the front, he personally led an attack on a Spanish launch containing thirty men. John Sykes, his coxswain, saved Nelson's life and lost his hand when he parried the blow of a Spanish saber that would have severed the admiral's head. Eighteen of the enemy were killed.

To prevent his men from plotting mutiny, St. Vincent forbade them to communicate with the shore or to visit other ships of his fleet. The marine detachments were quartered separately from the sailors, the use of the "Irish" language was barred, and the crews were mustered twice a day. Balancing severity with humanity, the admiral also made certain that adequate provisions were available and the men fairly treated, and he kept up a drumfire of representations to the Admiralty about delays in the payment of prize money and the deficiencies in the quantity and quality of supplies and clothing dispatched to the fleet.

Some of the ships sent to reinforce St. Vincent's fleet were on the verge

---

*In October 1799, two years after the mutiny, Captain Edward Hamilton led a cutting-out party from the twenty-eight-gun frigate *Surprise*, which seized the ship while she was anchored under the guns of Puerto Cabello, Venezuela. Hamilton was knighted for the daring exploit but was, himself, dismissed from the service a few years later for brutality.

of mutiny. When Nelson's flagship, *Captain,* was sent home for refitting, he was ordered to the newly arrived *Theseus,* seventy-four, along with Ralph Miller, his flag captain, to restore order. Nelson reacted to his new command with dismay. She was destitute of stores of any kind, and although the vessel had departed Spithead before the mutiny, her crew felt ill-used by their previous officers and were surly and uncooperative. Nelson and Miller begged and borrowed every type of store from nails to fresh vegetables while trying to impose a sense of order in the ship. Within a few weeks a crude note was found one night on her quarterdeck, which read: "Success attend Admiral Nelson. God bless Captain Miller. We thank them for the officers they have placed over us. We are happy and comfortable, and will shed every drop of blood in our veins to support them. . . ." It was signed "Ship's Company."

In contrast, mutiny broke out in *St. George,* seventy-four guns. St. Vincent surrounded her with the vessels of his fleet, with their guns run out. Four ringleaders were sentenced to hang, and the admiral insisted that they be executed the next day, even though it was a Sunday. Other mutinies were also sternly suppressed. In one case he forced the crew of a mutinous ship to hang their own leader by threatening to sink the vessel. Two homosexuals were also hanged in *St. George* for "an unnatural crime." They might have gotten off with a hundred lashes each on the lesser crime of "going to another man's hammock" in less trying times.

Not long after *London* arrived from Spithead to join the Mediterranean fleet, a man in her captain's gig called out to a seaman at a port of *Ville de Paris,* St. Vincent's flagship: "I say, there, what have you fellows been doing out here while we have been fighting for your beef and pork?" The old Mediterranean hand quietly replied: "If you'll take my advice, you'll say nothing at all about all that here; for by God if old Jarvie hears ye he'll have you dingle dangle at the yardarm at eight o'clock tomorrow morning."

ST. VINCENT HAD HOPED to provoke the Spaniards into making a sortie from Cádiz, but when this failed, he looked elsewhere to do harm to the enemy. Back in April, Nelson had conceived a plan for an amphibious attack on Santa Cruz de Tenerife in the Canary Islands, using a small squadron and the thirty-five hundred troops who had been evacuated from Elba. But the army refused to make the soldiers available, and Nelson backed away from the operation because the island was too well fortified to be taken unassisted. Not long after, word reached St. Vincent that a Spanish treasure ship from Manila had taken shelter at Santa Cruz. If the ship could be captured, it would be a blow to Spain's finances, a boost to

Britain's exchequer, and, not the least in the navy's eye, a fortune in prize money to those who captured it. Although Nelson had advised against a purely naval attack, he now agreed to carry it out when promised two hundred additional marines and Thomas Troubridge of *Culloden* as his second in command. "With 'General Troubridge' ashore and myself afloat, I am confident of success," he said.

Flying his flag in *Theseus* and accompanied by a pair of frigates, Nelson arrived off Tenerife on July 15, 1797. During the five-day voyage, the men trained with small arms and cutlasses as the carpenters built scaling ladders to be used in an assault on the fortifications. Once the cloud-covered volcanic peak of the island was sighted, the squadron lay below the horizon while a mixed force of marines and sailors under Troubridge manned the boats. They were towed in by the frigates under cover of darkness with the hope of surprising the island's two forts. At dawn, Nelson's ships were to move in and support the landing party with their broadsides.

Wind and current were adverse, however, and the plan miscarried. The frigates did not reach the line of departure until daylight, and with surprise lost, Troubridge delayed the landing. When Nelson's ships closed with the island, the admiral directed that the attack proceed as planned, but it was repulsed. Nelson's fabled luck seemed to have turned. A gale blew for two days, and the squadron was unable to get into position again for a landing until the night of July 24. With Nelson leading in person, the landing party, a thousand strong, was to come ashore at the mole that jutted out into the sea from the center of Santa Cruz itself. Nelson dined that evening on the frigate *Seahorse* with the newly married Captain Fremantle, who was to take part in the assault; Fremantle's wife, Betsey; and several of Nelson's captains. Nelson was full of confidence at the dinner table but privately regarded the enterprise as "a forlorn hope. . . . I never expected to return."

Packed with armed men, the boats pushed off at about eleven o'clock that night, roped together to preserve contact. The rise and fall of muffled oars carried them through the darkness into the harbor. In the stern of the admiral's barge sat Josiah Nisbet, now a lieutenant, who overcame his stepfather's objections to coming. "Should we both fall, what would become of your poor mother?" Nelson asked. But the young man replied, "I will go with you tonight, if I never go again."

Misty rain hid the boats, but the Spaniards were on the alert. With a flash and a roar, a gun boomed out with a long leap of flame that momentarily illuminated the oncoming boats. Others joined in spewing a hurricane of round and grapeshot in the direction of the invaders. The wild clanging of church bells sounding the alarm added to the uproar as the British sailors pulled frantically toward the mole through geysers of water thrown up by the enemy fire.

Leaping from their tossing boats onto the wet stone, some men gained a foothold on the mole and raced down it to capture several cannon at its end. Nelson quickly followed, but no sooner was he on the mole than he staggered and fell back into the boat, blood pumping from his shattered right arm. "I am a dead man," he muttered as he was caught by his step-son, who laid him in the bottom of the boat. Josiah ripped off his own black silk neck stock and hurriedly tied it as a tourniquet around Nelson's arm to stop the flow of blood from a severed artery.

The attack itself was a disaster. Only a few of the boats reached the mole; most were carried past it by the swift current and overturned in the surf or were stove in on the rocky shore. The water was full of floundering, drowning, shouting men. Troubridge and about three hundred others reached the main square of Santa Cruz, but much of their powder was wet, and they could penetrate no farther under intense sniper fire from the citadel and surrounding buildings.

Nelson was faint from loss of blood, and Josiah believed his life could be saved only by immediate medical attention. He ordered the boat's crew to pull for the one of the ships. By the light of the gun flashes, men could be seen struggling in the water. Nelson, now sitting upright although in considerable pain, ordered, no matter what the risk, that as many be pulled into the boat as it could hold. Eventually the overloaded craft reached one of the frigates. On learning that it was *Seahorse,* the admiral insisted on proceeding to another vessel. Josiah pleaded that his life was at risk if he did not receive immediate medical attention. "Then I will die," Nelson replied. "I would rather suffer death than alarm Mrs. Fremantle by her seeing me in this state when I can give her no tidings of her husband."* The boat sheered off toward *Theseus,* some distance away.

Midshipman William Hoste—at eleven too young to have joined the landing party—was astonished to see Nelson, "his right arm dangling by his side while with his left he jumped up the ship's side, and with a spirit that astonished everyone, told the surgeon to get his instruments ready." The amputation, performed by Dr. Robert Tainsh without anesthesia by dim lantern light in a rolling ship, was agonizing; the cutting of the flesh with a cold knife was even worse than the sawing of the bone, Nelson said later. The arm was cut off high up, near the shoulder.

With the coming of daylight, Troubridge and his force holed up in a thick-walled convent besieged by some eight thousand enemy troops and militia while the streets outside were strewn with dead and wounded. With superb effrontery, he told the Spanish commander that unless he and his men were given a safe conduct to their ships, they would burn down

---

*Fremantle also received a painful wound in the right arm, but recovered without the loss of the limb.

the town. The Spaniards refused to be bluffed. This was followed by a British promise to refrain from further attacks in the Canary Islands if they were released and, amazingly enough, the offer was accepted. Most of the boats that had brought the British ashore had been destroyed, so the Spaniards ferried them out to the waiting ships with parting gifts of bread and wine. Casualties were heavy: 153 men, including 7 officers, were killed, and 105 wounded—a quarter of the landing force.

As he returned to the fleet off Cádiz Nelson was enshrouded in gloom because of the loss of his arm and the defeat, for which he blamed himself. Frequent spasms of pain in his amputated stump bothered him, and he dosed himself with opium to sleep. "I have become a burthen to my friends and useless to my country," he wrote Lord St. Vincent in spidery, angular script with his left hand. "When I leave your command I become dead to the world; I go hence and am no more seen. . . . I hope you will give me a frigate to convey the remains of my carcass to England." St. Vincent tried to lift Nelson's spirits in his reply. "Mortals cannot command success; you and your companions . . . certainly deserved it by the greatest degree of heroism and perseverance that was ever exhibited." With these words, Nelson returned on sick leave to England—and to the wife he had not seen in four and a half years, having lost an eye and an arm in the interval.

⌒

THROUGHOUT THE SUMMER of 1797, Adam Duncan held grimly to his station off the Texel, where an army was waiting to embark for the invasion of Ireland. In the boardroom at the Admiralty, anxious glances were directed at the wind dial mounted on the wall to determine if the wind blew toward the west. But the Dutch fleet missed the opportunity to sortie provided by the mutinies because the enemy were as surprised by the upheaval as the British. In July the troops actually boarded the transports, only to be held in port by unfavorable winds and the failure of the Brest fleet to be ready.

Wolfe Tone, again calling himself "General Smith," was the guest of Admiral Jan Williem de Winter in the flagship *Vrijheid*, seventy-four. Both men were passionate whist players, and as the fleet waited to sail passed the time at cards. De Winter had entered the Dutch Navy in 1762 as a boy of twelve and had only reached the rank of lieutenant when the French Revolution broke out. A strong republican, he entered the French Army, and rose to the rank of general. When the French overran Holland and created the Batavian Republic, he returned home, to be appointed admiral of the Texel fleet even though he had never commanded so much as a single ship. Physically, he was almost as large a man as Adam Duncan.

As time passed, Tone fretted away his heart as the sailing encountered delay after delay. "The wind is as foul as possible this morning; it cannot be worse," he wrote in his diary. "Hell! Hell! Hell! Allah! Allah! I am in a most devouring rage." Soon it became worse. The troops on the crowded transports fell sick, and the best weather for an invasion came and went. The operation was dealt a fatal blow when General Lazare Hoch, the major supporter of Ireland's cause in France, died prematurely at twenty-nine from tuberculosis. Not long after, the enterprise was aborted.

Nevertheless, Duncan and his storm-battered ships maintained their long vigil off the Dutch coast. Every day, in all weather, his frigates reported on the state of the Dutch fleet of some twenty ships to Duncan, who remained in the Downs off the east coast of Kent, with the main fleet. The Admiralty repeatedly promised him replacements and reinforcements, but was seldom true to its word because the North Sea fleet was a stepchild compared to the Channel fleet and St. Vincent's squadrons off Cádiz. The Admiralty fobbed off its oldest and least seaworthy vessels on Duncan, and he openly despaired of even keeping them afloat. The aptly named *Venerable* was in such poor condition that when it rained, her great cabin leaked incessantly. "When she has much motion she cracks as if she would go to pieces," he informed the Admiralty. Early in October, after nineteen weeks at sea, Duncan took his worst ships into Yarmouth for refit and left a scouting force to keep an eye on the Dutch.

On the morning of October 9, 1797, the lugger *Speculator* dashed into Yarmouth Roads under a full press of sail with the news that a Dutch fleet of sixteen ships of the line was at sea, heading south along the Dutch coast. For what purpose? None that could be readily ascertained. The Dutch government, having gone through the expense of mobilizing a fleet, apparently ordered Admiral de Winter to take the fleet to sea merely because something had to be done with it. Leaving five of his ships behind to join at sea, Duncan weighed with eleven of the line and by noon was steering for the Dutch coast. While the two fleets were equal in numbers and the Dutch were justly proud of their naval traditions,* de Winter's ships were lighter built and less powerful than Duncan's. The British had seven ships of seventy-four guns, seven of sixty-four, and a pair of fifties. The Dutch had three of seventy-four plus a seventy-two, five sixty-eights, and two sixty-fours, three fifty-fours and a forty-four.

Having learned that the British were at sea, de Winter put about and was heading north with his ships close inshore in a loose line. Taking advantage of their shallow draft, he intended to steer close-in with the hope of

---

*In June 1667 the Dutch admiral Michael de Ruyter sailed up the Thames to within twenty miles of London, sinking and burning merchant ships and men-of-war and bringing out the British flagship as a prize.

luring the heavier British ships onto a lee shore. But he overlooked several factors: the high standard of seamanship in the British fleet and the excellence of British gunnery, plus the fact that the British ships were equipped with carronades—which would do deadly work at close range, and which were lacking on the Dutch ships.

Three days after sailing—on the morning of October 12*—Duncan sighted the enemy fleet and at about nine o'clock ordered a general chase. Holding the weather gage, he was determined to close with the Dutch before they could take shelter in the shoals. With all sails set, his ships pounded down on de Winter in considerable disorder and in two groups of eight ships each, one headed by Duncan, himself, in *Venerable,* the other, to the south, by Vice Admiral Richard Onslow. The two opposing fleets were now about nine miles off the seaside village of Kamperduin, anglicized by the British to Camperdown.

At about eleven o'clock Duncan noted that the Dutch had backed their sails, as if waiting to give battle. He signaled his own ships to shorten sail so the slower vessels could catch up and re-form a line of battle. Then he ordered the ships to wear simultaneously to engage their opposite numbers in the enemy line. Before they could get back into column, however, the admiral saw that the Dutch were slowly drifting toward the shoals, where his fleet would be unable to reach them without the danger of running aground. With no time to be lost, Duncan threw formality by the board and hurled his two groups of ships on the enemy line. As de Winter later told him, this decision determined the outcome of the battle: "Your not waiting to form [a] line ruined me. If I had got nearer to the shore and you had attacked, I should probably have drawn both fleets on to it, and it would have been a victory to me, being on my own coast."

The accidental British formation resembled that adopted intentionally by Nelson at Trafalgar eight years later—two roughly equal parallel lines that were determined to pierce the enemy line at two places. To prevent the Dutch from slipping into shoal water, Duncan hoisted the signal to break through the enemy line and engage from the leeward. Worried that some ships might not see the signal in the thick weather, he followed it with the signal for close action and kept it flying. Some of his captains were bewildered by this plethora of signals. Captain John Inglis, of the seventy-four-gun *Belliqueux,* and a hotheaded Scot, threw his signal book to the deck. "Damn! No more signals," he swore. "Up wi' the hel-lem and gang into the middle o' it."

In the meantime, de Winter had tightened his line, and as the two groups

*October 11 in the logbooks of the fleet because the nautical day then ran from noon to noon.

of British vessels approached bow on, implacable and silent, his ships poured shot after shot into them. Duncan saw a midshipman ducking his head as *Venerable* came under fire, and he patted the lad on the back. "Very well, my boy, but don't do it again," said the stately old giant. "You might put your head in the way of a shot." When the pilot warned that the flagship was in shallow water and might run aground, Duncan told him to continue on, "for I am determined to fight the ships on land if I cannot by sea."

Onslow's southern division was the first to break through the Dutch line. At about 12:30 P.M. *Monarch,* his flagship, passed between *Haarlem,* sixty-eight, third from the rear of the enemy line, and *Jupiter,* seventy-two, the fourth. Several raking broadsides were fired into them, with devastating effect. Unexpectedly, the forty-four-gun frigate *Monnikendam* threw herself in Onslow's way. She took the full blast of *Monarch*'s broadsides and drifted off, out of control. Followed by his eight ships, Onslow doubled against the five rear Dutch ships and a dogfight ensued, with the British firing three broadsides to two by the Dutch. William Bligh's *Director* took an active role in the struggle.

To the north, *Venerable,* closely supported by *Ardent,* sixty-four, and *Triumph,* seventy-four, struck *Vrijheid,* the Dutch flagship, lying fifth from the van, at about 12:45 P.M. Duncan was unable to break the line at first because *Staats Generaal,* seventy-four, moved up to fill the gap. Putting his helm aport, the admiral ran under the latter's stern and gave her such a battering that she was forced to drop out of line. At one point *Venerable* was all but surrounded by Dutch ships and it appeared she might be overwhelmed, but Duncan's other vessels came up to support him. Soon the battle turned into general melees at the van and rear of the Dutch line, while the center was almost unengaged. Later de Winter was critical of the admiral in charge of these ships for failing to come to his assistance.

Unlike the French, the Dutch followed the British practice of firing at the hulls of the enemy ships rather than their rigging. The carnage in Duncan's ship was so great that at one moment he and the pilot were the only men unwounded on *Venerable*'s quarterdeck, and the casualties were equally severe on his other vessels. One British ship was holed ninety-eight times. Inglis's *Belliqueux* lost a quarter of her complement. *Ardent,* which was locked yardarm to yardarm in combat with *Vrijheid,* had forty men killed, including her captain, master, and two lieutenants, and ninety men were wounded. One sailor's wife served at a gun with her husband until a shot carried off one of her legs. Surgeon Robert Young* gave a graphic account of the hellish conditions in *Ardent*'s cockpit:

*Quoted in Christopher Lloyd, *St. Vincent & Camperdown,* pp. 146–147.

The whole cockpit, deck, cabins, wing berths and part of the cable tier . . . were covered with [wounded]. For a time they were laid on each other at the foot of the ladder. . . . Numbers, about 16, mortally wounded, died after they were brought down, among them the brave and worthy Captain [Richard] Burgess. . . . Joseph Bonheur had his right thigh taken off by cannon shot close to the pelvis, so that it was impossible to apply a tourniquet; his right arm was also shot to pieces. . . . Melancholy cries for assistance were addressed to me from every side by wounded and dying, and piteous moans and bewailing from pain and despair. . . . An explosion . . . abreast of the cockpit hatchway filled the hatchway with flame and in a moment 14 or 15 wretches tumbled down upon each other, their faces black as a cinder, their clothes blown to shatters and their hats on fire. . . . I was employed in operating and dressing until 4.0 in the morning, the action beginning about 1.0 in the afternoon. So great was my fatigue that I began several amputations under a dread of sinking before I had secured the blood vessels. . . .

In such a close action, superior British gunnery, including the murderous fire of their carronades plus the mutual support the captains gave to each other, took their toll of an obstinate enemy. *Hercules*, a Dutch sixty-four-gun ship, was turned into a flaming torch when a powder cask on her poop exploded and set fire to her rigging. Other ships were pummeled into submission. *Vrijheid* was dismasted, her scuppers ran with blood, and torn sails hung over her guns. She surrendered to a British officer who hailed her quarterdeck—her colors had been shot away—at about 3:00 P.M., almost the same time as *Jupiter*, flagship of the rear division. In all, the British captured seven ships of the line, two fifty-gun ships, and a pair of frigates. Because of the damage to his own ships and the gathering darkness with his ships on a lee shore, Duncan did not pursue the remaining Dutch vessels.

The "butcher's bill" was formidable on both sides. The British lost 224 killed and 796 wounded; the Dutch had 540 killed, 622 wounded, and 3,775 taken prisoner. Three of the prizes were so badly damaged they foundered at sea, and the rest were "only worth bringing into port to be exhibited as trophies." Those remaining in the hands of the Dutch were of little further use for front-line service, and the navy of the Batavian Republic was finished as a striking force. There was still one ceremony to be completed, however. Brought on board *Venerable* in a blood-stained uniform, Admiral de Winter proffered his sword to Duncan, who refused it, saying: "I would much rather a brave man's hand than his sword." The Dutchman took his defeat with good grace. He challenged his captor to a game of whist, and when he lost, wryly remarked that it was indeed very hard to be beaten twice in a day by the same man.

◠

BELLS PEALED AND bonfires blazed across Britain in celebration of the victory. Duncan was made a viscount and Onslow a baronet. The triumph restored the faith of the British public in the Royal Navy, and a public subscription for the families of those killed in action raised five thousand pounds in a single day. Sailors who only a few months before had refused to follow their officers had fought like demons. Camperdown was soon eclipsed by Nelson's more famous victories, but it was then seen as a crowning deliverance from Britain's enemies.

However, another attempt at making peace was rejected by the Directory, which wanted a complete British surrender, and the war went on. Without a war, its members feared the very reason for its existence might be questioned. To boost British morale, a service of thanksgiving was held at St. Paul's. French, Spanish, and Dutch flags captured by Howe at the Glorious First of June, by Jervis at St. Vincent, and by Duncan at Camperdown were paraded through the streets of London before being placed on the altar of the cathedral.

Not long after, a slight figure with one eye, an empty right sleeve pinned to his coat, and the rolling gait of a sailor went to St. George's Church on Hanover Square from his temporary lodgings in Bond Street, and left his own brief thanksgiving prayer, to be read aloud by the vicar the following Sunday: "An officer desires to return thanks to Almighty God for his perfect recovery from a severe wound and also for the many mercies bestowed upon him."

CHAPTER 12

Proud New Frigates

ON THE MORNING OF September 20, 1797, while Britain was girding for an invasion, a new navy was making its appearance. A large and boisterous crowd had gathered at Edmund Hartt's shipyard in the North End of Boston to watch the launching of the U.S. Navy frigate *Constitution*. Shortly before noon, the tide reached flood, and Colonel George Claghorne, who had supervised the construction of the vessel, ordered the shoring timbers knocked out. A ragged cheer rose and then died. Instead of gliding gracefully into the water, the trim hull hung motionless on the ways. Claghorne ordered screw jacks and wedges applied to force the vessel to move, but she slid only a few feet before coming to a dead stop. Two days later another attempt was made to launch her, but this, too, ended in failure. Not until another month later, on October 21, 1797, did *Constitution* finally slip into the waters of Boston Harbor. A similar pattern of agonizingly fitful starts and stops marked the founding of the navy in which she served.

From the end of the War of Independence until the inauguration of George Washington as president in 1789, the United States had not been so much governed as maintained in caretaker status under the feeble Articles of Confederation enacted during the Revolution. There was no chief executive, and Congress functioned as little more than a council of ambassadors of an uneasy league of thirteen more or less sovereign republics. Funds were short, there was only a shadow of an army, and there was no navy at all. Moreover, most Americans had an inherent fear of a strong, centralized government, born out of the struggle for independence.

Once peace came, Yankee trading vessels carried the Stars and Stripes around the world. But no longer enjoying the protection of the British flag, they were prey for rapacious corsairs sailing from the Barbary states of Morocco, Algiers, Tunis, and Tripoli on the coast of North Africa. For two centuries these satrapies of the Ottoman Empire had levied tribute on the commerce of all nations. Unless paid bribes, they seized passing ships and enslaved their crews and passengers until they were ransomed. The

Europeans paid the tribute, arguing only over the amount, not the principle. Britain and France could have ended these depredations, but allowed the pirates to operate against the trade of their rivals while their own ships were protected by their navies. Thus, the corsairs viewed the American merchant marine—the second largest in the world—as fair game because the new nation neither paid tribute nor possessed a navy to protect its ships.

In 1785, the year in which *Alliance,* the last ship of the Continental Navy, was sold, Algerian corsairs captured two American vessels and enslaved their crews. Thomas Jefferson and John Adams, the American ministers to Paris and London, respectively, who had the task of negotiating treaties with the Barbary states, agreed that in the long run it would be cheaper to organize a navy to protect American shipping than to pay tribute. This, said Jefferson, would provide the government "with the safest of all instruments of coercion." But, as Adams noted, prospects for such a service were not bright owing to the lack of funds and sectional rivalries similar to those that delayed formation of the Continental Navy at the start of the Revolution. Consequently nothing was done to resist the demands of these seagoing brigands.

The Constitution, which went into effect in 1789, authorized Congress to "to provide and maintain a navy," but during Washington's first term there was little discussion of the issue. In 1790 General Henry Knox, who as secretary of war dealt with such naval matters as there were, secured estimates of the cost of several frigates. The next year Secretary of State Jefferson recommended that a naval force be fitted out to deal with the Barbary pirates. The sole result of his recommendation and Knox's estimates was a Senate report suggesting that a navy be organized "as soon as the state of public finance will admit."

The eruption of war between Britain and France in 1793 brought matters to a head. A truce between Portugal and the Algerians, negotiated with British help, ended a Portuguese blockade of the Strait of Gibraltar that had kept the corsairs bottled up in the Mediterranean. Pirate ships suddenly swarmed into the Atlantic, and within two months captured eleven American ships and more than a hundred American sailors. Many Americans were convinced that the truce was part of a British plot to destroy American commerce with the Mediterranean. Britain claimed, however, that its Portuguese ally had lifted the blockade so she could use her ships for other purposes.

Reacting to the seizure of the American vessels, the House of Representatives approved, on January 2, 1794, a resolution stating that "a naval force adequate to the protection of the commerce of the United States against the Algerian corsairs ought to be provided." This resolution, approved by a margin of only two votes, was referred to a committee dominated by pronavy congressmen. Eighteen days later it recommended the construction of four frigates of forty-four guns and two ships of twenty guns at a total cost of six hundred thousand dollars. Debate on the resolution followed sectional lines. Northern and tidewater representatives supported creation of a navy; inland and southern members, with the exception of representatives of South Carolina mercantile interests, were opposed.

Opponents of the measure charged that a navy would only fatten the pockets of northern merchants, embroil the new nation in foreign adventures, be a drain on the public purse, and saddle the country with an ever-expanding naval establishment that would be a touchstone of tyranny. Supporters argued that if the nation had a navy it would no longer have to pay tribute or ransom, maritime insurance would be less costly, and inasmuch as a navy operated offshore, it could scarcely be an instrument of domestic tyranny. A navy, they said, would not only protect American commerce but also force the warring French and British to respect the nation's rights as a neutral.

This struggle over the navy was the first of a series of running battles between the newly emerging political parties that marked the early days of the republic. The Republicans, advocates of states' rights and southern agrarian interests and ancestors of today's Democrats, largely opposed the formation of a navy, while the Federalists, who favored a strong central government and were supported by the northern commercial interests, advocated a navy.

As finally approved on March 27, 1797, the Navy Act authorized the procurement of six frigates—four of forty-four guns and two of thirty-six guns—and provided for the number, pay, and rations of the officers and crews. But the measure contained a "poison pill." To ensure approval, its supporters accepted an amendment providing that work on the ships would be summarily halted if peace terms were concluded between the United States and the dey of Algiers. Shortly after the bill was passed—as if to emphasize the deep division over the navy—Congress authorized the expenditure of eight hundred thousand dollars to obtain a treaty with the Algerians and to ransom the American captives.

PRESIDENT WASHINGTON and General Knox decided to provide the navy with newly built ships rather than convert lubberly merchant vessels into warships. Writing to Joshua Humphreys, a prominent Philadelphia Quaker shipbuilder who had a hand in the design of the Continental Navy's first frigates, Knox suggested that "the vessels should combine such qualities of strength, durability, swiftness of sailing, and force, as to render them superior to any frigate belonging to the European powers." Lacking quantity, the new navy would emphasize quality. Several other men worked on the project, but the final designs were basically the work of Humphreys.

Longer, wider in beam, and with stout sides and fine lines, the larger of these vessels resembled cut-down ships of the line rather than any existing frigate. They were designed to outrun any ship they could not outfight and were intended as commerce raiders as well as combat vessels. Humphreys was influenced by French designs, but to strengthen his outsize ships, added original features, such as diagonal "riders," to the internal structure that had not been seen before. They had wider gangways on the spar deck, transforming it into an upper gun deck. Although the larger vessels were rated at forty-four guns, these "superfrigates" sometimes carried as many as sixty. Unlike the Royal Navy's standard thirty-two-gun frigate, which was armed with eighteen-pounders, the American vessels carried a main battery of twenty-four-pound guns on their gun decks and another complete tier of guns, usually carronades, on the spar, or flush upper deck, which made them virtual two-deckers.

To distribute the financial benefits of the construction program and to encourage popular support of the navy, the work of building and outfitting the ships was spread up and down the Atlantic coast to privately operated shipyards, establishing a pattern of distributing defense contracts for political reasons that has endured. *Congress,* of thirty-six guns, was built in Portsmouth, New Hampshire; *Constitution,* forty-four, at Boston; *President,* forty-four, at New York; *United States,* forty-four, at Philadelphia; *Constellation,* thirty-six, at Baltimore; and *Chesapeake,* forty-four, at Norfolk. Knox stipulated that the ships were to be built of live oak and red cedar, which were five times as durable as the white oak commonly used in America.

Work on the ships proceeded in fits and starts because there was no reserve of seasoned timber and because of a shortage of guns. Between three hundred and four hundred cannons were bought from British foundries to fill the gap. Unfortunately for the navy's advocates, a treaty was signed with the dey of Algiers in September 1795, and in compliance with the Navy Act of 1794, all work on the frigates was to be suspended immediately. President Washington strongly opposed the stoppage on grounds that it would be wasteful. While it was true that the cost of completing the ships would be higher than originally estimated, Washington noted, the price of peace was also high. It cost almost $1 million, including $525,000 in bribes and ransom, the gift to the Algerians of a custom-built thirty-six-gun frigate, and an annual tribute of $21,000 in naval stores. After considerable debate, Congress allowed the completion of two forty-fours and a thirty-six—*Constitution, United States,* and *Constellation.*

〜

IN THE MEANTIME, relations with France had become strained. Under the terms of the Treaty of Alliance of 1778, which brought the French into the War of Independence, the United States agreed, in case of war between France and Britain, to help defend the French West Indies and throw open her ports to French privateers. The new French minister to the United States, Edmond Genêt, added to the tension through a series of unneutral acts, including arming privateers in American ports, meddling in domestic politics, and mounting filibustering expeditions against adjoining British and Spanish territory.

But with the Royal Navy dominating the sea lanes and with British troops, in defiance of the Treaty of Paris, occupying a line of forts along the western frontier, the new nation had no desire to risk a war with Britain by implementing the terms of the alliance, much to the anger of the French. Besides, America's sympathies were divided. Most ordinary Americans favored France because of their admiration for the French Revolution, while the more prosperous citizens, alarmed by the excesses of the revolutionary regime, sided with the British.

Yet no matter where their sympathies lay, the majority of Americans wanted to stay out of the war. Neutrality was profitable. Yankee farmers prospered as the French and British bid up the prices of foodstuffs and commodities. Shipowners reaped large profits carrying American goods to Europe, and gained a foothold in the trade with the French colonies in the Caribbean, from which they had been barred. To survive and prosper, the United States had to maintain a delicate balance between the belligerents. President Washington, who sympathized with the British, and Secretary of State Jefferson, who favored France, agreed that the Franco-American alliance of 1778 had outlived its usefulness and that neutrality was the best policy for the United States.

American anger was directed first at the British. Fighting for her life, Britain flatly refused to accept American arguments that neutral ships could trade freely with all the belligerents. The British contended that trade restricted in peacetime could not be open in time of war and seized goods carried in American ships from the Caribbean to France. Upward of 250 vessels may have been taken in the first year of the war. Moreover, Royal Navy captains used the right of search to impress likely hands into the king's service on grounds that they were really British subjects. It was a difficult thing to try to prove American citizenship in the face of a boarding party armed to the teeth and in search of prime seamen.

In 1794 Chief Justice John Jay, who was serving as a special envoy to Britain, negotiated a commercial treaty with the British. Under the terms of Jay's Treaty, the British relinquished the disputed frontier forts and opened the British home islands to American trade but gave no ground on American demands for the freedom of neutral trade. The treaty was unpopular in the United States, and Jay was hanged in effigy. Nevertheless, the agreement reduced tension between the two countries and the possibility that they might blunder into war. But reconciliation with the British complicated relations with France. The French Directory was aggrieved by Jay's treaty and tried to bully the United States into joining the war on their side. When the Americans refused, French commerce raiders harassed American shipping, seizing 312 vessels between October 1796 and June 1797.

As soon as John Adams, who had played a leading role in the organization of the Continental Navy, assumed the presidency on March 4, 1797, he called Congress into special session to deal with the crisis. "A Naval power, next to the militia, is the natural defense of the United States," he declared. Adams, a Federalist, sought authority to complete *Constitution*, *United States*, and *Constellation* and to procure several smaller vessels to help protect America's seaborne commerce. The Republicans, led by Jefferson, now vice president, suspected that Adams's request for approval of this naval program was but a step from a declaration of war against France and opposed the president's proposal. Nevertheless, with pronavy Federalist majorities in control of Congress, a new Navy Act was passed after acrimonious debate on July 1, 1797, enabling Adams to order the three frigates rushed to completion.

United States slid into the Delaware River on May 10. Work was speeded up on the other two ships, and *Constellation* was launched at Baltimore on September 7. After the two failures to get *Constitution* into the water, she joined the others six weeks later. Captains John Barry, Thomas Truxtun, and Samuel Nicholson, all veterans of the Continental Navy or successful privateersmen during the Revolution, had already been named to command the ships and helped supervise their construction. There were far more applicants for commissions in the new navy than berths, and would-be officers resorted to political influence to ensure appointment. The rules and regulations drafted by Adams for the Continental Navy were again put into effect. Building, arming, and maintaining the frigates cost about $2,510,730 from 1794 to 1798, but the savings in insurance charges paid by American shipowners during 1798 alone was estimated at $8,655,566—far more than the cost of the fleet.

In an attempt to head off a full-scale clash with France, Adams dispatched a three-man commission to Paris to negotiate an agreement with the Directory similar to the treaty Jay had reached with the British. For several months the commissioners were given the runaround, but just as they were packing up to return home, they were approached by three representatives of Charles Maurice de Talleyrand-Périgord, the apostate Catholic bishop who had become French foreign minister. These agents, accompanied by a woman—without whom no European intrigue was complete—demanded a $250,000 bribe for Talleyrand and a large loan to the French government as a prerequisite for negotiations. The Americans flatly rejected the proposal. One, Charles C. Pinckney, a South Carolina Federalist, is supposed to have declared, "No! No! Not a sixpence!," which was inflated into the patriotic "Millions for defense, but not one cent for tribute!"—even though the nation was paying tribute to the Barbary states.

When Adams issued a report in which the French agents were identified only as "X," "Y," and "Z," war fever swept the country. Although most leaders of the Federalist party wanted an all-out war with France so that New Orleans and Florida might be taken from France's ally Spain, Adams limited the struggle to a naval war. Beginning in early 1798, Congress appropriated new funds for the seemingly endless task of outfitting the three frigates already launched; ordered work resumed on the three left unfinished since the end of the Algerian crisis; and empowered the president to obtain an additional two dozen smaller ships. Logically, a declaration of a state of hostilities should have followed, but neither the United States nor France observed that formality. As a result, the two-and-a-half-year conflict that ensued was known as the Quasi-War.

THE UNITED STATES had acquired a navy—and a war in which it was to be used—but had no plans for deploying it. This was remedied on April 30, 1798, when Adams signed a bill creating the Department of the Navy. Benjamin Stoddert, a merchant and loyal Federalist living in Georgetown, then part of Maryland, was named the first secretary of the navy.* The choice was a good one. Stoddert was a wounded veteran of the Revolution, and later secretary to the Continental Board of War, predecessor of the War Department. Thus he was familiar with military logistics as well as ship design and construction, and had a smattering of knowledge of matters pertaining to the operation of a fleet. One officer called him "a man of few words." To assist him the new secretary had a chief clerk, Charles W. Goldsborough, who was to hold the post for almost fifty years; a half dozen junior clerks; and naval agents at the various ports to supervise construction and purchase supplies. In Philadelphia, the Navy Office, as it was commonly called, initially transacted its business at 139 Walnut Street and then at the corner of Eighth and Chestnut Streets.

*Adams's first choice, George Cabot of Boston, refused the post.

Under Stoddert's stewardship the U.S. Navy eventually grew to fifty-four vessels, including new vessels, converted merchantmen, revenue cutters, gifts from the patriotic citizens of seaport towns, and craft captured from the French. Navy yards were opened at Portsmouth, New Hampshire; New York; and Norfolk, Virginia. Stoddert also began work on a dozen seventy-four-gun ships, but they were never completed. At peak strength, "Stoddert's Navy" numbered about 750 officers and some 6,000 men, plus another 1,100 officers and men in the Marine Corps, which was established in July 1798. There was no difficulty in recruiting seamen because there were few privateers to compete for their services because French commerce was almost nonexistent. Unlike the Royal Navy, seaman signed on for a fixed enlistment, usually a year, commencing from the time when their ship left port. Able seamen were paid $17 a month—triple the rate in the British service.

Who were these men? Little information about them has survived, but certain conclusions can be drawn based on studies of merchant seamen at this time.* Most were young—running from the late teens to the late twenties—and remained at sea for only about fifteen years. Nearly 18 percent were black, probably freedmen, at a time when free blacks totaled only 2.5 percent of the American population. Blacks were allowed to enlist in the navy and were not segregated on board ship, although they were not accepted into the Marine Corps. Foreigners, especially English deserters from the Royal Navy, sometimes made up half the crews.

The French, blockaded for the most part in Brest and the Mediterranean by the Royal Navy, sent few large warships across the Atlantic. Instead they relied on a war against trade—the *guerre de course*—conducted by a handful of frigates and swarms of privateers. Commerce raiders darted out of Caribbean ports and plundered American shipping almost at will. Some were licensed by Victor Hugues, the "Caribbean Robespierre." To meet this threat, Stoddert concentrated his ships in coastal waters. Thus the story of the ensuing war is told not in heroic battles between great fleets but in the safe passage of convoys, the recapture of vessels taken by the French, and the driving off of commerce raiders from the major shipping lanes.

French privateer skippers were so brazen that they operated within sight of the American coast. In fact, the first prize captured by America's new navy was taken just outside Egg Harbor, New Jersey. She was the twelve-gun schooner *La Croyable*, which had taken several Yankee vessels before being captured on July 7, 1798, by the twenty-gun sloop-of-war *Delaware*, to the surprise of the French captain, who was unaware that the

*See Dye, "Early American Merchant Seafarers," *Proceedings* of the American Antiquarian Society 120. Also Bolster, *Black Jacks: African-American Seamen in the Age of Sail.*

Americans even had a navy. *Delaware* was a converted merchantman under the command of Captain Stephen Decatur Sr., an old privateersmen whose soon-to-be famous son was a midshipman on the frigate *United States*. Taken into the navy as *Retaliation*, the schooner was recaptured four months later by the French, and then again by the Americans.

These coastal operations allowed the captains of the new frigates to work out the problems inherent in any experimental design. Some officers were wary of these vessels because they thought them too large and too clumsy to handle easily, but with time and experience the ships achieved their full potential. Stoddert assigned twenty-one ships, including *United States*, *Constitution*, and *Constellation*, to the West Indies, with orders to "rid those seas . . . of French commissioned armed vessels. . . . We have nothing to fear but inactivity." By the end of 1798 the U.S. Navy had become so vigilant that the French retreated to the Caribbean.

Stoddert was convinced that concerted action by strong squadrons would be more effective than random patrols by one or two vessels, and organized his ships into four squadrons. Varying in size from three to ten ships, these units were commanded by Captains John Barry, Thomas Truxtun, Stephen Decatur Sr., and Thomas Tingley. To keep the ships on station as long as possible, without ruining their sailing qualities by loading them down with provisions or becoming dependent on the rapacious West Indies merchants, Stoddert sent out supply ships from the United States, and over time the U.S. Navy developed a long-legged capacity uncommon among the world's navies.

The assignment of these squadrons to the Caribbean brought the Americans into an area where war had been under way since 1793—and whether they liked it or not, they became unofficial allies of the British. The Royal Navy deployed four to five times more men-of-war in the West Indies than the U.S. Navy, and British ships chased and fought the same French cruisers and privateers. Both navies escorted each other's merchantmen, and exchanged recognition signals, while the American squadrons operated from British bases.

No man better personified the increasing professionalism and aggressive spirit of the fledgling navy than Thomas Truxtun, the captain of *Constellation*. Born on Long Island in 1755, he went to sea at age twelve. Three years later he was snatched from the deck of a merchantman and pressed into a British man-of-war. The youngster's abilities attracted the attention of his captain, who offered Truxtun the promise of advancement if he remained in the Royal Navy. Truxtun obtained his release, however, and by the time he was twenty had become a captain in the merchant service. During the War of Independence he captained several successful privateers and emerged from the conflict with a respectable fortune, which he invested with excellent results in the newly established China trade. Truxtun was not only a capable seaman but something of a scholar, too. In 1794, the same year in which he was commissioned a captain in the U.S. Navy, he published a treatise on navigation and wind currents. This was followed by books on signaling and naval tactics.

Under Truxtun's command, *Constellation* was a taut ship. Some of her crew, unused to the strict demands of the naval service, complained, but he was not a brutal man. Rather than having malefactors flogged, Truxtun preferred to withhold their rum rations.* One evening Midshipman David Porter was invited to dine with the captain and made the mistake of protesting the harsh treatment he had received from the captain and the frigate's first lieutenant, John Rodgers. He added that he was giving thought to resigning from the service.

"Why, you young dog!" Truxtun thundered. "If I can help it you shall never leave the navy! Swear at you? Damn it, sir—every time I do that you go up a round on the ladder of promotion! As for the first lieutenant's blowing up at you every day, why, sir, 'tis because he loves you and would not have you grow up a conceited young coxcombe. Go . . . and let us have no more whining."

Cruising alone off the island of Nevis at about noon on February 9, 1799, *Constellation* fell in with a large vessel that hoisted American colors as the Yankee frigate sailed up to inspect her. The stranger failed to respond to American and British recognition signals, and Truxtun was convinced she was a French man-of-war. As if to confirm his suspicions, the vessel broke out the French tricolor. She was *Insurgente*, a forty-gun frigate reputed to be one of the fastest ships in the French Navy. Although she carried four more guns than *Constellation*, her broadsides were less powerful. As the two vessels maneuvered for position, a sudden squall carried away the Frenchmen's main-topmast.

As soon as *Constellation*'s starboard guns began to bear on the enemy vessel, Truxtun unleashed a broadside into her. The French ship returned fire with spirit and swerved toward her adversary. "Stand by to board!" the French captain called to his men. Truxtun was alert to the danger, and his handier ship swept ahead of *Insurgente* and across her bow, pouring a murderous raking fire into her opponent's hull at close range. The battle raged for about an hour and a half, until the French vessel was a shambles. *Constellation* had just crossed her stern to rake her again when the French hauled down their colors.

A boarding party reported *Insurgente* "resembled a slaughterhouse,"

---

*One of the chief malcontents, Truxtun discovered, was an Englishman who proved to be one of the *Hermione* mutineers and was serving in *Constellation* under a false name. He was turned over to the Royal Navy and hanged.

with seventy of her crew dead or wounded. The French had fired high, and although *Constellation* was much cut up aloft, her total casualties were only one dead and two wounded.* *Insurgente* was taken into the U.S. Navy.† In his account of the action, Truxtun related that the French captain charged that "I have caused a War with France" and added, "if so, I am glad of it, for I detest Things being done by Halves."

Just about a year latter, *Constellation* engaged in another memorable battle. Following the encounter with *Insurgente*, Truxtun, dissatisfied with his vessel's sailing qualities, had altered her armament. The twenty-four-pound long guns of her main battery were replaced by eighteen-pounders, and to compensate for the loss of weight of metal, he substituted thirty-two-pound carronades for the long twelves on the quarterdeck. *Constellation* was now relatively weaker at long range but more powerful close in. She was sailing off Guadeloupe on February 1, 1800, when a lookout sighted a large ship on the horizon. Truxtun surmised that she was *Vengeance*, a fifty-four-gun French frigate, which he had been warned was in the area.

Although the French vessel outgunned *Constellation*, the enemy declined to give battle and clapped on all sail. Following a day-long chase that ran on into the darkness, the Yankee frigate closed with her. Night fell, and the men on both ships stood to their guns in the eerie light cast by the battle lanterns as the distance between the two vessels narrowed to little more than pistol shot. Without waiting to be hailed, the French fired first. *Constellation*'s guns, double-shotted at Truxtun's command, immediately replied with a broadside that slammed into *Vengeance*'s hull.

To make up for the deficiency in firepower, the American gun crews were ordered to "load and fire as fast as possible." In better trim than previously, *Constellation* repeatedly blocked attempts by the French to rake. Over the next five hours the two ships traded broadsides, and both suffered severe damage. The battle was "as close and obstinate an action as was ever fought between two ships of war," said an American officer. At close range, *Constellation*'s carronades wreaked havoc on her opponent.

Shortly before 1:00 A.M. Truxtun reported that "the Enemy's fire was completely silenced." Believing *Vengeance* had struck, he ordered *Constellation* laid alongside her, only to discover that his own mainmast was "totally unsupported by rigging." Truxtun broke off the action and made a last-minute effort to put up new rigging, but it was too late. The mast toppled

*The dead man was not a battle casualty but had been run through by Lieutenant Andrew Sterett—perhaps unnecessarily—for deserting his post at one of the guns.

†A year later, *Insurgente* was lost at sea with all her crew of 340 men.

A VIEW of the AMERICAN FRIGATE,CONSTELLATION,capturing the FRENCH NATIONAL FRIGATE,L'INSURGENTE,within fight of BASSETERRE,Feb'y9th1799.

The American frigate *Constellation* overpowers the French *Insurgente* in the West Indies on February 9, 1799. (Beverley Robinson Collection, U.S. Naval Academy Museum)

into the sea, taking with it a midshipman and three topmen. In the confusion, the shattered French frigate limped off into the darkness, with her crew at the pumps. Before arriving at Curaçao, she lost her mainmast, foremast, and mizzen-topmast. An American prisoner reported that she had been hit nearly two hundred times, with several shots plowing through both sides of her hull. In his report the French captain described *Constellation* as a two-decker—quite a compliment to the fighting qualities of the Yankee frigate and her officers and men.

Before the Quasi-War petered out, several other American naval vessels gave a good account of themselves, especially the twelve-gun schooners *Enterprise* and *Experiment*. In a single cruise in 1800, *Enterprise* captured seven French armed vessels, including a large fourteen-gun privateer. Later that year she bagged thirteen more vessels along with three hundred prisoners. *Experiment* was almost as lucky, capturing two privateers as well as seizing several American merchantmen that had been taken by the French. The frigate *Boston,* of twenty-eight guns, pounded the French corvette *Berceau,* twenty-four, into submission in a vigorous five-hour fight in which both vessels were repeatedly forced to draw off for repairs. The

American ascendancy in the Caribbean was reflected by a sharp drop in insurance rates for merchantmen traversing this area.

Having reaped such success, Stoddert settled on a more ambitious program of operations. Once the hurricane season hit the West Indies in 1799, he planned to send *Constitution* and *United States* to ravage the coast of France. The plan was a good one and might have produced dramatic results, but delays ashore prevented it from being carried out. Later, under the prodding of merchants doing business in the East Indies, the thirty-two-gun frigate *Essex*, built by public subscription by the citizens of Essex County, Massachusetts, was ordered to escort a convoy to Java, cruise for privateers in Sunda Strait, and then return home with another convoy. Under the command of Captain Edward Preble, she was the first American warship to cross the equator, double the Cape of Good Hope, and show the flag in the East Indies. U.S. Navy ships also supported the Haitian revolutionary regime of Toussaint L'Overture in his battles with the French for the island's freedom.

In the meantime, President Adams had begun negotiations with France for an end to hostilities. Leaders of the Federalist Party wished the war to continue, but Adams unselfishly put the nation's welfare above that of his party. Even though he fully realized that peace would result in the collapse of the Federalists' popularity and probably cost him reelection, he pressed ahead with the negotiations. Seven months of talks ended when the French, who recognized that the conflict was driving the United States into the arms of Britain, gave up their insistence that the Treaty of Alliance of 1778 was still in force and accepted the American view of neutral rights. On the other side, the United States dropped its claim for twenty million dollars in reimbursements for damages inflicted on American commerce. The settlement was unpopular, and as Adams had foreseen, he was defeated by Thomas Jefferson in 1800. But he was unbowed and regarded the successful conclusion of the war and the abrogation of the 1778 treaty as triumphs of his presidential team.

Before the Federalists relinquished control of the government, they took steps to protect the navy from the budgetary ax certain to be swung by the incoming Republican administration. On March 3, 1801, the day before the new president was inaugurated, Congress approved an act providing for a peacetime naval establishment. Based on Secretary Stoddart's recommendations, it authorized the president to dispose of the fleet but ordered the retention of the following frigates: *United States, Constitution, President, Chesapeake, Philadelphia, Constellation, New York, Boston, Adams, Essex, John Adams,* and *General Greene.* Six of the ships to be retained were to be kept in commission, while the rest were to be laid up.

With exception of 9 captains, 36 lieutenants, and 150 midshipmen, all the officers were to be dismissed from the service with four months' pay, although Stoddert had recommended the formation of a reserve of officers on half pay, following the practice of the Royal Navy. Frigates on active duty were allowed only two-thirds of their usual complements. These reductions were drastic, but as Charles Goldsborough said, "the existence of the [naval] establishment could be preserved by no other means than by reducing it to its lowest possible scale."

Nevertheless, for the U.S. Navy, the undeclared naval war with France had been a success. While some of the American commanders left over from the Continental Navy had proved superannuated, many had served with distinction. American ships and seamen had proven their worth in battle and provided protection for American trade. Benjamin Stoddert, with only a minimal staff and resources, had effectively established the navy as a fighting force with some claim to permanence. In all these activities, however, the U.S. Navy's secret ally was the Royal Navy, whose blockade of Europe denied the French Navy free movement to the theater of war in the Caribbean.

CHAPTER 13

"A Band of Brothers"

AN ADMIRAL'S FLAG snapping at her fore-topmast, the 120-gun three-decker *L'Orient* signaled to the huge convoy of transports and supply ships assembled in Toulon Harbor to make sail shortly after dawn on May 19, 1798. General Napoleon Bonaparte, already feeling queasy as the flagship rolled in the chop, watched from her quarterdeck as the 180 vessels struggled into some sort of order as they proceeded to sea. There were so many ships that numbers were painted on their sterns to identify them. Crammed belowdecks on the transports were 17,000 soldiers, 700 horses, and several hundred artillery pieces. Thirteen ships of the line deliberately plowed ahead as 7 frigates darted about the convoy like sheepdogs, trying to keep their clumsy flock in order. As it pressed on to the east, this fleet was swelled by convoys from Corsica and from Genoa and Civitavecchia on the Italian coast, bringing the total number of troops to 40,000. Only Bonaparte and his top commanders knew where they were bound.

Following the young general's stunning success in Italy and the death of Lazar Hoche, the Directory had named Bonaparte to command of the Army of England, with orders to prepare for a long-awaited, long-desired cross-Channel invasion. In early February 1798 he toured the ports of northern France, Belgium, and Holland to inspect preparations for the invasion. Barges and fishing boats were being converted to carry infantry, cavalry, artillery, and stores, and new craft were under construction. At each port he subjected the officers to questioning, and astonished them with the depth of his interrogation. In the cold, calm gaze of his gray eyes, they saw a quality that inspired devotion in some, fear in others. One day the dour winter sky cleared long enough for the general to catch his first tantalizing glimpse of the white cliffs of Dover on the far shore.

Unlike the civilian members of the Directory who looked on the deceptively narrow Channel—La Manche to the French—as merely an unusually wide river, Bonaparte knew that amphibious operations are the most complex in war. Vast amounts of shipping would be required to mount an invasion, and these vessels had to be protected as they crossed some of the most stormy, tideswept waters in the world. And more than one beachhead would be required, which meant that the arrival of the various landing forces would have to be coordinated with the differences in tides.

On his return to Paris, Bonaparte told the Directory that an invasion of Britain was impractical as long as the Royal Navy held command of the Channel. "To perform a descent upon England without being master of the seas is a very daring operation and very difficult to put into effect," he reported. Moreover, the military and naval resources available were totally inadequate. The Atlantic fleet was firmly blockaded in Brest, there were not enough landing craft to ferry the necessary troops, and the nights would soon be too short to cover the passage of the invasion force. With most of Continental Europe already subject to France, Bonaparte said that the nation should either make peace with England or create a second front where her navy could not interfere.

Bonaparte suggested an invasion of Egypt to cut Britain's lifeline to India. He had apparently been thinking about such an expedition for some time. From his earliest youth he was attracted by the mystery and lure of the East, and the year before, he had carried away all the books on the area from Milan's famed Ambrosian Library. Having played Caesar in Italy, he now dreamed of emulating Alexander and establishing an empire in the East. "This little Europe is too small a field," the general told an aide. "Great renown can only be won in the East."

Britain's industry and trade were closely bound to Asia, and India was the citadel of her power in the East, he observed. Without India, Britain could not carry on her lucrative commerce with China and the East Indies and would be unable to continue to finance the war. There were several favorable auguries for the expedition. The Royal Navy had been driven from the Mediterranean while the Ottoman sultan, who ostensibly ruled Egypt, was too weak to challenge any violation of his territory. Moreover, the self-perpetuating body of slave-soldiers, the Mamelukes, who actually controlled the country, could not withstand a French army. Impressed by Bonaparte's reasoning and aware of the danger of having a wolfishly ambitious hero on hand with nothing to do, the Directory acceded to his plan.

On April 12, 1798, Bonaparte was named commander in chief of the Army of the East and directed to take possession of Egypt for the French Republic. Only a man supremely confident of his own invincibility would have undertaken such risks. The expedition would have to travel the entire length of the Mediterranean to a hostile coast where the French had no base. By secrecy and evasive routing, he hoped to attain the surprise that was the key element of his plan. Napoleon's orders made no specific mention of Egypt or India, but he intended to occupy Egypt and then march through Syria and Persia to India and found a great new empire in the East.

To further this object, he enlisted a corps of antiquarians, chemists, artists, engineers, geologists, and naturalists to explore the captured territory and lay the foundations of the new imperial order.

The task of getting the expedition to Egypt was placed in the hands of Vice Admiral François-Paul Brueys d'Aigallieri. Unlike many flag officers of the postrevolutionary navy, he was an experienced sea officer. Brueys had served under the Comte de Grasse in the West Indies and was one of the few aristocratic officers not to flee France in the wake of the Revolution. He had served as captain of a seventy-four-gun ship, stood firm against mutinous elements in his crew, and as a rear admiral supplied naval support for Bonaparte's Italian campaign.

Brueys combed the ports of southern France, western Italy and Corsica for ships and seamen. Merchantmen were barred from sailing so both the vessels and their crews could be funneled into the expedition. Many of the troops were veterans of Bonaparte's old Italian command, and to confuse British spies, the gathering force was called "the left wing of the Army of Italy." That so much was accomplished in little more than a month is testimony to Bonaparte's skills and ruthless efficiency. On the eve of embarkation, he reminded the troops of past victories:

> Two years ago I came to take command of you. At that time you were on the Ligurian Coast, in the greatest want, lacking everything. . . . I promised to put an end to your privations. I led you into Italy. There all was given you in abundance. Have I not kept my word? [Shouts of Yes! Yes!] . . . I will now lead you into a country where by your future deeds you will surpass even those that are astonishing your admirers and you will render to the republic such services as she has a right to expect from an invincible army.

The soldiers cheered and shouted, "Long live the immortal Republic!" Fewer than half were to see their native land again.

⤳

BRITISH INTELLIGENCE WAS well aware of the powerful armament being assembled in southern France and on the Italian coast, but French operational security was so tight it was unable to fathom the expedition's destination. Rumors and tantalizing snippets of information flowed in. Some observers were convinced the French were going to attack Portugal; other targets included Naples; Sicily; Malta; Greece; Ireland, where rebellion was about to flare; or even Britain herself. Only Henry Dundas suspected that Bonaparte was going to Egypt, but the suggestion was ignored. To ascertain

the expedition's actual objective, a close watch was set at its point of departure. In the spring of 1798 the Admiralty directed Lord St. Vincent to send
a squadron into the Mediterranean to keep a watch on Toulon.

There were numerous risks involved such a move, however. If ships
were sent into the Mediterranean the vessels would have to be taken from
the squadrons blockading Cádiz and Brest even though there was the threat
of another French descent on Ireland. And not only was there a shortage of
ships, but also men were in short supply, with another eight thousand sailors
needed to man the existing ships and those being built. Nevertheless, Pitt
accepted these risks with the hope of encouraging a restive Austria, Russia,
and Naples into joining a new coalition against France. In April a Viennese
mob had torn down the tricolor from the French embassy; in May Naples,
terrified of a French invasion of the Papal States, secretly entered an alliance
with Austria. Not long after, the mad Czar Paul I of Russia, who regarded
himself as patron of the Knights of St. John, and unhappy with prospect of
French seizure of Malta, signed a military pact with Austria.

The Admiralty ordered St. Vincent to detach some of the ships blockading Cádiz and send them into the Mediterranean as soon as replacements
arrived. The admiral was also directed to place Horatio Nelson, having
recovered from his wound and recently returned to active duty, in command
of a few ships, and immediately dispatched him on an armed reconnaissance
of the Toulon area. St. Vincent, anticipating such orders, had already sent
Nelson, who was flying his flag in the seventy-four-gun *Vanguard*, along
with *Orion* and *Alexander*, two other seventy-fours, commanded by Captains
Sir James Saumarez and Alexander Ball, and three frigates, to those waters.
"The appearance of a British squadron in the Mediterranean is a condition
on which the fate of Europe may at this moment . . . depend," Lord Spencer,
the first lord of the Admiralty, told St. Vincent.

Nelson had been the hero of the hour in London and Bath during his
convalescence. Fanny saw to the care of his amputated arm, inspecting the
stump daily for signs of a recurrence of the inflammation that pained him.
She helped him manage his daily life, including buttoning his clothes and
cutting up the food on his dinner plate. Under her devoted care his wound
quickly healed and his energy was restored. Nelson was granted the freedom of the City of London and was presented at court for his investure in
the Order of the Bath.

"You have lost your right arm!" exclaimed King George in surprise on
meeting the admiral. Nelson quickly replied, "But not my right hand, as I
have the honour of presenting Captain Berry."* To this the monarch
responded, "Your country has a claim for a bit more of you."

*Captain Edward Berry, who had been first lieutenant in *Captain* and had
now been detailed as his flag captain in *Vanguard*.

Nelson's rank of rear admiral and knighthood plus the substantial sum of prize money that had accumulated in his account over the years and a disability pension of a thousand pounds a year not only gave him social confidence but also enabled him to be free of financial worries for the first time in his married life. Fanny's dream of "a neat cottage" to await the return of her husband from his next tour of duty was satisfied when Nelson spent two thousand pounds for a substantial house of eleven rooms called "Roundwood," situated on fifty acres near Ipswich.

Nelson was immensely popular with ordinary Englishmen. Unlike previous naval heroes such as Howe, Duncan, and St. Vincent, he enjoyed the limelight. The others were older men and authoritative and distant figures, while he was young and someone with whom the populace could identify. Not only was he brave, but also he had risen from modest circumstances and was approachable and generous. Widespread approval greeted reports that he had sought financial relief for the families of sailors lost in the sinking of the boats in the Tenerife debacle, insisting there should be no distinction between "those who are cut in twain by a shot and those who are drowned by a shot from the enemy."

Even grandes dames such as Lady Spencer, wife of the first lord, were captivated by Nelson. "The first time I saw him was in the drawing room of the Admiralty and a most uncouth creature, I thought him," she related. "He looked so sickly it was painful to see him and his general appearance was that of an idiot; so much so that, when he spoke, and his wonderful mind broke forth, it was a sort of surprise that riveted my whole attention."

As Nelson and his squadron neared Toulon, an encounter between history's greatest general and greatest admiral seemed imminent. But on May 20, the day after the French fleet sailed, the British ships were unexpectedly struck by a heavy gale. *Vanguard*'s sails were still being reefed when the main-topmast went over the side, taking the topsail yard, which was crowded with men, with it. It was followed by the mizzen-topmast, and then the foremast "gave an alarming crack . . . and went by the board with a most tremendous crash," Nelson reported. As a massive tangle of masts, sails, and rigging banged against *Vanguard*'s hull and the gale drove her toward a rocky shore, the vessel seemed lost. But Alexander Ball of Alexander took the flagship under tow, despite the danger to his own ship and the wind and surging sea.

Vanguard sought refuge from the storm in the harbor of San Pietro on the Sardinian coast. Riggers and carpenters from the entire squadron crawled over her. Surprisingly, she had lost only two men, and within four days she was ready for sea again under a jury rig. In the meantime, the gale had enabled the French fleet to complete its escape from Toulon without being seen by the watching British frigates. Unaware of the course being followed by the French, Nelson returned to the vicinity of Toulon with the hope of rendezvousing with the missing frigates, but they pressed on to Gibraltar without waiting for him to join them.

On June 5 Nelson fell in with the brig *La Mutiné* and received the welcome news from Captain Thomas Hardy that the Royal Navy was returning to the Mediterranean in strength. The scheduled reinforcements from England had joined St. Vincent off Cádiz and Nelson's puny squadron was about to be augmented by ten seventy-four-gun ships and a fifty-gun ship. A few days later the towering sails of these vessels were sighted: *Cullodon, Swiftsure, Majestic, Bellerophon, Defence, Minotour, Theseus, Audacious, Zealous,* and *Goliath,* as well as the smaller *Leander.* Unfortunately, there were no frigates because of the shortage of these vessels. Their captains included "the elite of the Navy of England"—Troubridge, Miller, Foley, Hallowell, a younger Samuel Hood of the ubiquitous Hood clan, and others known to Nelson or who soon would be. Like him, they were mostly self-made men, with an average age of under forty, and little given to hesitation.

With this powerful fleet flying his flag, Nelson itched "to try Bonaparte upon a wind," but without frigates Nelson could only grope blindly for the French expedition. For the next seven weeks the British fleet lurched about the Mediterranean on a wild-goose chase that was the most anxious and stressful period in Nelson's career. In the meantime, the enemy fleet, its various divisions having rendezvoused off Corsica, made its way placidly through Homer's "wine-dark sea." Bonaparte spent much of his time in a special bed that swung on casters and that was designed to alleviate the effects of seasickness. Seldom rising before 10:00 A.M., he passed the time discussing such topics as the age of the Earth and the interpretation of dreams with the savants accompanying the expedition. He was reassured by reports that Nelson's flagship had been dismasted in the gale and had put into Sardinia for repairs.

Having been told that the French fleet had been sighted off Sicily, Nelson was convinced the enemy was about to attack Naples and sailed eastward. He sent Troubridge into the Bay of Naples to confer with Sir William Hamilton, while the rest of the fleet remained off Ischia. The Neapolitans were uneasy with a French expedition loose in the Mediterranean, but Lady Hamilton is said to have urged Queen Maria Carolina to provide surreptitious help to the British in the form of provisions and water. But Sir William failed to inform Troubridge that the French, in an effort to relieve the fears of Naples, had made it clear the expedition was bound for Egypt. He thought it was misinformation intended to mislead and did not pass it on. On June 17 Nelson learned from a passing merchantman that the French had attacked Malta and immediately crammed on all sail for the island, taking the most direct route through the Strait of Messina.

Bonaparte had chosen Malta as his first objective because the well-fortified island and its fine harbor would serve as an excellent base for the protection of his communications between Continental Europe and Egypt. Malta had been under the control of the Knights of St. John, the last of the Crusading orders, since 1522, and had withstood a siege by the Ottoman Turks, but the knights had become decadent. Overawed by the power ranged against them and betrayed by some French knights, the grand master surrendered to the French on June 11. With a stroke of the pen, Bonaparte ended the order's centuries-old control of Malta, making it into a French colony, and then confiscated the priceless treasures he found on the island.*

The British fleet was at the southern point of Sicily, off Cape Passero, on June 22, when the captain of a Genoese brig informed Nelson that the French had captured Malta—which was true—and had left the island on July 16—which was not true. In fact, Bonaparte did not depart Malta until three days later, leaving a garrison of four thousand men behind. With the wind blowing steadily across the Mediterranean from the northwest, Nelson was now certain the French armada was bound for Alexandria and immediately set a course for Egypt.

Throughout the voyage, whenever the weather permitted, he invited groups of his captains to *Vanguard*'s great cabin, where, over dinner, as Captain Berry related, "he would fully develop to them his own ideas of the different and best modes of attack, and such plans as he proposed to execute upon falling in with the Enemy, whatever their position might be, by day or night." In this "school for captains" they came to know Nelson's intentions so well, Berry added, that in battle, signals were nearly unnecessary. Soon they became, in Nelson's words, "a Band of Brothers."

Unencumbered by wallowing transports, the British fleet overtook the French at sea—although the British did not know it. On the night of June 25 the two armadas actually crossed paths to the south of Crete in a mist, with the French able to hear British signal guns. The following day Nelson arrived off the Egyptian coast. He sent *La Mutiné* ahead to investigate, and two days later the remainder of the fleet sighted the Pharos, the great lighthouse of Alexandra, and the city's shimmering minarets and domes soon came into view.

But much to Nelson's chagrin, there was no sign of the French. Perhaps they had landed farther east on the Egyptian coast? Still blinded by the lack of frigates, he led his ships past Alexandria, along the low-lying Nile delta, and then northward along the eastern Mediterranean. Still no sign of the French. "The Devil's children have the Devil's luck," Nelson cursed. "I cannot find, or to this moment learn beyond vague conjecture, where the French fleet are gone to." Perhaps Naples and Sicily had been Bonaparte's objectives

---

*Most of this booty was lost when the French flagship *L'Orient* caught fire and blew up during the Battle of the Nile.

all along? With that, he turned his fleet westward, brooding over his mistaken judgment through the long, uneventful days at sea that followed.

↬

PARADOXICALLY, THE FRENCH reached Alexandria on July 1, just as the topgallant masts of Nelson's ships were dropping below the horizon. Aware of his narrow escape and fearing that the British might soon return, Bonaparte hastily disembarked his army and occupied the city. Admiral Brueys declined to bring his big ships into the Old Port of Alexandria because the harbor entrance was too narrow, so Bonaparte instructed him to take refuge at French-held Corfu, in the Ionian Islands. Instead, Brueys anchored in Aboukir Bay, inside the Rosetta mouth of the Nile about sixteen miles east of Alexandra where the sea curls over the shoals.

Three weeks after the capture of Alexandria, Napoleon, having advanced along the western bank of the Nile until he was opposite Cairo, drew up his troops in battle order within sight of the Pyramids. As the sun rose over the desert, he rode among his men, and overcome by a sense of history, shouted: "Soldiers, from the tops of these monuments, forty centuries look down!" With rolling volleys of musket fire, the disciplined French squares beat back a Mameluke cavalry charge and drove the enemy into the Nile, where many of the men and horses drowned. "The carnage was atrocious," reported a French soldier, who likened the affair to a massacre rather than a battle. Two days later, on July 23, Bonaparte entered Cairo in triumph.

While the French were overrunning Egypt, Nelson and his fleet were beating back toward Sicily. The admiral was now in a state of high anxiety and could neither sleep nor eat. Fearing that both Naples and Sicily had fallen to the French, he believed his career was finished. Half pay and unhappy retirement to Ipswich seemed his likely fate. On July 19, with the fleet's water nearly exhausted, he reached Syracuse. Nelson was relieved to learn that the French had not attacked Sicily or Naples, but he still had no idea where they were. Pausing only long enough to revictual, he steered eastward. Three days later, on July 28, Nelson learned from some Greek fishermen in the Gulf of Koron that four weeks before, the French had been seen sailing to the southwest—in the direction of Egypt. Both relieved and exhilarated, he immediately clapped on all sail for Alexandria.

↬

AUGUST 1, 1798, was a brilliant summer's day with light breezes and clear weather. Toward noon the British fleet edged in close to Alexandria, to find the tricolor flying over the battlements, and the harbor filled with a forest of masts. But Nelson was disappointed to find no sign of the enemy battle fleet. He sent two of his ships to probe ahead, and at 2:30 P.M. *Zealous* signaled that she had found the French—thirteen ships of the line and four large frigates plus some smaller vessels—at anchor along the shore of Aboukir Bay.

Sailors raced into the rigging to examine their long-sought quarry. In the flagship, Berry reported that "the utmost joy seemed to animate every breast," especially that of the admiral. Saumarez was dining in the wardroom of *Orion* with his officers when the report was received. "All sprang from their seats, and only staying to drink a *bumper* to our success, we were in a moment on deck," he said. Nelson made the signal "Prepare for battle" and sat down to enjoy his dinner. "Before this time tomorrow, I shall have gained a peerage or Westminster Abbey," he remarked to one of his officers.

Brueys was anchored in a strong defensive position, with his ships in a line ahead. The fleet's northern flank was near the small island of Bequieres, on which the French had placed a battery, while the remainder of the line bowed inward toward a sandbank off the mainland. *L'Orient*, his giant flagship, was at the center of the line. The frigates and several lighter craft were placed inboard of the ships of the line, between them and the shoals. The British would have to sail into the bay under the concentrated fire of the French ships, which had springs attached to their anchor cables, lines that would permit the ships to be hauled about and provide a wide angle of fire for their broadsides. An anchored, well-placed line of ships was a formidable obstacle, as had been made clear several times during the American War of Independence.

Both sides had thirteen ships of the line, but the French vessels were more heavily armed, carrying 1,026 guns, not counting those in the batteries, to the 740 in the British ships. In *L'Orient* the French not only had the sole three-decker present but also had four eighty-gun ships, and their seventy-fours were larger than their British equivalents. Brueys expected the British to pass along his line, fire a few broadsides at extreme range, and then withdraw before sunset. Having the advantage of weight of metal, he considered putting to sea, but changed his mind as topsail yards were being hoisted aloft. Many of his men, especially his most skilled gunners, had been assigned tasks ashore, and there were not enough hands available to sail the ships and fight the guns. In the end, he decided to await the enemy onslaught at anchor, confident that his position was impregnable.

Sunset was at 6:44 P.M., but with the wind at his back, Nelson decided to risk a night action. He had quickly discerned that the French admiral had committed two tactical errors. Brueys' ships were too far from the shore batteries to receive support from them, and he had left enough room between the shoals and his van for the British to round the head of his line and double it. "Where there was room for an enemy's ship to swing, there was room for one of his to anchor," Nelson reasoned.

On innumerable occasions, he had discussed his plans with his captains
for dealing with the French if he found them at anchor. To win the annihi-
lating victory he sought, he intended to throw the whole weight of his fleet
on part of their line and crush it before the rest could help. Then he would
move on to strike the rest of the enemy ships with overwhelming power.
There was no time for consultation or elaborate signals—and there was no
need for them. Every captain knew what was in the admiral's mind. At 5:30
P.M., when *Vanguard* was abreast of Bequieres, Nelson hoisted the signal for
his fleet to form a battle line in order of sailing. The flagship was in sixth
place, where the admiral could best exercise tactical control.

Although Nelson was a rear admiral of the Blue, he instructed his captains to fly the White Ensign, which was more recognizable in the falling
darkness. An officer noted the banter among his men: "There are thirteen
sail of the line and a whacking lot of frigates and small craft. I think we'll
hammer the rusk off ten of them if not the whole boiling," one sailor told
another. Then the talk turned to prize money. "I'm glad we've twigged them
at last. I want some new rigging damnably for Sundays. . . ." "So do I. I hope
we touch enough for that and a good cruise among the girls beside."

The Battle of the Nile began less than an hour later as *Guerrièr* and *Conquerant*, the two seventy-fours at the head of the French line, opened fire
on the two leading British ships, *Zealous* and *Goliath*. Hailing *Zealous*, Nelson asked Captain Hood if he could take his ship close to the shoals and
around the head of the French line and engage the enemy from the shore-
ward side. Hood replied that he would try, even though he had no chart of
those waters. Nelson raised his hat in salute, but as Hood raised his in
reply, a wind gust carried it over the side. "Never mind, Webley!" he said
as his first lieutenant scrambled for the hat. "There it goes for good luck.
Put the helm up and make sail." With a man in the foremast chains taking
soundings, *Zealous* felt her way through the gap.

But *Goliath* forged ahead of the rest of the fleet. Thomas Foley, her captain, is reported to have had a captured French chart that showed there
were five fathoms of water, just enough for a two-decker to squeeze pass
Guerrièr. Having seen an opportunity, Foley grasped it in a spontaneous
gesture, just as Nelson expected him to do. The French were surprised to
be attacked from the land side, and one of *Goliath*'s officers reported that
as they neared *Guerrièr*, "I saw her lower deck guns were not run out and
there was lumber such as bags and boxes on the upper deck ports."

Foley intended to anchor abreast of *Guerrièr*, but after he had poured a
broadside into her, his ship drifted down alongside *Conquerant* and he
opened fire on her. *Zealous* was next to round the head of the French line
and took on *Guerrièr*, bringing down her fore-topmast just as the sun was
setting. The thirty-six-gun French frigate *Serieuse* tried to interfere but was
turned into a floating wreck by the broadsides of *Orion*, the third ship to

round the French line. The frigate drifted ashore, the first casualty of the battle. Saumarez then anchored his vessel abreast of *Peuple Souverain*, seventy-four, and *Orion* was soon hotly engaged with her.

Captain Ralph Miller of *Theseus*, the next in line, noted that *Guerrièr* was firing high. "Knowing well that at such a moment Frenchmen would not have the coolness to change their elevation," he reported, "I closed them suddenly and running under the arch of their shot reserved my fire, every gun being loaded with two and some with three round-shot." *Guerrièr*'s mainmast and mizzenmast followed her fore-topmast into the water. Leaving *Guerrièr*'s dismasted hulk in her wake, *Theseus* next engaged *Spartiate*, seventy-four. Noting that the seaward side of the French line was unengaged, Nelson took *Vanguard* along it and opened fire from that side. *Minotaur* and *Defence* followed the flagship, and by 6:45 P.M. the five leading French ships were caught between the fire of five British ships to port and three to starboard. "Friendly fire" was one of the great dangers of a night battle, and with the coming of darkness, another sign of Nelson's thorough planning came into play as each British ship raised a prearranged recognition signal of four lanterns suspended horizontally to its mizzenpeak.

Bellerophon now came into action and audaciously stationed herself outboard of the 120-gun *L'Orient*, which was more than twice her size and carried double the weight of her broadside. Shortly afterward *Majestic* took on *Tonnant*, 80. But *Cullodon* ran aground on the shoals as she sailed into battle. Nothing that Captain Troubridge could do would budge her, and she came under fire from the French shore batteries, while her crew were unhappy witnesses to all that ensued. Nevertheless, the stranded vessel served as a beacon to guide *Swiftsure* and *Alexander*, the last British ships, safely over the shoals. Rear Admiral Pierre Charles Villeneuve, commander of the unengaged French rear, was later criticized for failing to capture *Cullodon* and come to the assistance of Bruey's battered van.

For more than an hour *Bellerophon* fought the gigantic enemy flagship alone. She lost two masts and nearly two hundred men, including her captain and every officer, were either killed or wounded. Crippled, *Bellerophon* drifted out of line under a ragged scrap of sail, but she had done her work well: *L'Orient* was severely damaged and ablaze. On the day before the battle, her crew had been painting her and had not jettisoned all the paint buckets before going into battle. Fires blazed out of control in several places. "The ship was burning fore and aft, and already the flames were reaching the twenty-four-pounder battery," reported a French officer.

Other ships took *Bellerophon*'s place, among them the fifty-gun *Leander*, which anchored in a position in which she could rake *L'Orient* and the eighty-gun *Franklin* while keeping out of their field of fire. Admiral Brueys had both legs shot away but refused to be taken below. "A French admiral should die on his quarterdeck," he declared. He was sitting in a chair with

The French flagship *L'Orient* blows up during the Battle of the Nile, August 1, 1798. From a painting by Philip James de Loutherbourg. (Beverly Robinson Collection, U. S. Naval Academy Museum)

tourniquets on the stumps of his legs when another shot almost cut him in two.

Flashes of gunfire and the flames of burning ships lit the night sky, revealing that four of the ships in the French van had already been battered into submission, including *Vanguard*'s opponent *Spartiate.* Putting the next part of his battle plan into operation, Nelson ordered his captains to move down the line to roll up the enemy center and rear. "Each knew his duty," said the admiral, who was "sure each would feel for a French ship."

Vanguard was drawing away from *Spartiate* when the French vessel unleased a final broadside into her. Nelson staggered and fell to the quarterdeck, his face covered in blood. A flying fragment of shot had laid open his forehead, and a strip of flesh hung down his face and over his good eye. "I am killed," he gasped in pain and shock to Berry, who was kneeling beside him. "Remember me to my wife." The fallen admiral was carried down to the crowded cockpit, where the surgeon immediately began to attend him. "No," he insisted, "I will take my turn with my brave fellows." The wound, although messy and painful, was determined not to be serious, and Nelson dictated to his clerk the opening words of his dispatch to St. Vincent even as the cannonade continued: "My Lord, Almighty God has blessed his Majesty's Arms by a Great Victory over the Fleet of the Enemy. . . ."

Nelson returned to the quarterdeck, a bandage wrapped around his head, just as *L'Orient* was undergoing her death throes. Flames were sweeping along her decks, and fanned by the wind, leaped up her rigging. Pitch was bubbling out from between her planks. Everyone knew the fire would soon reach her powder magazines. Both French and British ships cut their cables to get away from the explosion that was bound to come, but the cannonade continued, with *Swiftsure* firing directly into the heart of the blaze. It was "a most grand and awful spectacle," Captain Miller of *Theseus* later recalled. Louis Casabianca, the burning vessel's captain, was mortally wounded but his son, Giacoma, refused to leave his father—and was the inspiration for Felicia Hemans' much-quoted poem about "the boy who stood on the burning deck from which all but he had fled."

"At 10 *l'Orient* blew into the air!!!" reported Lieutenant Webley of *Zealous*. The darkness was rent by a brilliant flash and a shattering roar was heard sixteen miles away, in Alexandria. The scene was forever etched on the minds of those who witnessed it. Masts, yards, guns, splintered timbers, and broken bodies were hurled into the air and then fell back into the steaming sea. *Alexander* and *Leander* were set afire briefly by blazing wreckage. Sailors in the bowels of *Goliath* thought their own ship had exploded. Fewer than 100 of *L'Orient*'s crew of 1,010 men survived the blast.*

Both fleets were stupefied by the shock of the explosion, and Captain Berry noted "an awful pause and deathlike silence, for about three minutes." *Franklin* renewed the struggle with her few remaining guns, but to little avail. Two-thirds of her crew were dead or wounded, and she soon surrendered. With the French van and center all but destroyed, *Tonnant* became the focus of the British attack. She fought three British ships until battered into silence. Captain Astride Aubert Dupetit Thouars lost both arms and a leg to British round shot, but instead of being taken below, he insisted on being placed in a tub of bran to stem the flow of blood and continued to urge his men to fight on until he died. As the battle slackened, *Tonnant* slipped her cable, and the shattered hulk floated out of the battle.

By dawn the British crews were so exhausted after being in action for nearly twelve hours that some men fell asleep at their guns, but Nelson concentrated on Admiral Villeneuve's undamaged ships in the French rear. They had taken no part in the action—neither moving up to support their comrades in the van nor trying to escape. Soon only three—*Timoleon*, of

---

*Part of *L'Orient*'s shattered mainmast fell near *Swiftsure*, and Captain Hallowell had it fished out and fashioned into a coffin, which he presented to Nelson so that "when you have finished your glorious course in this world, you may journey into the next in one of your trophies." Nelson kept this bizarre memento propped up in his day cabin. He was buried in it at St. Paul's Cathedral after his death at Trafalgar in 1805.

seventy-four guns, *Guillaume Tell*, of eighty, and *Genereux*, of seventy-four—were still in good enough shape to try to get away. *Timoleon* ran aground and was set afire by her crew, and the remaining two vessels, accompanied by a pair of frigates, were the sole French vessels to survive the holocaust. *Zealous*, the only British ship sufficiently undamaged to carry sail, pursued them until recalled by Nelson. Both French ships were later lost in action against the Royal Navy.*

⌇

THE COMING OF DAY revealed a scene of silent, smoking desolation. "An awful sight it was," recalled John Nicol, a seaman in *Goliath*. "The whole bay was covered with dead bodies, mangled, wounded and scorched, not a bit of clothes on them but their trousers." No other victory of the Age of Fighting Sail was so astonishingly complete—not even Trafalgar. Of the thirteen French ships of the line that had cleared for action the day before, nine had been captured, two had burned, and only two escaped. The French lost 1,700 men killed, 1,500 wounded, and 3,000 taken prisoner. British casualties totaled 218 killed and 677 wounded, including the admiral himself. Nelson later attributed his failure to prevent the escape of two of the French ships to the grogginess resulting from his injury.

All the elements of what became known as the "Nelson Touch" were clearly visible at the Battle of the Nile: inspiring leadership, the intensive training of his captains, the delegation of crucial tactical decisions to them in the heat of battle rather than slavish adherence to the *Fighting Instructions,* and the taking of calculated risks to ensure that a battle would be not only decisive but devastating to an enemy fleet. Even more important, the battle changed not only naval warfare but the war against France itself.

Strategically, the British won control of the Mediterranean. Napoleon had suffered his first defeat, and his army was stranded in Egypt, cut off by sea from rescue or reinforcement. From that moment on, all his grandiose dreams of castles in the East were doomed. Nevertheless, he professed to be unconcerned about a British blockade and spent his time parceling out Egypt among his victorious generals and conducting an illicit affair with Pauline Foures, the pretty young wife of one of his officers. A truer picture of his army's prospects was to be seen along the shores of

*Six of the captured French ships were taken into the Royal Navy. *Franklin* was renamed *Canopus* and became the model for a new class of eighty-four-gun two-deckers. The others were deemed too damaged to repair and were burned. Marine archeologists have recently discovered the wreck of *L'Orient*.

Aboukir Bay, where the Bedouins looted the swollen corpses of the French dead that had washed shore and then threw them back into the Nile.

As a result of the battered condition of Nelson's fleet, he did not get his official dispatch off for a week. Two copies were sent. With no frigates available, one was carried by Captain Berry in *Leander,* but she had the ill luck to fall in with *Genereux,* one of the fugitive survivors of the battle, and was captured after a bitter struggle. The other copy was sent to the nearest British diplomat, Sir William Hamilton in Naples, in *La Mutiné** and reached there on September 4, where the news was greeted with wild celebration.

But at home, uncertainty and suspense prevailed throughout the summer of 1798. Nelson and his fleet appeared to have vanished over the horizon, and the Admiralty was criticized for entrusting such an important command to so junior an admiral. Public gloom was intensified by reports that Bonaparte had captured Malta and had arrived at Alexandria. Where was Nelson? Dark hints were received from European capitals of an action in which seven British ships had been lost. "I have seldom experienced a more severe disappointment than in the accounts which have lately reached us from the Mediterranean," said Lord Spencer.

Moreover, the long-festering unrest in Ireland erupted into revolution. This upheaval was accompanied by some of the most brutal carnage in Ireland's bloody history. Following a victory at Vinegar Hill, British troops overran a makeshift hospital and massacred the Irish wounded. At Scullabogue, County Wexford, rebels torched a barn, killing the two hundred Protestant men, women, and children inside. Then, on August 22, the unthinkable occurred: General Jean Joseph Humbert and a thousand French troops landed unopposed at Killala, County Mayo.

Expecting to light the flames of rebellion as he went, Humbert marched off to Dublin, but despite the optimism of the leaders of the United Irishmen, the dispirited peasantry of western Ireland failed to rally to the invaders in great numbers. The French were finally driven to ground by an overwhelming British force on September 8 and surrendered. Humbert and his officers were feted by Dublin society, while in contrast, their fleeing Irish adherents were hunted down like wild game.

Amid all this uncertainty, the dispatch announcing Nelson's victory arrived at the Admiralty on October 2—two months after the battle—and a relieved nation went mad. The bells of London pealed joyfully; the guns of the Tower fired triumphal salutes, and the streets were filled with uproarious crowds. Upon hearing the news, the king stood silent for a

---

*Thomas Hardy, *La Mutiné*'s former captain, replaced Berry as Nelson's flag captain, a post he held in most of the admiral's future commands.

minute, with his eyes turned toward heaven.* Lord Spencer fell to the floor in a dead faint. Public confidence in the certainty of victory over the French was restored. Nelson was created Baron Nelson of the Nile and Burnham Thorpe, given an additional pension of two thousand pounds a year, and the East India Company awarded him a purse of ten thousand pounds for saving India. Yet the ever-ambitious Nelson felt slighted—he thought he deserved an earldom.

Britain's cup of rejoicing was not yet full. Two weeks later, the Nile victory was crowned by the joyous news that Admiral John Borlace Warren had intercepted another French invasion force, off Lough Swilly on the northwestern coast of Ireland, taking a seventy-four-gun ship and four frigates. Wolfe Tone was among those captured. He was brought to Dublin, where he was tried for treason and sentenced to be hanged. Tone tried to kill himself by slashing his throat with a pen knife the day before his execution but botched the job and lingered for a week before he died at age thirty-five.

Nelson's victory had far greater ramifications than merely the destruction of the French fleet. Five weeks after the battle, the sultan of Turkey declared holy war on the infidel French for invading his territory. With the most dangerous and ruthless French general isolated in Egypt, new heart was pumped into Russia, Austria, and Naples. Encouraged by lavish financial subsidies provided by Pitt, they joined Britain in a Second Coalition against France and the Revolution. At the beginning of 1798, France had controlled the Mediterranean. Following the Nile, only two French ships of the line were at large in those waters, which now swarmed not only with ships of the Royal Navy but also with Russian and Turkish squadrons that had emerged in surprising amity from the Dardanelles. The French were driven from Minorca and its valuable base at Port Mahon. Corfu and the Ionian Islands were in the process of falling to the Russians and Turks, while Malta was under siege by a combined British and Portuguese fleet.

Horatio Nelson was ordered to Naples, which was deemed the most suitable port to repair his flagship, and it was hoped that it would be the center of resistance to the French. He dispatched seven of the ships of his victorious fleet to Gibraltar under Saumarez along with the six surviving prizes, and left Hood to blockade Alexandria with three ships. Still suffering from his wound, Nelson wrote Lord St. Vincent, "My head is splitting—splitting—splitting" as he sailed for Naples with his three remaining vessels. And there he became involved in both a scandal and a romantic legend forever linked with his name.

*In Vienna, Franz Joseph Haydn was composing his *Missa in Angustiis* (Mass in Time of Need) when he heard the news of the Nile victory. He added some triumphant trumpet calls at the end of the Benedictus in tribute to Nelson, and the work came to be called the Nelson Mass.

"Naples Is a Dangerous Place"

NO SOONER HAD *Vanguard*'s anchor splashed into the limpid waters of the Bay of Naples on September 22, 1798, than Horatio Nelson's battle-scarred flagship was surrounded by a multitude of small craft. Some were crowded with dignitaries including King Ferdinand, others bore women and musicians, and all were bedecked with flags and banners. The British ambassador's barge, carrying Sir William and Lady Hamilton, was the first to bump alongside and was greeted by a salute of thirteen guns. "Up flew her Ladyship, and exclaiming 'Oh God, is it possible!' she fell into my arms more dead and alive," Nelson later related in describing Emma's arrival. "Tears, however, soon set matters to rights. . . ."

The "Hero of the Nile" was accorded a lavish and theatrical reception. As he stepped ashore for the first time in nearly five months, a rainbow of caged birds was released, and flower petals were scattered at his feet. Flags and bunting bedecked the tier upon tier of houses, parchment-colored, terra-cotta, yellow, and coral, that climbed the hazy heights above the bay. But this welcome also contained a dash of Neapolitan cynicism. When a French fleet and Bonaparte's army were at large in the Mediterranean, the Kingdom of the Two Sicilies had been cool toward its on-again, off-again British ally. Now that the fleet had been destroyed and the French army safely marooned in Egypt, Naples overflowed with puffed-up patriotism and bellicose belligerence.

Nelson was well aware of the corrupting influence of the Neapolitan court, and he worried about becoming "Sicilified." "Naples is a dangerous place," he wrote soon after his arrival, "and we must keep clear of it." Originally he planned to spend only about four or five days there and then make Syracuse, on the southeastern coast of Sicily, his base of operations in the eastern Mediterranean. But Lady Hamilton clucked over his wounds and insisted that the admiral stay at the Palazzo Sessa.* Head throbbing

---

*The Palazzo Sessa and a beach house at Posillipo visited by Nelson and Emma still stand, although both are much altered.

and periodically racked by vomiting and chest pains, Nelson gratefully exchanged the limited comforts of his flagship for the soft pillows, delectable food, and exotic company of the Hamiltons. The British embassy, he could tell himself, was the center of affairs in that part of the world.

Nelson and the Hamiltons had not seen each other for five years, and he quickly developed a deep affection for both and a passionate—although as yet platonic—attachment to Emma. At this point she was still a friend about whom he could wrote home to Fanny: "I hope some day to have the pleasure of introducing you to Lady Hamilton. She is one of the very best women in the world. How few could have made the turn she has. She is an honour to her sex, and proof that even reputation may be regained."

Emma Hamilton had the effect of a drug on an exhausted man who was susceptible to pretty women. At thirty-three she was still strikingly beautiful and exuded a voluptuous sexuality even though she was coarse-tongued and growing fat. She had a taste for the theatrical and was fond of performing "Attitudes" in which she single-handedly created a living gallery of famous statues and pictures. Stage-managing Nelson's arrival, she arranged a celebration of his fortieth birthday to which eight hundred people were invited for supper and nearly eighteen hundred danced at a ball. The gowns of the guests were decorated with Nelson's monogram, and a victory column in the ballroom was inscribed with Caesar's *Veni, Vidi, Vici*. Gifts flowed in, and Nelson was particularly intrigued by one from the sultan of Turkey: a diamond plume of triumph called a *chelengk*, which was to be worn on the hat, the center of which, powered by clockwork, revolved to catch the shifting light.

A man far less susceptible to honors and flattery than Nelson probably would have had his head turned by Emma, and he was soon entranced. As a parson's son, he had a strict upbringing with little formal education and was captivated by the world of high living and low morals embodied by the Hamiltons. The straitlaced Lord St. Vincent must have been shocked to receive a dispatch from Naples stating: "I am writing opposite Lady Hamilton, therefore you will not be surprised at the glorious jumble of this letter. Were your Lordship in my place I must doubt if you could write so well. . . ."

Nelson was responsible for naval operations east of Corsica and Sardinia, including the blockade of Egypt, but he went to sea only rarely to show his flag and inspect his far-flung ships. Through Emma, a confidante of Queen Maria Carolina, whom Napoleon once described as "the only man in Naples," he became deeply embroiled in Neapolitan affairs, which annoyed his officers and eventually damaged his reputation.

Sir William Hamilton was under instructions not to encourage the Neapolitans to undertake actions beyond their means, but he and Nelson persuaded the vainglorious King Ferdinand to become the liberator of Italy from the French yoke. Earlier that year the French had seized Rome, expelled the pope, and established a republic. "Either advance, trusting to God and for His blessings on a just cause," Nelson advised the king, "or remain quiet and be kicked out of [your] dominion." An ill-trained army of thirty thousand men was organized, and an Austrian general, Baron Karl von Mack, whose zeal was exceeded only by his incompetence, was engaged to lead the march on Rome.

Nelson supported the operation by landing additional troops at Leghorn to cut enemy communications. The French were caught unprepared, and Ferdinand entered Rome in November 1798 at the head of his army, delightedly playing the part of conquering hero. This fantasy swiftly dissolved when the French rallied, and the gleaming, scented Neapolitan officers took to their heels at the first shot, and their men followed. "The Neapolitans did not lose much honour, for God knows they had not much to lose," said a disgusted Nelson, "but they lost all they had. Cannons, tents, baggage, all were left behind."

The Jacobins, with the support of the middle class and intellectuals tired of the autocratic Bourbons, rose in anticipation of the fall of Naples to the French. Nelson, who was instrumental in bringing about the fiasco, saw it as his duty to rescue the royal family and their hangers-on. Every available ship was gathered in the bay, and boats manned by armed sailors ferried the refugees out to them. Nelson and an escort of seamen carrying cutlasses supervised the escape of the king and queen through a hidden passage from the palace to the waterside. Two days before Christmas, *Vanguard*, carrying the royal family, the Hamiltons, and a treasury of two and a half million pounds in boxes marked "Stores for Nelson," sailed for the Sicilian capital at Palermo in a wild gale. "It blew harder than I have ever experienced since I was at sea," Nelson noted.

It was a terrible voyage. The king, queen, and most of the other passengers were nearly prostrate with seasickness and fear. Sir William Hamilton, expecting the ship to founder at any moment, braced himself in his cabin with a loaded pistol in each hand, prepared to shoot himself rather than drown with the "guggle, guggle, guggle of salt water in his throat." But Emma was at her best in the emergency. When the six-year-old Prince Carlo Alberto, the youngest of the many royal children, became sick, she nursed him until he died in her arms. The bond between her and Nelson was firmly sealed during the storm.

In Palermo, Nelson took up residence in the palazzo occupied by the Hamiltons—and there he and Emma became lovers, probably with the knowledge of Sir William. The envoy seemed more shaken by the loss of the ship carrying most of his collection of antiquities than the purported affair. English visitors to Palermo reported that a weary-looking Nelson spent his nights with Emma at the gaming tables drinking more champagne than was good for him and often fell asleep over the cards. He was angered when the Admiralty severed the Levant from his command and gave it to Sir William Sidney Smith,* a rival glory-hunter whom he heartily disliked—and a mere captain at that. And his letters to Fanny grew briefer and less affectionate.

～

As NELSON DALLIED IN Palermo, Napoleon, undeterred by his isolation in Egypt, was preparing to advance across two hundred miles of desert and seize Damascus. From there he reasoned he would be able to either drive to Constantinople and found a new Byzantine Empire on the ruins of the sultan's crumbling regime, or strike eastward along the old caravan route through Mesopotamia (now Iraq) toward the Persian Gulf. Word was sent to Tippoo Sahib requesting him to send emissaries to Suez to arrange plans for the overthrow of British rule in India. A true child of the Revolution, Bonaparte believed that to a man of will and energy such as himself, everything was possible.

On learning that the sultan was concentrating armies in Syria and Rhodes for an invasion of Egypt, Bonaparte struck first. In February 1799 he set out with thirteen thousand troops across the eastern desert and took El Arish, Gaza, and Jaffa in Palestine with ease. The three thousand Turks captured at El Arish were shot and bayoneted as a warning against resisting the invader. Resuming the march, the young conqueror headed for the poorly defended port of Acre, about sixty miles north, which barred the road to Damascus. And there, he again encountered the Royal Navy.

First, Sidney Smith, with a squadron of two ships of the line and several smaller vessels, captured a flotilla of gunboats carrying the French siege train as it crept up the coast from Egypt. And then the energetic Smith put his sailors and marines and the three thousand Turks of the garrison to work restoring the walls of Acre and its Crusader castle and mounted the captured guns on them. Full credit for the fortification of Acre should be given to Colonel Louis-Edmond Le Picard de Phelipeaux, a onetime Royalist officer who was a classmate of Bonaparte at the École Militaire in Paris.† Several frontal assaults by the French failed with heavy casualties, and an angry Bonaparte settled down to starve out the garrison. "The whole fate of the East hangs from this little quarter," he declared. Follow-

*Smith's knighthood was Swedish, not British, and Nelson contemptuously referred to him as "the Swedish knight."

†Phelipeaux was killed during the defense of Acre, so Smith reaped all the glory.

ing a sixty-two-day siege, the French launched a final assault across the stinking, corpse-lined ditches surrounding Acre. It failed, and having lost more than a quarter of his men and with the rest infected with bubonic plague or mutinous, Bonaparte retreated into Egypt.

Fortune had turned against France in Europe and in India as well as in the Levant. The Directory had dispersed the French Army into dozens of garrisons to make it easier to extort enough loot from the conquered provinces to finance the regime. In the meantime, the Austrian Army had been reorganized following its trouncing by Bonaparte two years before, while the grasping politicians in Paris had starved and neglected their own legions. Faced by superior numbers, the French were driven back in Germany and then in Italy, where a Russian army led by the redoubtable Marshal Alexander Suvorov reconquered Piedmont and Lombardy. At home, the Vendée was again in revolt. In India, a British-Sepoy army stormed Seringapatam, the capital of Mysore, in May 1799, killed Tippoo Sultan, and destroyed his French-trained army as he vainly awaited Bonaparte's heralded arrival. The campaign had been planned by a twenty-nine-year-old lieutenant colonel named Arthur Wellesley.

With the republic in its greatest danger since 1793, the Directory ordered Vice Admiral Eustache Bruix, the minister of marine, to take the newly refitted Atlantic fleet to the Mediterranean to challenge British naval supremacy, from which all these disasters stemmed, and to rescue Bonaparte from Egypt—the one man who could save the nation. Although the Admiralty had ample notice of a formidable force fitting out at Brest, Lord Bridport, still in command of the Channel Fleet despite past failures, did not maintain a close blockade. Nursing his ships against buffeting by storms, Bridport kept them too far offshore or in port. In fact, a lugger sent out by the French to mislead the British with false dispatches indicating that an attack on Ireland was being prepared had to cruise for several days before it could find a vessel that was obliging enough to capture her. On April 25, 1799, Bruix escaped from Brest with twenty-five of the line and ten frigates and headed south.

While the befuddled Bridport was mobilizing every ship to defend Ireland against another invasion despite reports from merchant captains that the French were headed in the opposite direction, Bruix appeared off Cádiz. There, Lord Keith, now in command in place of St. Vincent, who was in poor health and ashore at Gibraltar, was blockading a superior Spanish force with fifteen ships of the line. Bruix hoped to join forces with the Spaniards, but with a westerly gale blowing on a lee shore, they declined to come out. Uncertain about the ability of his untrained crews to cope with such adverse weather conditions, the French admiral headed for Gibraltar and in a thick haze slipped through the strait. Keith pursued

Bruix, lifting the blockade, and seventeen Spanish sail-of-the-line emerged from Cádiz and followed their French allies.

The sudden and unexpected appearance of a powerful French fleet in the Mediterranean imperiled British naval operations from Gibraltar to the Levant. Britain's fleet was divided into several squadrons: Sir John Duckworth was off Minorca with four of the line, Ball had three blockading Valletta, Sidney Smith had two at Acre, Troubridge had four off Naples, and Nelson was at Palermo with his flagship. If Bruix had taken advantage of a favorable wind, he could have defeated the various elements of the British fleet in detail. "It is scarcely too much to say that never was there a greater opportunity than that offered to the French fleet," Admiral Mahan observed.

But Bruix was haunted by the French disaster at the Nile and saw himself as the hunted rather than the hunter. Instead of attacking the scattered British squadrons, he made for the safety of Toulon, anchoring there on May 14. For its part, the Spanish fleet, badly damaged by the storm, put into Cartagena. By his flight to Toulon, Bruix gave Lord St. Vincent time to mobilize his fleet. Nelson played an unusually passive role in these operations. He ordered his ships to join Keith in barring the way to Egypt, but personally declined to leave Palermo—and Emma. "You may depend on my exertion and I am sorry too that I cannot move to your help," he wrote Keith in an astonishing letter, "but this island appears to hang on my stay. Nothing could console the Queen this night but my promise not to leave them unless the battle were to be fought off Sardinia."

At Toulon, Bruix received new orders. Suvorov and a Russian-Austrian army had captured Turin with a large haul of guns, and the Directory abandoned its plan to rescue Bonaparte in favor of the defense of France itself. Late in May the fleet was sent to Genoa with reinforcements and provisions for a French army under siege there. St. Vincent plowed along in Bruix's wake, but declining health forced him to again turn over command to Lord Keith, this time for good. Nelson was angered that Keith rather than himself was named commander in chief in the Mediterranean, and he obeyed orders from Keith only reluctantly.

Hugging the coasts of France and Spain after leaving Genoa early in June, Bruix showed remarkable skill in eluding capture, but not much else. He picked up the Spanish fleet at Cartagena and returned in mid-August to Brest, where the Spanish ships were held hostage for the wavering loyalty of Spain. The Directory's attempt to restore the naval balance in the Mediterranean had failed. Despite his opportunities, Bruix accomplished little except to force the Admiralty to bring Keith's fleet up from the Mediterranean to meet public clamor for the defense of Ireland against a nonexistent threat. This made Nelson temporary commander in chief of the naval forces in those waters.

❦

NELSON HAD PLAYED A curious role in the operations against Bruix. By refusing to leave Palermo, he committed two errors. He tied Britain to a comparatively unimportant and not particularly worthy cause, and he made promises that he, as a subordinate commander, was not entitled to make. His owed his loyalty to King George III, not Maria Carolina of the Two Sicilies. Gossips were already suggesting openly that the real reason for his devotion to the queen lay in his relationship with Lady Hamilton, Her Majesty's closest friend. Some people joked that Emma was the real commander of the fleet. St. Vincent and later Keith were unwilling to break with the war's major hero so they reluctantly went along with this unhappy state of affairs. With no public rebuke of his actions coming his way, Nelson immersed himself even more deeply in Neapolitan politics. "The poor Queen . . . made me promise not to quit her side," he wrote Fanny.

In an effort to spark a counterrevolution in Naples, Ferdinand had sent Fabrizio Cardinal Ruffo, a shrewd and popular prelate, to the mainland to plot the overthrow of the Vesuvian Republic, which had been established by the French. Ruffo mobilized the peasants of Calabria, and by summer 1799 his partisans controlled Naples except for a pair of castles still held by the French and their sympathizers. Royalist mobs were pillaging the homes of those suspected of supporting the French, and dead bodies were left stripped naked in the streets. Suspecting Ruffo might come to terms with the rebels, the king and the queen sent Nelson to Naples to demand that the French surrender unconditionally. Sir William and Lady Hamilton, who saw herself as Maria Carolina's "deputy," accompanied him in his new flagship, *Foudroyant,* of eighty guns, on what was to be the most unsavory incident of Nelson's career.

The admiral was in a fierce, unforgiving mood and was determined to teach the Neapolitans, whom he regarded as "fiddlers and poets, whores and scoundrels" a sharp lesson. Arriving off Naples, he found that Cardinal Ruffo had indeed reached a truce with the rebels holding out in the castles. In return for surrender, they were promised safe conduct to France. "The republicans are vile traitors and must throw themselves on the Royal mercy," Nelson declared, and annulled the agreement. An orgy of bloodshed followed. Some of the rebels were beheaded, while hundreds of others, women included, died on the gallows as dwarfs capered obscenely on their shoulders and drunken mobs howled approval.

Nelson had the former head of the Neapolitan navy, Admiral Prince Caracciolo, who had switched sides, court-martialed for treason and hanged that same day from a yardarm of his former flagship. The body was then cut down to splash into the Bay of Naples like a piece of garbage. Several days later, Caracciolo's bloated corpse with the noose still around its neck bobbed to the surface near *Foudroyant,* to the consternation of the recently arrived King Ferdinand, who blanched at the sight and immediately went below. A boat towed the body ashore.

For his efforts on behalf of the Bourbons, Nelson was rewarded with the dukedom of Brontë and an estate on the volcanic slopes of Mount Etna in Sicily that supposedly produced an income of three thousand pounds yearly. He was especially pleased when told that the original Bronte was the Cyclops who had forged the thunderbolts of Zeus, and from then on signed himself "Nelson and Brontë."* But true to nature, the king and the queen shortchanged him: most of the estate's thirty thousand acres were strewn with volcanic rock, the manor house was an uninhabitable ruin, and the estate produced little revenue.

As the century drew to an end, the curtain was coming down on Nelson's career in the Mediterranean. Lord Elgin, passing through Palermo on his way to Constantinople, reported that the admiral "looks very old, has lost his upper teeth, sees ill of one eye, and has a film coming over both of them. He has pains pretty constantly from his late wound." Tongues in London were clacking with the latest gossip about the scandalous *ménage à trois,* while some of his officers thought he was making himself ridiculous with the Hamiltons. To remove Nelson from Emma's clutches, Lord Keith, who had again assumed command in the Mediterranean, ordered him to take charge of the siege of Malta.

In one of Nelson's rare excursions from Palermo, *Foudroyant* encountered the seventy-four-gun *Genereux,* one of the two French survivors of the Battle of the Nile. The French vessel opened fire first, and as one of her shots passed through a sail, the admiral noticed that one of the younger midshipmen had flinched. He patted him on the head, jokingly asked how he liked the music, and told the lad that although King Charles XII of Sweden had run away from the first shot he heard, he was later called "The Great" because of his bravery in action. "I therefore hope much from you in the future." he added. Here was the Nelson the Royal Navy remembered and adored.†

Nelson claimed that he was not well enough to remain on station off Malta and insisted on returning to his "friends in Palermo"—where Emma was now carrying his child—and did so. Sir William, with true diplomatic

---

*The name Brontë lives on today because a Yorkshire parson named Patrick Brunty altered his name to Brontë in homage to Nelson, and it was carried on by his literary daughters, Charlotte and Emily.

†Not long after, the eighty-gun *Guillaume Tell,* the other survivor of the Nile, also fell into British hands.

sangfroid, took no notice of her attacks of morning sickness. This escapade confirmed the Admiralty's worst fears about Nelson. Lord Spencer sent him an icy letter stating that if the admiral's health was so poor, it would be better for him to return home at once "than to be obliged to remain inactive at Palermo. . . . You will be more likely to recover your strength and health in England than in an inactive situation at a foreign Court."

Learning that Sir William was being replaced as British envoy to Naples, Nelson concluded he had no further reason for remaining in Palermo. He struck his flag and joined the Hamiltons on a trip overland across unoccupied Europe, during which he was both hailed as a conquering hero and snickered at behind his back. In Dresden an observer noted that Nelson, who insisted on wearing his glittering decorations and orders everywhere, seemed "a little man without dignity. . . . Lady Hamilton takes possession of him, and he is a willing captive. . . . Sir William is old, infirm, all admiration of his wife and never spoke. . . ."

❦

IN EGYPT, Bonaparte bounced back from his repulse at Acre in July 1799 to destroy an army of fifteen thousand Turks landed by Sidney Smith at Aboukir. Every man was either killed, driven into the Nile, or captured. But the armies of the republic were meeting defeat on every other front. An Anglo-Russian expeditionary force commanded by the duke of York had invaded northern Holland, while the Russians and the Austrians were advancing along the Rhine. In Paris, the Directory was wallowing in indecision and confusion. Smith taunted his stranded opponent by sending him newspaper accounts of these disasters, but they had an opposite effect than intended. Now that he had his recent victory to offset the Nile and Acre disasters, Bonaparte judged the time ripe for a return to France.

Without informing General Jean Baptiste Kléber, his second in command, of his plan, he abandoned his army. On August 23, 1799, Bonaparte slipped out of Alexandria in a frigate with only a few supporters—one would become a king, one a prince, and three would be made dukes—and escaped through the loose British blockade. Once the vessel was sighted by Lord Keith's fleet but was thought to be a British ship and allowed to pass. Upon such threads does history hang. After a passage of forty-seven days, Bonaparte landed in the South of France and was immediately acclaimed by the populace as their savior.

Yet, even as he arrived in Paris, the coalition of France's enemies was falling apart, making the indispensable man a little less indispensable. The invasion of Holland and the Austro-Russian offensive in Switzerland had been turned back. But there was no dimming of Bonaparte's star. Within three weeks of his return—on the eighteenth of Brumaire in the Revolutionary calendar, or November 9, 1799—he overthrew the Directory in a coup d'état and as first consul became the virtual dictator of France at age of thirty.*

Over the next ten months Bonaparte, in a masterful display of statesmanship, gave France a new Constitution, pacified the rebellious Vendée, stabilized the franc, signed a concordat with the Vatican, and laid the foundation for a new Civil Code. As a sop to the French people's desire for peace, he offered Britain and Austria, his last two remaining active enemies, terms that he knew they would reject. And then he was ready to take the field again. Crossing the Alps at the head of fifty thousand men, he defeated an Austrian army of double that size at Marengo in northern Italy on June 14, 1800. Following further defeats, the Austrians sued for peace. Moreover, Spain invaded Portugal and drove British shipping from Lisbon. Restrictions were also placed on Britain's trade, designed to bankrupt her. With all of her major Continental allies out of the war, Britain was left, once again, to fight on alone.

---

*Throughout Bonaparte's time in Egypt his wife, Josephine, had openly carried on affairs and had run up substantial gambling debts, and he was determined to divorce her. Arriving in Paris, he ordered her out of their house and had all her belongings packed and placed at the entrance. She cried, pleaded, and pounded on the door to his study all day, and at last, when his tearful stepchildren joined her, he relented. Next morning, Bonaparte's brother, Lucien, found them in bed together.

CHAPTER 15

Of Nelson and the North

NAPOLEON BONAPARTE'S crushing victory over the Austrians at Marengo and his subsequent triumphs regained for France the mastery of western and southern Europe, but the Royal Navy still held dominion over the sea. In eight years of war it had grown, losses notwithstanding, from 15,000 to 133,000 men, and from 160 ships of the line and 131 frigates to 192 and 181, respectively. If Bonaparte's own estimate that a fleet of 30 sail of the line were equal to 120,000 troops, Britain had a sea force equal to a land army of almost 800,000 men. Against this, the French navy had been reduced by 50 percent. In 1801, France had only 39 ships of the line and 35 frigates left, and only a few of the battleships were in condition to take to the sea.

The advent of Lord St. Vincent to command of the Channel fleet in 1800, in place of the ineffective Lord Bridport, marked the establishment of a continuous and close blockade of Brest for the first time in the war. The old man brushed aside the vehement protests of his physicians to take the post. "The king and the government require it and the discipline of the British Navy demands it," he declared. "It is of no consequence to me if I die afloat or ashore." Neither men nor ships were spared in a determined effort to prevent anything that floated from entering or leaving France's Atlantic ports.

St. Vincent found the Channel fleet "at the lowest ebb of miserable and wretched discipline." The fault, he declared, lay with the quality of the officers he had inherited. "I am at my wits' end to meet every shift, evasion, and neglect of duty. Seven-eighths of the captains who compose this fleet are practicing every subterfuge to get into the harbour for the winter." Under St. Vincent they had scant success. Even when their ships were driven by storms into Plymouth or Falmouth, no officer was allowed to sleep onshore or put his vessel into the dockyard for repair without the permission of the admiral. Angered by the time-honored corruption in the dockyards, he forced through reforms in naval administration with the same unyielding sternness with which he had dealt with mutiny in the fleet.

The duty division of the squadron blockading Brest, where the combined navies of France and Spain lay inert, was increased from fifteen to thirty ships. Five ships of the line were always on patrol within ten miles of the harbor. Frigates and sloops worked inshore, while the main fleet stood in close to Ushant. Other frigates ranged the Bay of Biscay, intercepting coastal traffic and making raids on French ports. This unrelenting, year-round blockade ruined France's maritime trade and destroyed the morale of the French Navy.

Naval blockade is one of the most onerous duties that can be imposed on a fleet. The routine is boring and wearing on ships and crews alike. The storms and cold of the Bay of Biscay took their toll, and the men suffered from scurvy and influenza. As in the Mediterranean, St. Vincent insisted that attention be paid to the health and morale of his crews, and he revived a system of floating supply and refit established by Admiral Sir Edward Hawke during the Seven Years' War. Victualing ships arrived from England at fixed times with fresh supplies of bread, beef, water, and rum, and carried away the empty casks to be refilled. Scurvy was extirpated by issuing daily doses of lime juice. As a result of these measures, the fleet was able to maintain its relentless vigil for months on end, and the threat to England and Ireland was diminished. "Of all the services I lay claim to," St. Vincent later declared, "the preservation of the health of our fleets is my proudest boast."

In an effort to exploit their control of the sea and the option of amphibious operations conferred by it, the British embarked an army of twenty-two thousand men under the joint command of Lieutenant General Sir Ralph Abercromby and Lord Keith for service in the Mediterranean. Several objectives were considered, but the strategists in London failed to fix on a target. As a result, the great convoy of transports wandered about like Gypsies throughout the summer of 1800—from Minorca to Leghorn, from Leghorn to Malta, from Malta to Minorca, and from Minorca to Gibraltar. Plans were broached for an attack on Ferrol and then against Cádiz to knock Spain out of the war. But these, too, were abandoned. Abercromby and Keith returned to Gibraltar the "laughingstock of friends and foes"—to find a new plan awaiting them.

They were now directed to take part in a risky three-pronged venture designed to destroy the orphaned French Army in Egypt. First, Abercromby was to invade Egypt from the sea; second, a Turkish army would work its way across Asia Minor; and third, an Anglo-Indian force was to be brought from India by way of the Red Sea, where it would cooperate with troops sent from England around the Cape of Good Hope. Prospects for the plan were not bright. Abercromby's force had been reduced to some sixteen thousand troops, ill-equipped and without cavalry, and he was invading a territory of which intelligence was lacking and occupied by a battle-hardened enemy numbering twenty-four thousand men, a third greater than calculated, and much more willing to fight than the London strategists realized.

In December 1800 Abercromby's army arrived from Malta at the staging area on Marmaris Bay on the southern coast of Turkey opposite Rhodes, where they expected to find horses and provisions. The Turks had been lavish with promises, but the only mounts to be had were of poor quality. Yet the six weeks the expedition spent in Marmaris Bay were to prove crucial to the campaign. Abercromby and Keith staged rigorous rehearsals of the landing under conditions that were as realistic as possible. Each man—soldier, sailor, and marine—was put through his part in the intended operation so many times that they eventually performed their tasks almost automatically.

On March 2, 1801, the expeditionary force, under escort by Keith's fleet, anchored in Aboukir Bay after steering among the sunken wrecks that were mute testimony to the completeness of Nelson's victory. Abercromby found no sign of the forces due by way of the Red Sea; in fact, the units coming from India were still at Bombay. For five days, gales and heavy swells made a landing impossible, while French infantry and artillery were seen digging in on a ridge of sand dunes overlooking the landing place, a narrow strip of beach on the Aboukir peninsula.

The operation began at two o'clock in the morning of March 8 with the firing of a rocket from *Foudroyant,* Keith's flagship. Because of shoal water, the transports had to anchor five miles offshore, but the problem had been anticipated during the exercises at Marmaris. To a remarkable extent, the techniques used foreshadowed modern amphibious landings. The first of three waves of fifty-five hundred troops was to be ferried directly to the beach in special flat-bottom boats from the transports, while the backup second wave, in regular ships' boats, was prepositioned at the line of departure, which was about two miles from shore and marked by a pair of gunboats. They would come in as soon as a beachhead was secured. The third wave was to consist of launches carrying the expedition's field guns and gunners.

At 9:00 A.M., under the cover of a cannonade by gunboats and armed launches, the first wave headed toward shore in a well-ordered line. The French met them with a cloud of round shot and grape that whipped up the waters of the bay and drenched the soldiers and marines who, packed fifty to a boat, sat patiently with their muskets between their knees. Several boats were sunk, yet they continued to come in as the sailors pulled at the oars. Once the boats grounded, there was a tremendous cheer as the men leaped ashore, established a beachhead, and rapidly formed up in companies and battalions, as so often rehearsed in Marmaris Bay.

Waving his hat, Major General Sir John Moore led them up an almost perpendicular sand ridge and drove off the two thousand French defenders at the point of the bayonet. They looked "like a heavy wave rolling over a beach," said one officer. Reinforcements repulsed an enemy cavalry charge. The whole operation was over in little more than half an hour. The bruised French withdrew to Alexandria. British losses totaled about seven hundred killed or wounded, while French casualties were about half that number.

The energetic General Kléber, Bonaparte's successor, had been assassinated by a Muslim fanatic, so command of the French army had passed to General Abdullah Jacques Menou, who was not only less competent but also, as a Muslim convert, was something of a laughingstock to his troops. Over the coming months several battles were fought along Egypt's northern coast, all won by the British, although at heavy cost to both sides. Abercromby, who led from the front, was mortally wounded early on. The French divided their forces, one part holed up in Alexandria, while the other withdrew to Cairo, and the campaign settled down to a pair of sieges interrupted by periodic firefights.

⌐

WHILE THESE EVENTS were unfolding in Egypt, the Royal Navy was mobilizing a powerful fleet amid the snow and gales at Great Yarmouth to meet a new threat to Britain's security from the north. In 1800 the cunning Bonaparte, assisted by the unstable Czar Paul, so recently allied with the British and now alienated because they refused to present him with Malta, succeeded in organizing a coalition of Baltic states—Russia and Denmark, which then included Norway, Sweden, and Prussia—called the Armed Neutrality, which like its predecessor of the American War, challenged the Royal Navy's right to stop and search neutral shipping for goods bound for France.

Alarmed, the British feared these nations would exclude their ships from the Baltic trade, thereby striking at the foundation of British sea power by denying the Royal Navy the masts, spars, and other naval stores necessary for operations. Britain would also be deprived of badly needed grain at a time when the domestic harvest had failed following several years of poor crops, and in many places in England, people were in want. Additionally, it was feared that the fleets of Russia, Sweden, and Denmark might be added to the forces arrayed against Britain and tip the balance in Bonaparte's favor. Several clashes occurred as British warships continued to search neutral vessels for contraband, the most serious in July 1800, when a Danish frigate and her convoy were captured by a British squadron.

This incident was resolved by diplomacy, but the Danes, rashly following the lead of the Russians, who had seized British shipping in their ports, placed an embargo on all British merchantmen and declared the Elbe closed to British trade. William Pitt answered the challenge by ordering a powerful fleet to the

Baltic to overawe these nations before they became a menace. The Admiralty entrusted command of this expedition to Admiral Sir Hyde Parker. At sixty-two, Parker was long on seniority and short on recent combat experience. For the previous four years he had been on the Jamaica station, where he had amassed a fortune from the prizes taken by his captains and had married an eighteen-year-old girl. To offset the defects of this appointment, the Admiralty named Horatio Nelson as his second in command.

Nelson had arrived in England three months before with the Hamiltons under a cloud of scandal. Although the admiral was as popular as always with ordinary Englishmen, Nelson and the Hamiltons found themselves welcome only among the most raffish members of high society. The rigorously moral King George turned his back on Nelson at a levee after the briefest greeting. Emma was about to give birth, but the high-waisted dresses of the period and her stoutness concealed her condition. After a chilly meeting with Lady Nelson and a misguided attempt by Nelson to induce her to accept Emma as a friend rather than his mistress, Nelson and his wife reached the end of their marriage. Holding out her hand to him at what was to be their last meeting, Fanny plaintively asked whether she had ever given him cause for complaint or suspicion, and Nelson ruefully acknowledged that she had not. With that they parted, although he continued to provide for her.

It was the low point of Nelson's life. The final break with his wife must have been a blow for a man of Nelson's religious convictions. Moreover, his wounds were troubling him, and he was having difficulty with his remaining eye. Having just reached the rank of vice admiral and hoping to escape his troubles by returning to sea, he notified the Admiralty that he was ready for active service and was given a command under Lord St. Vincent in the English Channel. On January 13, 1801, he broke out his flag on the three-decker *San José,* which he had personally captured from the Spanish at Cape St. Vincent nearly four years before. There were reports that he was going to the Dardanelles to chastise the Russians.

Soon after, Nelson was informed that Emma had given birth to their daughter, who was named Horatia Thompson—Thompson being the pseudonym they used in their letters. Every precaution was taken to avoid a public scandal, and the baby was spirited away to live with a nurse.* At almost the same time, Nelson was assigned to the Baltic expedition, with *St. George,* ninety-eight, as his flatship. On the way to Yarmouth, the excited father stopped off in London to see his new daughter. Later he poured out his heart to Emma. "Now, my own dear wife, for such you are in my eyes

---

*Some writers state that there is evidence the child may have been a twin. The second baby girl was said to have been sent to the Foundlings' Hospital, while Nelson was told that she had died.

and in the face of heaven, I can give full scope to my feelings. . . . You know, my dearest Emma, that there is nothing in the world that I would not do for us to live together, and to have our dear little child with us. . . ."

While the Baltic fleet was being mobilized, the nation was shaken by the unexpected resignation of Pitt, who had been prime minister without a break since 1784. In an effort to end revolutionary violence in Ireland, he had supported Catholic emancipation, or the removal of bars to participation by Catholics in the political life of the nation. When the proposal was rejected by the king on grounds that it would violate his coronation oath as defender of the faith, Pitt resigned. Henry Addington, the Speaker of the House of Commons, was invited by the king to form a new ministry, primarily because he opposed Catholic emancipation.* Addington was an amiable nonentity who owed the Speakership to Pitt, and wits observed that "Pitt is to Addington what London is to Paddington." Several members of Pitt's cabinet, including Lord Spencer, declined to serve in the new government, which was largely staffed by mediocrities. To bolster the ministry, St. Vincent was asked to become first lord of the Admiralty and he brought Thomas Troubridge to the Board of Admiralty as a junior sea lord.

Upon his arrival at Yarmouth, Nelson was angered to find that Sir Hyde Parker was living ashore and was making little effort to get his ships to sea. "Consider how nice it must be lying in bed with a young wife, compared to a damned, cold raw wind," he remarked. Admiral Parker appeared more interested in an elaborate birthday ball being arranged by Lady Parker than the affairs of the fleet. Realizing that the Baltic nations must be attacked before they could organize a defense, Nelson wrote Troubridge, describing conditions at Yarmouth, knowing full well that the letter would be shown to St. Vincent—and it had the desired effect. Parker was ordered by the first lord to immediately put to sea. He suspected that Nelson was behind this peremptory order, and relations between the commanders were so cool that Parker failed to call even a single council of war to outline his plan for operations—if any—before sailing.

THE FLEET THAT SAILED on March 12, 1801, consisted of fifteen ships of the line, including two three-deckers, Parker's *London*, and Nelson's *St. George*.

---

*It is worth noting that in an age of profligacy, Pitt, who had made the British government solvent while neglecting his own financial affairs, was heavily in debt but refused a gift of a hundred thousand pounds from his supporters in the City and a royal grant of thirty thousand pounds from the Privy Purse. With some difficulty, friends persuaded him to accept a loan to keep his furniture and personal effects from being seized by creditors.

It was later increased to eighteen, as well as two fifty-gun ships and numerous frigates, brigs and bomb vessels. Such a strong armada was deemed necessary because if the Baltic nations concentrated their fleets, Parker would face a battle line of ten Danish, eleven Swedish, and twenty Russian vessels. Denmark was chosen as the first target because the British hoped to chastise the Danes before their Russian allies could come to their rescue, and she controlled the Sound, the narrow passage between Denmark and Sweden that served as an entrance to the Baltic from the Kattegat and the North Sea.

Following a stormy passage, the fleet arrived in the Skaw, off the northern tip of Denmark, or Jutland, as it was known, on March 20. There they awaited word from the British envoy, Nicholas Vansittart, who had been sent ahead to Copenhagen in a frigate with an ultimatum warning the Danes to withdraw from the Armed Neutrality or accept the consequences. Everyone was in a somber mood. The weather was bitterly cold, and half the fleet seemed to have a hacking cough. Nelson was much annoyed at the delay. "A fleet of British ships are the best negotiators in Europe," he declared. "While negotiation is going on, the Dane should see our flag waving every time he lifts up his head."

Vansittart returned on March 23 with a negative reply to the ultimatum, and Parker at last summoned Nelson to a council of war to make plans to reduce the capital of a nation with which Britain was not at war. "Now we are sure of fighting," he wrote Emma, "I am sent for." He arrived late on *London* to find the council in a state of gloom. The defenses of Copenhagen, Vansittart reported, were stronger than expected. Parker was reluctant to send in his ships to attack these powerful batteries and favored blockading the Kattegat until the allied navies emerged to give battle. That was not Nelson's style. He was for pressing home an attack before the enemy could organize a defense.

Pacing the great cabin of the flagship, Nelson lucidly presented a plan of battle. The Danish defenses were strongest to the north, where the guns of Hamlet's Elsinore Castle and Swedish batteries on the opposite shore barred the approach to the Sound, so Nelson suggested that the fleet follow the longer route by way of the Great Belt around the island of Zealand, thereby attacking the enemy in the rear, where he was least expecting it. Once the Danes had been dealt with, the bulk of the fleet could press on to smash that half of the Russian fleet that was at Reval while the rest were frozen in the ice at Kronstadt. But the main thing, Nelson insisted, was to attack—and to attack at once. "Go by the Sound or by the Belt or anyhow, only lose not an hour," he declared.

Even the cautious Parker was unable to resist Nelson's enthusiasm, and he agreed to pass through the Belt and attack the Danes but declined to launch an assault against the Russians until later. It is one of the ironies of history that had Nelson's plan been followed through, there would have been no Battle of Copenhagen. On March 26 the fleet weighed anchor, but Parker again changed his mind after his flag captain, William Donnett, warned of the danger of attempting a passage of the Belt with its dangerous shoals without adequate charts. He now decided to brave the narrow northern passage into the Sound despite the Danish and Swedish batteries.

With danger in the offing, Nelson volunteered to lead the way and transferred his flag to the lighter draft *Elephant,* of seventy-four guns. Headwinds delayed the fleet for three days, until March 30, but the passage proved absurdly easy. The Swedes turned out to have mounted only a few large cannon on their side of the passage, so Nelson ordered his ships to hug the Swedish shore, out of range of the Danish guns. That afternoon the entire British fleet anchored safely in the Sound five miles northeast of Copenhagen.

Nelson and Parker at once reconnoitered the defenses of the Danish capital in a schooner. From the sea, Copenhagen was a picturesque city of copper-green spires and steep-pitched roofs. But it was surrounded by walls and batteries and could be approached only by two channels on either side of a large shoal known as the Middle Ground. The inner, narrower passage, called the King's Channel, was heavily defended, most notably by the great Trekroner Battery—named for the three crowns of Denmark, Norway, and Sweden—which blocked an attack from the north. Running south from it was a mile-and-a-half-long line of eighteen fighting ships, with hulks and floating batteries moored among them. To make it even more difficult to attack from this direction, the Danes also had removed buoys and other navigational markers from the channel.

The alternative was to pass through the Outer Channel around the Middle Ground and attack from the south, thereby avoiding the Trekroner's guns. This plan offered the advantage of assaulting the Danish defenses from the direction least expected and at their weakest point. Copenhagen would also be cut off from reinforcement by a Swedish or a Russian fleet sailing in from the Baltic. A northerly wind was required for the first part of the operation and a southerly wind for the second, but Nelson chose this option despite the tricky navigational problems involved. Although naval doctrine of the time held that ships could not stand and fight against fortifications, he wrote that the Danish line of defense "looks formidable to those who are children at war but . . . with ten sail of the line I think I can annihilate them; at all events I hope I am allowed to try."

Parker was only too happy to assign the attack to someone willing to take the risk. He gave Nelson the ten lightest ships of the line, later augmented to twelve, plus six hundred troops, who were to be landed once the guns of the Trekroner Battery had been silenced while he remained with the deeper-draft ships to the north of the city. The nights of March 30 and 31 were passed in sounding and buoying the channel around the Middle Ground. This task was handled with great skill by Captain Edward Riou of the frigate *Amazon*. At about 1:00 P.M. on April 1, Nelson made the signal to weigh, and a great cheer went up as the fleet, led by Riou, moved slowly down the outer passage. By sundown most of the ships had rounded the Middle Ground and anchored at the tip of King's Channel, about two miles to the south of the Danish line. "I will fight them the moment I have a fair wind," Nelson told his officers.

As soon as the fleet anchored, the admiral, as was his custom before a battle, invited his captains to dinner in *Elephant*'s great cabin. They were all in high spirits and drank to a fair wind and victory over the Danes the following day. In the meantime, Thomas Hardy, Nelson's flag captain, was making a daring reconnaissance of the Danish fleet. He went out in a small boat with muffled oars to sound the depth of the water right up to the sides of the enemy vessels. Once the dinner was over, Nelson; Thomas Foley, *Elephant*'s captain; and Captain Riou began to draft and dictate orders for the battle.

Nelson's plan and the presence of Foley recalled the Battle of the Nile. Like the Danes, the French had been anchored in Aboukir Bay, and Foley had led the British fleet around the head of the enemy line to double it. Although the Danish fleet could not be doubled because of shallow water inshore of their fleet, Nelson intended to use the same doctrine of concentration of force to subdue part of the enemy line and then to attack the rest. *Edgar*, of seventy-four guns, the first ship in the British line, was to leapfrog the first four Danish ships to take on the sixty-four-gun *Jylland*. The sixty-fours *Ardent* and *Glatton*, the latter under the command of Captain William Bligh, were to pass *Edgar* on her unengaged side and engage a frigate, a floating battery, and the sixty-four-gun *Dannebrog*, the flagship of Commodore Johan Olfert Fischer. *Isis*, fifty, and Nelson's old *Agamemnon*, sixty-four, supported by a frigate, were to anchor opposite the first three ships of the Danish line, which had been bypassed.

The remaining British ships were to sail along the unengaged side of these vessels and attack the rest of the Danish line and the forts, which were to be hammered by seven bomb ketches. On paper, the attacking force was stronger than that of the defenders, but the Danish line was reinforced by floating batteries and its northern end was covered by the Trekroner Battery and other bastions. Moreover, the Danes were fighting in defense of their capital and homeland. Exhausted by the tensions of the past few days, Nelson dictated his final instructions to his captains from his cot. There would be little opportunity for maneuvering and individual initiative, so every captain was allotted an exact task. Periodically, he broke off his dictation to urge the battery of clerks copying his orders to hurry with their work so the captains would have their copies by daylight.

◡

AS DAWN BROKE on morning of April 2, 1801, the wind veered around to blow from the south, fair for an attack on Copenhagen. At 7:00 A.M. all captains were called to *Elephant* and given their written orders, but there was a last-minute hitch. Much to Nelson's anger, the fleet's pilots, mostly civilians recruited from Baltic trading vessels, refused to take such deep-draft vessels up King's Channel. They had "no other thought than to keep their ship clear of danger, and their own silly heads clear of shot," he declared. The master of *Bellona*, seventy-four, who had been with Nelson at the Nile, volunteered to lead the column, and a boat took him to *Edgar*. At 9:30 A.M. signal flags flew up *Elephant*'s halyards—first to weigh anchor and then to make sail.

The lids of every ship's gun ports snapped open, and the ominous black muzzles of the cannon were run out. Under topsails, the fleet glided toward the anchored line of enemy ships and batteries in silence. "A more beautiful and solemn sight I never witnessed," said Midshipman William Millard of *Monarch*, seventy-four, as *Edgar* moved ahead to take her assigned position. "We saw her passing on through the enemy's fire, and moving in the midst of it to gain her station. Our minds were filled with a sort of awe. Not a word was spoken . . . save by the pilot and helmsman, and their commands, being chanted in much the same manner as the responses in a Cathedral service, added to the solemnity."

As so often happens in war, little went according to plan. *Agamemnon* failed to weather the Middle Ground and got stuck in the mud. *Polyphemus*, sixty-four, took her place. She and *Edgar* were unsupported for some time and aborbed such heavy fire that they had to anchor farther from the Danish line than the 250 yards specified by Nelson. The seventy-fours *Bellona* and *Russell*, which were closely following, swept too far to starboard and also grounded. Both kept firing, but their fire was ineffective because of the distance from their objectives. Nelson had lost the use of a quarter of his largest ships, even before the battle had begun. *Elephant* was saved from a similar fate when the admiral had her helm put over at the last moment, and she steered safely past the stranded *Russell* to take the place designated for *Bellona* opposite *Dannebrog*. Nelson's other captains reacted with commendable independence, especially Captain Riou, whose frigates engaged the Trekroner Battery. *Monarch* passed along the entire Danish line firing broadside after broadside at the ships at the northern end of the Danish line.

The action began just after 10:00 and by 11:30 A.M. had become general. The Danes fought with the utmost ferocity, and the battle developed into a series of duels, with both sides deafened by the roar of the guns and half blinded by smoke. For a time the outcome was uncertain. "*Here* was no manoeuvering," Nelson observed afterward. "It *was* downright fighting."

The gallant Riou's frigates, which were dueling the Trekroner Battery in place of the grounded battleships, were particularly cut up. Each ship was marked by sudden scenes of horror as shot plunged through their sides, filling the air with deadly splinters.

"When I arrived on the maindeck, along which I had to pass," reported Midshipman Millard of *Monarch*, who was sent below on an errand, "there was not a single man standing the whole way from the mainmast forward, a district containing eight guns, some of which were run out ready for firing; others lay dismounted; the others remained where they were after recoiling. . . . I hastened down the foreladder to the lower deck and felt really relieved to find someone alive."

Throughout the engagement, the Danes sent in boatloads of volunteers from the shore to replace casualties and keep their guns firing. A seventeen-year-old lieutenant named Peter Willemoes, who commanded a small floating battery, placed his frail craft under *Elephant*'s counter and fired into the flagship's tall sides until most of his men had been cut down. Following the battle, Nelson asked to meet young Willemoes, congratulated him on his performance, and told Crown Prince Frederick, the Danish ruler, that he should be made an admiral.

Anxious spectators crowded the church towers and rooftops of Copenhagen. They saw little of the battle except for the stabbing flashes of gunfire in the heavy smoke and the mastheads of Nelson's ships. Twice, the Danish commander, Commodore Fischer, was forced to shift his flag, first to another ship and then ashore to the Trekroner Battery. Two-thirds of *Dannebrog*'s crew of 336 were killed or wounded, and several of the British ships suffered similar casualty rates. *Monarch* lost more than 200 men; *Isis* suffered heavy casualties when some of her guns exploded. "Hard pounding," remarked Nelson to Colonel Edward Stewart, the commander of the embarked troops as they paced *Elephant*'s quarterdeck while enemy shot whistled overhead. "But mark you, I would not be elsewhere for thousands!"

Firing fast and accurately, the British were gaining the upper hand despite the battering being taken by their ships. By noon, several of the floating batteries had struck their flags, and some of the enemy craft were aflame. But for Admiral Parker, who had remained to the north of the Middle Ground, where his heavy ships were having difficulty in beating against the wind to come to Nelson's assistance, everything was shrouded in smoke, and the situation appeared confused. *Agamemnon* could be seen aground, while *Bellona* and *Russell* were flying distress signals. At about 1:15 P.M. Parker, fearing that Nelson was being fought to a standstill but was unwilling to withdraw without orders, ordered Signal 39 hoisted to *London*'s masthead: "Discontinue action."

The signal was reported to Nelson, who was still pacing *Elephant*'s quarterdeck with Colonel Stewart. Nelson took no notice and made another

Nelson destroys the Danish fleet and bombards Copenhagen on April 2, 1801. (Beverley Robinson Collection, U.S. Naval Academy Museum)

turn or two on the deck. Lieutenant Frederick Langford, Nelson's signal officer, asked whether it should be repeated, and the admiral replied: "No, acknowledge it."* A moment later he called to Langford, "Is signal 16 [close action] still flying?" Told that it was, he said, "Mind you keep it so." He resumed his pacing, the stump of his right arm twitching in involuntary agitation.

"Do you know what is shown on the commander in chief?" he asked Stewart. "Number 39."

The colonel asked Nelson what that meant, and the admiral replied: "Why to leave off action! Leave off action!" And then he added with a shrug, "Now, damn me if I do!"

It was maddening. Nelson had fought a bitter fight to bring the enemy to bay, and now that he had accomplished it, Parker was ordering him to break off and retreat. But how could he ignore a direct order? Carefully extending his telescope to full focus, Nelson put it to his blind eye and exclaimed to *Elephant*'s captain: "You know, Foley, I have only one eye—I

*In Nelson's time, to "acknowledge" a flag signal meant no more than that it had been seen. To show that its meaning had been looked up in the signal book and was "understood," the signal had to be repeated or hoisted by the ship for which it was intended.

have a right to be blind sometimes. I really do not see the signal!" The battle went on.

Unfortunately, Riou saw the signal and had no choice but to obey. "What will Nelson think of us?" he asked as he ordered his battered frigates to withdraw from action. As the stern of *Amazon* wore around, he was cut in two by an enemy shot. Lieutenant John Quilliam, later the first lieutenant of *Victory* at Trafalgar, took over command and got the frigates away. No other ship obeyed the signal. Had they done so, they would have had to run the gantlet of the whole Danish fleet and the shore batteries as they sailed northward to join Parker's squadron.

Between 1:00 and 2:00 P.M., the enemy's fire slackened. The Danish flagship drifted out of line in flames and exploded like *L'Orient* at the Nile. Two floating batteries sank trying to escape into the harbor, and many of the enemy ships and batteries were smoking wrecks. The British also had suffered heavily, with six ships aground and the others cut up aloft. There was no sign of a Danish surrender, however, and just as boats from the British fleet pulled toward the Danish ships that were thought to have surrendered to take possession of them, they were fired on. Nelson angrily determined to end the battle with a ruthlessness that recalled his dealings with the Jacobins in Naples two years before.

Using the head of the flagship's rudder post as a desk, he penned a note "To the Brothers of Englishmen, the Danes," and sent it under flag of truce to Crown Prince Frederick. Unless the Danes ceased fire immediately, he wrote, "Lord Nelson will be obliged to set on fire all the floating batteries he has taken without having the power of saving the brave Danes who have defended them." He sealed it carefully with his coat of arms so the enemy would not think it had been written in a hurry. The note had the desired effect, possibly because the Danes knew that Czar Paul had been assassinated—a fact as yet unknown to the British—and realized that the Armed Neutrality would soon collapse.

The next day, Nelson went ashore to negotiate an extension of the armistice, and it was extended on a day-by-day basis. Later it was extended for fourteen weeks, and the Danes agreed to resupply the British fleet before it pressed on to deal with the Swedes and the Russians. In return, Nelson refrained from bombarding the Danish capital. The Battle of Copenhagen, observed Admiral Mahan, was "the severest and most doubtful [Nelson] had ever fought." Nonetheless, he had all but annihilated an enemy fleet for the second time in three years and won a battle that, except for his refusal to obey Parker's recall signal, might well have ended in disaster. Casualties were heavy, with the British losing 253 men killed in action and 688 wounded, while the Danes had 790 killed, 900 wounded, and 2,500 taken prisoner. Twelve Danish ships were captured, but they were in such bad shape that all but a sixty-gun vessel were burned.

Repairs having been made to his fleet, Parker entered the Baltic on April 12 with seventeen sail of the line. To Nelson's annoyance, he did not press on, but waited off the Swedish coast for new instructions from the Admiralty. Nelson urged an immediate attack on the Russian fleet at Reval before it could escape, which would convince the new Russian Czar, Alexander I, to abandon the Baltic alliance. Parker cautioned that a too-rapid advance might expose the fleet to a combined Russian and Swedish armada, to which Nelson replied, "I wish there were twice as many; the more numerous, the easier the victory!" By this he meant that a multinational fleet unused to joint operations would be fair game for a disciplined British battle fleet.

Fresh orders arrived on May 5—Parker was recalled, never to be employed at sea again—and Nelson was named to command the fleet. "Your Lordship's whole conduct from your first appointment to this hour," wrote St. Vincent, "is the subject of our constant admiration. . . . All agree there is but one Nelson." Perhaps he recalled that Nelson's disobedience of orders at the Battle of Cape St. Vincent had given him a victory and his title.

Wasting not an hour, Nelson sailed for Reval, but because of Parker's procrastination, it was too late. Three days before the arrival of the British, the ice had broken, enabling the Russian fleet to escape to Kronstadt. Czar Alexander, who had no wish to continue the quarrel with Britain, reversed his father's pro-French policies, raised the embargo on British shipping, and accepted the legality of the right of search and seizure of contraband in neutral bottoms. Upon hearing the news, Napoleon got into a shouting rage.

In Britain, Nelson's victory was greeted with relief, and he was raised one step in the peerage and created Viscount Nelson. Parker, in pointed contrast, got nothing. For the second time, Nelson returned home a popular hero. The admiral's first act on his arrival in England was to visit the naval hospital at Yarmouth, crowded with sailors wounded at Copenhagen. A doctor who made the rounds with him reported that Nelson stopped at every bedside for a brief word. With a sailor who had lost an arm, he had the following conversation:

Nelson: "Well, Jack, what's the matter with you?"

Sailor: "Lost my arm, Your Honour."

Nelson paused, looked down at his own empty sleeve, then at the sailor, and said playfully, "Well, Jack, then you and I are spoiled for fishermen." And then he was off to London—and Lady Hamilton.

BRITAIN'S CUP OF rejoicing was not yet full, however. Alarmed by the desperate situation of the Army of the Orient under siege in Egypt, Bonaparte made several attempts to relieve it. Urged on by the first consul, Vice Admi-

Admiral Horatio Viscount Nelson. An engraving based on a portrait by Sir William Beechey. (U.S. Naval Academy Museum)

ral Honoré Ganteaume slipped out of Brest during a storm in January 1801 with five thousand troops and seven ships of the line. Once into the Mediterranean, however, he took fright like Admiral Bruix at the proximity of the British and put into Toulon. "You must, at whatever price whatever, bring aid to the Army of the Orient," Bonaparte admonished him. Under this threat, Ganteaume set out again early in June, but finding Alexandria under blockade, returned to Toulon, having dared nothing and accomplished nothing.

Bonaparte tried again. While Ganteaume was making for the Mediterranean, the British blockading squadrons had left their stations off Cádiz and Ferrol to pursue him, and a dozen Spanish ships of the line were able to concentrate at Cádiz under a French admiral. Another squadron, this one of three of the line and a frigate under Rear Admiral Durand Linois, escaped from Toulon on June 13, with orders to join the Cádiz fleet and then to make another effort to resupply the troops in Egypt. Running into a superior force under the command of James Saumarez at Gibraltar, Linois took refuge in Algeciras Bay. The British attacked on July 4, but the wind failed, and the Spaniards deliberately grounded their ships in shallow water under the guns of some nearby shore batteries. *Hannibal,* a British seventy-four-gun ship, was lost in this frustrating action, and Saumarez's other ships were cut up.

Linois was joined by a Franco-Spanish squadron of five of the line from Cádiz, and on July 12 again headed for the strait. Working around the clock, Saumarez had refitted his five remaining seventy-fours, and as they sailed from Gibraltar the musicians of his flagship *Formidable* played "Heart of Oak" and the garrisons's band replied with "Britons, Strike Home!" Outnumbered nearly two to one, Saumarez attacked that night. In the darkness and confusion, two Spanish three-deckers, *Real Carlos* and *San Hermenegildo,* both of 112 guns, fired into each other, collided, caught fire, and blew up within a few minutes of each other, with the loss of nearly two thousand men. A French seventy-four also was captured.

In Egypt itself, French plans were going equally awry. The British, having bypassed Alexandria, were joined by four thousand Turkish troops and twelve hundred Mamelukes and were advancing on Cairo. At the same time, six thousand men long due from India had arrived by way of the Red Sea and were crossing the desert from Suez to join in operations. Homesick and dispirited, the French troops in the Egyptian capital surrendered on June 27, 1801, and those locked up in Alexandria capitulated about two months later. In all, about twenty-four thousand men, along with more than six hundred guns, had been routed by a far inferior force. So ended Bonaparte's bold oriental adventure—rendered a total failure by Britain's naval power.

For all this, Britons were proud, yet they were also worn out. "I wish all these victories may lead to peace," sighed Betsey Fremantle, whose husband was serving with Nelson. Britain had been struggling against France's attempt to impose its hegemony on Europe for nine years, yet the coalitions of Continental powers painfully and expensively knit together had been easily crushed by the French. The British people were weary of high taxes, spiraling prices, and the unending sacrifice of money and blood. Britain and France had proved that neither could prevail over the other, it was said. Britain controlled the sea; France, the land. Moreover, Bonaparte, after eighteen months in power, seemed less "the last adventurer in the lottery of revolution," whom Pitt had so contemptuously described, than a reasonable leader who desired stability and tranquillity for his nation.

Responding to the demand for peace, Addington opened secret negotiations with the French. Napoleon, faced with the collapse of the Baltic alliance and the destruction of the Army of the Orient, saw in these overtures the possibility of winning at the peace table what he had been unable to gain on the battlefield. As masterful a negotiator and practitioner of psychological warfare as he was a general, he hid his own eagerness for a settlement and exploited Addington's desire for a quick end to the war.

Bonaparte's most brilliant ploy was to concentrate a bogus "invasion" army on the Channel coast—much to the consternation of the British. Having investigated the possibility of invading England in 1798 and concluding it was impossible without command of the sea, he had no intention of carrying out the operation, but a gullible Addington convinced himself that a landing was imminent. The Paris newspapers, so anxiously scanned by British politicians, were filled with boastful proclamations, and troops and small boats were being gathered at Boulougne and other ports.

A warier man than Addington might have suspended negotiations until these ominous preparations ceased, but he was like a rabbit hypnotized by a boa constrictor. It never occurred to him that Napoleon was bluffing. Once again, Britain was gripped by an invasion alarm. Volunteers drilled on every village green, French spies were suspected of lurking in the shadows, and Britons were urged to be ready to repel the invader. "Billy" Pitt, in retirement at Walmer, carried out his duties as lord warden of the Cinque Ports by drilling an assortment of yokels.

As a public relations gesture, Nelson was dragged away from the arms of his mistress and appointed to the command of a grab bag of light craft guarding the Channel. Nevertheless, he took up his new task with his usual enthusiasm and prepared an elaborate plan for the defense of the mouth of the Thames, Kent, Sussex, and Suffolk. As always, believing the best defense was an offense, Nelson bombarded Boulogne and the bogus invasion flotilla for sixteen hours on August 4. Little damage was done, however. Eleven nights later he sent in a raiding party that attempted to "cut out" the barges and other landing craft, but the assault was repulsed with heavy casualties and recalled the disastrous attack on Tenerife in 1797.

Nelson's rank forbade him from leading the raid in person, so he had awaited the outcome in a frigate offshore. Miserable over the results, he resolved to never again to engage in an operation in which he was not in personal command. "My mind suffers much more than if I had a leg shot off," he wrote St. Vincent.

Napoleon's war of nerves against Britain was a brilliant success. In his eagerness to end the threat of invasion, Addington agreed to the French offer of a truce on October 2, 1801. For reasons unknown to the British, the first consul was also anxious for a quick peace. He had been informed of the defeat of his Egyptian army while the British had not yet received the news, and wished to reach a settlement before they learned of this disaster. Under the terms of the armistice, Britain recognized France's predominant position in Europe and abandoned to France, Spain, and Holland all the conquests she had made during the war with the exception of Trinidad and Ceylon. For a nation dependent on an overseas empire and sea power, this was folly. Malta, Elba, and Minorca in the Mediterranean; Tobago, St. Lucia, and Martinique in the West Indies; and the Cape of Good Hope and various military and commercial stations in India were given up. These terms were formally ratified by the Treaty of Amiens five months later. Not long after, Bonaparte, with the approval of a plebiscite of the French people, made himself Consul for Life.

Neither side expected peace to last very long, however, for the British could not accept the Frenchman's ultimate goal of the domination of Europe and perhaps Asia as well, nor could he accept the existence of an undefeated England. But in the brief interval of peace among the great powers of Europe, the infant U.S. Navy made its first bow on the European scene.

CHAPTER 16

"To the Shores of Tripoli"

WREATHED IN THE acrid smoke of her salutes, the strange warship swung to her anchor off Constantinople on the morning of November 9, 1800, as the rising sun brightened the domes and minarets of the old city's countless mosques. She had slipped into the Golden Horn during the night, and when daylight revealed her presence, it created consternation, for she was flying a curious flag with stars and stripes never before seen in the heart of the Ottoman Empire. A harbor boat came alongside, and Captain William Bainbridge identified his ship as the twenty-four-gun frigate *George Washington* of the U.S. Navy, and said he had official business with Sultan Selem III.

Despite this brave show, *George Washington* was on a mission that was obnoxious to her captain. While the rest of the U.S. Navy was fighting the French in the Caribbean, the frigate had been dispatched two months before by President Adams to Algiers, one of the Barbary states, with an installment of tribute. The local ruler, the dey of Algiers, had angered the sultan, his nominal sovereign, by entering into a treaty with France at the very moment the French were despoiling the Turkish ruler of his empire in Egypt. In an effort to placate the sultan's anger, the dey had ordered Bainbridge to carry his ambassador and a tribute of his own to Constantinople.

When Bainbridge refused, he was told: "You pay me tribute, by which you become my slaves. I have a right to order you as I may think proper." With heavy guns trained on his ship, the chagrined American had no choice but to hoist Algerian colors and carry out this distasteful mission. As soon as *George Washington* was out of sight of land, Bainbridge again raised the American flag, but the voyage to Constantinople was not a happy one. Besides the Algerian envoy, a large retinue of aides and slaves, and $1 million in gold and jewels, the frigate carried a menagerie worthy of Noah's Ark—twenty lions, three tigers, five antelope, four horses, and a herd of sheep and cattle and as well as a pair of ostriches and twenty parrots.

She soon smelled like a barnyard, and the overcrowded conditions

239

created considerable ill will between the American crewmen and their passengers. Five times a day, the devout Muslims assembled on the spar deck to prostrate themselves in prayer to Allah, sometimes making it difficult to work the ship. *George Washington* had to tack frequently because of shifting winds in the Mediterranean, which caused considerable scurrying about as the faithful frantically shifted position to face toward Mecca. Thus everyone greeted the frigate's arrival at Constantinople with considerable relief.

Luckily, the sultan, who had never heard of the United States, noted that the American ensign, like the Turkish flag, contained a constellation of stars and was favorably impressed by this omen. He received Bainbridge warmly, presented him with gifts, and sent him on his way with a firman guaranteeing him the respect of all the nations of the Ottoman Empire, including the Barbary states. It came in handy, for upon *George Washington*'s return to Algiers, the dey attempted to seize the vessel and hold her crew for ransom. Bainbridge produced the sultan's firman, and as he later recounted, the "blood thirsting tyrant became a mild, humble and even crouching dependent."

On his return home, Bainbridge's account of his humiliation excited a public uproar and created problems for Thomas Jefferson, the new president of the United States. The American people demanded that Algiers be punished for its insult to the flag, but such punishment could only be administered by a navy, and Jefferson had been cutting away at that service. On becoming president in 1801, he espoused a policy of economy in government and reduction of the national debt. Looking for areas where spending could be curbed, the eyes of Jefferson and his major ally in this task, the Swiss-born secretary of the treasury, Albert Gallatin, had fallen on the U.S. Navy, which was linked in their minds to their Federalist predecessors.

Under President Adams, government expenditures had averaged about $11 million a year, $2.5 million of which were earmarked for the navy—a service that Gallatin, as a Pennsylvania congressman, rigidly opposed on grounds that it was wasteful and superfluous. Jefferson's view was more ambiguous. While minister to France and secretary of state, he had advocated a navy to chastise the Barbary pirates rather than trying to bribe them. By the time of his elevation to the presidency, however, he had adopted some of the antinavy ideology of his supporters. Jefferson intended to rely on "such a naval force only as may protect our coasts and harbors" and not on a seagoing fleet "which by its own expenses and the eternal wars in which it will implicate us, grind us with public burthens, & sink us under them."

The Jeffersonian ideal of a purely defensive navy was epitomized by a fleet of some two hundred gunboats that took up station in the nation's major ports from Maine to Louisiana. Ranging in length from about fifty feet to seventy feet, propelled by oars and sails, and armed with one or two cannons, these craft were intended to provide harbor defense in conjunction with fixed batteries. Cheap to build and operate, they could not become "an excitement to engage in offensive maritime war," according to the president.

But for all its appeal to logic and economy, Jefferson's gunboat policy was a failure. Gunboats could not convoy merchant shipping on the high seas, could not prevent the coast of the United States from being blockaded and could not ward off an invasion. They were costly to maintain and drained the treasury of some $1.85 million that could have been used for building frigates. Even worse, critics charged, they were "subversive to good morals, discipline and subordination" by confining officers and men to harbor duty. In almost all respects, the gunboat policy ignored the hard-bought lessons of naval warfare. As Admiral Mahan pointed out, a "true defense consists in imposing upon the enemy a wholesome fear of yourself."

So dim were the U.S. Navy's prospects under the Jeffersonian Republicans that the first four men to whom the president offered the post of secretary of the navy refused it. "I believe I shall have to advertise for a secretary of the navy," he declared, probably more in desperation than jest. Robert Smith, who finally accepted the office, was an admiralty lawyer from Baltimore whose family was prominent in Republican politics. The historian Henry Adams has described him as "easy and cordial, glad to oblige and fond of power and show, popular in the Navy, yielding in the Cabinet, but as little fitted as Jefferson himself for . . . administering with severe economy an unpopular service."

Reductions in the size of the navy had begun even before Smith assumed the duties of his office in July 1801. With the exception of the thirteen frigates the government was required to keep by the law passed at the end of Adams's term, all the remaining ships were stripped of their gear and sold. Only $276,000 was realized from the sale of sixteen ships, an amount that would barely cover the cost of a single frigate. Work ceased on a seventy-four-gun ship that had been laid down under Benjamin Stoddert's regime as navy secretary, and timber acquired for others was placed in storage, where some of it rotted. Naval constructors were dismissed, and Jefferson and Gallatin gave serious thought to closing the navy yards established by the Federalists and to consolidating most shore operations at the Washington Navy Yard.

Once the government had settled in Washington, the Navy Office was housed in a two-and-a-half-story brick building where the Eisenhower Executive Office Building now stands. It shared the thirty-four rooms in the structure with the War and State Departments. The secretary of the navy and his staff were housed in three offices on the second floor. The stairs leading to the secretary's room, it was said, constantly creaked under the tread of officers seeking appointments and senators and congressmen trying to finagle government contracts for political friends.

Jefferson considered dividing the frigates into two groups, one of six ships, which were to remain in commission with reduced crews, while the other seven were to be mothballed in a huge, covered dry dock designed by the president himself, an inveterate tinkerer. Referring to the corruption said to flourish in the dockyards, he said that there "they would be under the immediate eye of the [Navy] department, and would require but one set of plunderers to take care of them."

THE NAVY WAS SAVED from being dismantled by the insolence of the Barbary pirates. Bainbridge's account of his treatment at Algiers became public at the same time the American consuls at Tripoli and Tunis reported that these satrapies were becoming increasingly belligerent. Yusuf Karamanli, the pasha of Tripoli, was jealous because the United States was paying higher tribute to Algiers than to him, while the bey of Tunis was restive because no bribes had come his way in three years. On May 10, 1801, the Tripolitans declared war on the United States in their own picturesque way—by chopping down the flagstaff in front of the American consulate.

Even though he was unaware of the Tripolitan declaration of war, Jefferson decided to send what he called "a squadron of observation" to the Mediterranean. Bribing the corsairs was "money thrown away," he declared. "There is no end to the demands of these powers, nor any security in their promises." The frigates *President*, forty-four, *Philadelphia*, thirty-eight, and *Essex*, thirty-two, plus the schooner *Enterprise*, twelve, were readied for sea. And so began Thomas Jefferson's long, frustrating, and ultimately less than successful attempt to suppress the Barbary pirates.

THOMAS TRUXTUN, the hero of the Quasi-War, was first offered command of the squadron, but his head may have been turned by the adulation he had received, and he would not accept the appointment unless offensive action was contemplated against the corsairs. Informed by Secretary Smith that the squadron would see action only if war had been declared by the Tripolitans, he declined the appointment. It was offered then to Richard Dale, who nearly a quarter century before had been John Paul Jones's first lieutenant in *Bonhomme Richard*.

Dale sailed on June 2, 1801, flying the broad pennant of a commodore in *President*, with James Barron as his flag captain. Dale was directed to proceed first to Gibraltar to ascertain the state of affairs in the Mediterranean. If all were well, he was to show the flag and return home at the end of the year, when the enlistments of most of the crews would be up. But if any of the Barbary pirates had declared war on the United States, Dale was instructed to "protect our commerce and chastise their insolence—by sinking, burning or destroying their ships & Vessels wherever you shall find them."

Following a stormy Atlantic crossing, Dale arrived a month later at Gibraltar, where he hoped the British would allow the U.S. Navy to establish a base, as they had in the West Indies during the Quasi-War. The British agreed to accommodate the Americans, but to his surprise, the commodore also found two Tripolitan vessels riding at anchor at Gibraltar. They were the twenty-six-gun *Meshouda,* commanded by Murad Reis, a Scottish adventurer formerly known as Peter Lisle, who had become a Muslim; and a sixteen-gun brig, both awaiting the opportunity to slip out into the Atlantic to attack American commerce. Dale left *Philadelphia* to keep an eye on the corsairs and pressed on into the Mediterranean.

Although the sudden and unexpected appearance of Dale's ships evoked expressions of devoted friendship from Algiers and Tunis, Yusuf Karamanli, the ruler of Tripoli, remained undisturbed behind his stout fortifications, built by generations of Christian prisoners. Having learned of the Tripolitan declaration of war, Dale blockaded Tripoli, but the blockade was ineffective because there were not enough ships to maintain it when some of the vessels had to return to Gibraltar and Malta for water and fresh supplies.

The only thing accomplished by the squadron was the capture by *Enterprise* of a fourteen-gun Tripolitan cruiser after a spirited, three-hour fight. Repeated attempts by the Tripolitans to board were beaten off, and superior American gunnery took its toll. The carnage on board the enemy vessel was dreadful: twenty of her crew of eighty men were killed, and another thirty were wounded. The Americans suffered no casualties. No provision had been made for dealing with prizes, so Lieutenant Andrew Sterett, *Enterprise*'s captain, ordered the vessel stripped and turned her loose. When the battered craft made port, the furious dey had the captain paraded around Tripoli astride an ass and then bastinadoed—given five hundred blows on the soles of his feet. As soon as the news reached Gibraltar, the crews of the two ships under observation of *Philadelphia*, fearing similar treatment, abandoned their vessels.

With the enlistments of most of his men running out, Dale headed for home near the end of the year, blaming the failure to achieve permanent results on the lack of sufficient ships to simultaneously conduct a blockade, convoy merchantmen, and deploy vessels for replenishment, as well as on the one-year enlistments. Dale's return was delayed when a pilot ran *President* aground and seriously damaged her. It was an ignominious ending to the first appearance of an American naval squadron in the Mediterranean. Nevertheless, the harassment of American shipping by the Tripolitans ceased at least temporarily, and it is reasonable to assume that the presence of the squadron gave pause to the other Barbary states when they thought of attacking American ships.

Now drawn deeper into a conflict with the Barbary pirates, President Jefferson abandoned his efforts to liquidate the navy, and early in 1802 dispatched a slightly more powerful squadron to the Mediterranean. Once again command was offered to Truxtun, who requested that a captain be appointed to handle *Chesapeake,* forty-four, his flagship, while he dealt with the squadron. He pointed out that Dale had received such assistance, and inasmuch as the new squadron contained numerous young, inexperienced, and contentious officers, he would be in even greater need of help. Smith agreed but later turned down the request, saying there was a scarcity of ranking officers. As a result, Truxtun angrily stomped off the flagship and went ashore.

The Navy Department then gave the appointment to Captain Richard V. Morris, who may have been chosen because of his political connections. In addition to *Chesapeake,* the squadron included four other frigates and several smaller craft, which made it more formidable than the flotilla sent out under Dale. The crews of these ships had signed on for two years, double the previous enlistment, which meant the ships could remain on station for a longer period. Morris took his wife with him, and some of his officers who thought she controlled the squadron's movements called her the "commodoress." She probably was not alone because women, usually the wives of warrant and petty officers, frequently sailed in U.S. Navy ships. The Navy Department usually left it to the discretion of the individual squadron commanders.

Although everyone was convinced that the Tripolitan resistance would collapse under the first determined assault by the American squadron, Tripoli was far less vulnerable to attack than it appeared. The city was protected by walls that bristled with cannon and was impervious to most of the shot that could be fired by the squadron's guns. Further, the attackers had no light-draft craft that could operate among the reefs off the North African coast to make the blockade effective. And the theater of operations was more than three thousand miles from home, which meant that the squadron would have to depend on the goodwill of the various European powers for repair facilities and supplies, especially after merchant ships dispatched to replenish it refused to venture past Gibraltar for fear of capture by the corsairs. Faced with these difficulties, only a commodore with imagination and independent judgment stood a chance of success—and these were qualities sadly lacking in Morris. As Charles Goldsborough, the Navy Department's chief clerk, later noted, "he might have acquitted himself well in the command of a single ship, under the orders of a superior, but . . . was not competent for the command of a squadron."

While the squadron, which arrived at Gibraltar in bits and pieces near the end of May 1802, provided added protection for American shipping, it was largely ineffective. The major operation conducted by Morris's squadron was a raid on a dozen small grain ships trapped in a bay near Tripoli. Lieutenant David Porter led several small boats crowded with sailors and marines along with two craft loaded with combustibles to burn the enemy vessels. Under a hail of bullets from about a thousand soldiers ashore, the raiders fired the grain boats and made their getaway. Fifteen of the Americans were killed or wounded, including Porter, who was hit in both legs, and only about half the grain, which was difficult to burn, was destroyed.

Nevertheless, Morris was satisfied with the exploit, but when he tried to capitalize on it with a message proposing peace negotiations, the pasha of Tripoli was not impressed. "I do not fear war," he boasted. "It is my trade." He demanded two hundred thousand dollars to end the conflict plus complete reimbursement for all its costs. Morris angrily rejected the demand, and the war continued. For the most part, the squadron sailed from port to port, accomplishing little, while the officers took in the sights and fought duels among themselves—at least one with fatal consequences. "What have they done but dance and wench?" asked William Eaton, the outspoken American consul at Tunis. Morris must have recognized his inadequacies, because he sent few reports to Washington, once remaining silent for nearly six months. When he did send dispatches, they were often short and cryptic.

Wearying of the squadron's inaction, which was proving an embarrassment to his administration, Jefferson relieved Morris in June 1803. "From his inactivity hitherto, I have no expectation that anything will be done against Tripoli by the frigates in the Mediterranean under his command," the exasperated president declared. Morris later faced a court of inquiry, which found that he "did not conduct himself and his command of the Mediterranean squadron with the diligence or activity necessary to execute the important duties of his station," and he was dismissed from the navy.

⌐⌐

CASTING ABOUT FOR a commodore who would at last humble the Barbary corsairs, the eye of Secretary Smith fortunately fell on Edward Preble. A native of Maine, Preble had served as a youth in a privateer during the

Revolution and as a midshipman in the Massachusetts State Navy. After the war he sailed for fifteen years in various merchantmen before joining the newly organized navy in 1798 as a lieutenant. When the Quasi-War broke out, Preble was promoted to captain and given command of the frigate *Essex*. Unlike most of the navy's officers, he did not serve in the Caribbean during that conflict, but escorted some Yankee trading vessels around the Cape of Good Hope on a long and lonely voyage to the East Indies and back. He contracted malaria and stomach ulcers, which prevented him from taking an active role in the opening phase of the Barbary war and plagued him for the rest of his life.

Preble had considerable difficulty getting his new command to sea. For one thing, *Constitution*, his flagship, had been laid up since the end of the war with France and required extensive repairs. And for another, Albert Gallatin's economy measures made it difficult to recruit crews for the squadron because the monthly pay of able seamen had been slashed to ten dollars. To obtain sailors, Preble offered volunteers four months' pay in advance and hoped they would not desert before he sailed. International events also conspired against him. The Peace of Amiens, which ended the long-running war between Britain and France, was showing signs of breaking down, and the demand for America's produce was soaring—along with the wages of merchant seamen, making it even more difficult to secure men for the navy. Preble fell back on foreign seamen trying to avoid impressment by roving British cruisers by serving in the U.S. Navy. "I do not believe that I have twenty native Americans on board," the commodore said of the *Constitution*'s crew. Similar conditions prevailed throughout the squadron, and about three-quarters of *Philadelphia*'s complement were listed as British subjects.

Preble's ships put to sea as each ship completed fitting out, rather than as a unit, and the last of them did not reach Gibraltar until November 1803. The squadron had only two frigates, *Constitution* and *Philadelphia*, which was under the command of William Bainbridge, but unlike his predecessors, Preble had several smaller ships capable of operating close inshore—the sixteen-gun brigs *Argus* and *Siren* and the twelve-gun schooners *Vixen* and *Nautilus*. Preble was also given authority to purchase shallow-draft gunboats in the Mediterranean.

Immediately after putting to sea, Preble placed *Constitution* on a war footing. The men were repeatedly exercised at the guns and drilled in the use of small arms and cutlasses, and boarding pikes. Swearing and "immorality" were forbidden. Preble inspected the ship from stem to stern and from spar deck to hold every day. Beards, long hair, and dirty and slovenly clothes were not permitted. Rebels and malingerers were quickly dealt with. The flagship's logbook records numerous floggings. Preble was stingy with praise and he had a temper that was frightening to behold.* But the victims of his rages usually found, as one man observed, that they "did not last long enough for him to take a turn of the quarterdeck," and he usually apologized as quickly as the storm had blown up.

Neither Preble nor his officers, who regarded him as an unfeeling martinet, liked each other. Keeping largely to himself, he dined with his senior officers only once a week. When he strode the weather side of the quarterdeck, no one was permitted to approach him unless summoned or bearing an urgent message. Sectional prejudice may have been a factor in his unpopularity. He was a New Englander, and most of his officers were from the middle and southern states. Youthful, high-spirited, and dreaming of glory, they contrasted sharply with their captain. Preble, then forty-two years old, noted unhappily that most of his officers were half his age. "They have given me nothing but a pack of boys!" he exploded. Among them were Stephen Decatur Jr., Isaac Hull, David Porter, James Lawrence, and James Biddle—all of whom would soon be proud to call themselves "Preble's boys."

Sailing off the coast of Spain in the failing light of evening on September 10, 1803, Preble sighted a strange vessel that had the look of a ship-of-war. He ordered *Constitution*'s crew to quarters and had her guns run out. After hailing the stranger several times and receiving unsatisfactory answers, Preble, operating as always on a short fuse, seized a speaking trumpet and shouted: "I am now going to hail you for the last time. If a proper answer is not returned, I will fire a shot into you!"

"If you fire a shot, I will return a broadside!" replied the strange vessel, which was enveloped in darkness.

"What ship is that?" demanded Preble.

"This is His Britannic Majesty's ship *Donegal,* eighty-four guns, Sir Richard Strachan, an English commodore. Send a boat on board!"

Leaping atop the hammock nettings and steadying himself against the shrouds, Preble cried: "This is the United States ship *Constitution*, forty-four guns, Edward Preble, an American commodore, who will be damned before he sends his boat on board of any vessel! Blow [on] your matches, boys!"

---

*Fully aware of his volatile temper, Preble usually waited a day or two before he decreed the extent of a culprit's punishment. Even though he was known for his strict discipline, he was less notorious than some captains, notably John Rodgers, for use of the lash. In contrast, Isaac Hull and Stephen Decatur were known for their fair-minded leniency.

The creak of yards and the squeaking of ropes in their blocks sounded louder than usual as the ships ran side by side. After a few minutes, the sound of an approaching boat was heard. A British lieutenant came on board to sheepishly explain that he was not from *Donegal,* a two-decker, but from *Maidstone,* a mere thirty-two-gun frigate. He explained that his captain had delayed in answering Preble's challenge because he was certain the larger ship was an enemy vessel and he needed time to get his crew to quarters. The incident delighted Preble's "boys" and helped create a bond between them and their commander.

Preble arrived at Gibraltar a few days after the encounter with *Maidstone,* to find the situation in the Mediterranean not good. Tripoli was actively at war with the United States, Tunis had expelled the American consul, and Morocco had evidently decided to disregard the treaty made with the United States in 1786 and was seizing the few Yankee vessels found in the area. The commodore decided to meet force with force. Soon after his arrival, he wrote Secretary Smith: "I believe a firm and decided conduct in the first instance toward those of them who make war against us would have a good effect."

Philadelphia and *Vixen* were sent to blockade Tripoli, while Preble took *Constitution,* two frigates diverted from Morris's old squadron that were returning home, and several smaller vessels to Tangier. Overawed by this show of force, the Moroccan emperor immediately pledged eternal peace with the United States. With Morocco now under control, Preble established a base at Syracuse in Sicily and turned his attention to Tripoli without having to worry about trouble in his rear.* But this excellent beginning to Preble's tour of command was suddenly clouded by the sickening news that *Philadelphia* had run aground off Tripoli and been captured by the enemy.

The frigate was pursuing a small Tripolitan vessel inshore on October 31, 1803, and was making a good eight knots under full sail. Bainbridge knew that these waters were shallow and had three leadsmen in the bow calling out the depth. Once his quarry had escaped into shallow water, he put about and headed for the open sea. Suddenly *Philadelphia* shuddered and ground to a stop. She had struck the uncharted Kalusha Reef, barely five miles off Tripoli itself.

Bainbridge tried to push the vessel over the shoal by crowding on sail, but only succeeded in driving her farther onto the rocks. In an attempt to lighten the frigate, he ordered her fresh water pumped out, all her guns jet-

---

*Sir Alexander Ball, the British governor of Malta, offered Preble the use of a base on the island, but supplies there were short because of the needs of the Royal Navy.

BURNING of the FRIGATE PHILADELPHIA in the HARBOUR of TRIPOLI 16 Feb. 1804. by y Gallant Tars of Columbia commanded by Lieut Decatur

The destruction of the captured American frigate *Philadelphia* on February 16, 1804. (Beverley Robinson Collection, U.S. Naval Academy Museum)

tisoned except for a few aft, and finally, her foremast was cut away. As it fell, it carried away the main-topgallent mast. Nothing helped, and *Philadelphia* remained stuck. With Tripolitan gunboats circling around and a pronounced list preventing him from bringing the frigate's few remaining guns to bear, Bainbridge was unable to flee or fight. He destroyed his signal books, ordered holes chopped in the frigate's bottom, and struck her colors.

Unfortunately, the work of scuttling the vessel was bungled. Two days after her capture a storm blew up, and the Tripolitans refloated her. *Philadelphia* was towed into the harbor for refitting under the guns of the citadel and in full view of her 309 former crewmen, who were to remain captive for nineteen months. Despite the widely circulated tales of Tripolitan barbarity, for the most part the captured officers were decently treated. Bainbridge and David Porter, his first lieutenant, were allowed to conduct a school where the junior officers were taught navigation, tactics, and languages. The men were put to work on the fortifications and sometimes beaten, but were probably treated little worse than the pasha's own people. What few comforts they had were due to the generosity of Nicholas Nissen, the Danish consul. Only five "went Turk"—or converted to Islam.

Painted by T. Sully. Eng. by A.B. Durand from a Copy by James Herring.

STEPHEN DECATUR

Stephen Decatur

Commodore Stephen Decatur. An engraving based on a portrait by Thomas Sully. (U.S. Naval Academy Museum)

The loss of *Philadelphia* was a body blow to Preble's plans for offensive action and to the prestige of the infant navy. His force of frigates, already inadequate to the squadron's task, had been cut in half, and the enemy had added a powerful ship to their fleet. The prisoners also gave the Tripolitans an important bargaining chip in future negotiations. Preble said nothing critical of Bainbridge's conduct in public, although he was less reserved in private. "Would to God that the officers and crew of the *Philadelphia* had, one and all, determined to prefer death to slavery!" he wrote Smith. "It is possible that such a determination might save them from either." Somehow or other, the ship had to be retaken or destroyed.

Preble's problem was solved by Lieutenant Stephen Decatur, the youthful commander of *Enterprise*. Handsome, dashing, and ambitious, Decatur volunteered to sail a recently captured Tripolitan ketch loaded with combustibles into the harbor of Tripoli and set the captured frigate afire. Decatur had already impressed everyone, both officers and men, with his bravado and the quality of his leadership.* "The intrepid Decatur is proverbial among sailors, for the good treatment of his men, as he is for valor," said one man. Preble approved the plan, even though he told Secretary Smith "it will undoubtedly cost us many lives. But it must be done."

Decatur mustered *Enterprise's* crew and asked for volunteers. Every man stepped forward. Seventy officers and sailors were selected—later increased to eighty-four—and on the night of February 16, 1804, with most of the men crammed below the hatches, Decatur set out for Tripoli in the ketch, now aptly named the *Intrepid*. Under cover of darkness, the lateen-rigged vessel, which flew the British flag, crept up to the anchored *Philadelphia*. The frigate's guns, which had been fished out of the sea, were loaded and run out in case of a surprise attack. Salvatore Catalano, the ketch's Sicilian pilot, hailed the frigate in Arabic, identified his craft as a Maltese vessel, and asked permission to tie up to the larger ship for the night because she had lost her anchors in a recent storm. Lines were being passed between the vessels when one of the guards cried out, "Americans! Americanos!"

"In a moment we were near enough, and the order 'Board!' was given," reported Midshipman Charles Morris. "With this cry our men were soon on the decks of the frigate." Wielding cutlasses, pikes, and tomahawks and with Decatur in the lead, the Americans swarmed over the vessel. Few of the guards tried to meet the Yankee charge across the *Philadelphia's* deck; most jumped over the side and swam ashore. No firearms were used, but Decatur estimated that about twenty Tripolitans were killed before resistance was

*There is a story—perhaps apocryphal—that Decatur had entered the navy as a relatively old nineteen-year-old midshipman at the urging of his attorney after being acquitted of the murder of "a woman of doubtful integrity."

crushed. The raiders quickly passed bundles of combustibles over to the ship and placed them in strategic places. Within twenty minutes flames were licking up *Philadelphia's* mastheads. The heat set off the ship's loaded guns, and her shot, as well as that of shore batteries, splashed around *Intrepid* as she made her getaway. Only one American was wounded in the affair.

The raid caused panic in Tripoli. The burning *Philadelphia* drifted ashore near the dey's castle, and the explosion shook the city. "Tumult, consternation, confusion, and delay reigned in every section of the town and castle," reported one of the American prisoners. When news of the exploit reached the United States, there was a tremendous outpouring of popular support for the navy, and Decatur was hailed as a hero. Lord Nelson, a connoisseur of swashbuckling, called the exploit "the most bold and daring act of the age." Decatur was promoted to captain, at twenty-five the youngest man ever to hold that rank in the U.S. Navy, and Congress awarded the *Intrepid's* crew an extra two months' pay.

⌒

THE SPECTER OF the *Philadelphia* in enemy hands now exorcised, Preble turned to the problem of dealing with Tripoli. With only a few ships under his command, it was obvious that he could not mount an effective blockade, so the commodore elected to batter the Tripolitans into making peace. Shallow-draft gunboats were required for such an operation, and he obtained a half dozen from the Kingdom of Naples. These craft, each armed with a single twenty-four-pound gun, as well as a pair of bomb ketches that mounted powerful thirteen-inch mortars, were towed across the Mediterranean to join the American squadron off Tripoli in the summer of 1804.

Before unleashing his attack, Preble attempted to secure the release of the *Philadelphia's* crew by negotiation, but the pasha flatly rejected his overtures. The commodore concluded that he would have to "endeavor to beat & distress his serene highness" into a more reasonable attitude. The prospects for achieving such an end were not all that bright. In addition to the pair of mortars, the squadron carried only 42 guns that were capable of breaching the Tripolitan fortifications, while arrayed against it were the 115 guns of the shore batteries, plus a large number of cannon mounted by a flotilla of 19 gunboats and other armed vessels. The battlements and ships were manned by no fewer than 25,000 men. But the Tripolitans were neither disciplined nor good marksmen, and the American gunners were well trained.

Preble launched his attack on Tripoli on the afternoon of August 3, 1804. With a fair east wind, he moved his vessels to within two or three miles of the enemy fortifications. For his part, Murad Reis, the Tripolitan naval commander, divided his gunboats into two divisions and advanced beyond the reefs that guarded the harbor, as if taunting the Americans. Perceiving an opportunity to attack enemy craft while they were out of range supporting gunfire from the shore batteries, Preble also divided his own gunboats into two divisions, of three boats each, one under Stephen Decatur and the other commanded by Lieutenant Richard Somers. Decatur was ordered to attack one enemy formation, while Somers was to go after the other. While these maneuvers were taking place, the bomb ketches moved in close to shore to be ready to lob shells into the city while the brigs and schooners supported the gunboats. Mindful of the fate of *Philadelphia*, Preble kept *Constitution* offshore, and communicated with the gunboats through signal flags.

At 2:30 P.M. the commodore gave the order for a general engagement. He wryly noted that the rooftops of Tripoli, which had been crowded with spectators, suddenly emptied as the shot began to fly. Command and control of Preble's force immediately broke down, however, as none of the gunboat captains made any effort to observe the flagship's signals. Moreover, Somers's own gunboat was too far to the lee, and even though he pressed forward under oars and sails, he was unable to join his other two vessels in the attack. As enemy shot splashed about them, the bomb ketches sent their shells arching into the city, with the pasha's castle the main target, while the Yankee brigs and schooners concentrated on the shore batteries.

The Barbary corsairs favored boarding and hand-to-hand fighting, and with the Americans eager to oblige, the two groups of gunboats swept forward to engage each other. Decatur sprayed the nearest enemy craft with grape and musket fire, felling her captain and sending her crew to cover. As the two vessels bumped against each other, a screaming, yelling band of Americans swarmed on board the enemy craft and quickly carried her. Most of the Tripolitans were cut down, while the rest either jumped over the side or surrendered.

Decatur took the captured gunboat in tow and went after another prize. Again he led a slashing attack, which cleared the deck of the vessel, but her captain, a huge Turk, stood his ground. Decatur lunged at him with a boarding pike, but his adversary snatched it away. Decatur drew his cutlass and slashed at the pike, only to have his weapon break at the hilt. He was now unarmed, and the Turk slashed at him, cutting his arm. Fighting for his life, Decatur grabbed at his adversary's throat and wrestled him to the deck. As they fell with Decatur on top, another Tripolitan came to his captain's assistance and raised his scimitar, ready to cut off the young officer's head.

At that moment, a sailor named Daniel Fraser,* although wounded in both arms, lunged between Decatur and the scimitar. Another Yankee seaman shot the Tripolitan, and as he fell, his scimitar only glanced off Fraser's head, cutting his scalp. In the meantime, the big Turk had rolled onto Decatur and was trying to stab him. Decatur seized his wrist, and as they arm-wrestled, managed to slip a pistol out of his jacket, pressed it against the Turk's back, and fired. Rising from the pile of dead about him, Decatur calmly picked up his adversary's elaborately decorated dagger as a souvenir. Fifty-two Tripolitans were killed or wounded, eight were taken prisoner, and an uncounted number were swimming for their lives. Only a half dozen Americans were wounded.

As Decatur was preparing to send his prizes out to Preble, the gunboat commanded by his younger brother, Lieutenant James Decatur, came alongside, but he was nowhere to be seen. The older Decatur was enraged when he learned that James had forced a Tripolitan gunboat to surrender, but when the young officer stepped on board to claim his prize, the Tripolitan captain treacherously shot him in the head and fled. Maddened by this report, Decatur pursued the boat he thought was commanded by his brother's murderer and crashed his craft into it. Although outnumbered, the Americans boarded the vessel, and Decatur killed her captain in a hand-to-hand struggle.

Smeared with blood and powder, Decatur reported to Preble on the quarterdeck of *Constitution.* "I have brought you three of the enemy's gunboats," he declared.

"Three, sir!" the commodore snapped. "Where are the rest of them?"

Preble seemed ungrateful, but in truth the strength of the Tripolitans had been only marginally reduced. *Constitution* and the other vessels had battered the shore batteries, but Tripoli's fortifications were largely undamaged. And, although Decatur had performed well, the other gunboats, with the exception of one commanded by Lieutenant John Trippe, had accomplished little. Followed by ten men, Trippe leaped on board an enemy craft, only to see his own boat drift away before reinforcements could join them. Facing thirty-six Tripolitans, he was, as Preble reported, "compelled to conquer or perish." Trippe and his little band killed fourteen and captured twenty-two of the enemy.

Preble removed his squadron six miles off to the northeast for repairs, and the captured gunboats were refitted and added to the American force. A French privateer was sighted coming out of Tripoli, and the commodore persuaded its captain to return with a message to Yusuf Karamanli: The

---

*The deed is sometimes mistakenly credited to another seaman, Reuben James.

Americans offered to exchange their prisoners for *Philadelphia*'s crew, and because more Americans than Tripolitans were involved, Preble sweetened the deal with the promise of a fifty-thousand-dollar payment. If the offer was not accepted, he promised to destroy Tripoli. "I would rather bury myself under the ruins of my country than basely yield to the wishes of my enemy," the pasha replied.

Four days later, on August 7, Preble again bombarded Tripoli. This time the bomb ketches had the range, and shell after shell poured down on the pasha's castle. The gunboats attacked the shore batteries, and the flagship joined in. When the Americans withdrew that evening, some of the batteries had been silenced, and clouds of smoke were rising from Tripoli. Nevertheless, Preble was disappointed. One gunboat with most of its crew was lost, and some of the mortar shells turned out to be duds. And just as the attack was ending, *John Adams* arrived from home with the news that he was to be relieved of his command.

The loss of *Philadelphia* had apparently raised questions in President Jefferson's mind of Preble's competence, and he decided to replace him with Samuel Barron, another of the superannuated Revolutionary War captains who still encrusted the Navy List. Jefferson had also decided to dispatch "a force which would be able, beyond the possibility of a doubt, to coerce the enemy to a peace upon terms compatible with our honor and our interest." Five frigates, three brigs, and three schooners, as well as several smaller craft, were placed under Barron's command. Before the squadron sailed, however, Jefferson received news of the prompt action taken by *Philadelphia* to the Tripolitans, but it was too late to countermand Barron's orders.

The Navy Department tried to placate Preble with assurances that his replacement reflected no dissatisfaction with his conduct of the squadron's operations. Naval officers were deeply sensitive to seniority, and Preble was told that there were not enough captains junior to him available for the commands in the reinforcing squadron, so he had to be replaced by the more senior Barron. "How much my feelings are lacerated by this supercedure at the moment of Victory cannot be described and can be felt only by an Officer placed in my mortifying situation," an angry Preble confided to his private journal.

Preble bombarded Tripoli three more times, with the hope of forcing the pasha into making peace before Barron arrived. Although some damage was inflicted on Tripoli—William Bainbridge was almost buried in the rubble of one attack—these assaults were in vain. Everything else having failed, Preble decided to transform the *Intrepid* into a floating bomb and send her into Tripoli harbor to destroy the city's defenses. About 100 barrels of powder and 150 mortar shells as well as other combustibles were crammed into the ketch, which was manned by Richard Somers and a dozen volunteers. Once in position, they were to light the fuses and make their escape in a small boat.

On the night of September 4, 1804, the *Intrepid* disappeared into the darkness. Nothing more was heard from her until shortly after 10:00 P.M., when the harbor was suddenly rocked by a tremendous explosion that momentarily turned night into day. Throughout the rest of the night the squadron anxiously awaited some sign of Somers and his crew, but nothing was heard of them. It was presumed that either the vessel had exploded prematurely by accident or that Somers had blown her up with all hands to prevent her from being captured. Flotsam, burned timbers, and bits of fire-blackened canvas were all that was found of the craft. Six days later, Samuel Barron arrived to assume his new command.

As SOON AS Preble struck his flag,* much of the spirit went out of the naval side of the war against Tripoli. Barron's squadron included the frigates *President, Constitution, Congress, Constellation,* and *Essex,* and several smaller vessels, but he did not follow up on Preble's vigorous campaign. Stricken with a near-fatal liver ailment, he spent most his tour of duty ashore in Sicily, while his squadron conducted a desultory blockade of Tripoli. The focus of action, in the meantime, switched to a land campaign aimed at deposing Yusuf Karamanli.

William Eaton, the swashbuckling former American consul in Tunis, had convinced President Jefferson to support a bold scheme to replace Yusuf with his older brother Hamet, whom Yusuf had ousted from the throne a few years before. Eaton was America's own "Lawrence of Arabia." He had joined the Continental Army at age fifteen, fought throughout the Revolution, emerging as a sergeant, studied oriental languages and philosophy at Dartmouth, and married a rich widow. To escape from her, he became an officer in the U.S. Army, where he fought Indians on the frontier for five years. Eaton then persuaded the State Department to send him to North Africa, where he immediately went "native," wearing Arab dress, attending Muslim religious services, and eating with his fingers while sitting cross-legged on the floor.

Eaton sought out Hamet, who was hiding in Egypt, and Hamet agreed

---

*Preble was given a hero's welcome when he arrived home and was asked to dine at the White House by Jefferson, who undoubtedly regretted his decision to replace him. But Preble's health soon failed. In addition to malaria and ulcers, he also had contracted tuberculosis, and he died in 1807 at age forty-six.

to allow the Americans to put him back on the throne. Early in 1805, with the self-styled "General" Eaton in command, a ragtag band of four hundred adventurers of mixed nationality, including Marine lieutenant Presley N. O'Bannon and seven enlisted marines from the brig *Argus*, began an epic march across nearly six hundred miles of Libyan desert to Derna, a port second only to Tripoli itself. Food and water ran short, and Eaton's "army" was on the verge of mutiny—the marines slept on their arms to prevent them from being stolen—when *Argus* and two other U.S. Navy vessels were sighted offshore. Reinforced by desert tribesmen who now scented victory, Eaton captured Derna on April 27, 1805, with the support of the cannon of the American ships and held it against several counterattacks by Yusuf's men.

Back in Washington, Jefferson had come to the reluctant conclusion that force would not bring a favorable end to the war with Tripoli. Eaton was organizing further operations, but before they could begin, a peace treaty was negotiated with Tripoli by Tobias Lear, who had been dispatched to the Mediterranean by the president for that purpose. Faced with the twin threats of Eaton's army and Barron's ships, Yusuf dropped his demand for American tribute and accepted sixty thousand dollars—about half what he previously demanded—as a ransom for *Philadelphia*'s crew.

Lear's peace at a price received a mixed reception at home. Critics charged that the treaty was ill timed because resumption of the naval bombardment, combined with an attack by Eaton's force, would have brought the war to an end without the payment of ransom. Others argued that Lear's treaty was the best ever extracted from the Tripolitans, and as long as *Philadelphia*'s crew remained in enemy hands, no better one could have been obtained without endangering their lives. Under American pressure, Yusuf permitted Hamet to remain as governor of Derna, but later fell out with him again. Hamet fled to Egypt and lived out the remainder of his life in poverty. For a time, he received a small pension obtained for him by Eaton, but it was soon discontinued. Like so many who have tied their fates to American policy, he was cut loose when the political winds changed.

Thus the war in Barbary ended with a whimper rather than a bang. One by one, the vessels kept in the Mediterranean to protect American commerce were withdrawn until only a skeleton force remained. The Barbary corsairs were not to be finally humbled until 1815, when a powerful squadron was sent to the Mediterranean. Nevertheless, the five years of struggle had positive results. The U.S. Navy was established as a permanent force with its own traditions and standards of professionalism. And the young officers who learned their trade under Edward Preble provided the navy and the nation with leadership that was to prove invaluable in trying years to come.

CHAPTER 17

". . . He Will Not Come by Water"

A WAVE OF RELIEF swept over Britain following the Treaty of Amiens in 1802, like a comforting summer breeze. Wearied by nine years of strife, people rejoiced in the return of peace and set to work rebuilding their lives. Like William Wordsworth and his sister, Dorothy, seeing the Lake Country woods full of daffodils, they felt an impulse of hope and joy. The war against France had left Britain richer and stronger than ever before. Despite the depredations of French privateers and cruisers, the annual value of Britain's foreign trade had risen from 50 million pounds to 73.5 million pounds in the two years before the peace. And as a result of the ingenuity of her people, Britain had become the world's workshop. The whirling wheels of Manchester and Birmingham were spinning the pattern for a new world.

Although Cassandra-like voices railed against relaxing the nation's guard, reasonable men were convinced that Napoleon Bonaparte thought the same as they did and the world was truly on the threshold of a new age of international goodwill and expanding commercial opportunity. Looking across the Channel, Britons were, for the most part, willing to regard the once-dreaded "Corsican ogre" on his own terms as the man who had liquidated the Revolution and saved France—and Europe as well—from Jacobin violence and lawlessness. Bonaparte, himself, watched, waited, and planned for the future. He had made peace only to secure a better position from which to wage war.

Ten days after the signing of the treaty, Prime Minister Addington, who espoused an appeasing policy of "Peace and Plenty," abolished William Pitt's hated income tax. The army was halved, and the militia was demobilized. At the Admiralty, Earl St. Vincent, who seems to have been the only naval officer to believe in permanent peace, slashed the Royal Navy with the same ruthlessness he had used to maintain it at war. More than sixty of Britain's hundred ships of the line were paid off, and the dockyards were reduced to skeleton staffs. Half-pay officers vied for the few billets available in the peacetime navy, and eighty thousand experienced seamen—veterans of the First of June, Camperdown, St. Vincent, the Nile, Copenhagen, and the unceasing blockade—were discharged without so much as a thanks. Surplus stores were sold to the highest bidders, often French, who shipped them across the Channel.

Horatio Nelson retired to a newly purchased estate at Merton Place near Wimbledon in Surrey, where he lived contentedly with Emma, Sir William Hamilton, and little Horatia, who was described as Nelson's ward. *Tria juncta in uno*—three joined in one—is the way they described their *ménage*. Emma turned the place into a shrine to her lover's fame and filled it with pictures and memorabilia of his victories. Nelson reveled in the role of country squire. He took time to stop and chat with the local people, and he and Emma attended the local church. Sir William enjoyed the fishing in the nearby streams and said nothing about Horatia's parentage. "I am determined that my quiet shall not be disturbed," he declared. Emma nursed him in his last illness, and Nelson held his hand as he died in March 1803. Both were greatly distressed by his passing.

In the immediate glow of peace, those who could afford the luxury of foreign travel were eager to end a long-enforced insularity behind their gray-white cliffs. Paris was crowded with visitors who sampled the city's long-denied sensual pleasures, shops, and culinary delights. Rather than the bloodthirsty revolutionary rabble they expected, tourists were greeted by friendly faces, clean streets, fine goods, and orderly citizens. They were overwhelmed by the Louvre, now stocked with the finest pictures and sculptures of Italy—the plunder of a hundred battles and sieges.*

Before this shimmering background moved the diminutive figure of General Bonaparte, with his abrupt manner and Byronic, searching eyes. His coming was invariably heralded by the clatter of cavalry. Foreign visitors seeing him taking the salute of his brilliantly uniformed troops immediately fell under his spell, and a legend was born. Like Nelson, he exuded the supreme quality of genius—unlimited energy. On all that he had wrought, however, he left a strong authoritarian cast. In the Place Vendôme, a pillar like the column of Trajan was being erected to commemorate his victories. The press was muzzled, and the French always seemed to be conscious of the presence of the secret police. And in an imperial gesture, the first consul required that he be addressed by his first name alone: Napoleon.

He had a new dream as well, of conquering a world whose sun would rise and set over Paris. Most of Europe was already under his control, and French agents were again meddling in Egypt, Greece, and India. But there was one hurdle in his way—that damned nation of insolent shopkeepers across the Channel and their thrice-damned navy. Even as Napoleon pre-

---

*A British collector who applied to Napoleon for the return of some of his pictures seized by the French in Venice was told that they were too fine to be given up, and was assured that he could always view them at the Louvre.

sented a smiling face to the world, he regarded peace as merely a temporary armistice in the struggle against Britain.

To bring about the final victory, Napoleon was convinced he had to invade Britain. If the Royal Navy was a thousand-headed hydra, he reasoned, its heart was London. Destroy that heart and the heads would die. "Let us be master of the strait for six hours, and we shall be masters of the world," he declared. Vice Admiral Denis Decres, his talented minister of marine, was directed to use the time afforded by peace to build as many as twenty-five new battleships a year over the next five years and to train officers and crews to sail in them. By then, Napoleon reasoned, with two hundred sail of the line he would be as invincible on the sea as he was on land. Naval morale and discipline were improved, and efforts were made to restock the storehouses and arsenals that were depleted after years of blockade.

War came sooner than Napoleon had planned, however. Very early on, he began to violate his treaty pledges to respect the territorial boundaries of Europe and those overseas. Large numbers of troops were sent to San Domingo to put down Toussaint l'Overture's slave revolt and in preparation for a takeover of the vast and largely unknown territory in North America called Louisiana, which had secretly been ceded to France by Spain.* In Europe he conducted a bloodless offensive that raked in Piedmont and Liguria in Italy, and he added the Austrian Netherlands to his domain, and along with it French control of the coastal ports, which Britain had gone to war in 1793 to prevent. Next, the French began intriguing in Switzerland.

When Addington eventually protested against the Swiss adventure, Napoleon countered with a demand that the British leave Malta and Egypt, as stipulated in the Treaty of Amiens. The British agreed to abandon Egypt, but no British government could give up Malta, especially with a war brewing. In March 1803 Napoleon told Admiral Decres to prepare for an attack on British commerce and gibed openly at Britain's military weakness. Nothing could have been more calculated to unite the British people, and on May 16, 1803, they again grasped the sword. And, as always, its keenest edge was the Royal Navy.

⤷

FIVE SHIPS OF THE line sailed from Tor Bay on May 17, under the command of Admiral Sir William Cornwallis, to take up the familiar station off Ushant and renew the watch on Brest. On that same day, Lord Keith raised his flag at the Nore. And three days later, Nelson sailed in *Victory* for the

---

*On learning of Napoleon's intentions, President Jefferson observed that the moment that France took over New Orleans, "we must marry ourselves to the British fleet."

Mediterranean to begin the blockade of Toulon. Before leaving London, he accompanied Emma to the parish church in Marylebone, where their child, now two years old, was christened Horatia Nelson Thompson. Once embarked on his flagship, the admiral did not set foot ashore again for nearly two years.

Britain's naval mobilization was hampered, however, by a campaign that had been waged by Lord St. Vincent to reduce long-standing corruption and other abuses in the dockyards. "All the master shipwrights ought to be hanged, every one of them, without exception," growled Thomas Troubridge, a member of the Admiralty Board. The same went for many of the contractors. The *Naval Chronicle*, a journal devoted to naval affairs, estimated the losses up to 1802 due to "speculation or negligence" at twenty million pounds. But the entrenched ring of bureaucrats, contractors, and the "Timber Trust" resisted every effort to force them to forgo their financial fiddles. As a result, there were only about thirty-two ships of the line in commission or in good repair, and there was a timber shortage.

But patriotic fervor took hold, and within a few weeks another twenty-eight big ships were ready for sea, plus a clutch of frigates. Each day saw new vessels sail on active service. Even the master craftsmen dropped their surly attitude and worked overtime to prepare vessels for sea. At the same time, press gangs swept up large numbers of experienced seamen to fill the newly commissioned ships. In the Thames, alone, merchant vessels were stripped of a thousand hands in a single night. Parliament voted funds for a sizable increase in the number of sailors and marines, the cost to be borne by extra taxes on letters, horses, and salt, the common food preservative.

But Addington had no strategy for conducting the war. Having come to power with the goal of making peace, he was bankrupt of ideas now that peace with France had proved an illusion. He was obsessed with fear of Napoleon and psychologically unprepared to take the offensive. Pitt the Elder and his son had demonstrated that the unsurpassed mobility of the Royal Navy provided Britain with the opportunity to make sudden, damaging blows against the enemy and challenge Napoleon's hegemony of the Continent. It could give range and effect to even a small military striking force that was ready for rapid response whenever a foe exposed a weakness. For example, a properly trained British army had overrun Egypt in cooperation with the navy and compelled the surrender of numerically superior French forces. But Britain remained on the defensive under Addington, which meant abandoning the rest of the world to the French.

On the other side, the British declaration of war caught Napoleon, who had expected war in September, not May, unprepared. Although Admiral Decres had laid down new men-of-war—thirty in 1802 alone—the French Navy was deficient in ships and men. In all, France could muster only a dozen of the line at the outbreak of hostilities; by September 1803 the number was increased to thirty. Work proceeded slowly on the vessels on the stocks because the supplies of timber and other stores in French dockyards and arsenals had been only partially replenished. More than half of Napoleon's available ships were scattered over the oceans of the world, from India to the West Indies. Experienced seamen were at a premium because many were captured at sea immediately after the outbreak of war. When the French ships in the Caribbean returned to European waters, they were forced to run into Ferrol, where they were blockaded by a squadron flying the flag of the redoubtable Sir Edward Pellew. French trade was also driven from the sea by British cruisers.

Napoleon's recall of his warships from the Caribbean left the area to the mercies of the British. A small amphibious force from Barbados captured St. Lucia, Tobago, Demerara, and Essiquibo. Surinam followed in the spring of 1804. The isolated remnants of the French army in San Domingo—decimated by guerrilla attacks, yellow fever, and other diseases—surrendered to the British as an alternative to massacre at the hands of the blacks.* In India, Sir Arthur Wellesley crushed the French-trained armies of the restless Mahratta chiefs at Assaye.

News of the capture of two French ships at sea on May 18 threw Napoleon into a towering rage. He ordered the arrest of all British travelers in France—some ten thousand people—and decreed the Continent, including the free ports of Hamburg and Bremen, closed to British shipping. Hanover was invaded and capitulated after token resistance. Yet nothing but a blow at Britain's heart could satisfy the First Consul's craving for vengeance against Perfidious Albion. He visited the Channel ports, looked across to England, and said, "They want us to jump the ditch and we *will* jump it."

Within a few days of the war's beginning, Napoleon ordered a renewal of the preparations for an invasion of the island kingdom that had been made in 1801.† This time he was serious, and he suspended all other military activities in favor of the preparation for the invasion. Nearly 160,000 veteran troops of the Grand Army were mobilized on the cliffs at Boulogne

*Of the thirty-four thousand troops sent to San Domingo, fewer than a third remained. The loss of this army caused Napoleon to have second thoughts about keeping Louisiana, and he sold the territory to the United States for the bargain price of fifteen million dollars, which doubled the size of the new nation.

†In 1940 a victorious Adolf Hitler ordered preparations for an invasion of Britain: Operation Sea Lion. But unlike Napoleon, the evidence indicates that he was skeptical from the start about the feasibility—or necessity—of a landing in England. Landing craft were massed in the Channel ports, but the actual invasion was delayed until the Luftwaffe, the German Air Force, could seize control of the air from the Royal Air Force. When this failed, Hitler abandoned Sea Lion and turned his attention to the east, to settle old scores with the Soviet Union. See Miller, *War at Sea,* chapter III.

and from Havre to the Texel in readiness for embarkation. This huge force was to be carried by a fleet of some 2,300 landing craft under construction at ports all along the coast and as far east as the Rhine. Three different types of flat-bottomed vessels were built, ranging in length from 70 to 100 feet, each carrying from 55 to 120, troops and propelled by simple sails and oars. The roads leading to the Channel ports were soon crammed with men, horses, guns, and equipment as preparations for the landing heated up.*

The First Consul went to Boulogne to supervise the preparations for the invasion, and as a talisman, brought with him the Bayeux Tapestry, which portrayed William of Normandy's successful descent on Britain in 1066. There were endless reviews and parades. At Calais, toasts were drunk to a review of the Army of England in St. James's Park. But the Royal Navy put on a display of how it still ruled the Channel before his very eyes when a frigate ignored the guns of Boulogne and captured seven landing craft heading into the harbor.

For all his brilliance as a soldier and strategist, Napoleon had little understanding of the realities of war at sea. He made the fundamental error of assuming that naval forces could be handled like armies and that ships could be moved around like regiments on a parade ground without regard to the winds and the sea. He intended to cross the Channel on a foggy night or in the sudden calm after a gale when the British blockaders had been driven off and his battle fleet could slip out to sea to guard the invasion force. With the mastery of the world at issue, Napoleon reasoned, it would matter little if ten thousand or even twenty thousand men were lost. "One loses that number in battle every day," he remarked, "and what battle ever promised such results as a landing in England?"

Throughout the summer and autumn of 1803, an alarmed British public never went to bed without peering into the darkness to see if the beacons warning of a French landing were lighting up the sky. French cavalry were momentarily expected to come galloping down the country lanes.

*Robert Fulton, an American artist and inventor living in France, tried to interest the French in the *Nautilus,* a three-man submarine he had developed that was powered by a hand-driven propeller. He said it could be used to destroy British ships blockading French ports or to blockade British harbors by attaching "torpedoes"—in reality mines with delayed-action fuses—against the hulls of the vessels. A test run was made at Brest in which an anchored ship was sunk. The French, however, were dilatory in supplying financial help, and Fulton crossed the Channel in 1804 and offered his invention to the British government. Not surprisingly, the Admiralty was loath to develop weapons that would endanger Britain's maritime supremacy. Fulton returned to America, where he put aside his plan for a submarine and became active in the development of the steamboat.

Rumors circulated that Napoleon was building a bridge from Calais to Dover, or that he was going to transport his army in giant hot-air balloons or through a Channel tunnel. Church doors were placarded with blood-curdling posters warning of imminent pillage, rape, and the slaughter of innocent children. "Boney," himself, was reputedly seen lurking in various parts of the nation. Nurses threatened obstreperous charges with warnings of the Corsican ogre's imminent advent:

Baby, baby, naughty baby,
Hush your squalling thing, I say;
Hush your squalling, or it may be
Bonaparte may pass this way.

Fortifications and a chain of Martello towers were erected at key points on the Kent and Sussex coasts, and defensive works were placed across the main roads to London. Captain Frederick Austen, one of Jane Austen's three sailor brothers, was among those assigned to readying the seaside defenses. But there were only 28,000 regular troops to protect the entire island, with another 20,000 tied down in rebellious and sullen Ireland. A panicked Addington filled the gap by enrolling large numbers of untrained volunteers in the local militias; no fewer than 340,000 men were soon under arms in England and another 70,000 in Ireland. Pocket drill books became best-sellers; recruits drilled in town squares and on village greens to the rattling of fife and drum and swore heartfelt oaths to stand firm against the invader. Addington appeared on the floor of the House of Commons in uniform. The chief result of the mobilization, however, was to dry up recruits for the regular army who could have been used in offensive operations that would have upset Napoleon's plans. Thus, Addington's England, by ensuring its own safety, made certain it could do nothing to defend the safety of other nations.

Thanks to Lord St. Vincent's steady hand, the Admiralty kept its head, however, and refused to succumb to invasion panic. Naval officers believed that the nation's first line of defense lay not on the English coast, but outside the enemy's ports. "As to the possibility," said Pellew, "of the enemy being able in a narrow sea to pass through our blockading and protecting squadrons with all the secrecy and dexterity and by those hidden means that some worthy people expect, I really, from anything I have seen in the course of my professional life, am not much disposed to concur in it."

The passage of a large force over the Channel presented difficulties that not even Napoleon's genius could overcome. Weather in the Channel was notoriously treacherous, and as any experienced mariner could tell, the ungainly invasion barges were not only unmanageable in any kind of a sea but also could not possibly be kept in order in rain and fog. It was also impossible to float the entire army over in one tide, so the troops would have to be committed piecemeal. And there was no cover plan, nothing to distract attention from the major operation. Nor was there any chance of surprise, with all the invasion ports under daily observation by the Royal Navy.

Nothing seemed to go as Napoleon expected. He was accustomed to ordering troops to march on a specific date in a particular direction, knowing that they would do so. Yet even though gunboats and transports lay nine deep along the quays at Boulogne, lack of wind, contrary winds, even a gale prevented his admirals from carrying out his orders. The time needed to command the Channel was extended to twelve hours, then to twenty-four hours, then to several days, and finally to several weeks. "I do not say the French cannot come," St. Vincent grimly declared, "I only say he will not come by water."

                                          ~

THE KEY TO Britain's defense, as always, was its wooden walls. To the extreme north, Lord Keith kept eleven ships of the line in readiness off the Texel, while numerous frigates and smaller craft watched and harassed the invasion coast and guarded the Strait of Dover. With twelve of the line in winter and twenty-four in summer, Cornwallis secured the approaches to the English and Irish Channels and closely invested Brest to prevent a hostile concentration of enemy squadrons. Sir Robert Calder had eight off Ferrol, Sir John Orde guarded Cádiz with six in case Spain should enter the war, while at the southern extremity of the long chain of blockading squadrons Nelson kept watch on Toulon with nine. Unless these ships were destroyed or dispersed, the invasion barges could not move—and they could not be brushed aside as long as French battleships lay immobilized in port.

The Channel fleet and sixty-year-old "Billy-go-tight" Cornwallis, as his men called him because of his florid countenance and country squire's manner, held the pivot of the British defense. The main body of the fleet, including Cornwallis' flagship *Ville de Paris*, cruised off Ushant. An inshore squadron of frigates, brigs, and cutters worked close in to Brest, Rochefort, and Lorient in good weather and foul. Others harassed French and Dutch coastal shipping. The blockade of Brest from May 1803 to November 1805 is one of the Royal Navy's supreme achievements. As Mahan so eloquently put it, "Those far-distant storm-beaten ships, upon which the Grand Army never looked, stood between it and the dominion of the world."

Life on the blockade was grim. Cornwallis' ships were lashed by gales that fractured masts, carried away spars, and ripped sails to tatters. The men were usually cold, wet, and without fresh provisions. And there was the constant threat of running aground on the rocks of a lee shore. *Atalanta,* seventy-four, was wrecked on an uncharted reef; *Impetueux*, also a seventy-four, was almost laid on her on beam ends by a gale and survived only by jettisoning her guns. No blockade could be permanently maintained in such conditions, and on several occasions Cornwallis was forced to run into Tor Bay for a few hours' shelter from the terrible buffeting. Nevertheless, he quickly resumed his unremitting watch. Some of his ships were unsound because of the economies made in the dockyards by St. Vincent during the armistice and the slowness in making repairs. "We have been sailing for the last six months with only a sheet of copper between us and eternity," reported Collingwood, who led one of the squadrons.

Salt beef ten years in the cask, stinking water, and maggoty biscuits constituted the diet of the men on the long watch. "O! for a draught of fresh water, I cry out, for our water stinks enough to poison a person," eleven-year-old Midshipman Bernard Coleridge wrote his mother, "and we are generally forced to drink two glasses of wine or brandy to one glass of water to take off the stink." Vessels going into port for repairs were required to transfer their supplies to other ships and come out again with fresh beef and vegetables for distribution throughout the squadron. Eventually, special victualing craft loaded with supplies were sent out to rendezvous with the fleet. Through it all, young Coleridge thrilled at the glimpse of the French shore and the distant, unmoving masts of the enemy fleet in Brest, frolicked in the rigging of his ship, and played marbles on the poop with his fellow midshipmen—"good fellows but they swear rather."

At the other end of the great loop of ocean that encloses western Europe, Nelson kept guard in the Mediterranean, effectively barring Napoleon's egress to the south and the west. Specifically, his task was to prevent a union of the French fleet at Toulon with the Spaniards should they enter the war and to defend Malta, Gibraltar, and Naples, Britain's always uneasy ally. With the rest of Europe terrified of the French, his task was made more difficult by the lack of a nearby dockyard. Unlike the Channel fleet, he could not send ships into Plymouth or Portsmouth to refit, and even though some of his vessels were desperately in need of repair, they had to remain on station until they could be replaced by ships from England. "My crazy Fleet are getting in very indifferent state," the admiral said in December 1803, and conditions were expected to worsen.

Nelson's objective, however, was not to keep the enemy locked in port but to lure him out to fight. While a chain of frigates was on the alert to warn* of French movements at Toulon, the main elements of his fleet voyaged to and

*The Royal Navy was now using a new signal system devised by Sir Home Popham in which flags meant different words, enabling a fleet commander to signal his intentions in his own words within the limits of the vocabulary chosen by Popham.

fro across a wide patch of sea—between the Balearics on the west and Corsica and Sardinia on the east—through which the enemy, wherever bound, would have to pass. Nelson established a base for revictualing and watering in Agincourt Sound at Maddalena Island, off the northern tip of Sardinia. "The great thing in all military service is health and . . . it is easier for an officer to keep men healthy, than for a physician to cure them," Nelson observed. Sometime during this period he ordered the fleet painted what was to be called "Nelson fashion"—black sides with varnish-yellow bands along the gunports, the lids of which were painted black, giving the vessels a checkerboard effect.

Nelson was prone to seasickness in the frequent gales of the Gulf of Lion, but in good weather he invited his captains to *Victory* for dinner in rotation according to seniority. Although the admiral was usually on some kind of self-imposed diet, he was hospitable and spared no expense in setting a good table. He usually served three courses, a desert of fruit, three or four fine wines, sometimes champagne, followed by coffee and liqueurs. Overlooking all was a pastel of a wistful Lady Hamilton. Following dinner, the visitors strolled on the quarterdeck as the flagship's band serenaded them. Most of his captains were strangers to the admiral, so he used these affairs to take their measure. "Day by day, my dear friend," he wrote his prize agent, "I am expecting the French to put to sea—every day, hour and moment; and you may rely that, if it is within the power of men to get at them, it shall be done."

In July 1804 Napoleon ordered his best admiral, Louis de Latouché-Tréville, to give Nelson the slip, pass through the Strait of Gibraltar with his eight ships of the line, release the French vessels in Ferrol, Cádiz, and Rochefort, proceed up the Channel or around Ireland, and appear off Boulogne in September to cover the French army's crossing to England. In anticipation of this triumph, Napoleon ordered a victory medal to be struck, inscribed with the legend *Descent en Angleterre, Frappe à Londres en 1804*. Latouché-Tréville, encouraged by Nelson's efforts to lure him out by remaining over the horizon, edged out of port and chased the watching British frigates. Soon, however, he realized he was being led into a trap and put back into Toulon.

⸏

THREE SIGNIFICANT EVENTS occurred in mid-1804: William Pitt returned to power, Napoleon made himself emperor, and the turning point came in his invasion project. Late in the previous year, King George had shown signs of madness—now believed to be the result of mind-altering porphyria—and his courtiers had to restrain him from opening Parliament with the words "My Lords and Peacocks!" Visions of a regency by the bloated and disreputable prince of Wales, bigamist and hero of a thousand battles with the bottle, were enough to convince Pitt that the government could not be left in Addington's flaccid hands.

Soaring above party politics, Pitt called on Britons to unite to preserve not only their own liberty but those of other countries as well. "Amid the wreck and the misery of nations it is our just exultation that we have continued superior to all that ambition or that despotism could effect," he told an uncommonly silent House of Commons. "Our still higher exultation ought to be that we provide not only for our own safety but hold out a prospect for nations now bending under the iron yoke of tyranny." The next day, Addington resigned, and Pitt returned to Downing Street. Prospects for a coalition government were dashed, however, when the king refused to accept the dissolute Charles James Fox, Pitt's great rival and the leader of the Whig Opposition, as a member of the government.

On the day that Pitt again became prime minister—May 14, 1804—Napoleon had himself proclaimed emperor of the French by the Senate in the wake of a clumsy Royalist plot to assassinate him (there was evidence of the involvement of British intelligence in the conspiracy). There could not have been a greater contrast between national leaders. Pitt was frail and worn out by his previous exertions, leader of a precarious majority in the Commons, and the servant of a half-crazed monarch. Napoleon was master of France, at the height of his remarkable mental and physical powers, supported by the greatest army in the world, and enjoying untrammeled power. Yet it was his arrogant exercise of this power that caused him to commit a fatal error.

French agents mistakenly believed that a young Bourbon, the Duc d'Enghien, was involved in the assassination plot. He was kidnapped from his home in Baden, and Napoleon had him shot on trumped-up charges. The execution horrified the royal houses of Europe and played into the hands of Pitt, who was trying to assemble another alliance against France. To Europe's crowned heads, Napoleon now appeared to be nothing less than a Jacobin in imperial ermine who must be exterminated.

Pitt persuaded the Russians that Napoleon, hemmed in to the north, west, and south by the sea and the Royal Navy, had only one direction in which he could expand—to the east. Austria and Sweden were next convinced to join Britain in what became a Third Coalition against France. With the hope of seizing the initiative from Napoleon, Pitt planned joint operations in the Mediterranean with a Russian army based on Corfu. Some seven thousand troops were scratched up and dispatched to Malta under the command of Lieutenant Geneneral Sir James Craig to begin such operations. To prevent spies from discovering its existence, it was labeled the Secret Expedition and covered by a tight security blanket.

Before risking troops so far from home, Pitt had to protect the lines of communication between Britain and its bases at Gibraltar and Malta. And across his path lay Spain. Left to themselves, the Spaniards would have remained neutral, but Manuel Godoy, the virtual dictator of Spain, was beholden to Napoleon. In the autumn of 1804 the British feared that the French were about to demand the assistance of the Spanish fleet, and it was expected that Godoy would give his approval. It was also learned that fifteen hundred French troops had been sent to Spain to man the French warships at Ferrol.

Pitt decided to force Godoy's hand. Britain's envoy in Madrid was instructed to demand an explanation for the presence of French troops in the country and to seek the demobilization of the Spanish fleet. Simultaneously, Cornwallis was ordered to detach four frigates to intercept a treasure fleet carrying gold and silver from the mines of Spanish America before it reached Cádiz. Unfortunately, Pitt failed to reckon with Spanish pride. The Spaniards refused to surrender to this small force, and one of the treasure ships blew up in the ensuing fight, with the loss of three hundred lives. The cargoes of the remaining vessels were valued at a million pounds and brought instant wealth in prize money to the captors. An angry Spain declared war against Britain in December 1804. At the same time, Napoleon crowned himself emperor by seizing the crown from the hands of the trembling pope.

Aware that his enemies were gathering against him, Napoleon secured his rear by cowing the Austrians into submission. And he reevaluated his plans for the conquest of Britain. Invasion had failed in 1803 and 1804 because the Royal Navy controlled the Channel. With the addition of the Spanish fleet, he had on paper, at the beginning of 1805, more than 70 sail of the line to deploy against an estimated 105 British battleships. If the number of British ships being refitted is deducted, the Royal Navy had about 80 such vessels available for active service. From these, however, squadrons had to be supplied for the defense of the East Indies, the Caribbean, and Newfoundland. As a result, the two opposing fleets were for all practical purposes of comparable size.

Napoleon decided that a successful invasion of Britain hinged on decoying Cornwallis' fleet from off Brest. If he could somehow be lured away from his station, Britain would be left momentarily unguarded. What threat would bring this about? Napoleon was convinced that an attack on the West Indies would have such an effect. The sugar islands were so important to Britain's economy, he reasoned, that the West India merchants would demand that the Royal Navy defend the Caribbean islands even at the cost of the defense of Britain itself.

The first part of the new invasion plan enjoyed some success. In January 1805 Vice Admiral Comte de Missiessy escaped from Rochefort with five of the line and an equal number of frigates and sailed for the

Caribbean. On his own initiative, Rear Admiral Alexander Cochrane lifted the blockade of Ferrol and followed him with six of the line. Vice Admiral Pierre de Villeneuve, a survivor of the holocaust at Aboukir Bay, slipped out of Toulon a week later with eleven of the line and nine frigates. Warned by his frigates of Villeneuve's departure, Nelson believed the French were heading for the Levant. Repeating the experience of 1798, he headed eastward to defend Sicily, Naples, and Egypt, but there was no trace of the French. Unknown to Nelson, they had already been driven back into Toulon because the seamanship of Villeneuve's crews was inadequate to battle the gales of the Gulf of Lion. Upon the admiral's return, he begged the emperor to relieve him of command, but the request was refused.

Undeterred, Napoleon tried again, this time on a bigger scale, which he called the Grand Design. In essence the plan called for Vice Admiral Honoré Ganteaume to sail from Brest with twenty-one of the line, release the Franco-Spanish squadron at Ferrol, and steer for Martinique, where he was to meet Missiessy, who had been ordered to remain in the Caribbean, where he was to wait for Villeneuve for thirty days. For his part, Villeneuve was to escape from Toulon, raise the blockade of Cartagena, release the ships at Cádiz, and after adding the squadrons in these ports to his own, make for the Caribbean.

Once the three fleets—more than fifty ships in all—had rendezvoused at Martinique, they were to recross the Atlantic, enter the Channel between June 10 and July 10, and sweeping all before them, cover the invasion of Britain. If Ganteaume failed to appear, Villeneuve was to wait forty days at Martinique, cross the Atlantic, liberate Ganteaume from Brest, and guard the passage of the invasion fleet. Napoleon convinced himself that the way would be clear because the British would send the Channel fleet to save the West Indies. The plan was a bold one, but it was based on assumptions that any experienced naval officer would have found unacceptable:

1. The Toulon and Brest fleets would be able to evade the blockading squadrons within a reasonable time of one another, and then would enjoy favorable winds that would carry them to their rendezvous without hindrance.
2. While Villeneuve would be chased, his pursuers would never catch him.
3. Cornwallis' fleet, if met, would be defeated, as would the British inshore squadrons, thereby ensuring safe passage of the troops.
4. Napoleon also failed to realize that the defeat of the home islands was Britain's major strategic objective. Nothing—not even the defense of their Caribbean possessions—had a higher priority.

Meantime, Nelson had returned to the blockade of Toulon from his fruitless search to the east. With the hope of luring the French out of Toulon, he shifted his cruising ground to the southwest, off Barcelona, seemingly leaving Toulon uncovered. After showing the flag, he left the seventy-four gun *Leviathan* on this station to continue the ruse, while the rest of his ships went to the Gulf of Palmas, to the southwest of Sardinia, to provision from transports newly arrived from Britain. A pair of frigates, *Active*, thirty-eight, and *Phoebe*, thirty-six, remained at Toulon to keep an eye on the French.

Ganteaume, learning that the Channel fleet had been reduced to fifteen of the line by the need to send ships into port to reprovision and make repairs, told Napoleon he would fight his way out of Brest. But the emperor replied: "A naval victory in existing circumstances can lead to nothing. . . . Get to sea without an action." So Ganteaume endeavored to escape from Brest on March 26, as a fog covered his departure. But he had gotten only a few miles to seaward when the mist lifted and Cornwallis' ships were sighted. Having been ordered not to fight, Ganteaume returned to port.

Taken in by Nelson's ruse and believing that the British were off Cape San Sebastian, not nearby, Villeneuve sailed from Toulon on March 30. He flew his flag in the eighty-gun *Bucentaure* and was accompanied by three other eighties, seven seventy-fours, eight frigates, with more than three thousand soldiers on board. *Phoebe*, one of the watching British frigates, sped off to warn Nelson that the French were out, while *Active* shadowed the enemy fleet. In the falling darkness, Villeneuve shook her off. He planned to go east of the Balearic Islands—a course that would have brought him directly under the guns of the British fleet. Fortunately for Villeneuve, he learned on April 1 from a neutral vessel that the enemy was actually to the south of Sardinia, and steered sharply westward to pass north of the Balearics and out of harm's way.

The six Spanish ships at Cartagena were not ready when Villeneuve arrived there on April 6, so he pressed on, passing through the Strait of Gibraltar into the Atlantic two days later in good order. "May fortune fulfill the hopes which the Emperor has founded upon the destination of this squadron," he wrote Admiral Decres. The events that were to lead to Trafalgar, the climactic sea battle of the Age of Fighting Sail, had now been set in motion.

CHAPTER 18

The Long Watch

FOUR DAYS AFTER the French slipped out of Toulon, on the morning of April 4, 1805, one of *Victory's* lookouts sighted a frigate with every sail set driving headlong toward the fleet through a drizzling rain. From *Phoebe's* masthead whipped the distant signal: "Enemy at sea." Having completed provisioning that morning, Nelson was midway between Sardinia and the coast of Africa. Upon learning that the French were at sea again, he quickly spread out his ships to cover the widest possible area as he launched a fresh search for the Toulon fleet.

Nelson was uncertain about Villeneuve's destination. British spies had previously reported that the French ships were loading troops and saddlery intended for cavalry, which indicated that the enemy was heading for Naples, Sicily, or Egypt. But he was more cautious than he had been earlier in the year. Instead of dashing off in that direction, he established a cruising ground midway between Sardinia and Sicily to cover both islands and the route to the Levant. "I shall neither go to the eastward of Sicily nor to the westward of Sardinia," he wrote, "until I know something positive."

Day after day, he sailed between the two islands without finding any trace of the enemy fleet or sign that it was trying to break through to the east. Nelson had violated a basic strategic principle: he had considered only what he thought the enemy would do, not what he was capable of doing. Soon, he began to have doubts about his reading of French intentions and now believed Villeneuve was bent on leaving the Mediterranean. On April 9—as the French were passing through the Strait of Gibraltar— Nelson, having fulfilled his responsibility to defend the Mediterranean, turned westward, leaving five frigates behind to protect Naples. But the foul bottoms of his ships made it difficult to make much headway against the strong winds that were blowing dead against him.

Nelson's vessels tacked and tacked and tacked again, yet in a two-day period they made only fifteen miles to the west. Once again the admiral experienced the gnawing anxieties he had felt during the search for Bruey's fleet in 1798. Nelson's stomach bothered him, he was often seasick, he suffered from gout and rheumatism in the stump of his right arm, and he was worried about the sight of his good eye. He found it difficult to sleep more than two hours a night. Awakened by coughing spasms, he would throw a greatcoat over his nightshirt and pace *Victory*'s quarterdeck.

On April 16 the fleet encountered a neutral vessel that reported that Villeneuve had been seen off the Spanish coast more than a week before. Soon afterward, Nelson learned that the French fleet was out in the Atlantic. "If this speaks true, they may be halfway to Ireland or Jamaica by this time!" he declared. "Oh, that I could but find them!" Not long after, the agitated admiral wrote: "My good luck seems flown away. I cannot get a fair wind, or even a side wind. Dead foul! Dead foul!"

On his way to Gibraltar, Nelson received orders that added to his burdens—to cover the lightly defended convoy of forty-two transports carrying the troops of the Secret Expedition to Malta. The convoy was nowhere to be seen, and he feared that General Craig's little army had been snapped up by one or another of the French squadrons on the loose.* Nelson did not sight the Rock until April 30, and even there, his vessels were held back by adverse winds. The fleet finally anchored in Mazari Bay, on the North African coast, and took on water and provisions. Nelson learned that Villeneuve had passed Cádiz, where his fleet was reinforced by the French seventy-four-gun ship *Aigle* while five Spanish ships of the line under Vice Admiral Don Federico de Gravina straggled out in Villeneuve's wake. These reinforcements brought the French fleet to eighteen of the line plus several frigates.

Also, much to Nelson's anger, he learned that Admiral Orde, who had been watching Cádiz with six of the line, had failed to follow and keep track of the Combined Fleet. Unlike Alexander Cochrane, who had unhesitatingly left his station off Ferrol to pursue Missiessy to the Caribbean, Orde, who believed the enemy's destination was the Channel, had taken the safe course and fallen back on Cornwallis. Nelson, however, was now certain Villeneuve was bound for the Caribbean.

On May 5, a light breeze from the east caused Nelson to hurriedly get his ships out of Mazari Bay, but just as they were approaching the Strait of Gibraltar, the wind died away. With some difficulty, the fleet got into Rosia Bay, Gibraltar. "I believe easterly winds have left the Mediterranean," observed a frustrated Nelson. *Victory* and some of the larger ships had just anchored, and the admiral had sent his laundry ashore to be washed when cat's-paws from the east ruffled the waters of the anchorage. The signal to sail was broken out by the flagship. Leaving his laundry behind, Nelson led

---

*In fact, the convoy had not left Portsmouth until April 17. While still in the Atlantic, it received warnings of Villeneuve's movements, and put into Lisbon until certain the French were well out to sea.

his fleet toward the straits, propelled by the first breaths of a long-awaited easterly breeze. By nightfall his ships were riding the Atlantic swells.

On May 9 Nelson anchored in Lagos Bay in Portugal, where he received confirmation from Rear Admiral Donald Campbell, a Scottish mercenary serving in the Portuguese Navy, that Villeneuve was indeed heading for the Caribbean.* That settled the matter as far as Nelson was concerned. "I was in a thousand fears for Jamaica, for that is a blow which Buonaparte would be happy to give us," he later wrote. "I flew to the West Indies without any orders. But I think the Ministry cannot be displeased. . . . I was bred, as you known, in the good old school and taught to appreciate the value of our West India possessions. . . ."

Nelson's decision to go to the West Indies without orders can be compared in audacity to his decision to leave the battle line at St. Vincent. In that case, he disregarded the *Fighting Instructions*; in this one he disregarded standing Admiralty orders to fall back upon the Channel fleet in the event of losing touch with the enemy. Nelson reasoned that Britain was amply guarded by Cornwallis and Keith with forty ships of the line while the West Indies were endangered. Moreover, he thought it his paramount duty to seek out and destroy the enemy wherever he might be. With communications slow and unreliable, it was, in the final analysis, this readiness of Nelson and other British naval commanders to shoulder responsibility in the absence of orders, coupled with their experience and understanding of war at sea, that played havoc with Napoleon's Grand Design.

Nelson sailed on May 11, and four hours later fell in with the Secret Expedition. Regarding its escort as inadequate, he covered the convoy past Cádiz and as far as the strait of Gibraltar. In a gesture much appreciated by the convoy commander, he detached Rear Admiral Sir Richard H. Bickerton, now designated commander of the Mediterranean station and the hundred-gun *Royal Sovereign*, to temporarily bolster the escort. With his fleet reduced to ten of the line and three frigates, Nelson now headed for the Caribbean to deal with a force of nearly double his strength. He was discouraged neither by the relative weakness of his fleet nor by the month's head start possessed by Villeneuve. "Although I am late, yet chance may have given them a bad passage, and me a good one," he wrote. "I must hope for the best."

↜

WHILE THESE OPERATIONS were unfolding, Pitt's ministry was in crisis, with the management of the Admiralty at the vortex. Lord St. Vincent had

---

*The French complained to the Portuguese about Campbell's conduct, and he was dismissed from his post.

gone out of office with Addington, and Pitt had appointed his old friend Henry Dundas, now Lord Melville, to head the Admiralty. But St. Vincent had left a time bomb ticking at the Admiralty by demanding a parliamentary inquiry into the operation of the dockyards, and it exploded under Melville. Pitt's political enemies struck at him through Melville by accusing his old friend of corruption during a previous term as treasurer of the navy. The appearance of Missiessy's squadron in the West Indies—he attacked Dominica* and bagged a significant number of trading vessels—added to the outcry against Melville's management of the Admiralty. He was forced to resign as first lord just as Villeneuve and Gravina were disappearing into the Atlantic.

For two weeks, the ailing and harassed Pitt searched for a replacement who would be politically acceptable and capable of exercising effective strategic control of naval affairs. On April 21, despite the objections of the king and his cabinet, Pitt appointed seventy-eight-year-old Admiral Sir Charles Middleton as first lord of the Admiralty. Middleton, who had been Melville's unofficial naval adviser, took the post reluctantly and only after he was elevated to the peerage as Lord Barham. As comptroller of the navy he had done much to restore the service following the American War, and he was responsible for the good state of the fleet when the new war began. The appointment was widely criticized, however, because of Barham's age—he was a captain when Nelson was still in his cradle—and had spent most of his career on the administrative rather than the fighting side of the navy. But he was vigorous and in good health and proved himself a strategist of the highest order. Few men did more to lay the foundation for the eventual victory over Napoleon.

Four days after Barham took over his new office, on April 25, he learned the dreadful news of Villeneuve's escape and that he and Gravina had linked up. Moreover, Orde no longer guarded Cádiz, and Craig's expedition might be sailing to its destruction. Barham immediately began evolving a strategy to deal with the crisis. Working far into the night over his charts and memorandums, the old man produced a flood of orders designed to save the Secret Expedition from destruction, guard Ferrol, and protect the Western Approaches should Orde's guess about the Combined Fleet's destination be correct.

Sir Robert Calder's squadron at Ferrol was reinforced by the ships blockading Rochefort, and every vessel that could be made ready for sea was sent to Lord Gardner, who had temporarily replaced Cornwallis. Under no circumstances, Barham decreed, should the Channel fleet—which he called "the main spring from which all offensive operations must

*The French captured much of Dominica, but the British garrison continued to hold out in a corner of the island.

proceed"—be allowed to fall below eighteen of the line. Collingwood was ordered to take the Secret Expedition under his wing and conduct it as far as Cape St. Vincent. If he met Nelson, he was to place himself under his command. And if he learned Nelson had not followed Villeneuve to the Caribbean, Collingwood was himself to pursue the Combined Fleet.

The news that the fleets of France and Spain were in motion created a panic in the City. The price of government bonds plunged, while insurance rates on ships and cargoes bound for the West Indian islands doubled. And where was Nelson? Had he gone to Egypt? Or had he gone to the West Indies? The general belief, shared by Napoleon, was that he had gone to the Levant. "The cry is stirring up fast against him," observed Admiral Lord Radstock, whose son was serving in *Victory*, "and the loss of Jamaica would at once sink all his past services into oblivion." On June 4 the nation was relieved by the arrival of a dispatch from Nelson at Madeira, dated May 14, revealing that he was on Villeneuve's trail. Once he had resupplied his ships with provisions for five months, he sailed for Barbados.

VILLENEUVE DROPPED ANCHOR in the roadstead at Fort de France in Martinique on May 16 and began the wait for Ganteaume's fleet, which was still penned up in Brest by the British. On his slow, five-week passage, he and Admiral Missiessy had passed each other without making contact. The latter was returning to Europe after having missed the latest instructions ordering him to remain in the Caribbean. Villeneuve's first task was to unload a thousand sick from his ships, many of them suffering from dysentery and scurvy because the French had not as yet followed the British practice of serving lime juice to their crews.

New orders from the emperor awaited. Rear Admiral Magon de Medine, with two ships of the line from Rochefort, would soon join him and Gravina, and he was to await the arrival of the Brest fleet for seven weeks. If there was no sign of Ganteaume, he was to cross the Atlantic to Ferrol, and release the French and Spanish ships under blockade there by Calder. With this force—which Napoleon estimated would reach fifty vessels—Villeneuve was to enter "the Strait of Dover and join me off Boulogne" for the long-awaited "descent upon Britain." Magon arrived at Martinique on June 4, bringing the Combined Fleet to twenty of the line.

With no news of Ganteaume or the British, Villeneuve sent out two frigates to cruise to windward in search of them. Almost immediately he dispatched a letter of explanation to the Ministry of Marine in Paris—and in this can be readily seen the wide gulf between the French and the British navies. Nelson made his own decision to cross the Atlantic; Villeneuve was terrified of even sending out frigates to scout without explaining it to the emperor. For want of something better to do while running out the time before he returned to Europe, he decided to threaten some of the British islands to the north of Martinique. But he accomplished little except for the easy capture of a convoy of fourteen merchantmen and H.M.S. *Diamond Rock,* a tiny island from which the British kept an annoying watch on Martinique. From some prisoners he learned the disturbing news that Horatio Nelson had followed him to the Caribbean and was anchored at Barbados.

A British naval officer who once met Villeneuve described him as "a tallish thin man, a very tranquil, placid, English-looking Frenchman" and said he was "gentlemanly" and "a good officer." A veteran of Suffren's campaign in the Indian Ocean during the American War, he was one of the few aristocrats to serve the Revolution, and he had been rewarded for his loyalty with command of the Toulon fleet. But memories of the fiery holocaust at the Nile haunted him, and the very mention of Nelson's name made him nervous. Learning that the feared admiral was hot on his heels, Villeneuve ignored his orders to wait for Ganteaume and sailed on June 10 for Europe. A departing French officer bitterly summed up Villeneuve's stay in the Caribbean: "We have been masters of the sea for three weeks with an army of seven thousand and have not been able to attack a single island."

On his passage across the Atlantic, Nelson had dipped south to pick up the trade winds, and they held steady to Barbados. Even though his ships were badly in need of refitting, he pushed them to the limit and made the crossing in little more than three weeks. In contrast to the French fleet, his men were healthy, and morale was high. On some days, reported Nelson, his fleet covered 135 miles, often reaching a speed of five or six knots. *Superb,* eighty, was in the worst condition of the ships, but her captain, Richard Keats, kept all sails flying and lashed his studding-sail booms to the yards to keep up with the rest of the fleet while his men worked day and night at the pumps.

Villeneuve and Gravina might be found at anchor in any Caribbean bay, and if so, Nelson planned to repeat the devastating doubling-up tactics of Aboukir Bay and Cophenhagen. If the fleets met at sea, he told his captains that no man could do wrong who laid his ship close alongside an enemy vessel. "Take you a Frenchman apiece and leave me the Spaniards," he wrote. "We shall not part without a fight." At Barbados Nelson found two of Cochrane's ships—the other four were at Jamaica—and with his fleet strengthened to twelve of the line, again took up the search for Villeneuve.

The Combined Fleet was only a hundred miles away to the north, but misled by a report that it had been spotted sailing south toward Trinidad, Nelson embarked some troops and immediately headed for the threatened island. Following a fruitless search, he followed his original hunch and turned northward, toward Martinque. His course took him through the same cobalt-blue seas where Rodney had brought de Grasse to bay, and he passed Antigua, his base nearly two decades before when he had been an unknown frigate captain, and Nevis, where he had courted and married Fanny Nisbet.

Unable to find any trace of Villeneuve, Nelson concluded that the Frenchman had left the West Indies and was headed for the Mediterranean. He followed on June 13 with eleven of the line, setting a course for Gibraltar. Nelson had spent only nine days in the Caribbean, but in that brief time he had prevented the French from seizing the sugar islands and protected a convoy of some two hundred merchantmen waiting to sail for England until it was safely out of range of the enemy. Before leaving the area, he dispatched the speedy brig *Curieux* to inform the Admiralty of Villeneuve's return to Europe and Nelson's intention to follow.

Curieux's captain, George E. Bettesworth, brought with him more than Nelson's dispatches when he arrived at the Admiralty late on the evening of July 8. On his passage, he had overhauled the Combined Fleet about nine hundred miles to the east of Antigua, and determined that it was standing to the northward on a course that would take it to the Bay of Biscay rather than the Mediterranean, as Nelson had surmised. But Lord Barham had gone to bed and no one dared disturb him, so the first lord did not receive Bettesworth's vital intelligence until the next morning.

Furious at the delay, Barham began issuing orders while he was still in his dressing gown. Making use of the interior lines of communication that were the key to British control of the Channel, he disposed his squadrons to prevent the junction of the fleets that was central to Napoleon's invasion plan. Uncertain as to whether Villeneuve and Gravina were heading for Brest or Ferrol, Barham provided for both contingencies. Cornwallis, who was back with the Channel fleet, was directed to cruise to the southwest of Brest and to send Rear Admiral Charles Stirling and the five ships blockading Rochefort to reinforce Sir Robert Calder at Ferrol. With fifteen of the line, Calder was ordered to take up a station about a hundred miles off Cape Finisterre and intercept Villeneuve. Collingwood, who had six of the line off Cádiz, where it was supposed Nelson was heading, covered the entrance to the Mediterranean to prevent a union of the Cádiz and Cartagena squadrons.

In Britain, the threat of invasion had again become a reality. Boulogne was said to be packed with waiting barges, and the Combined Fleet was expected momentarily in the Channel. Napoleon placed his marshals on notice to embark for Britain early in August. Ganteaume was ordered to use the shift in British forces as an opportunity to get out of Brest and join Villeneuve and a squadron of five of the line under Rear Admiral Zacharie de Allemand that had escaped from Rochefort, and cover the invasion force. If the navy could win control the Channel for only three days, the emperor declared, he could "end the destiny of England." With twenty-two ships of the line, Ganteaume outnumbered Cornwallis, but as soon as he saw the mastheads of the blockading squadron, he dropped anchor. And so, as Napoleon fumed against his admirals, the Brest fleet remained in port, and Villeneuve and Gravina ran into Calder.

The encounter that took place in the fog off Finisterre on July 22, 1805, is one of the great might-have-beens of the Age of Fighting Sail. The odds favored Calder even though he had only fifteen ships of the line while the enemy had twenty. Three of his ships were three-deckers, while the allies had none; moreover, the enemy vessels were unseaworthy after their Atlantic crossing and were crowded with sick. The weather was so thick that the rival gunners, unable to make out their targets in the mist and the smoke, fired at their opponent's gun flashes.

By nightfall, Calder had captured two Spanish ships, one of eighty guns and the other of seventy-four, while only one of his ships had suffered severe damage. Over the next two days the two fleets lay to, making repairs, but Calder, intent on protecting his prizes, failed to press home his advantage. Villeneuve eventually broke off contact and took his fleet into Vigo on July 28, where he claimed to have won a victory. The repair facilities there were inadequate, and four days later he crept into Ferrol after Calder had been driven off station by a gale.

Like the Glorious First of June, "Calder's Action," as it was called, was a failed interception. In the former, Lord Howe had defeated the enemy fleet but failed to capture the grain convoy that was his primary objective. Calder had prevented Villeneuve from entering the Channel but had missed the opportunity to destroy the Combined Fleet. He was much criticized by a public that had come to view naval actions in the light of Aboukir and Copenhagen. Rather than removing the menace of Villeneuve's fleet, critics charged, Calder had merely driven the enemy into port, and the threat of invasion remained. "We are all raving mad at Sir Robert Calder," wrote one lady from the comfort of her country house. "I could have done better myself." Had Lord Nelson been in command off Finisterre rather than Calder, it was said, the decisive naval battle of the war against France would have taken place there rather than off Cape Trafalgar three months later.*

Part of the reason for the outcry against Calder was that the Combined Fleet and Allemand's squadron represented a serious threat to the nation's trade. The outward-bound East India convoy had to be detained in Plymouth, and the Lisbon convoy could not leave Portugal. Also, the homecoming West Indies sugar fleet, which had been saved by Nelson, and a rich convoy from China were both somewhere out in the Atlantic. At Cork, five

---

*Angered by these rumors, Calder demanded a court-martial to investigate his conduct at Finisterre. It censured him for failing to act more aggressively.

thousand British soldiers were waiting to embark for the capture of the Cape of Good Hope. From the center of his vast strategic spiderweb, Lord Barham made new dispositions to meet the new crisis. Calder and Stirling were dispatched to Cornwallis to defend the Channel. Nelson, who had arrived with his fleet at Gibraltar on July 19 and found no trace of Villeneuve, joined them, bringing the Channel Fleet to an imposing thirty-nine ships of the line.

Napoleon was at Boulogne, readying the Grande Armée for the invasion. On August 8 he learned that Villeneuve was at Vigo but not yet that he had taken refuge at Ferrol, and ordered him to come north and seize control of the Channel. Reluctantly, Villeneuve left Ferrol with twenty-nine of the line two days later. For several days his ragged fleet sailed northward into the Bay of Biscay, avoiding all contact with other ships and while the admiral's resolution oozed away. His ships were short of stores and water, their crews suffered from scurvy and dysentery, and the Spaniards were almost in mutiny.

With Villeneuve and Gravina supposedly on the way to Brest to lift the blockade, Napoleon ordered Ganteaume to be ready to put to sea at a moment's notice. "Never did a fleet face danger for a grander object," he declared. "Never [did] soldiers and sailors risk their lives in a greater goal." But Villeneuve, whose nerve had failed him, had already put about and was shaping a course for Cádiz. Pushing aside Collingwood's small squadron, he dropped anchor there on August 20. Eager to wipe out the stigma of his earlier caution, Calder put the stopper in the bottle, bringing the British blockading fleet off Cádiz to twenty-six ships. Napoleon's plan for invading Britain, which had been evolving over two years, had collapsed.

Overlooking his own contribution to the debacle, the emperor blamed his naval commanders for the failure of the invasion plan. He raged that "Villeneuve has not the courage to command even a frigate. He is man without resolution or moral courage." In point of fact, however, even before Napoleon had received word that Villeneuve was heading away from a junction with Ganteaume, he was giving consideration to breaking camp and turning his army eastward to deal with the menace of Russia and Austria before they could fully mobilize their armies. Villeneuve's failure to come north was merely the final straw that caused him to call off the invasion. In effect, Pitt had forced him from the Channel by setting Europe at his back. The threat of a French landing in Britain was over—at least for 1805— and the initiative had passed to Britain.

⌐⌐

WEARY AND AILING after more than two years at sea, Nelson was allowed a long-sought leave, and proceeded in *Victory* to Spithead, where he struck his flag on August 19. Within a few hours he was on his way by post chaise to Merton Place—"Paradise Merton"—where the woman he loved and their child eagerly awaited his return. The next twenty-five days were among the most pleasant of his life. He was surrounded by admiring relatives and friends, and Horatia, now four and a half and learning French and Italian, was a delight. And, as always, Emma fascinated him. Lord Minto, who dined at Merton, was impressed with the improvements Emma had made in Nelson's absence—"she is a clever being after all"— and noted "the passion" between the lovers "is as hot as ever."

Having unsuccessfully pursued Villeneuve for fourteen thousand miles, Nelson was worried about his reception by both the Admiralty and the public. He went up to London, where he found that he was still Britain's premier naval hero. An American visitor, a Yale professor named Benjamin Silliman,* observed that "Lord Nelson cannot appear in the streets without immediately collecting a retinue, which augments as his proceeds, and when he enters a shop the door is thronged until he comes out."

At the Admiralty, Nelson was taken aback by Lord Barham's unusual request for the journals of his transatlantic voyage, a request that hardly would have been made of an officer he trusted. But the first lord apparently found enough in them to henceforth place his full confidence in Nelson, who was assured his services would soon be required again. Nelson conferred repeatedly with Pitt and his ministers, who eagerly sought his opinion, and he played a prominent role in the making of British strategy. Together with Barham, he helped reorganize the positioning of frigates and other cruisers for improved trade protection in the Western Approaches.† Nelson also tried to obtain a pension for Emma in recognition of her services to the nation while in Naples, but these pleas were met with silence.

Years later, the future duke of Wellington, then Major General Sir Arthur Wellesley, who had just returned victorious from India, recalled a chance meeting with Nelson in a waiting room at the Colonial Office. Wellesley immediately recognized his companion, who "entered at once into conversation with me, if I can call it conversation, for it was almost all on his side and all about himself and, in reality, a style so vain and so silly as to surprise and disgust me.

"I supposed that something that I happened to say may have made him guess that I was *somebody*," Wellesley continued, "and he went out of the room for a moment, I have no doubt to ask the office-keeper who I was, for when he came back he was altogether a different man, in both in manner

---

*He was soon to be recognized as a distinguished chemist.

†Perhaps Nelson had a premonition that he would not come back alive from his forthcoming assignment. He visited the London upholstery shop where his coffin was stored and ordered it be made ready, "for I think it highly probable that I may want it on my return."

and matter. All that I had thought a charlatan style had vanished and he talked of the state of the country and . . . of affairs on the Continent with a good sense . . . that surprised me. . . . I don't know that I ever had a conversation that interested me more."

British strategists, unaware of Napoleon's abandonment of his plan to invade England, were concerned with the whereabouts of the Combined Fleet. No one knew whether it had gone to Brest to join Ganteaume or had sailed into the Mediterranean. The mystery was not resolved until dispatches were received from Collingwood on September 2, reporting that Villeneuve had put into Cádiz. The news was brought by Captain Henry Blackwood of the frigate *Euryalus,* of thirty-six guns. Merton was near the Portsmouth–London road, and Blackwood, certain that Nelson would be immediately recalled to active duty, stopped off to inform the admiral of the latest developments. "Depend upon it, Blackwood, I shall yet give Mr. Villeneuve a drubbing," Nelson told him.

Summoned to the Admiralty, Nelson was told he was to reassume command of the Mediterranean fleet, which was blockading Cádiz, as soon as *Victory* was ready for sea. He was to have Collingwood as his second in command, Thomas Hardy as his flag captain, and forty ships of the line. Nelson's precise task was to prevent the Combined Fleet, now estimated at thirty-three of the line, from getting into the Mediterranean, where it would threaten Craig's force and the Russian transports preparing to sail from Odessa on the Black Sea with an army that was to fight in Italy.

Gloom enshrouded the household at Merton as Nelson took his leave on the night of September 13. Emma's eyes were puffed and reddened with weeping, and she nearly fainted as the carriage that was to take her lover to Portsmouth was heard crunching up the gravel driveway. Just before leaving, the admiral slipped into Horatia's room, kneeled at the bedside of his sleeping daughter for a brief prayer, and tiptoed away.

VICTORY BEAT DOWN the Channel in company with *Euryalus* from St. Helens on the morning tide two days later in spite of dead foul winds. Nelson was rowed out to his flagship from the beach at Southsea instead of Portsmouth Point to avoid the crowds, but he was nevertheless cheered by a sizable gathering. In his novel *The Trumpet Major,* Thomas Hardy described the flagship's passage along Portland Bill, based on eyewitness accounts: "The great silent ship, with her population of bluejackets, marines, officers, captain and the admiral who was not to return alive, passed like a phantom. . . . Sometimes her aspect was that of a large white bat, sometimes that of a grey one. . . . [Presently] the courses of the *Victory* were absorbed into the main, then her topsails went, and then her

Admiral Cuthbert Lord Collingwood, Nelson's friend and second in command at Trafalgar. (U.S. Naval Academy Museum)

topgallants. . . . The admiral's flag sank behind the watery line, and in a minute the very truck of her last topmast stole away. . . ."

Nelson's arrival off Cádiz on September 28 galvanized the fleet, although he ordered that no salute be fired so as not to alert the enemy to his presence. "Lord Nelson is arrived," Captain Edward Codrington of *Orion* wrote his wife. "A sort of general joy has been the consequence, and many good effects will shortly arise from our change of system." His prediction was correct, because Nelson immediately replaced the close block-ade ordered by Collingwood with one similar to what he had maintained off Toulon, which was designed to tempt the Combined Fleet out of the harbor. Accordingly, the main fleet took up station fifty miles off Cádiz, while his only two frigates, *Euryalus* and *Hydra*, thirty-eight, remained close inshore. Between them, Nelson stationed four or five of his two-deck-ers within signaling distance of each other so information from the frigates could pass to the flagship within minutes.

As Napoleon moved the Grande Armée into Germany to deal with the Russians and the Austrians, he issued new orders for Villeneuve on Sep-tember 16. The Combined Fleet was to weigh anchor as soon as possible; pick up the Spanish ships at Cartagna; proceed to Naples, where the troops on board were to be landed to resist the expected Anglo-Russian attack on southern Italy; and then return to Toulon. But the emperor did not inform the unhappy Villeneuve—whom he unjustly regarded as a coward—that he was being sacked and replaced by Vice Admiral François Rosily, who was carrying the order relieving Villeneuve with him to Spain.

In Cádiz Bay, the conditions faced by Villeneuve were bad. Although his fleet had grown to thirty-three of the line with the addition of four Span-ish vessels already in port, the ships were in poor condition; there was a poverty of resources; and the local authorities refused to provide provi-sions, shot, and powder unless paid in advance. There was friction between the allies, with the Spaniards claiming the French had treacher-ously abandoned the two Spanish ships captured by Calder during the action off Finisterre. Nevertheless, Villeneuve did his best to prepare his ships for sea.

On September 29—Nelson's forty-seventh birthday—he invited his captains to dinner. Most were young, with only a few having reached their midforties, and *Victory*'s great cabin soon echoed with their laughter. Codrington was thirty-five, Hardy thirty-six, George Duff of *Mars* and John Cooke of *Bellerophon* were forty-two, Blackwood was thirty-four, and Charles Tyler of *Tonnant* was, at forty-five, one of the oldest present. There was much gaiety, for the admiral had been thoughtful enough to bring per-sonal letters from wives and families for his captains.

When Thomas Fremantle, now captain of the three-decker *Neptune* and expecting word of the birth of a child, came on board, Nelson greeted his old friend warmly and asked whether he wanted a boy or a girl.

"A girl," replied Fremantle, who already had two sons.

"Be satisfied," the admiral replied, handing over a letter announcing that Betsey Fremantle had given birth to a daughter.

Following dinner, Nelson unveiled his plan for attacking the Combined Fleet should it come out—a plan designed to annihilate the enemy. He intended to form his ships into three divisions, two of which, sailing in parallel columns, would strike the enemy line about one-third of the way behind the leading ship and an equal distance from the rear. While the van tried to come about, those in the center and rear would be overwhelmed in a pell-mell battle, in which superior gunnery and ship handling would give the British the advantage. The third (reserve) division would engage the enemy van if it entered the battle.

This plan was well received, according to Nelson. "When I came to explain to them the *Nelson Touch* it was like an electric shock," he wrote Emma. "Some shed tears, all approved—'It was new—it was singular—it was simple!' and, from the admirals downward it was repeated—'It must succeed, if ever they will allow us to get at them! You are, My Lord, surrounded by friends, whom you inspire with confidence.'" On October 9 Nelson followed up by sending each of his captains a detailed memorandum outlining his plan.*

Over the next three weeks, reinforcements brought the British fleet off Cádiz to twenty-seven ships of the line, including seven three-deckers. Nelson also received three additional frigates, which were added to the picket line commanded by Blackwood. As they arrived, each ship was painted black with yellow strakes in the Nelson style. If the enemy did not soon come out, the admiral began thinking about an attack on the Combined Fleet in Cádiz Bay itself, by a flotilla of fire ships and the newfangled Congreve rocket. While waiting to get at the enemy, Nelson made certain morale remained high. Pursers were directed to supply more fresh meat and green vegetables for the ships' soup, and the men were encouraged to send letters home. With typical kindness, Nelson, upon learning that *Victory*'s coxswain had been so busy filling the mailbags he had forgotten to include his own letters, he ordered the mail ship recalled so they could be included.

Gloom enshrouded the French and Spaniards, however. With the dreaded Nelson now known to be offshore, Villeneuve and his senior officers discussed their next move at a council of war held in the cabin of *Bucentaure* on October 8. Following a turbulent debate, they resolved to do nothing until "a more favorable opportunity" presented itself. Such an opportunity failed to appear because of bad weather, but Villeneuve's hand was forced by rumors that Admiral Rosily, who was already in Madrid, was on his way to relieve him. At the same time, he learned that

---

*Nelson had already outlined the essentials of his plan to Captain Richard Keats of *Superb*, who visited him at Merton. Former prime minister Addington also reported that the admiral had told him, "'Rodney broke the line at one place; I shall do it at two,'" and demonstrated what he intended with his fingers on a small table. Nelson's Memorandum appears in Appendix II.

Nelson's command had been reduced: four British ships of the line had been diverted to escort a convoy carrying reinforcements for General Craig to Malta, and two more, under Rear Admiral Thomas Louis, had been sent to Gibraltar for water and repairs. Rather than return to Paris in disgrace, the troubled Villeneuve saw an opportunity to salvage his honor by escaping into the Mediterranean.

On the morning of October 19 the frigate *Sirius*, thirty-six, which was watching Cádiz, hoisted signal 370—"The enemy's ships are coming out." Within minutes the signal was repeated to *Euryalus* and she to *Phoebe*, and so on until at 9:30 A.M. Nelson was warned that his prey was making a bolt from its lair. At once the jubilant admiral hoisted the signal "General chase, southeast," but kept his own ships out of sight below the horizon with the intention of placing his battle line between Villeneuve and the entrance to the Strait of Gibraltar. But the Combined Fleet's seamanship was unequal to the task of getting to sea in one tide, and only twelve ships had emerged from Cádiz by late afternoon.

Nelson was surprised to find no sign of the enemy fleet during the night, and as he closed in on Gibraltar in heavy rain and thick weather, he feared the foe had put back into Cádiz. In reality the ships that had gotten out had anchored a little to the north of the port to await their consorts. As he was setting course to regain his previous station fifty miles west of Cádiz on the morning of October 20, one of Blackwood's frigates reported that the rest of Villeneuve's ships were straggling out and heading toward Gibraltar. It was a Sunday, and a large crowd grimly watched the departure of the Franco-Spanish fleet. Cádiz's cathedrals and churches were filled with families praying for their men who were going into danger.

Nelson remained continually on *Victory's* poop while Blackwood's squadron provided fresh reports. To a nearby group of midshipmen Nelson observed, "This day, or tomorrow, will be a fortunate one for you young gentlemen"—obviously meaning the survivors would step into the shoes of their superiors who were killed in action. At dinner that evening the admiral showed no sign of foreboding and stated that he expected to capture between twenty and twenty-two of the enemy ships. "The twenty-first will be our day," he said more than once.

Throughout the night the British frigates hung on to the Combined Fleet despite repeated efforts to brush them off. Alarmed by the hollow thud of signal guns and the sinister glow of blue lanterns, Villeneuve worried that Nelson might suddenly strike his unwieldy fleet in the darkness. After all, Nelson had attacked during the night at the Nile, and the admiral, who had vivid memories of the fiery aftermath, was skittish about another such encounter. Such was Nelson's reputation for the unexpected that Villeneuve seems to have given up even before the battle.

CHAPTER 19

"England Expects . . . "

By 5:30 A.M. on October 21, 1805, the rain squalls that had fallen during the night had given way to a light breeze from the west-northwest, but heavy swells rolled in from the Atlantic. As the pale light appeared through the slow-moving clouds, the white cliffs of Cape Trafalgar loomed up twenty miles to the east. Many eyes watched them appear, measuring their chances, the margin of life and death. Twenty minutes later, a group of flags ran up to the main masthead of *Achille*, seventy-four, signaling that she had "discovered a strange fleet." A massive French and Spanish armada—its masts appearing to one of *Victory*'s sailors like "a great wood on our lee bow"—revealed itself about nine miles away following the curve of the coast to the southeast. Men swarmed into the rigging or stared from the gun ports to catch a glimpse of the ships they had been trying to bring to battle for more than two years.

Nelson, a slight, one-armed figure on the weather side of *Victory*'s poop, examined the multicolored hulls of the enemy fleet through his long glass. Their ensigns drooped: the red and gold of Spain looked like twisted curtains, while the French tricolor hung so the red stripe obscured the rest. The count of vessels silhouetted across the horizon rose steadily: fifteen . . . twenty . . . twenty-five . . . finally reaching thirty-three—seventeen French and sixteen Spanish. Gaps in the enemy line showed where ships were dropping astern, and it sagged away to leeward. Nelson's own command was smaller—twenty-seven of the line, five frigates, a schooner, and a cutter. The admiral, who wore a threadbare uniform frock coat with the stars of his four orders of knighthood embroidered on the left breast, seemed in "excellent spirits," according to Dr. William Beatty, *Victory*'s surgeon. Notwithstanding the inferiority of his fleet, he assured Captain Hardy "he would not be contented with capturing less than twenty sail of the line."

In *Royal Sovereign*, Collingwood's flagship, the admiral's servant, a man named Smith, entered his master's cabin at daybreak to find him already up and dressing. Asked if he had seen the enemy fleet, Smith replied he had not and was told "'to look out at them. . . . In a very short time we should see a great deal more.'" Looking through one of *Royal Sovereign*'s quarter galleries, Smith said he "observed a crowd of ships to leeward" but was more impressed by the fact that the admiral was shaving himself with an astonishing composure. "It was a beautiful sight when their line was completed," related Midshipman William Badcock of *Neptune.* "Their broadsides turned toward us, showing their iron teeth."

At 6:10 A.M. Nelson ordered his ships to form up in order of sailing into two columns, a weather division of fifteen of the line led by *Victory,* and a lee division of twelve, with Collingwood's *Royal Sovereign* in the van. Because Nelson had fewer ships than he had expected, he abandoned the idea of a reserve division embodied in his original plan. *Victory*'s bow began to swing into the path of the rising sun. In all the vessels of the fleet, the order was repeated. Helmsmen heaved on the great steering wheels, the braces were manned to trim the yards and sails, and every one of the great ships flying Nelson's flag* altered course—slowly, implacably, and silently—toward the enemy. Some had names that were already famous; others were to become famous that day: *Téméraire, Bellerophon, Dreadnought, Revenge, Colossus, Ajax,* Nelson's old *Agamemnon*—all the great names that symbolized Britain's mastery of the seas. Shortly afterward, at 6:22 A.M., Signal 13—"Prepare for battle"—was hoisted.

Every scrap of canvas was set—courses, topsails, topgallants and royals. There was little wind but a heavy swell, a sign of bad weather to come. As the pale and watery sun grew warmer an almost festive air pervaded the fleet. Bands on some of the ships played "Rule Britannia" and "Britons, Strike Home!" The tunes danced across the water to be taken up by other ships. Captains hailed their fellows to wish each other good luck and a captured enemy ship in tow before night fell. And down in the gloom of the gun decks, the crews chalked defiant slogans on their cannon. "One would have thought that the people were preparing for a festival rather than a combat," wrote Midshipman John Franklin of *Bellerophon.*

Nelson had gone below to write a new codicil to his will in which he made one last attempt to secure a pension for Emma for her services at the Neapolitan court. "Could I have rewarded these services, I would not now call upon my Country; but as it is not in my power I leave . . . Emma Lady Hamilton . . . a Legacy to my King and Country, that they will give her ample provision to maintain her rank in life." He also expressed the desire

---

*Nelson was a vice admiral of the White, so the ships of his division flew the white flag, but Collingwood was a vice admiral of the Blue, so his ships should, according to regulations, fly the blue flag. Nelson ordered the entire fleet to wear the White Ensign because it was easier to distinguish it from the French tricolor.

that his adopted daughter, Horatia Nelson Thompson, would henceforth use the name Nelson. Hardy and Blackwood, who had come to the flagship to make a report, witnessed his signature.

Villeneuve, in the center of the allied line, stood on the poop of *Bucentaure* in undress uniform, his hair freshly powdered, and closely observed the British fleet steering toward him under a cloud of sail. He was not surprised by its unorthodox configuration, for he had already perceived Nelson's plan of action. "The enemy will not confine himself to forming on a line of battle parallel with our own," he had told his captains before departing Cádiz. "He will endeavor to envelop our rear, to break through our line, and to direct his ships in groups upon such of ours as he shall have cut off, so as to surround them and defeat them." Yet the French admiral had prepared no plan to counter the attack except to order his fleet to form up in a long, single line on a southerly course for the Strait of Gibraltar.

But he changed his mind at about 8:00 A.M. If the fleet continued on its current course he would be committed to passing through the Strait of Gibraltar, where he might be trapped between Nelson and Admiral Louis' squadron in the Mediterranean. Villeneuve signaled his ships to wear together, or reverse course, to return in the direction of Cádiz. This put Admiral Gravina's ships, which had been in the van, in the rear. By the time the Combined Fleet had floundered through the evolution in the light airs it was nearly 10:00 A.M. and they were in considerable disorder. Rather than forming a single column, some vessels were bunched together two and three deep in a line that was bowed toward the land. "Our fleet is doomed," observed Commodore Don Cosme de Churruca of the Spanish seventy-four-gun *San Juan Nepomunceno* as he viewed the disorder all around him. "The French admiral does not understand his business."

Midshipman Badcock reported that the full array of enemy ships, stretching some four miles along the horizon, were now clearly in view. "Some . . . were painted like ourselves—with double yellow sides, some with a broad single red or yellowish streak, others all black, and the *Santisima Trinidad* with four distinct lines of red, with white ribbons between them, made her seem to be a superb man-of-war. . . . She was lying head-to under topsails, topgallants, royals, jib and spanker; her courses were hauled up, and her lofty, towering sails looked beautiful as she awaited the onset."*

At 11:15 Villeneuve signaled: "Open fire as soon as the enemy is within range," which roused the spirit of his crews. A roar of cheers passed along his battle line, and the bands struck up patriotic tunes. On the British ships, which were approaching the enemy line at a walking pace, their crews were piped to a dinner of cold salt pork followed by a tot of grog. Nelson

---

*With 140 guns, she was the largest warship in the world. Nelson had hoped to capture her at St. Vincent eight years before.

again went below. "Take care of my Guardian Angel!" he told the sailors dismantling his cabin as they carried Lady Hamilton's portrait to a secure place. The admiral kneeled in front of his desk—the chairs having been removed—and penned a final prayer in his private journal:

> May the Great God, whom I worship, grant to my Country, and for the benefit of Europe in general, a great and glorious victory; and may no misconduct in anyone tarnish it; and may humanity after Victory be the predominant feature in the British fleet. For myself, individually, I commit my life to Him who made me, and may His blessing light upon my endeavours for serving my Country faithfully. To Him I resign myself and the just cause which is entrusted to me to defend. Amen, amen, amen.

Returning to the deck, Nelson ordered two signals to be made. One was to Collingwood, whose division was closest to the Combined Fleet, reiterating his intention to break the enemy line. The other instructed his captains to anchor at the close of day, for the light airs, rising swell, and falling barometer indicated a storm that could drive any damaged ships onto the rocky shore of Cape Trafalgar. Shortly before noon the admiral informed Hardy that he wished "to amuse the fleet." Summoning his signal officer, Lieutenant John Pasco, he declared: "I want you to say to the fleet, 'England confides that every man will do his duty.' You must be quick, for I have one more signal to make, which is for close action."

"If Your Lordship will permit me to substitute 'expects' for 'confides,' the signal will be sooner completed," replied Pasco, "because the word 'expects' is in the vocabulary [Popham's signal book], and 'confides' must be spelled out."

"That will do, Pasco," Nelson answered. "Make it directly."

Some men cheered as they read the most famous signal in naval history. Others shrugged it off as a statement of the obvious. "I wish Nelson would stop signaling," growled Collingwood. "We all know what to do."

"England expects" was briskly followed by Signal 16—"Engage the enemy more closely"—which was kept flying until shot away.

⌐

SUDDENLY A ROW OF glowing red dots appeared along the side of the French seventy-four *Fougueux* as she opened the battle with ranging shots at *Royal Sovereign,* which was still about a mile away. Collingwood calmly munched an apple as the enemy's shot kicked up thin waterspouts about his flagship. Unshaken, she grimly plowed on, the thin edge of a wedge of ships that seemed likely to strike the fifteenth ship from the enemy's rear, the 112-gun Spanish-three decker *Santa Ana,* which had also opened fire, her cannon spouting out their vivid orange tongues. "See how that noble fellow Collingwood takes his ship into action!" declared Nelson, whose own vessel had not yet come under enemy fire. "How I envy him!"

The next few minutes were crucial. Had the French and Spanish gunnery been good, *Royal Sovereign* and *Victory* would have been raked from stem to stern without being able to reply. Such a concentration of broadsides might have been sufficient to force them to turn away from the allied line. But Nelson had gambled that the enemy gunners were inexperienced and unskilled and that his ships would be in a position to retaliate before suffering serious damage—and he won. The enemy gunners were not only unskilled, but their aim was spoiled by the heavy swells, which caused their ships to roll. One minute the gun captains saw blue sky; the next, green sea.

Just as the ship's bell of *Royal Sovereign* tolled noon, she shouldered her way between *Santa Ana*'s ornately decorated stern and across the beaked bow of *Fougueux* and unleashed double-shotted broadsides into both vessels. The enemy ships appeared to roll over as if struck by a mountainous sea. Nearly four hundred men were either killed or wounded in these vessels. *Santa Ana* had fourteen guns dismounted, and her stern disintegrated into splinters. *Royal Sovereign* then ranged alongside *Santa Ana* so closely that their yardarms locked, and they continued a furious duel muzzle to muzzle. *Fougueux, San Leandro*, sixty-four, and other vessels poured a crossfire into Collingwood's ship, which ceased after they realized they were hitting each other as often as the enemy.

Royal Sovereign fought on alone for about fifteen minutes and was taking a heavy beating before *Bellisle*, seventy-four, followed her through the enemy line. Captain William Hargood told the men on deck to lie down while he directed the steering of his ship. "The silence on board was almost awful," related one officer. "As we got nearer and nearer to the enemy, this silence was, however, broken frequently by the sadly stirring shrieks of the wounded, for of them, and killed, we had more than fifty before we fired a shot; and our colours were three times shot away. . . ."

Bellisle was engaged successively by five Spanish and French ships. She was totally dismasted and unable to fire her guns out of fear of setting the wreckage afire. *Swiftsure*, seventy-four, and *Polyphemus*, sixty-four, came to her rescue and took up positions covering the shattered vessel. The allied rear was now becoming jumbled and confused, with some of the ships pressing forward to support the center while others hesitated, their sails shivering or aback. Soon they were covered by thick smoke that rolled downwind from hundreds of guns of the British lee division.

Mars, seventy-four, next in the British line, had difficulty finding a gap in the French line. Under fire from four ships, she was soon unmanageable, and her captain, George Duff, had his head ripped off by a cannonball. The arrival of more British ships drove off her assailants, but the stricken vessel was an awful warning to the rest of the British fleet of what might have happened had the Spanish and the French been better gunners, or even luckier. Nevertheless, by 12:30 P.M. more than half of Collingwood's ships were in action and giving better than they received. The rest followed, precipitating the pell-mell sought by Nelson.

The eighty-gun *Tonnant*, which had been captured by Nelson at the Nile, fought yardarm to yardarm with *Monarca*, seventy-four, until the latter struck her colors. *Tonnant* next engaged *Algesiras*, seventy-four. Sharpshooters in the French vessel's tops cleared *Tonnant*'s quarterdeck, but eventually her assailant's masts were brought down by cannon fire and the snipers were thrown into the sea. *Algesiras* was taken by boarding. Seventy-seven of her crewmen were killed and another 142 wounded.

Bellerophon came under fire from four French and Spanish ships and was twice nearly boarded by men from *Aigle*, seventy-four, who were beaten back in hand-to-hand fighting. The French tossed grenades through her gunports, which ignited powder on the lower deck. More than a hundred men were killed or wounded in the explosion. But the crew of *Bellerophon* kept firing, pulling wreckage and wounded men aside to keep the guns in action. Two-thirds of *Aigle*'s crew were cut down. She drifted off with her rigging ripped apart and her masts tottering, but *Bellerophon* was too badly damaged to follow. The crippled *Aigle* was next engaged by *Defiance*, seventy-four, and forced to surrender.

The gunners of *Dreadnought*, 98, had been trained so well that they could fire three broadsides in three and a half minutes, and she gave a good account of herself against Admiral Gravina's flagship, the 112-gun *Principe de Asturias*, and *San Juan de Nepomunceno*, 74. The latter was maneuvering to rake *Bellerophon* when *Dreadnought*'s broadsides wreaked such devastation that she surrendered ten minutes later. *Principe de Asturias* was badly battered and Gravina was mortally wounded, but *Dreadnought* was such a slow sailer that the Spanish flagship managed to drift away from the battle toward Cádiz with other survivors.

⌒

IN THE MEANTIME, Nelson's column plowed on toward the allied line in the sickly light airs, as if they were held together by some irresistible force. Captain Hardy urged the admiral to allow *Neptune* and *Téméraire*, the vessels just behind *Victory*, to assume the leadership of his line and absorb the full effect of the enemy broadsides, but Nelson refused. When *Téméraire*'s captain tried to push ahead, Nelson sharply ordered him to keep his place in line. Hardy also suggested that he change his coat because his decorations would make him a target for sharpshooters. Nelson replied that "he was aware it might be seen but it was now too late to be shifting a coat."

The ships of the allied van and center began firing ranging shots at the oncoming *Victory* at about 12:20 P.M. By this time Villeneuve had realized that Nelson's target was his center and sought the assistance of the eight unengaged ships of his van. But instead of directly signaling these ships to wear and support him, he made only a general signal directing them to take whatever steps were necessary to get into action. Rear Admiral Pierre Dumanoir le Pelley, who led the van, ignored the signal, and his ships held their northerly course toward Cádiz.

A shot passed through *Victory*'s main-topgallant sail, showing that the range had been found, and almost all the allied vessels now opened up on the slow-moving British flagship. The heavy shot screeched overhead and punched dozens of holes in the her sails. Nelson told Captain Blackwood that it was time for him to return to *Euryalus*. As he prepared to step over the side, Blackwood took the admiral's hand and said: "I trust my Lord, that on my return to the *Victory*, which will be as soon as possible, I shall find your Lordship well and in possession of twenty prizes."

"God bless you, Blackwood," replied Nelson. "I shall never speak to you again."

Victory breaks the French line at Trafalgar on October 21, 1805. (Beverley Robinson Collection, U.S. Naval Academy Museum)

Victory, surging bow-on toward the enemy line, was unable to bring her own guns to bear and was repeatedly raked, according to one historian, with "such a fire as had scarcely before been directed at a single ship."[*] Several shot struck the lower hull like battering rams. One shot howled across the quarterdeck and mangled the body of John Scott, the admiral's secretary, who had been conversing with Hardy only moments before. "Is that poor Scott?" Nelson asked as the bloody corpse was thrown overboard. Another shot killed eight of a file of marines stationed on the poop to deal with enemy sharpshooters. Nelson ordered the rest to be dispersed on the main deck rather then sent aloft to combat snipers—a decision that may have ultimately cost him his own life.[†] Within a few minutes the flagship had suffered fifty killed and wounded, had lost her mizzen-topmast, and her wheel was smashed. For the rest of the battle she was steered by forty men who manned the tiller in the gun room and carried out orders brought down to them from the quarterdeck. Wooden splinters whirled in the air, and one bruised Hardy's foot and tore a silver buckle from his shoe. Hardy and Nelson stopped and exchanged an inquiring look. "This is too warm work to last too long," the admiral observed with a bleak smile.

As *Victory* neared the enemy line, she hauled to starboard, which carried her and the vessels following her to the allied center. There, the great *Santisima Trinidad,* Villeneuve's flagship *Bucentaure,* and *Redoubtable,* seventy-four, the most efficient vessel in the Combined Fleet, barred the way. Hardy spotted a small gap in the line and took *Victory* between *Redoubtable* and *Bucentaure.* Successive broadsides from her double- and triple-shotted guns erupted like a volcano, dismounting about twenty guns, and killing and wounding more than a hundred of the French flagship's crew. Once having cleared *Bucentaure, Victory* ran alongside *Redoubtable* and did even greater damage to her. Soon *Victory* was dueling not only with these vessels but also with *Santisima Trinidad, Neptune,* eighty-four,[§] and *San Justo,* seventy-four, and was enshrouded in a cloud of swirling smoke. The air was filled with noise, gun captains yelling and gesturing to their crews who heaved the smoking guns toward the enemy. Overhead, seamen called to one another while severed rigging flapped in the wind and defied their grasping fingers. Shattered yards and masts plummeted down from aloft.

Téméraire followed *Victory* through the gap, engaged *Neptune* in a hot action, and then drifted across the bow of *Redoubtable,* where she supported the battered flagship. Behind her in quick succession came the British *Nep-*

[*]William James, *The Naval History of Great Britain,* vol. IV, pp. 53–54.

[†]Nelson is reported to have believed that the flash of their muskets might set the flagship's sails on fire.

[§]Both fleets had ships named *Neptune* and *Achille,* and the Spaniards had a *Neptuno,* eighty.

tune, Leviathan, seventy-four, and *Conqueror,* seventy-four, backed by *Britannia,* one hundred, *Ajax,* seventy-four, and *Agamemnon.* By one o'clock the center and rear of the allied line were a cauldron of flames and smoke and falling top hamper. The ships crowded together, broadsides crashing into their blazing hulls at point-blank range, while some French captains vainly tried to put boarding parties on the decks of their opponents. It was not a struggle between opposite fleets but a series of single combats of the utmost ferocity.

"We were engaging on both sides; every gun was going off," observed Lieutenant Lewis Rotely of *Victory.* "A man should witness a battle in a three-decker in the middle deck, for it beggars all description: it bewilders the senses of sight and hearing. There was the fire from above, there was the fire from below, besides the fire from the deck I was upon, the guns recoiling with violence, reports louder than thunder, the decks heaving and the sides straining. I fancied myself in the external regions, where every man appeared a devil. Lips might move, but orders and hearing were out of question; everything was done by signs."

Sharpshooters in *Redoubtable*'s tops and rigging swept *Victory*'s decks, and again and again broadsides from *Bucentaure* and *Santisima Trinidad* struck home, turning *Victory* into "a butcher's shambles." Men lay buried under overturned guns and shattered timber. Having brought the fleet into close action, there was little for Nelson to do and he paced the quarterdeck with Hardy, stopping now and then to give orders or lend encouragement. At about 1:15 P.M. Hardy turned to see Nelson on his knees and about to collapse. He crouched over the admiral and anxiously asked:

"I hope you are not severely wounded, my Lord?"

"They have done for me at last, Hardy," Nelson gasped.

"I hope not!"

"Yes," gasped the admiral, "my backbone is shot through."

Nelson had been hit in the left shoulder by a bullet from aloft that had driven downward into his chest, torn through his left lung, severed a major artery, and then fractured his spine. He was carried below to the cockpit, his face and medals covered with handkerchiefs so the men on the gundecks would not recognize him and become discouraged.

Victory's surgeon, Dr. William Beatty, examined Nelson and quickly determined that he was beyond helping. Nothing could be done except to make the dying man as comfortable as possible. He could feel no sensation in his lower body but was in severe pain at the point where the ball was lodged against his spine, and his breathing was difficult. Believing that he had not long to live, the admiral told the Reverend Alexander Scott, his personal chaplain, in agitated and hurried sentences: "Remember me to Lady Hamilton! Remember me to Horatia! Remember me to my friends!"

For three hours, Nelson lay dying in *Victory*'s dimly lit cockpit, jarred by the broadsides of his ship, amid the screams and moans of the other wounded and the sounds of hoarse cheers as one after another of the French and Spanish ships struck their colors. The admiral desperately wanted news of the battle and repeatedly asked that Hardy come down to see him. But the battle had reached a crescendo of fury, and the captain was delayed on deck. "Is Hardy killed?" asked Nelson. "Beatty, why does Hardy not come?"

Having sent an officer in a boat to inform Collingwood that Nelson had been wounded, Hardy took command of the windward division and fought the final stages of the battle. At 2:25 P.M. Villeneuve ordered the flag of *Bucentaure,* all three masts and bowsprit shot away, hauled down. "Our ship was so riddled that it seemed to be no more than a mass of wreckage," said her captain. *Redoubtable* had lost five-sixths of her crew and was sinking, while *Fougueux* fell to *Téméraire* soon afterward. *Santisima Trinidad* tried to escape but was completely dismasted and lay an unmanageable wreck on the water. "Blood ran in streams about the deck, and in spite of the sand, the rolling of the ship carried it hither and thither until it made strange patterns on the planks," recalled a crewman.

At about this time, Admiral Dumanoir, commander of the unengaged French van, finally ordered his ships to sail to the assistance of the center of the fleet. Hardy ordered his division to re-form in preparation for this new onslaught, and once again British seamanship carried the day. The regrouping was carried out so rapidly that *Leviathan, Conqueror, Neptune, Ajax, Agamemnon,* and *Britannia* blocked Dumanoir's squadron from interfering and began to pick off his ships. In the rear, *Santa Ana,* filled with more than three hundred dead, surrendered. *Achille* caught fire and blew up with an explosion that sent "a prodigious tree of flame" into the air.* On the other side, *Royal Sovereign* was a wreck, with fragments of spars, fallen blocks, and rigging littering her deck, and was taken under tow by *Euryalus.*

Hardy reported to his dying friend and chief that the British fleet was winning a great victory—taking perhaps fourteen or fifteen enemy ships without the loss of any of its own. "That is well," Nelson responded, "but I bargained for twenty.

In spite of his pain, Nelson's feeling for the sea remained. Worried about the rising wind and its effects on the damaged ships on both sides, he implored Hardy to anchor at the end of the day. *"Anchor,* Hardy, *anchor!,"* he cried out, abruptly trying to raise himself in a spasm of energy. He was assured that such orders would be given.

Falling back weakly and now breathing with some difficulty, Nelson mumbled "Take care of my dear Lady Hamilton, Hardy." And then in a show of affection, "Kiss me, Hardy."

---

*Among *Achille*'s survivors was a young woman pulled naked from the sea who said she had joined her sailor husband in handing up cartridges from the magazine when the ship blew up.

Hardy knelt and kissed the dying man's cheek.* "Now I am satisfied," he murmured. "Thank God, I have done my duty."

Not long after, as the dismasted *Victory* rolled in the growing Atlantic swell while surrounded by an increasing number of prizes, an entry was made in pencil in the flagship's log: "Partial firing continued until 4.30, when a victory having been reported to the Right Honourable Lord Viscount Nelson, K.B. and Commander in Chief, he then died of his wound."

⌒

"TRAFALGAR WAS THE MOST decisive and complete Victory that was ever gained over a powerful Enemy," wrote Collingwood a few days after the battle. "The Combined Fleet is annihilated." Of the thirty-three French and Spanish ships that took part in the battle, eighteen were captured that day—only two fewer than Nelson had wanted. The four that had slipped away under Dumanoir were taken two weeks later in the Bay of Biscay by Captain Sir Richard Strachan.† Of the eleven survivors who reached Cádiz under the mortally wounded Admiral Gravina, none ever put to sea again as a fighting ship. The allies suffered an estimated 6,000 men killed or wounded and another 7,000 taken prisoner. No British ships were lost, despite heavy damage to many, and casualties were remarkably light—437 dead and 1,242 wounded—considering the battle's fury.

Even worse was to come. Nelson's concern that the fleet anchor following the battle, which Collingwood for some unknown reason chose to ignore, was not misplaced. For four days a gale blew from the west, sweeping the dismasted prizes before it to their destruction on the reefs and beaches of the Spanish coast, while others fought under storm canvas to ride out the wild and mountainous seas racing in from the Atlantic. Only four of the captured ships remained in British hands when the storm blew itself out, the rest having foundered with heavy losses among their crews or been scuttled because they were too badly damaged to be saved.

The news of Trafalgar did not reach London until November 5, 1805, where it was received with a mixture of joy and a remarkable outpouring of public grief over Nelson's death. "The country has gained the most splendid and decisive Victory that has ever graced the naval annals of England, but it has been dearly purchased," intoned *The Times:* "The great and

---

*It was not uncommon then for Englishmen to kiss or embrace. Some writers have contended that Nelson said "Kismet, Hardy," but it seems unlikely.

†All were taken into the Royal Navy. The seventy-four-gun *Duguay Trouin* was renamed *Implacable* and survived until 1949, when beyond repair, she was taken out into the Channel and scuttled while flying both the White Ensign and the Tricolor. *Victory's* victory was now complete.

gallant Nelson is no more." After an elaborate state funeral, Nelson was interred in St. Paul's in the coffin made from the mainmast of *L'Orient*. A grateful nation awarded his parson brother William an earldom, and annuities and pensions were given his sisters and to Fanny, who survived her husband by twenty-five years. Collingwood was made a baron, Hardy a baronet, and most of the officers were promoted.* But for Emma and Horatia, Nelson's "gift to the nation"—there was nothing. "My heart is broken," Emma wrote after his death. "Life to me now is not worth having. I lived but for him. . . ."†

Trafalgar did not end the invasion threat to Britain—Napoleon, himself, had already done that by breaking camp at Boulogne and sending his troops across the Rhine, where he crushed the armies of Austria and Russia at Ulm and Austerlitz. Nor did it destroy the French Navy or mark the end of the war at sea. The Brest fleet remained "in being," and Admiral Decres created a new one over the years. But even though the French and the Spaniards had fought with great bravery and tenacity, the élan of their navies had been destroyed by Nelson's smashing victory, and Napoleon never again seriously challenged Britain's control of the seas.

The emperor, in his only public reference to Trafalgar, remarked that "storms caused us the loss of several ships after an imprudently undertaken engagement." But the strategic results of the battle outweighed this contemptuous dismissal. Trafalgar cushioned the shock of Ulm and Austerlitz, which destroyed the Third Coalition. Moreover, it slammed shut the door on any plans for action he had in the Mediterranean, Egypt, and the East. Unable to take direct action against Britain, he thrashed about Europe, overextending the Grande Armée, and engaged in rash adventures that led to his bloodying in Portugal and Spain and eventually to crushing defeat on the frozen plains of Russia.

As for Horatio Nelson, his victory—and his death—made him immortal.

---

*Villeneuve met a mysterious end. Following his release from captivity by the British, the defeated admiral returned to France, where he expected to be court-martialed for the loss of his fleet. He was found dead in his room on the night of his return. Officially his death was ruled a suicide, although there were those who believed he had been done away with at Napoleon's order.

†Emma had been adequately provided for by Nelson and Sir William Hamilton, but she was extravagant, became raddled with drink, and was eventually arrested for debt. She fled to France with Horatia and died in utmost poverty in Calais in 1815. Hard as it may be to believe, Horatia insisted that Emma never acknowledged to her that she was her mother. Following Emma's death, the child was cared for by the Nelson family, married a country parson with whom she had nine children, and lived until 1881.

CHAPTER 20

". . . The Beautiful Precision
of our Fire"

OUTWARD BOUND FOR the Mediterranean with the broad pendant of Commodore James Barron snapping at her masthead, the U.S. Navy frigate *Chesapeake* slipped past Cape Henry at the mouth of Chesapeake Bay on the morning of June 22, 1807. Signal flags fluttered from a cluster of British men-of-war that lay in the distance. The fifty-gun *Leopard* immediately weighed and shadowed the Yankee vessel. Although the more or less peaceful coexistence between Britain and the United States that had prevailed for most of the war was breaking up under the pressures of a global trade war after Trafalgar, Barron saw nothing threatening in these movements.

Newly designated as commander of what was left of the American force in the Mediterranean, Barron was regarded as one of the navy's ablest officers. He was probably grateful for the long voyage that lay ahead as he glanced around *Chesapeake's* main deck. She was a shambles of unstowed gear and supplies. Some of her forty cannon were not properly mounted, oversize sponges and wads had been issued, and most of the crew were green hands who did not know their battle stations.

Shortly after 3:00 P.M., when *Chesapeake* was about ten miles south of Cape Henry Light and in international waters, *Leopard* bore down with a request to send dispatches on board. Such a procedure was not unusual, because British and American warships often carried dispatches to foreign stations for each other. Ushered into Barron's cabin, a British lieutenant gave the commodore two communications. One was a copy of an order from Vice Admiral George Cranfield Berkeley, commander of the North American station, requiring captains of all British ships meeting *Chesapeake* to search her for deserters from the Royal Navy. The other, from *Leopard's* captain, S. P. Humphreys, expressed hope that the matter could be "adjusted" without disturbing "the harmony subsisting between the two countries."

Barron flatly refused to agree to such a search. He anticipated nothing more than an angry exchange of notes, but as the British officer was being

301

rowed back to his ship, he noticed that *Leopard*'s gunports had been triced up and her guns run out. He immediately ordered *Chesapeake's* captain, Master Commandant Charles Gordon, to clear for action, but in an attempt at secrecy to omit the customary drumroll. Unfortunately, through some foul-up, the drummer sounded his urgent beat long enough for it to be heard on the British vessel, only a cable's length away. A shot was fired across *Chesapeake's* bow, and when that was disregarded, three rapid broadsides were poured into the defenseless vessel. As British shot smashed into her and tore her sails and rigging to tatters, some men ran below while others huddled at the guns, cursing the fact that they had no means of firing them.

Throughout the carnage, the anguished Barron tried to get his ship into action. "For God's sake, gentlemen," he cried to his officers, "will nobody do their duty?!"

Finally, after about ten minutes of pounding, in which *Chesapeake* was hit twenty-two times and did not fire a single shot, the slightly wounded Barron ordered her colors struck, but not before imploring his crew "to fire one gun for the honor of the flag!" Plucking a hot coal from the galley, an officer juggled it in his bare hand and touched off a gun just as the Stars and Stripes were hauled down. Three Americans were killed by British fire and eighteen wounded.

A boarding party from *Leopard* rounded up *Chesapeake's* crew and arrested three Americans—two of them free blacks—who were identified as deserters from the Royal Navy. A British deserter who had enlisted in the U.S. Navy under a false name was discovered cowering belowdecks. The shattered *Chesapeake* was left to limp homeward with her tidings of humiliation and defeat. The British deserter was summarily hanged from the yardarm of his ship, and the Americans were sentenced to five hundred lashes, which was a death sentence, but it was remitted.*

An unprecedented wave of anger swept the United States following this unprovoked attack on an American man-of-war. British officers ashore fled to the safety of their ships; infuriated mobs destroyed water casks belonging to British vessels; the governor of Virginia called out the militia to repel

---

*Barron was made the scapegoat of the affair in place of the Navy Department, which had sent his ship to sea in such unready condition. Tried by a court-martial, he was convicted of "neglecting on the probability of an engagement to clear his ship for action" by judges prejudiced against him, and he was suspended from the navy for five years without pay.

The Barron case split the navy's officer corps and ultimately led, in 1820, to a duel in which Stephen Decatur, who had served on the court-martial that convicted Barron, was killed by Barron. Barron was seriously wounded, although he recovered.

an invasion. Americans in all sections of the country demanded war to avenge the insult to American honor and neutrality. "Never since the Battle of Lexington have I seen this country in such a state of exasperation as at present," observed President Jefferson, "and even that did not produce such unanimity."

Not even Britain contended she had the right to halt an American man-of-war and seize crewmen from her deck, and two of the three American sailors taken from *Chesapeake* were eventually released, the third having died in the meantime. But the incident was a sign of the mounting tensions between the two countries as Britain and France stepped up the trade war against each other. The United States, as the most neutral with the most dynamic carrying trade, was caught between them.

Even before Trafalgar, Napoleon had abandoned, at least temporarily, his efforts to contest command of the sea and to invade Britain. With the French fleet in decline, fleet actions were less important—there was only one major sea battle between 1806 and 1815—and the belligerents, unable to defeat their rivals by military or naval means, sought victory by undermining each other's economies through a trade war or *guerre de course*. Napoleon issued his Berlin and Milan decrees, by which he declared Europe closed to British trade, and Britain retaliated in May 1806 with Orders in Council that established a blockade of European ports "where French influence prevails to exclude the British Flag." Napoleon, hoping to "conquer the sea by the land," now intensified his Continental System, which was designed to bring the "nation of shopkeepers" to her economic knees and destroy the fiscal foundation of the Royal Navy. "The struggle is between her and me," the Emperor declared. "The whole of Europe will be our instruments. . . ." Instead of Britain blockading Europe, Europe would blockade Britain.

For the Royal Navy, power projection became more important than sea control. It ruthlessly hunted down those enemy ships that did escape to sea; seized whatever colonies remained to the French; supported amphibious operations; and, above all, went about the patient, unglamorous work of trade protection. Angered by the fact that while they were engaged in this life-and-death struggle with Napoleon, Yankee traders were getting rich by supplying their enemy, the British sent cruisers to take up stations off the American coast. There they seized merchant vessels carrying cargoes bound for France and impressed American sailors into the Royal Navy—and laid the foundations for a new war.

⤶

IF HORATIO NELSON WAS the epitome of the Royal Navy before Trafalgar, probably no person better filled this role in the years following the battle

Admiral Thomas Lord Cochrane, later earl of Dundonald. (U.S. Naval Academy Museum)

than Thomas, Lord Cochrane. Well over six feet tall, handsome, red-haired, and with a temper to match, he was the most dashing British frigate captain of the Age of Fighting Sail. Bold to the point of recklessness, gallant and courageous, Cochrane was a master of commerce raiding and the daring inshore commando strikes that were key elements of the post-Trafalgar naval war. *Guerre de course* was made to order for Cochrane. To Napoleon he was the "Sea Wolf," while the Spaniards called him El Diablo.

Readers of Patrick O'Brian and C. S. Forester will recognize aspects of

Cochrane's career in the adventures of Jack Aubrey and Horatio Horn-blower, for both authors made use of his deeds. Yet he was also expelled from the House of Commons, struck from the Navy List, degraded from the Order of the Bath, imprisoned for stock market fraud, and was the last man sentenced to the pillory in England. Disgraced at home, he commanded the revolutionary navies of Greece, Chile, Peru, and Brazil, and eventually returned to the Royal Navy to become admiral of the fleet, a favorite of Queen Victoria, and is buried in Westminster Abbey.

Cochrane was the eldest son of the earl of Dundonald, but there was more honor in the name than fortune, for his eccentric father had frittered away the family money with a series of inventions, such as road-paving materials and rain-proof clothing, that appeared before their time. The family estate in Scotland was sold to pay the old man's debts. To give his son a leg up on a naval career, the earl had his name inscribed on the muster books of four different men-of-war while he was about five years old and on the roster of the Household Cavalry as well. Young Cochrane was nearly eighteen, old by the standards of the day, when in 1793 he went to sea as a midshipman in a vessel commanded by an uncle, Sir Alexander Cochrane. Using his rather dubious seniority, he took the lieutenant's examination after only three years' service at sea—rather than the usual six—and passed on the first try.

Cochrane's adventures began in 1800, when he was appointed master and commander of the fourteen-gun brig *Speedy* in the Mediterranean.* Never was a ship more inappropriately named, for she was a pitiably slow old coasting vessel. She was so small that the only way the towering Cochrane could shave in comfort was to poke his head through the sky-light of his cabin and place the mirror before him on the deck. *Speedy*'s four-pound popguns were so ineffectual that he carried most of her broadside about in his coat pockets.

A natural corsair, Cochrane made himself the terror of the Spanish coast. Over a thirteen-month period he scooped up more than fifty vessels, filling his pockets—and those of his chief—with prize money. Most of the prizes were small, but these depredations paralyzed the coastal trade on which the Spaniards were dependent because of the lack of good roads. His most audacious escapade occurred in March 1801, when *Speedy* was chasing some Spanish gunboats near Barcelona. Suddenly she encountered a thirty-two-gun Spanish frigate, *El Gamo,* which had been sent in search of Cochrane and his ship. She mounted a broadside of 190 pounds compared to *Speedy*'s 28 pounds and mustered a crew of 319 men to only 54 in the British vessel.

*Much of Patrick O'Brian's first Aubrey-Maturin novel, *Master and Commander,* is drawn from Cochrane's adventures in *Speedy.*

Unable to flee, Cochrane chose to fight. To confuse the enemy captain, he raised American colors, and gambling that the ruse would not be discovered until too late, he edged up on *El Gamo's* leeward side. As Cochrane lowered the American flag and raised the British ensign, a flash of flame spouted from *El Gamo's* triced-up gunports. But as Cochrane had known, a ship to leeward was a difficult target, since her attacker heeled toward her with the wind, depressing her guns and making her liable to fire into the sea.

While the Spanish gunners reloaded, Cochrane swung *Speedy* alongside her opponent. The frigate's guns roared out again, but her shots hissed over the heads of Cochrane and his crew. He ordered *Speedy's* four-pounders double-shotted and angled upward. The results were devastating. The British shots ripped upward through the frigate's gun deck, causing heavy casualties among the gunners and killing her captain. *Speedy's* little guns were devastating at close range while the aim of the Spanish was poor. On three occasions, the Spaniards tried to board *Speedy*. Cochrane allowed them to muster on the frigate's deck and then fired bursts of grapeshot and musket fire into their ranks and withdrew. Improbable as it may have seemed, *El Gamo* was fought to a standstill. But Cochrane wanted more—a victory. He told his crew that they must "either take the frigate or be themselves taken, in which case the Spaniards would give no quarter." To a man they replied that they would follow him "to Hell itself" if that was where he intended to go.

Leaving the surgeon at the wheel, Cochrane sent half his crew, their faces blackened, up *El Gamo's* bows while he led the remaining score of men in scaling the frigate's side. This party struck first, and while they were battling with pistols and cutlasses amidships, the Spaniards were suddenly surprised by the black-faced, screaming devils coming over the bow. Steel clashed on steel, and in the darkness men staggered and reeled. Calling over to the surgeon, the only man left in *Speedy*, Cochrane loudly ordered him to send over the next wave of attackers. Some three hundred Spaniards, convinced the brig was a decoy loaded with Royal Marines, surrendered to forty-eight British sailors.

The capture of *El Gamo* was hailed as the finest single-ship action of the Napoleonic Wars. Cochrane instantly became a public hero, but the Admiralty's reaction was restrained. Lord St. Vincent, the first lord, disliked Scotsmen in general and Lord Cochrane, whom he regarded as flippant toward his superiors, in particular, and only after a delay was he given a well-deserved promotion to captain. Cochrane thought his officers also deserved promotion, but St. Vincent replied that the casualties suffered by *Speedy* did not merit such awards. Cochrane wrote back that his casualties were higher than those suffered by the first lord's flagship at the Battle of St. Vincent, which gained him his peerage. Cochrane's colleagues were amused, but the old man was not—and neither were the old hands at the Admiralty, who had long and unforgiving memories.

⟿

WHILE THE MORALE of the French Navy was at its nadir after Trafalgar, Napoleon still possessed a substantial fleet. He had 32 ships of the line afloat in 1806 and 21 under construction. To these vessels must be added the ships of the satellite states of Spain, Holland, Portugal, Venice, and Denmark. Moreover, he was building ships of the line in every port under French control from the Baltic to the Adriatic. Napoleon set a target of 150 battleships, and by 1813 had 80 in commission and 35 being built. Although many of these ships were landlocked behind choke points such as the Baltic Narrows, controlled by the Royal Navy, Admiral Sir Thomas Byam Martin observed that as late as 1814 the British had "to strain our efforts to the utmost to keep pace with French building. . . . Had the war continued, the French . . . would in a short time have outnumbered us. . . ."

In Brest at the beginning of 1806, the French had a fleet of thirteen ships of the line, and there were eight more at Rochefort. Both fleets were under watch by the Channel fleet, but the blockade was not as stringent as before. "It is to little purpose now," declared Lord Barham, "to wear out our ships in a fruitless blockade in winter." Frigates maintained watch on the Biscay ports in all weather, but the big ships now sheltered against storms in Tor Bay or Falmouth. If enemy ships escaped, flying squadrons were to be sent in pursuit.

These tactics received a test early in 1806, when a French squadron of eleven ships of the line escaped from Brest after the watching British vessels were driven off station by bad weather. The French divided into two squadrons, one of six led by Rear Admiral Juan Baptiste Willaumez, which sailed for the South Atlantic, where he raided British shipping with some success.* The other, commanded by Vice Admiral Corentin Leissègues in

---

*Jerome Bonaparte, Napoleon's youngest brother, was one of Willaumez's captains. Jerome destroyed six enemy merchantmen, for which he was promoted to admiral. But he had abandoned Willaumez without telling him his intentions, and the admiral wasted considerable time waiting for him before returning to Brest in February 1807. Later, Napoleon made Jerome king of Westphalia.

While in America, Jerome became infatuated with Elizabeth Patterson, the beautiful daughter of a Baltimore merchant. They married, but an angry Napoleon had the marriage annulled. Following Jerome's departure, Betsey had a child. Their grandchild, Charles Joseph Bonaparte, was a leading civil service reformer, and secretary of the navy and attorney general in the administration of Theodore Roosevelt.

the 130-gun *Imperial,* made for the Caribbean with a thousand soldiers for Santo Domingo. Such sorties offered rich pickings and illustrated what might have happened had the French used their navy to strike at the sources of British wealth and to tie down the enemy's battle squadrons instead of letting it rock uselessly in port.

Vice Admiral Sir John Duckworth, who was watching the remnants of the Combined Fleet in Cádiz, learned that an enemy force had been sighted near Madeira—it was actually that of Admiral Allemand, which was returning home safely to Rochefort after capturing four British men-of-war and forty-two merchantmen—and gave chase. Duckworth saw no Frenchmen and sailed on to St. Kitts, where he was joined by Sir Alexander Cochrane's two seventy-four-gun ships, bringing his total to six of the line. Duckworth learned that Leissègues' squadron was at Santo Domingo and sailed in search of the enemy ships. At daybreak on February 6, 1806, the French ships were was sighted in Occa Bay, at the southeastern end of the island.

Leissègues slipped his moorings and headed for the open sea, where he organized a line of battle running to the west. Following Nelson's example, Duckworth formed his own ships into two columns and steered toward the enemy van with the intention of cutting off the first three ships—*Alexandre,* eighty, and *Impérial* and *Diomede,* seventy-four each. *Superb,* seventy-four, Duckworth's flagship, supported by *Northumberland,* seventy-four, and

Sir John Duckworth defeats the French off Santo Domingo on February 6, 1806, in the last major fleet action of the Napoleonic wars. (Beverley Robinson Collection, U.S. Naval Academy Museum)

Agamemnon, sluggish and now showing her age, took on *Alexandre,* which, after absorbing repeated broadsides, fell off, creating considerable confusion in the rest of the French line.

On the other side, *Impérial* badly mauled *Northumberland* and then engaged *Superb* and *Agamemnon.* Superior British seamanship and gunnery soon settled the issue. The French flagship lost her mainmast and then her mizzenmast. With only her foremast still standing, Leissègues headed for shore, and at noon the three-decker piled up on the jutting rocks. The shock sent her remaining mast tumbling backward onto her deck. *Superb,* now in only seventeen feet of water, put about in haste, but *Diomede,* hoping to aid her admiral, ran aground and was dismasted. In fewer than two hours Duckworth had destroyed the entire French squadron. Besides the two vessels that were wrecked and later burned by the victors, three were captured, ending the Battle of Santo Domingo—the last major fleet action of the war.

～

"MR. PITT IS DEAD! Mr. Pitt died at four o'clock this morning!" Within a few weeks of Nelson's funeral, the dire news of William Pitt's death spread rapidly across London on January 23, 1806, amid thick fog, blazing torches, and shouting coachmen. The prime minister died at forty-seven, worn out by his labors and his heart broken by the shipwreck of the Third Coalition. Napoleon's victory at Austerlitz was so overwhelming that the dying man, seeing a map of the Continent, supposedly called out: "Roll up the map of Europe, for it will not be wanted for ten years." And then he turned his face to the wall.

Pitt personified Britain's political will to defy Napoleon—if need be, alone—and the ever-vigilant emperor saw in his death the opportunity to end the standoff with the British and gain by guile what he was unable to win by war. The new government, a coalition "ministry of all-the-talents," was headed by Lord Grenville, but Charles James Fox, Pitt's longtime adversary and champion of a speedy end to the war, was the key figure. As foreign secretary he immediately undertook peace negotiations with Napoleon, only too delighted to accommodate him.

Napoleon spoke grandiosely of dividing the world between Britain and France and offered—verbally—to allow Britain to retain all her conquests. Even King George III was disarmed by the promise of the return of his ancestral home of Hanover, with which Prussia had been bribed by the French into joining an alliance. But Napoleon remained a trickster. As soon as serious negotiations got under way, he insisted on the return of all French colonies and the relinquishment of Sicily to France to round out his conquest of Italy. Fox wanted peace, but not at the price of everything that had been gained by the war, and he refused. Negotiations lagged and finally collapsed with Fox's death in September 1806—and the war went on.

The scene of action shifted to the Mediterranean, where Lord Collingwood, who had succeeded Nelson, bore naval and diplomatic responsibilities for an area that stretched from Cádiz to Constantinople. Hardly ever going ashore, he kept an eye on the enemy fleets at Cádiz, Cartagena, and Toulon, and as Britain's representative, dealt with the nations fringing those waters. He faced "an active and powerful enemy," the admiral wrote, "always threatening, and though he seldom moves, keeps us constantly on the alert." Under the arduous strain of the blockade and the spinning of a delicate web of political and diplomatic intrigue, Collingwood wore himself out and died at sea in 1810, while on the way home for a well-earned rest.

Napoleon, having imposed French hegemony on northern and central Europe and Italy—which British sea power could do nothing to hinder—was seeking new areas for imperial expansion. Once again, his eye turned toward the faltering Ottoman Empire and the East. And as before, his ambitions were thwarted, this time by Collingwood's fleet and the small British army commanded by General James Craig, which had been sent to Naples to buoy the Bourbon regime. Craig, along with a Russian force, had tried to prevent the French from overrunning southern Italy but was forced to withdraw. He crossed the narrow Strait of Messina to Sicily, which was transformed into a barrier to Napoleon's eastern ambitions while the Russians retreated to Corfu.

WITH THE FRENCH NAVY unable to protect France's colonies, the British swept up those that had previously escaped their grasp: Martinique, Guadeloupe, St. Croix, St. Thomas, and Cayenne (now French Guiana) in the Caribbean; Sénégal in West Africa; Mauritius and Réunion in the Indian Ocean; and Sir Edward Pellew raided Java, the jewel of the Dutch islands in the East Indies. A French attempt to seize the Portuguese Navy was forestalled by the appearance of Lord St. Vincent, now more than seventy years of age, and the Channel fleet at Lisbon, even before Napoleon had time to organize an invasion force.* And Major General John Stuart, new commander of the British army in Sicily, crossed over into Calabria with five thousand men and repulsed a much larger French force at Maida with disciplined musket fire and a bayonet charge. Outnumbered, the British withdrew to Sicily, but they had broken the legend of the invincibility of the French Army in Europe.

*This was St. Vincent's last active service, for soon after, he struck his flag for the final time. He died in 1823 at eighty-eight.

Foremost of the British conquests was the retaking of the Cape of Good Hope by Commodore Sir Home Popham, the signals expert,* in an operation intended to not only protect the India and China trade but also to block Napoleon's persistent ambitions in the East. Popham next reembarked a force of some seventeen hundred troops for a quixotic mission. Having heard that the Spanish colonies at Buenos Aires and Montevideo on the River Plate were eager for liberation, he sailed across the South Atlantic with visions of the vast booty to be harvested in the New World. Weakly defended Buenos Aires, a city of seventy thousand people and capital of an area half the size of Europe, was attacked first, and on June 27, 1807, the Spaniards quickly surrendered.

Popham heralded his victory with a flamboyant circular to the merchants of England announcing that trade with the Plate, from which they had been barred, was now open. But he overplayed his hand. Greed overwhelmed his political instincts, and he seized a million Spanish dollars from the public treasury and goods from privately owned warehouses worth an equal sum. This so angered the *Porteños* that, aided by Spanish troops from Montevideo, across the river, they rose and overwhelmed the small detachment of Redcoats. Although the Admiralty angrily recalled Popham for exceeding his authority, the acquisitive appetites of the British merchants led to more troops and ships being deployed to the Plate. Wild schemes, which came to nothing, were also hatched for the invasion of Chile and Mexico. Over the next several years, successive expeditions turned the Plate into a quagmire from which no one emerged with much credit.[†]

But an effort by Britain early in 1807 to keep Russia in the war by encouraging her to pinch off part of the Ottoman Empire failed. Sir John Duckworth—the victor of Santo Domingo—was ordered to seize the Turkish fleet, numbering twelve ships of the line and nine frigates. If the Turks refused to turn over the vessels, Constantinople was to be bombarded, as Nelson had done at Copenhagen. Duckworth was no Nelson, however. He might have bagged the Turkish fleet had he acted vigorously, but he delayed to bargain with the wily sultan, and made other mistakes that were to be repeated a century later during the Dardanelles campaign in World War I. While Duckworth dallied, the Turks improved their defenses.

*Popham was hardly the typical British naval officer of the era. He was born in Tétouan in North Africa, where his father was British consul, was educated at Cambridge, had commanded an Austrian East Indiaman, served on land under the duke of York, been knighted by the Russian Czar, was a fellow of the Royal Society, and spoke several languages.

[†]Among the ships lost in the Plate was Nelson's old *Agamemnon*, which sank off Punta del Este, in what is now Uruguay, in 1809. The wreck was found by divers in 1993.

In the end, he was forced to withdraw under fire, escaping with only the thinnest margin of safety. An attempt to occupy Egypt was also repulsed with severe losses, and stakes along the roads were crowned with the rotting heads of British soldiers.

⌐

LORD COCHRANE WAS punished for his flippancy toward Lord St. Vincent by being assigned to the command of a lumbering ex-collier, but he was soon promoted to the new thirty-two-gun frigate *Pallas*. In her he took so many rich prizes that she became known as the "Golden *Pallas*." On his first cruise, around the Azores and the Spanish coast in 1805, his prize money totaled more than seventy-five thousand pounds. As a symbol of victory, she arrived in Plymouth with three candelabra intended for a cathedral in Spain lashed to her mastheads. They were five feet high and solid gold. Unlike most captains, Cochrane never again had to resort to the sweepings of the press gang for a crew, for whenever he put to sea, he was inundated with volunteers. Strict but fair, he was loved by his men and careful with their lives despite his daring escapades. All he needed to do to fill out a crew was post a sign on a dockyard wall reading: "WANTED. Stout, able-bodied men who can run a mile with a sackful of Spanish dollars on their backs."

With the country on the eve of a general election, Cochrane decided to run for a seat in Parliament.* His main purpose in entering politics was to end corruption in the naval dockyards and other aspects of the service.† Honiton, the constituency he decided to contest, was generally recognized as the most corrupt in the country. Popular though he was, Cochrane was defeated by a small margin because he refused to match the five guineas a vote offered by his opponent. But when the election was over, he made a public relations gesture guaranteed to ensure his election the next time: the ballot was not secret, and with the names of those who voted for him known, he gave each ten guineas as a reward.

Cochrane returned to *Pallas* and was assigned to patrol the Bay of Bis-

---

*The number of people allowed to vote in a parliamentary constituency was severely limited, and the eligible electors of some "rotten boroughs" sold the seat to the highest bidder. Some boroughs had as few as a dozen electors. There were also "pocket boroughs" owned by landed families who handpicked the winning candidate.

†For example, Cochrane reported that while one of his ships was being refitted in a royal dockyard, some wretch stole the copper bolts securing the compass and substituted iron ones. The vessel was almost wrecked before the defect was caught.

cay, where he played havoc with coastal commerce. The Gironde estuary, which led to Bordeaux, was covered by a half dozen French corvettes—equal to British sloops-of-war—and Cochrane sent in a raiding party to deal with them. One of the vessels was immediately captured, and three others gave chase to the escaping ship. By skillful seamanship, Cochrane lured them onto the rocks, where they were destroyed. Whereas only hours before there had been six vessels guarding the Gironde, now only two remained. On the way home, Cochrane attacked and disabled a French frigate and then led his marines ashore to blow up an artillery battery and signal station. Even Lord St. Vincent expressed grudging approval of these exploits. And even greater glory was to come.

⟿

As ANNOYING AS THESE pinpricks were to Napoleon, they had little effect on his hegemony over Europe. While the British harried him on the fringes of his empire, he struck from the center. In October 1806 he crushed the Prussian Army at Jena and Auerstadt, and he smashed the Russians at Friedland in June 1807. Not long after, he met with Czar Alexander I on a raft in the middle of the Niemen River at Tilsit, in what is now Lithuania. "I hate the English as much as you do," Alexander is reported to have said. "In that case," replied Napoleon, "peace is made." The czar, now under the tutelage of Napoleon, agreed to ally Russia with France, while Denmark, Portugal, and Austria were to be coerced into joining the common cause against Britain.

To Napoleon, Tilsit was a stop on the road to London. Following the treaty, he extended the ban on British trade imposed by his Continental System to Russian ports and then to Spain and Portugal. The whole of Europe from the Baltic to the Hellespont was closed to British ships. Soon there was a shortage in Britain of Prussian oak, Russian masts, and naval stores from the Baltic that were fundamental to both naval and mercantile shipbuilding. British exports to Europe, particularly along the shores of the Baltic, were greatly reduced, dropping in two years from ten million pounds to two million pounds. French privateers also levied an ever-increasing toll on British shipping. Two hundred operated in the West Indies alone.

Warehouses were filled with goods that had no market and as mills and factories closed, thousands of starving weavers rioted in Manchester and other industrial towns. Insurance rates on cargoes that did get to sea climbed to prohibitive levels. "The game, we fear, is decidedly lost," announced the *Edinburgh Review,* soberly echoing the theme of newspapers and peace movements throughout the country.

A total disaster was averted because the Continental System was never applied long enough or consistently enough to be fully effective. The restrictions were also counterproductive because the Continental nations soon became as desperate for British manufactured goods and colonial produce such as coffee and sugar as the British were for naval stores from the Baltic. Smuggling, sometimes with the connivance of corrupt French officials, became rampant. The most significant gaps were in Sweden, which continued to trade with Britain, and in the Iberian Peninsula, where Portugal did not take part in the embargo and where Spain was only a half-hearted participant. As long as some countries on the European mainland continued to trade with Britain, the blockade could not succeed as an instrument of policy. To tighten it, Napoleon intervened, first in Spain and then in Russia—and both ventures ended in catastrophes for France.

⟿

IN 1807 THE "Talents" were replaced by a hard-line government headed by the aged duke of Portland that was described as "Mr. Pitt's friends without Pitt." Worried that Napoleon might grab the Russian, Swedish, and Danish fleets, which would give him an additional sixty ships of the line, George Canning, the foreign secretary and strongman of the new cabinet, decided to beat him to the punch. In July 1807 Britain demanded that Denmark immediately surrender the nineteen ships of the line and seventeen frigates in its fleet in return for a British alliance and an annual rent of a hundred thousand pounds. Having learned from the Dardanelles fiasco, the Admiralty provided Admiral Sir James Gambier with a strong force of seventeen of the line and thirty thousand troops to put teeth into the ultimatum.

Great secrecy enshrouded the expedition, and no hint reached France. In fact, on July 31, the day Gambier's fleet anchored in the Skaw, off the northern tip of Denmark, Napoleon offered the Danes the choice of war or an alliance with France and ordered thirty thousand of his own troops to assemble at Hamburg for an invasion of Denmark.* British security was so tight that he was completely unaware that he had already been trumped. The Danes rejected the ultimatum, and troops under the command of Sir Arthur Wellesley swarmed ashore on the morning of August 16, near Copenhagen, under the protection of the fleet's guns.

Gambier was reluctant to open fire on Copenhagen because of religious scruples,† but lengthy negotiations failed. Without a declaration of war,

---

*Curiously, this situation was repeated in the early months of 1940 during World War II, when Britain and Germany were in a race to see which would invade Norway first without the other knowing about it. See my *War at Sea*, chapter II.

†Gambier was well known throughout the fleet for distributing Methodist tracts and other religious exhortations to his men. He contributed funds for the founding of Gambier College in Ohio.

British batteries afloat and ashore began pounding the city on the evening of September 2 with red-hot shot and Congreve rockets. Copenhagen was soon in flames, but the Danes held out for three days. Three Danish ships of the line were destroyed on the stocks, and Gambier sailed away with the remaining sixteen. Of these, only four were considered seaworthy enough to be taken into the Royal Navy. The immense amount of loot captured in the Danish arsenals—yards, masts, timber, cordage, and other naval stores—was far more valuable and filled the holds of ninety-two vessels. This blow was followed soon afterward by the seizure of the Danish island of Helgoland, at the mouth of the Elbe, which became an important center for smuggling British goods into central Europe.

The attack on Copenhagen marked the beginning of a lengthy period of delicate naval and diplomatic arrangements in the Baltic. Early in 1808 the Russians, supported by Napoleon, seized the Swedish province of Finland, and war broke out between the two countries. Inasmuch as the Swedes had not supported the Continental System, the British encouraged them. But she was no longer the first-rate power she had once been and was no match for Russia. In 1810 Sweden was forced into war with Britain, but Sir James Saumarez, the British admiral commanding in the Baltic, scrupulously respected Swedish trade and held open the door for eventual reconciliation between the two nations. Like Collingwood and his successor in the Mediterranean, Sir Edward Pellew, Saumarez understood that there was more to the exercise of sea power than the vigorous pursuit of enemy fleets.

~

FURIOUS AT BEING OUTFOXED by the British in the Baltic, Napoleon threatened to assemble a hundred thousand men at Boulogne for an immediate invasion of the island kingdom. These were idle threats because the harbor had silted up and the invasion barges were neglected and unseaworthy. When his temper cooled, he realized that an invasion was out of question and the only way he could hope to bring Britain to heel was to slowly strangle her by eliminating her trade. "We must close all the ports of Europe, even those of Austria, against them, drive every British minister from the coast and even arrest all Englishmen," he declared.

Napoleon angrily turned on Portugal, Britain's remaining ally on the Continent, and demanded that the Portuguese join his embargo of British trade. "If Portugal does not do what I wish, the House of Braganza will not be reigning in Europe in two months," he ranted. "I have three hundred thousand Russians at my disposal, and with that powerful ally I can do everything. The English declare that they will no longer respect neutrals on the sea; I will no longer recognize them on land!"

Mindful of the example of Copenhagen, Prince João, the regent for the mad Queen Anna, tried to steer a middle course between France and Britain, but the scale was tipped when he learned that a French army of thirty thousand men under General Androche Junot was being assembled in Bayonne to invade Portugal and seize the Portuguese fleet. The French also had the support of a Russian squadron commanded by Admiral Dimitri Nicolaevitch Seniavin, then operating in the Mediterranean. On the last day of November 1807, Junot's army, having marched more than three hundred miles in two weeks despite heavy rains and nearly nonexistent roads, straggled into Lisbon with fewer than two thousand men still in its ranks. The rest had fallen exhausted by the wayside.

Junot found that his quarry had flown the coop. Two days before, Prince João and the entire Portuguese court, escorted by a squadron of Royal Navy ships, had sailed for Rio de Janeiro in the Portuguese colony of Brazil, accompanied by the eight ships of the line of the Portuguese Navy. Along with the descent on Copenhagen, this operation demonstrated that Britain not only had the resolution to continue the struggle against Napoleon but also the naval power to strike counterblows where needed.

NAPOLEON NEXT TURNED his immense energy to planning for an offensive at both ends of the Mediterranean aimed at paving the way to the Orient. A Franco-Russian expedition was to strike at the Ottoman Empire and the approaches to India. In the central Mediterranean, British forces in Sicily were to be attacked by an army from Naples. To the west, a third and even greater French army was to march across Spain, besiege Gibraltar, and jump over to North Africa to deprive the British blockading squadrons off Cádiz, Lisbon, and Cartagena of their source of supplies. As soon as these ships were withdrawn, French and Spanish raiding squadrons would sail for the Cape of Good Hope and the Indian Ocean. "By the last of May our troops can be in Asia," Napoleon told the Czar. "Then the English, threatened in the Indies and chased from the Levant, will be crushed under the weight of events."

Napoleon struck at Spain first. Already angry at Manuel Godoy, the Spanish dictator, for perceived betrayals, in February 1808 he sent some hundred thousand French troops pouring across the Pyrenees into Spain. He had other than military reasons for the invasion. British goods were flowing unrestrictedly into Spain and Portugal, and the assault was designed to plug the most serious leak in the Continental System. King Ferdinand VII was swept from the throne and replaced by Napoleon's older brother, Joseph, who was "transferred" from Naples, where he had been set up as king. To keep Naples in the family, its crown was given to Marshal Joachim Murat, the emperor's brother-in-law. At a stroke Napoleon appeared to have won control of the entire Iberian Peninsula and the Spanish colonial empire as well.

All seemed to go as planned, but beneath the surface the hatred of the deeply conservative, nationalistic Spaniards for the invader was festering. They may not have liked their own rulers, but they saw them as preferable to a foreigner imposed from the outside. A revolt spontaneously erupted in Madrid on May 2, 1808, in which the French garrison was almost massacred. But Murat, who was in the city, gathered enough troops to ruthlessly suppress the rebellion. "Tranquillity is everywhere established," said Napoleon as the dead lay piled in heaps in the streets. But trouble soon broke out all over the country, and Spain became an enraged nation in arms.

Pro-French governors at Badajoz, Cartagena, and Cádiz were dragged through the streets by raging mobs and slaughtered. At Baylen, a French army of eighteen thousand men was forced to lay down its arms. By August the revolt had spread to Portugal. A revolutionary junta was established at Seville that appealed to the British governor of Gibraltar for money and arms. Napoleon had blundered into a war in the Iberian Peninsula whose savagery, portrayed in Goya's drawings, was not to be matched until the twentieth century. It steadily drained his resources, and soon he was to ruefully call it his "Spanish ulcer."

Seizing the opportunity to nip at Napoleon's heels, Collingwood attempted to assist the Spanish insurgents after leaving a division of ships to continue the blockade of Toulon. The revolt ended the threat of the French fleet holed up at Cádiz. Trapped between a British blockading squadron and the now hostile Spanish batteries, Admiral Rosily, Villeneuve's successor, surrendered his ships. The Royal Navy was relieved of the need to blockade Cádiz, Ferrol, Vigo, and Cartagena. British cruisers escorted Spanish troops from the Balearics for duty on the mainland. British intelligence officers were clandestinely put ashore at numerous points along the coast and made their way to the mountains to join the guerrilla bands.

In August 1808 an expeditionary force of 13,500 British troops under Sir Arthur Wellesley was landed in Portugal at Mondego Bay, about eighty miles north of Lisbon. General Junot asked the Russian admiral, Seniavin, whose vessels lay in the Tagus River, for assistance, but he refused, saying his country was not at war with Spain. The following month, Seniavin, an Anglophile, turned his nine ships of the line and single frigate over to the British.

Three weeks after his landing, Wellesley resoundingly defeated Junot at Vimiero, a village not far from the beach, and secured his bridgehead. Offshore, Jane Austen's brother, passing down the coast in his ship—

a white-sailed embodiment of the remote force that made the victory possible—watched it unfolding through his long glass. Although greatly outnumbered, the disciplined British troops carried the day at the point of the bayonet. Unhappily, Wellesley's superiors snatched away the fruits of his victory by signing the Convention of Cintra, which allowed the return of the twenty-four thousand beaten French troops to France on British ships with all their booty. Although Wellesley had nothing to do with this agreement, he was recalled with the other commanders for an inquiry from which only he emerged without blame.

Sir John Moore replaced Wellesley and thrust into Spain with some 40,000 troops, with the intention of joining the Spanish armies trying to encircle the French. Before he could reach the rendezvous with the Spaniards at Burgos in central Spain, Napoleon surprised the British and the Spaniards by personally leading an army of 120,000 of the finest troops in Europe into the country. Before mounting the expedition, he had received assurances from the Russians that they would keep an eye on Austria, which was showing signs of again taking up arms.

Napoleon had little difficulty in dealing with the Spanish armies, which threw themselves on the French with greater gallantry than skill. Resistance in northern and central Spain collapsed and the French were between the British and Burgos. With his communications with Portugal cut, Moore realized that any further advance would be suicidal. Sensibly, he ordered a retreat in the latter part of December 1808 toward the port of Corunna on the Atlantic coast, where the Royal Navy was to meet him with transports to take off his men. "The English are running away as fast as they can," the emperor wrote to Paris. "They have abandoned the Spaniards in a shameful and cowardly manner. Have all this shown in the newspapers. . . . Have them circulated in Italy and Germany," where the people were restive and thinking of throwing off French rule with British support.

The retreat to Corunna over the mountains was harrowing. Wet, cold, hungry, and demoralized, the troops mercilessly ransacked the villages along the way for food, ripped up furniture for firewood, and looted at will. In some cases they became openly mutinous. Only the British rear guard maintained discipline, repeatedly driving off harassing attacks by the French cavalry. What was left of the army straggled into Corunna on January 10, 1809, and was elated to see the masts of 140 ships riding in the harbor. But these turned out to be hospital and store ships; the transports were windbound at Vigo. When they would arrive at Corunna was an open question.

Reports having reached Napoleon that war with Austria was imminent, he turned over command of his army to one of his ablest marshals, Nicholas Jean Soult, and hurried to Paris to deal with the crisis to the east. Poor roads and weather delayed Soult from immediately bringing up his artillery, and Moore used the time to embark his sick and wounded on the ships available and to prepare the defenses of Corunna. The transports and their escort finally worked their way up from Vigo on the evening of January 14, 1809, and the troops embarked as the French forced the pace.

Leaving only pickets to hold their front, regiment after regiment marched down to the quays and beaches to be taken off. Some of the boat crews had had no food or sleep for two days as they labored at the oars. Moore was fatally wounded as he fought a last-ditch holding action and died soon after. The final task of his troops before pushing off in the last boats was to bury their fallen leader in their ramparts. Once again, a naval force had performed one of its classic roles: saving a beaten army so it could fight another day. But as Winston Churchill was to say in a later age, wars are not won by evacuations.

⤴

SURROUNDED ON THREE SIDES by the sea, the Iberian Peninsula was an ideal theater for amphibious operations. The French troops deployed there were dependent for supplies on coasting vessels or wretched roads that followed the shore, and it was a perfect situation for the depredations of Lord Cochrane. Having finally achieved election to Parliament, he was a bitter critic of Admiralty abuses and a supporter of such radical causes as broadening the eligibility to vote. To remove him from the scene, the Admiralty sent him to sea in the thirty-eight-gun frigate *Imperieuse*, with a crew that had largely followed him from *Pallas*, and he was put to work in the Mediterranean in humdrum convoy escort duty.

In the spring of 1808, with the beginning of the Spanish revolt, Cochrane was ordered by Lord Collingwood to assist Britain's new ally "with every means in his power." Over the next six months he conducted commando raids on the French line of communications along the coast of Catalonia that are a model of such operations. Moving faster than the roadbound French, Cochrane blew up bridges and roads, demolished batteries and signal posts, seized codebooks, interrupted the flow of supplies, and harassed columns of enemy troops on the march. With the assistance of Spanish guerrillas, he assaulted enemy fortifications.

Cochrane's deeds were recorded by an admiring midshipman named Frederick Marryat, and he later appears under various names in Marryat's popular nautical novels *Mr. Midshipman Easy, Peter Simple,* and *Frank Mildmay.* Here is the way Marryat recalled those days:

> The cruises of the *Imperieuse* were periods of continual excitement, from the hour in which she hove up her anchor till she dropped it again in port; the day that passed without a shot being fired in anger was with us a blank day; the boats were hardly secured on the booms than they were cast loose and out again; the yard and stay tackles were for ever hoisting

up and lowering down. The expedition with which parties were formed for service; the rapidity of the frigate's movements day and night; the hasty sleep, snatched at all hours; the waking up at the report of the guns, which seemed the only keynote to the hearts of those on board; the beautiful precision of our fire, obtained by constant practice; the coolness and courage of our captain, inoculating the whole of the ship's company, the suddenness of our attacks . . . even now my pulse beats more quickly with the reminiscence.*

Cochrane's most spectacular escapade was to block for several weeks at the end of 1808 the passage of a column of six thousand French troops who were proceeding along the coastal highway from the French frontier to Barcelona. With only about a hundred sailors and marines and about eighty guerrillas, he occupied the ruins of an old tower known as Fort Trinidad that dominated the road on the heights above the town of Rosas. Provisions and ammunition were ferried in from *Imperieuse* and hoisted up the steep cliffs. Unwilling to leave a strong British force in their rear as they advanced into Catalonia, the French resolved to drive the British from their position.

French artillery pounded the outer defenses of the fort for several days, and Cochrane's aristocratically ample nose was broken by a piece of flying stone. A breach was finally punched into the wall, but the twelve hundred troops of the advance guard who surged through it met an unpleasant surprise. Cochrane had built a steep wooden incline inside the wall and thickly greased it with "cook's slush" from *Imperieuse*'s galley. Slipping and sliding, the confused attackers tumbled into a deep pit dug by Cochrane's men, who poured musket fire and a deadly hail of hand grenades into them. Others were blown up by an enormous mine. "Up they went in the air, and down they fell buried in the ruins," related Midshipman Marryat. "Groans, screams, confusion, French yells, British hurras, rent the sky!"

Several more attacks were repelled over the next week, but Cochrane received a message from *Imperieuse* that with a gale blowing up, the frigate would have to put to sea with no assurance of when she could return. Having held the now ruined Fort Trinidad for more than a month despite repeated assaults, Cochrane accepted the inevitable and evacuated his men. They got down the cliff to the beach by rope ladders and were taken off by the ship's boats. Cochrane was the last to leave the fort, remaining behind to light the fuses for the charges that blew the place skyward. Total British casualties for the entire operation were, amazingly enough, only three killed and three seriously wounded. Collingwood expressed "the highest admiration" for Cochrane's "zeal and energy" in his report to the

*C. S. Forester also used these activities in his Horatio Hornblower novels.

Admiralty, but their Lordships ignored this praise. They reprimanded him for "excessive use of powder and shot."

⌐⌐

WHILE THE BRITISH AWAITED an opportunity to send an army back to the Iberian Peninsula, where Lisbon, Seville, and Cádiz were unconquered by the French, a naval crisis flared on the Atlantic coast. Napoleon's squadrons at Brest and Lorient were increasing in size and showing signs of activity. In the Schelde estuary, where the shipyards were described by Napoleon as a pistol pointed toward the head of England, there were ten French ships of the line in service, and ten more were being built at Antwerp and Flushing. The cabinet proposed a raid on Walcheren, an island that dominated the estuary, to destroy these vessels, but sufficient troops were unavailable and the project was shelved.

In mid-February 1809 Lord Gambier's ships blockading Brest were driven off by a westerly gale, and Admiral Willaumez, who flew his flag in the 120-gun *Ocean*, slipped out with seven ships of the line. The news caused consternation in London, where it was feared the fleet was bound for the Caribbean to reinforce Martinique, then under attack by a British force. Willaumez did not cross the Atlantic, however. He sailed down the French coast, where he rendezvoused with three ships of the line from Lorient before joining the Rochefort squadron at anchor in the Basque Roads near the Gironde estuary. Before Willaumez could get out again, a British squadron arrived on the scene and held the French there until Gambier arrived with the rest of the Channel fleet to impose a blockade.

Even though the enemy ships were now under blockade again, the Admiralty was concerned about the concentration of a large segment of the French fleet in one place. The vessels were also a threat to communications with Portugal and to the West Indies trade. Lord Cochrane, who had recently returned from the Mediterranean, was assigned the task of destroying the enemy vessels with a flotilla of fire ships. He would be backed up by Gambier's large ships. Relations between the two commanders were tense from the start. Gambier, who disliked the flamboyant Cochrane and whose religious sensibilities had already been violated by the bombardment of Copenhagen, decried the use of fire ships as "a horrible mode of warfare." Moreover, he was opposed to using his ships against shore defenses in shoal water, especially under the initiative of a subordinate.

The attack was launched on the night of April 11, which was described by Marryat as very dark with a high wind blowing down on the enemy fleet. Cochrane led the way into the Basque Roads with two old transports, each packed with fifteen hundred barrels of powder and three thousand grenades and other explosives, and was followed by about twenty fire ships. He commanded the first, and Marryat was in the second. Because of delays resulting from Gambier's indecision, the French were alert to the British plan. Admiral Allemand, who had replaced Willaumez, had struck the topmasts and yards of the big ships and stowed their sails to reduce the amount of exposed flammable material. A line of frigates also had been placed between them and a stout boom across the harbor entrance.

Once he had reached the boom, Cochrane lit the fuse of his vessel, and he and his handful of men swarmed into their boat, only to discover that they had left their pet dog behind. They returned to rescue the animal and furiously pulled back against the wind and tide to the waiting *Imperieuse* before being engulfed by the explosion. Minutes later, the transport blew up, lighting the sky with a lurid, red glare. The second vessel exploded shortly afterward, destroying the boom. But most of the fire ships were prematurely abandoned before they entered the channel and drifted harmlessly ashore.

Nevertheless, terror gripped the French fleet. Unable to see clearly in the smoke, the panicked gunners fired into the line of protecting frigates. Anchor cables were cut to escape the surge of flames, and without sails, the ships piled up on the shoals. At dawn Cochrane surveyed the scene from *Imperieuse* and was elated to see that all but two of the enemy battleships were stranded, some listing so badly they could not use their guns. But Gambier, a dozen miles away, made no effort to attack the grounded French ships despite repeated signals from Cochrane that they were at his mercy:

5:48 A.M. Half the fleet can destroy the enemy. Seven on shore.

6:40 A.M. Eleven on shore.

7:40 A.M. Only two afloat.

9:30 A.M. Enemy preparing to heave off.

There was no answer from *Caledonia*, Gambier's flagship. Finally, unable to restrain himself any longer, Cochrane decided to attack the enemy vessels before they could be refloated by the turning tide. With *Imperieuse* and a handful of small craft, he attacked several of the French vessels that had gotten afloat, forcing one to strike. Some of Gambier's ships eventually made an appearance and captured three of the French seventy-four-gun ships. Cochrane urged that the work of destruction be completed, but his pleas for an assault against the remainder of the fleet were ignored, and the enemy escaped upriver.

Basque Roads was hailed as a victory for the British and not without reason, for the Brest fleet had been virtually destroyed. Cochrane was made a knight of the Bath, but he thought a more stinging defeat could have been administered to the French and announced his intention to vote against a parliamentary motion of thanks to Lord Gambier. The Admiralty tried to bribe him into silence with his choice of commands, but the stubborn Scotsman was adamant. Reports also appeared in the press questioning Gambier's conduct—perhaps inspired by Cochrane—and the admiral demanded a court-martial to clear his name. The court was rigged in Gambier's favor, and he was whitewashed. Cochrane, however, was faulted for disloyalty to the service by exposing its dirty linen to the public. Gambier might be an old woman, it was said, but did not deserve public disgrace. Cochrane had committed professional suicide, and his career as Britain's greatest frigate captain was over.* And so the great weapon of sea power, so potent in the hands of Nelson, Barham, St. Vincent, Cornwallis, Pellew, and Cochrane, fell into the hands of irresolute and unimaginative men such as Duckworth and Gambier.

~

LESS THAN A WEEK AFTER the Basque Roads affair, Britain showed its determination to continue the war in the peninsula. Arthur Wellesley, absolved of all blame in the Cintra Convention matter, landed at Lisbon with 20,000 British troops and 3,000 Hanoverians. This force was far outnumbered by the approximately 250,000 French troops in Portugal and Spain, but on examining the strategic situation, Wellesley saw that most of the French were in garrison, guarding convoys, and trying to maintain some sort of order in the face of a disruptive guerrilla war. Some of the best units had been sent to Germany to deal with the Austrians.

The terrain was ideally suited for a force that had command of the sea.

*Cochrane maintained his seat in the House of Commons, where he continued to support radical political causes and to attack Admiralty abuses. In 1814 he was convicted of complicity in a stock exchange fraud in a case in which his guilt is still debated, and imprisoned and expelled from the Royal Navy, Parliament, and the Order of the Bath. Even as he was being stripped of his honors, he eloped with a beautiful girl to mark the beginning of a completely happy marriage. Then he went off to glory—and, as always, new disagreements—as commander of the revolutionary navies of Chile, Peru, Brazil, and Greece. Having outlived most of his enemies and become earl of Dundonald, he was granted a pardon for the crime he claimed he had not committed and was reinstated in the Royal Navy as an admiral in 1832—when, most delicious of ironies, Lord Gambier was Admiral of the Fleet. Cochrane became commander of the North American station in the 1840s and during the Crimean War put forward a plan for the conquest of the besieged Russian port of Sebastopol by the use of poison gas that was regarded as too horrible to be used. He died in 1860.

While the British army could be supplied by ship, the French were dependent on two wretched roads through the rugged mountains of northern Spain for reinforcements, provisions, and ammunition. One, running along the coast of Catalonia, could, as Cochrane and others had demonstrated, easily be cut. Thus the highway leading from Bayonne in France through Burgos and Madrid and then on to Lisbon was the only reliable road. Even so, it did not run directly to Lisbon but to the Tagus estuary, where it could be interdicted by the Royal Navy.

Two French armies opposed Wellesley, one of twenty-three thousand troops to the north, near Oporto, and headed by Marshal Soult, while another, of twenty-five thousand men under the command of Marshal Claude Victor, threatened from the east. Wellesley chose to attack Soult first. Moving quickly and reinforced by about six thousand ill-trained Portuguese regulars, the British took the unsuspecting enemy by surprise and fell on his rear. Oporto was liberated, and a beaten Soult retreated into Spain over the rugged mountains with the loss of all his artillery and stores. Rape, looting, and murder marked the route of his escape, and the vengeance of the hill folk was terrible. French stragglers were nailed alive to the doors of barns; others were emasculated and their penises stuffed into their mouths; the wounded were burned alive.

Wellesley set about reorganizing his army for an advance into Spain while Britain prepared to assist the hard-pressed Austrians with a strike across the North Sea to Walcheren and the Schelde estuary. By menacing Antwerp, the British hoped to force Napoleon to divide his forces in the East and send troops to the Low Countries. The expedition might have been brought off by someone with the flair and dash of Lord Cochrane or Edward Pellew. For political reasons, however, it was entrusted to Pitt's older brother, the earl of Chatham, who, after being dismissed as first lord of the Admiralty earlier in the war, had become a part-time soldier.

With a cabinet reshuffle in the offing, George Canning, its guiding genius, planned to make Chatham prime minister in place of the ailing duke of Portland and thus enhance his own power. A glorious military triumph would ensure Chatham the job. But Chatham lacked the sense of urgency that was the central core of military success. He was slow in thought and in action—at the Admiralty he had been known as the "late" Lord Chatham. In fact, the naval commander of the expedition, Sir Richard Strachan, could barely restrain his anger at Chatham's lackadaisical way of doing business.

Napoleon, however, never gave his enemies time to combine against him. Even as the British dawdled, he fought a whirlwind series of battles on the Danube that made the fighting in the Peninsula look like a skirmish. He finally crushed the Austrians at Wagram on July 6, 1809, entered Vienna in triumph, and dictated a peace in Schönbrunn Palace by which Austria lost her outlet to the sea and a fifth of her population. Having divorced Empress Josephine for failing to give him an heir, Napoleon sealed his victory by marrying Archduchess Marie Louise, eighteen-year-old daughter of Emperor Francis I and a niece of the dead Queen Marie Antoinette.*

Three weeks after Wagram, nearly forty thousand men—the largest army yet sent abroad by Britain—sailed from the Kentish coast for the Schelde in four hundred transports guarded by thirty-seven ships of the line, even though the reason for the expedition no longer existed. This armada crossed the North Sea in less than a day, but as Strachan fumed, Chatham wasted three days surveying the situation before disembarking the troops on Walcheren, robbing the operation of its chief assets: speed and surprise. The French withdrew their ships up the Schelde to Antwerp, where they lay mockingly behind a boom. Flushing was easily taken with the assistance of the navy's gunboats, but Chatham's procrastination gave the enemy ample time to improve Antwerp's defenses and increase the garrison to thirty-five thousand men. As a contemporary versifier put it:

Lord Chatham, with his sword undrawn,
Stood waiting for Sir Richard Strachan;
Sir Richard, longing to be at 'em,
Stood waiting for the earl of Chatham.

The British advanced to within sight of the spires of Antwerp, but the boats and gunboats that were to ferry them up the last stage of the East Schelde did not arrive until the opportunity had passed for an assault. The enemy blew up the dikes, which flooded the area, and the troops were trapped in a nightmare of mud, marshes, and malarial fevers. Typhoid, typhus, and "polder fever" were rampant, and half the army was stricken. The military hospitals—"miserable, stinking holes"—were so crowded the men had to lie atop one another.

Having wasted whatever chance he had of taking Antwerp, and with the campaigning season growing late, Chatham ordered the bulk of the troops reembarked for England. An attempt was made to hold on to Walcheren, but even that failed because of the fevers. In one regiment, the Royal Welch Fusiliers, not a single man was fit for duty. At the end of the year the last troops were withdrawn, with nothing accomplished except for the destruction of the dockyard and arsenal at Flushing. For the second

*Marie Louise bore him a son in March 1811. The boy, known as the king of Rome during the Empire, was brought up in Vienna as the duke of Reichstadt after its fall. Following the death of Napoleon I in 1821, he was accepted by Bonapartists as Napoleon II. He died in 1832.

time in 1809, a British army had returned from a foreign shore in defeat—
and Walcheren became a byword for fiasco.*

⟿

ON THE SAME DAY that the Schelde expedition sailed for Holland—July
28—Arthur Wellesley turned a disaster in the making at Talavera in Spain
into a smashing victory. He had advanced into Spain in conjunction with
the Spaniards who proposed a combined assault on Madrid. Nothing went
as planned. The Spanish junta failed to provide the British with promised
provisions, and the troops were on half rations. And they were amazed by
the first sight of the Spanish army as it moved across the barren plain in a
huge cloud of dust—a bewildering array of half-armed brigands, regular
regiments in blue and scarlet marching in perfect order, cavalry with lances
and pennants, guns, staff officers, priests, women, carts, artillery wagons,
mules, pigs, sheep, and herds of cattle. To a British officer, it appeared as if
a medieval army had marched out of the pages of history to do battle with
Napoleon's veteran legions.

Rather than waiting to be attacked, the French commander, Marshal
Claude Victor, who had forty-six thousand troops, nearly double the number believed, struck the unwary Spaniards at Torrijos on the Madrid road
and routed them. The British army of twenty thousand men now found
itself in as perilous a state as any since the morning of Agincourt. Wellesley took up a defensive position on a line of hills near Talavera and awaited
the attack. Repeated French charges were beaten back by the half-starved,
outnumbered Redcoats, and at the end of the day, the enemy fell back
under attack by British cavalry. Casualties were heavy on both sides. To
add to the horror, the parched grass on the slopes caught fire, and hundreds of the helpless wounded were engulfed in the flames.

Wellesley, raised to the peerage as Viscount Wellington for his victory at
Talavera, fell back with Britain's last army to its ultimate base—the sea. In
an area of the Lisbon peninsula called Torres Vedres, between the Tagus
and the Atlantic, he put an army of Portuguese laborers to work erecting
three great lines of redoubts, trenches, batteries, palisades, ditches, and
barriers. Roads were torn up, bridges mined, and rivers diverted to create
impassable marshes. The whole fifty-mile system was bound together by

---

*Chatham's hope of becoming prime minister vanished in the miasma, and
Canning was dropped from the cabinet in the wake of the disaster. The post
went to Spencer Perceval, whose major distinction is that he was assassinated
in the lobby of the House of Commons in 1812 by a man with a grudge against
the government.

signal stations manned by sailors from the fleet. In 1810 Wellington withdrew within the lines of Torres Vedres as the new French commander, Marshal André Massena, advanced like an avalanche. Before withdrawing, however, the British systematically denuded the area outside their lines of crops, orchards, animals, and houses—anything that might provide sustenance for the enemy.

Massena, who had promised "to drive the leopards into the sea," now discovered that the British position was impregnable and settled down for a siege. As Wellington had planned, this turned out to be a death trap for the French army. Over the next seven months the French, who traditionally lived on the land, found themselves occupying a desert. They were reduced to eating their pack animals while the British and their Portuguese allies were amply supplied by sea, including large amounts of flour from America. Royal Navy gunboats in the Tagus estuary also supported Wellington's flanks and harassed the French.

Having lost thirty-five thousand men to hunger and disease, Massena withdrew into Spain with the remnant of his demoralized and exhausted army, leaving Portugal unsubdued. Throughout the remainder of 1810 and into 1811, Wellington alternately advanced and retreated in an attempt to wear down and harass his adversary. At the same time, Marshal Victor was checked before Cádiz, which was also supplied from the sea, and then his army suffered a serious defeat at Barrosa at the hands of a force landed behind his lines by the navy. British ships under Commodore Edward Coddrington enabled the garrison of Tarragona to withstand a siege.

Like a stone tossed into a pool, Wellington's defense of the line of Torres Vedras created ever-widening ripples. It encouraged the resistance of the Spanish irregulars, whose bands were coalescing into small armies; stifled the murmuring among the Opposition at home about the cost and waste of life in the peninsula; and encouraged resistance to Napoleon among the Russians, whose relations with France were souring. The Russians resented the restrictions of the Continental System, Napoleon's recreation of Poland as the Duchy of Warsaw,* and his refusal to join them in aiding their fellow Slavs in driving the Turks out of the Balkans.

No matter what Napoleon did in the peninsula, he was unable to hold Wellington in check or crush the guerrillas. The Peninsula War is one of the most striking examples of the influence of sea power on military strategy. Throughout the campaign, the British army's defensive and offensive operations turned on the hinge of Britain's command of the sea—which Nelson had won at Trafalgar. The Royal Navy provided it with strategic

*Napoleon supported an independent Poland because he had promised this to his Polish mistress, Countess Marie Walewska.

mobility, communications, and logistical support, and stood ready to assist it when it suffered reverses. Without the navy, Wellington's vastly out-numbered army could not have conducted the campaigns that eventually undermined Napoleon's power. No one recognized this more than Well-ington himself. "If anyone wishes to know the history of this war," he declared, "I will tell him that it is our maritime superiority that gives me the power of maintaining my army while the enemy are unable to do so."

As 1812 opened, Wellington was at last ready to challenge the French, and he marched into Spain to storm the frontier fortresses of Ciudad Rodrigo and Badojoz. At the same time, the war was taking a new turn as it spread to Russia and the shores of North America.

CHAPTER 21

Free Trade and Sailors' Rights

CAPTAIN JOHN RODGERS PACED the quarterdeck of the forty-four-gun U.S. Navy frigate *President* with a stride that betrayed even more anger than usual. With a face like a clenched fist and a domineering manner, he was not a man to be trifled with. Now, as dusk was falling on the evening of May 16, 1811, he was confronted off the Chesapeake Capes by a vessel that stubbornly refused to identify herself. Only few days before, Rodgers had sailed from Annapolis with orders to protect American shipping from the roving British cruisers that were harassing Yankee trade despite the nation's neutrality. As soon as the strange ship was sighted, he ordered his crew to quarters and ran out his guns.

Four years had passed since the *Chesapeake-Leopard* affair, and even though the British had paid reparations for the unprovoked attack on the American frigate and the seized American sailors had been released from the Royal Navy, relations between the two nations had continued to sour. In fact, British warships had all but established a blockade of the American coast and with impunity searched merchantmen for cargoes bound for French ports. Even more galling, American sailors were being seized from the decks of those vessels and impressed into the British service.

The Navy Department, determined that there would be no repetition of the *Chesapeake* incident, had issued a general order to all captains that stated: "What has been perpetrated may again be attempted. It is therefore our duty to be prepared and determined at every hazard to vindicate the injured honor of our Navy. . . ." For his part, Rodgers had told his officers, "I should consider the firing of a shot by a vessel of war of either nation [France or Britain] . . . at one of our public vessels as a menace of the grossest order, and in amount an insult which it would be disgraceful not to resent by the return of two shot at least."

The strange ship had come into view that afternoon. Rodgers was wary because he knew the British frigate *Guerrière*,* which had recently impressed

---

*Guerrière had been captured from the French in 1806 and taken into the Royal Navy under her original name.

Commodore John Rodgers. (U.S. Naval Academy Museum)

a sailor from an American merchant vessel, was in the area. *President* broke out the Stars and Stripes, but Rodgers claimed he could not make out the colors of the other vessel. She altered course and bore away to the south. Believing the other ship to be *Guerrière,* Rodgers said he took up the chase with the hope of obtaining the release of the impressed man. But the two vessels did not come within hailing distance of each other until 8:15 P.M., as darkness was closing in.

"What ship is that?" Rodgers inquired.

"What ship is that?" replied the stranger.

Rodgers made no reply, taking the position that inasmuch as he had issued the first challenge, he had the right to receive the first answer.

What happened next is subject to debate. Rodgers claimed that the stranger fired a shot that struck one of *President*'s masts. She responded immediately with a shot, and the other ship countered with a broadside. The engagement became general and, within fifteen minutes, the opposing vessel was silenced and drifted away. Rodgers kept his men at their guns and cruised for the rest of the night without finding any trace of his opponent. When dawn came, she was sighted lying a short distance away in great distress. The vessel, which proved to be the British sloop of war *Lille Belt*,* twenty, refused assistance and made its way to Halifax with eleven dead and twenty-one wounded.

Captain A. B. Bingham, *Lille Belt*'s commander, challenged Rodgers' account of the encounter. He told a court of inquiry that he had been the first to hail and *President* had been first to fire and then he had fired only after being fired upon. A deserter from the American vessel testified that one of *President*'s guns had fired accidentally. No matter what the cause of the incident, Rodgers was hailed by Americans as a hero for having avenged the attack on *Chesapeake*. Once more, war talk was in the air.

ONLY NAPOLEON BENEFITED from an Anglo-American confrontation, but the events leading to the outbreak of war between Britain and the United States in 1812 are a study in how nations can conduct their affairs in a way contrary to their own best interests. Neither side understood or appreciated the difficulties faced by the other. Like most adolescent nations, the United States was sensitive to issues of national sovereignty and independence and refused to see any justice in Britain's attempts to defend herself by preventing American flour, cotton, and tobacco from reaching Napoleon, and to man its ships—"the knife at the throat of Napoleon"— whether by fair means or foul.

With their hands full in Europe, the British had no wish to become embroiled in a war with the United States, even though she was weak and insignificant. Nevertheless, successive British governments helped to create the atmosphere that led to the conflict. There was a strong undercurrent of anti-Americanism in Britain because of what was viewed as the pro-French attitude of the Yankees, and British response to American complaints was foolishly harsh and unyielding. Even if Britain believed it could not give way on the fundamental issues of impressment and trade with the enemy, there was ample room for conciliatory gestures and concessions on details.

---

*Her name is usually given as *Little Belt*.

Unfortunately, after years of dealing with Napoleon, the British were convinced that concessions would be seen as weakness and open the way for further demands.

Using the right of a belligerent to inspect neutral vessels to establish their identities and to see if their cargoes were contraband bound for France, the British established a virtual blockade of the American coast. Often British officers seized ships merely suspected of irregularities and sent them off for adjudication by the Admiralty court in Halifax. This was sometimes the last an owner might see of his vessel and cargo. As Basil Hall, then a midshipman in *Leander*, fifty, on patrol off New York, recalled:

> Every morning at daybreak during our stay off New York we set about arresting the progress of all vessels we saw, firing off guns to the right and left, to make every ship that was running in heave-to, or wait until we had leisure to send a boat on board to "see" in our lingo, "what she was made of." I have frequently known a dozen, and sometimes a couple of dozen ships lying a league or two off the port, losing their fair wind, their tide, and worse than all, their market for many hours, sometimes the whole day, before our search was completed.

Sometimes the British were none too careful in laying warning shots across the bows of Yankee vessels. Once, reported Hall, "a casual shot from the *Leander* hit an unfortunate ship's main boom; and the broken spar striking the mate, John Pierce by name, killed him instantly."

British captains also used such opportunities to impress likely hands into the Royal Navy. Probably about a quarter of the hundred thousand seamen employed on Yankee merchant ships were of British origin and the Royal Navy took the position that these men were dodging naval service. In the death grapple with Napoleon, neutral rights were of secondary importance to obtaining adequate crews for its men-of-war. If American citizens were picked up in these dragnets, it was the fortunes of war.

A Royal Navy boarding officer in need of an experienced topman was unlikely to inquire too deeply into a man's background. If a man looked like an Englishman and sounded like an Englishman, he was fair game. Britain denied Englishmen the right to renounce their citizenship, and naturalization papers were of little value. "Once an Englishman, always an Englishman" was the simple doctrine of the quarterdeck. Some sailors carried "protections" identifying them as native Americans, but when they presented them, press gangs laughed in their faces. Such documents, it was claimed, could be obtained for a dollar in any port. If a man resisted, he was knocked unconscious and dragged on board the man-of-war, where death or the end of hostilities was his only release. Up to ten thousand American sailors may have been forced into such servitude between 1799 and 1812.

Nevertheless, trade with the belligerents was so lucrative that Yankee shipowners ignored the perils and did their best to deal with, or evade, the restrictions imposed by both sides. The American merchant marine grew from 558,000 tons in 1802 to 981,000 tons in 1810, and the value of American trade leaped from $60 million annually before 1793 to nearly $250 million in 1807. Inasmuch as France could do little to enforce its decrees barring trade with Britain because its navy had all but been driven from the high seas—although French privateers were active—Britain bore the brunt of American anger.

〜

FOLLOWING THE ENCOUNTER between *Chesapeake* and *Leopard*, Thomas Jefferson thought economic coercion could accomplish as much as war. He had ordered an embargo on trade with the belligerents, with the hope of forcing them to adopt a more reasonable attitude toward the United States. But the results of the president's alternative to war were hardly what he anticipated. American commerce stagnated, vessels rotted at their piers, jobless sailors thronged the streets, and cargoes were piled high on the wharves. Smuggling became big business, especially along the Canadian border, and the government repeatedly violated the civil rights of its citizens in an effort to stamp it out. Exasperated New England and New York merchants and shipowners—mostly Federalists—likened the embargo to "cutting one's throat to cure a nosebleed."

Jefferson was forced after a year of the embargo to recognize the bankruptcy of his policy. Albert Gallatin, the treasury secretary, reported that revenues from customs duties had shrunk from $16 million to $8 million—a disaster worse than war itself in the eyes of that thrifty gentleman. On March 1, 1809, three days before James Madison was inaugurated as president, Congress repealed the embargo and replaced it with the Nonintercourse Act. Trade was restored with all nations with the exception of Britain and France, and Madison was empowered to reopen commerce with those countries should they agree to end their harassment of American trade.

Nonintercourse proved to be as much a failure as the embargo, however. The British and the French toyed with the United States, now one and then the other raising false hopes that their restrictions on American trade would be removed. Impressment also continued to be an irritant, as the Royal Navy persisted in stopping American ships almost within sight of land and grabbing hands where it could. In the face of American protests, British officials argued that these policies were aimed not at America but at Napoleonic France. Once the French had been beaten, all infringements on American rights would cease.

Yet, New England, which had suffered most from the depredations of the Royal Navy, stoutly resisted the drift toward war. In spite of all the problems facing their trade, the Yankees were making money. If one cargo in three reached its destination safely, a merchant could still show a profit—and that was of more importance than idle talk of preserving the national honor. Paradoxically, the loudest demands for war to protect sailors' rights came from the landlocked West. Led by a group of hot-blooded young congressmen known as "War Hawks," westerners blamed British trade restrictions for a depression in the South and the West and held the British responsible for Indian uprisings that had set the frontier ablaze. The "War Hawks" saw war as a golden opportunity to wrest Canada from Britain and Florida from Spain. With the cry "On to Canada!" they predicted an easy victory because most of Britain's naval and military strength was engaged in the death struggle with France.

Under the inexorable pressure of the West, the nation was borne along to war. On June 1, 1812, President Madison sent a message to Congress asking for a declaration of war against Britain. Impressment, interference with neutral trade, and British intrigues with the Indians were cited as causes of the conflict. "Mr. Madison's War" was not at all popular, however. Congress did declare war on June 18—but only on a vote of 79 to 49 in the House and by the closer margin of 19 to 13 in the Senate. New England and the Middle Atlantic states were strongly opposed to war, even though it had been declared supposedly to protect the maritime commerce on which they depended for their livelihoods, while the agrarian West and the South were wholeheartedly for it. A Boston newspaper noted bitterly that "we . . . whose ships were the nursery of Sailors, are insulted with the hypocrisy of a devotedness to Sailors' rights . . . by those whose country furnishes no navigation beyond the size of a ferryboat or an Indian canoe." Ironically, Britain had five days before suspended the obnoxious Orders in Council, which were alleged to be a major cause of the conflict.

"AN INFANT HERCULES, destined by the presage of early prowess to extirpate the British race of pirates and free-booters!"

So went the toast to the U.S. Navy at a gala formal dinner in Washington on July 4, 1812, attended by President Madison and most of his cabinet. But cantankerous old John Adams took a different view. Writing to his grandson, he said: "Our Navy is so lilliputian that . . . Gulliver might bury it in the deep by making water on it." Of these two appraisals, that of the former president was closer to the existing reality.

The U.S. Navy consisted of twenty ships, ten of them frigates, and the rest a ragged assortment of smaller vessels and nearly useless gunboats.

President was considered the best of the "super frigates," while the sailing qualities of *United States* were so poor that she was called "the Old Wagon." Many of the ships were in need of extensive repair, and all were short-handed. The Washington Navy Yard was the only functioning base, and timber, naval stores, and munitions stock were depleted. Only seven months before the outbreak of war, Congress had balked at a proposal to build a dozen seventy-four-gun ships and twenty frigates, with most of the opposition coming from the Westerners, who were vociferously demanding war. In the years since the Tripolitan War, the navy's prospects had fallen so low that some officers—William Bainbridge, for one—thought of resigning their commissions and joining the merchant service.

Britain, in contrast, had more than 600 men-of-war, among them some 250 ships of the line and frigates. In fact, it was said, the Royal Navy had more ships than the Americans had guns. Most of this fleet was in European waters, but it was thought that no more than a few two-deckers and a handful of frigates would be enough to deal with the upstart Yankees. While the North American squadron, commanded by Admiral Sir John Borlase Warren, consisted only of the sixty-four-gun *Africa,* seven frigates, and some smaller vessels, there were a hundred more ships within easy call off Newfoundland and in the West Indies. In the years since Trafalgar, however, there had been a decline in readiness. The Admiralty was tight with funds for target practice, and many British captains now placed greater emphasis on speed of fire rather than accuracy.

Some American officials were convinced that it would be useless to oppose such an overwhelming force. Paul Hamilton, the hard-drinking South Carolina rice planter and politician who was serving as secretary of the navy, thought the larger ships should be laid up in various ports where they could serve as floating batteries, and as receiving ships for men recruited to serve in the gunboats. President Madison insisted, however, that the ships be sent to sea. The basic strategy was clear: to protect the nation's maritime frontiers and to disrupt British naval and commercial operations. But how was the meager force available best used to accomplish these strategic ends?

A few days before the actual declaration of war, Secretary Hamilton put this question to his ranking captains. They differed in approach, but all favored offensive operations at sea. Stephen Decatur suggested that the "best use of the Navy would be to send single ships out . . . no more than two frigates together." Bainbridge supported his position. John Rodgers argued that the navy should operate in squadrons built around the heavy frigates, while lighter vessels could harass British commerce in the Caribbean.

Hamilton supported Rodgers' proposal, and on June 22, 1812, he divided the naval force at New York into two squadrons: one under Rodgers' command and the other under Decatur. One squadron was to cruise off New York and the other in the vicinity of the Chesapeake Capes, to protect the large number of American merchantmen that had rushed off to Europe in anticipation of the declaration of war and that were now homeward bound. Hours after learning that hostilities had begun, Rodgers put to sea. Flying his commodore's pennant in *President* and accompanied by *United States,* forty-four, *Congress,* thirty-eight, and the sloop of war *Hornet* and brig *Argus,* both eighteen, he sailed southeastward in search of a rich Jamaica convoy that was reported to be on its way to Britain.

Two days out, Rodgers sighted the thirty-six-gun British frigate *Belvidera* and, forgetting about the convoy, gave chase. *President* fired several ranging shots with her bow chasers, one of which struck *Belvidera* and killed or wounded nine men. It looked as if the frigate would soon be bagged, but one of *President's* guns exploded, hurling sailors about like tenpins. Sixteen men were wounded, including Rodgers, who had been observing the work of the gun crew and suffered a broken leg. In the confusion, *Belvidera* escaped.

Having lost his squadron, Rodgers pressed on alone in search of the convoy, which was sighted and followed almost into the English Channel. No prizes were taken, but on turning southward *President* captured seven merchantmen off Madeira. Rodgers returned to port after seventy days at sea and claimed that even though the pickings were slim, the British had been forced to divert a significant force to search for his squadron. As a result, he said, the enemy had been delayed in establishing a blockade of the American coast and most of the returning Yankee trading vessels had arrived home safely. In the meantime, the thirty-two-gun *Essex,* under the command of David Porter, carried off a troop-laden British transport from a Québec-bound convoy, as well as nine other vessels, valued at three hundred thousand dollars, including the sixteen-gun sloop-of-war *Alert.*

Constitution was lying at Annapolis, taking on a crew and stores, when war came. She was rated at forty-four guns but actually carried fifty-two. Captain Isaac Hull, fearing that his ship might be trapped in Chesapeake Bay, hastily filled out her complement and put to sea on July 12, 1812. Most of the new men were green hands who signed on for two years and were paid twelve dollars a month. Some were free blacks. "The crew are as yet unacquainted with a ship of war, as many have but lately joined and have never been on an armed vessel before," Hull wrote Secretary Hamilton. "We are doing all we can to make them acquainted with their duties, and in a few days we shall have nothing to fear from any single-decked ship."

Five days later *Constitution* was off the New Jersey coast when a British frigate was sighted. Twilight was falling, and Hull followed her throughout the night. At daylight he was surprised to make out no fewer than three sails on his starboard quarter and four astern. On learning of the encounter between *Belvidera* and *President,* the British commander at Halifax had sent out a squadron consisting of the sixty-four-gun *Africa* and four frigates plus a brig and a schooner to deal with Rodgers. Any attempt to fight would have been suicidal, so Hull decided to run. A towering cloud of canvas billowed on *Constitution*'s tall masts, promising one of the most exciting chases of the age of fighting sail.

Constitution showed her heels to the British vessels, but soon a dead calm set in and both sides bent every effort to coax a few knots from their vessels. With the hope of catching a breeze, the various captains ordered out their boats and tried to tow their vessels into the wind. Then they resorted to the backbreaking task of kedging. The boats carried anchors ahead of the ships, where they were dropped. Men hove in on the cables to pull the ship forward. Then the process was repeated . . . and again and again. When Hull noted that one of the British vessels was gaining slightly, she was discouraged with a few well-aimed shots from a stern chaser. After three days of this, Hull took advantage of a sudden squall that reached his ship first, and *Constitution* made her getaway. She ran into Boston, where despite the unpopularity of "Mr. Madison's War," a warm welcome awaited her.

⤳

LESS THAN A MONTH later, on August 19, *Constitution* was off Cape Race, athwart the main route for Atlantic shipping, when the British frigate *Guerrière* was sighted. Just a few days before, her commanding officer, Captain James R. Dacres, had challenged John Rodgers in New York, daring *President* "or any American frigate of equal force" to come out for a "few minutes tête-à-tête." *Constitution* was a much more powerful ship than his own—mounting thirty twenty-four-pound long guns and twenty-four thirty-two-pound carronades to *Guerrière*'s thirty eighteen-pounders, two twelve-pounders, and eighteen thirty-two-pound carronades. Moreover, *Guerrière* was badly in need of a refit. But Dacres unhesitatingly offered battle. Over the past two decades, the Royal Navy had fought some two hundred single-ship engagements and had lost only five, and those to superior force, so he had no fear of what *The Times* called "a handful of fir-built frigates under a bit of striped bunting."

For three-quarters of an hour the ships maneuvered for position, *Guerrière* firing her starboard broadside at long range and then wearing or zigzagging downwind and firing her portside battery. Shortly before 6:00 P.M. Hull gave the order to fire. "Now boys, pour it into them!" he shouted. A line of flame spread along the Yankee frigate's side as her double-shotted cannon poured death and destruction into her lighter-built opponent. *Guerrière* "reeled and trembled as though she had received the shock of an earthquake," Hull reported. Within fifteen minutes her mizzenmast was shot away, her sides riddled, and her sails and rigging reduced to a tangle of wreckage. "We've made a brig out of her!" cried Hull. A Yankee sailor is reported to have seen a British shot bounce off *Constitution*'s side and into the water. "Her sides are made of iron!" he yelled. After that the frigate was known as "Old Ironsides."

Drawing ahead of the wallowing British vessel and crossing her bow, *Constitution* raked her with a port and then a starboard broadside. A fluke of wind caused *Guerrière*'s bowsprit to catch in the American vessel's mizzen rigging, and for a few moments the two ships clung together. Boarding parties gathered on the decks of both but were dispersed by small-arms fire. And then, as suddenly as they had come together, the ships drifted apart. *Guerrière*'s foremast toppled over the side, carrying the mainmast with it. She was now a mastless hulk, nearly rolling the muzzles of main-deck guns into the sea. Nevertheless, the white ensign still waved gallantly from the stump of her mizzen.

At about 7:00 P.M., little more than an hour after the engagement started, Hull ordered his guns to cease fire and sent an officer over to *Guerrière* to inquire if she had struck her colors. Dacres was in a daze, and when the question was put to him, he stood puzzled for a moment. "Well," he finally replied, "I don't know. Our mizzenmast is gone, our mainmast is gone; an upon the whole, you may say we *have* struck our flag."

Guerrière was a shambles. Fifteen of her crew were dead and sixty-three were wounded. *Constitution* suffered only fourteen casualties, half of whom were killed. Damaged beyond salvaging, the prize was abandoned and set afire.* In his official report, Hull paid special tribute to the courage of his black seamen. "I never had any better fighters . . . they stripped to the waist & fought like devils, sir . . . utterly insensible to danger & . . . possessed with a determination to outfight white sailors."

Constitution returned to Boston to a celebration made even more enthusiastic by the fact that her victory had come amid a rising tide of disasters in the war on land. The conquest of Canada, which Jefferson had considered "a mere matter of marching," had gone awry because of poor planning and inferior leadership. Fort Dearborn (now Chicago) had been captured by the Indians, who promptly massacred the garrison. And only a few hours before Hull's arrival in Boston, word had been received that

---

*There is a story, perhaps apocryphal, that Hull and Dacres had met before the war and the British officer claimed that his ship could defeat any American frigate. He was so certain of the outcome of such an encounter that he offered to bet a hat on it, and Hull accepted. After the battle Dacres offered his sword to Hull, but the American refused it and asked for the hat.

his uncle, General William Hull, had surrendered Detroit to the British after only a perfunctory defense.

Congress awarded Captain Hull and his crew fifty thousand dollars in lieu of prize money. But the affair did more than lift American spirits in a time of defeat; it also provided popular support for an expansion of the U.S. Navy. In January 1813, Congress authorized four seventy-four-gun ships of the line and six heavy frigates of forty-four guns, as well as an assortment of smaller vessels. The ineffectual Paul Hamilton, who was said to have been drunk in public on several occasions and to have been "incapable of working in the second half of the day," was dropped as secretary of the navy. He was replaced by William Jones, a Philadelphia merchant with considerable experience in maritime affairs.

To the British, the loss of *Guerrière* was a profound shock. *The Times* said the news "spread a degree of gloom through the town, which it was painful to observe." But there was worse to come. While *Constitution* owed her victory to superior size and weight of metal, superior gunnery and seamanship should be credited for the victory of the next American vessel to encounter a British man-of-war. The eighteen-gun sloop-of-war *Wasp,* commanded by Master Commandant Jacob Jones, met the brig *Frolic,* eighteen, off Bermuda on October 18, 1812, in a boisterous sea. *Frolic* fired far faster than *Wasp*—in fact, so fast that she seemed to carry more guns than the Yankee vessel. But *Wasp*'s gunnery was far more accurate, and in less than an hour her adversary was so badly cut up that she was taken by boarding. Later in the day, however, *Wasp,* slowed by the damage she had suffered in the fight, was taken by a British two-decker.

Realizing that in time the Royal Navy would try to impose a blockade on the American coast, the Navy Department used the window of opportunity afforded it to inflict the severest possible damage to British commerce. Taking up John Rodgers' suggestion, Jones sent all available ships to sea in three squadrons under the command of Rodgers, Decatur, and Bainbridge. The flamboyant Decatur, who was sailing in the frigate *United States,* was the first to score a victory.

On October 25, 1812, Decatur sighted the British frigate *Macedonian* off the Canary Islands. He had put to sea in company with the brig *Argus,* but preferring to cruise alone, he had parted company with his consort. Even so, *United States* was more than a match for the British frigate. Rated as a forty-four, *United States* actually carried fifty-four guns, including twenty-two forty-two-pound carronades rather than the usual thirty-twos. *Macedonian* was rated as a thirty-eight, but she mounted eleven more guns. Newly refitted, she was considered a crack ship. Captain John S. Carden had laid special emphasis on gunnery at a time when such training was neglected in the Royal Navy. But she was anything but a happy ship. Samuel Leech, one of the few sailors of the era who wrote his memoirs, described Carden as "a heartless, unfeeling lover of whip discipline." Ignoring the pleas of several impressed American sailors that they not be forced to fight against their countrymen, he ordered them to their battle stations under pain of death. Some were killed in action.

Instead of closing with *United States,* Carden made the fatal error of engaging her at long range. The twenty-four-pound long guns on the American vessel's gun deck were more than a match for *Macedonian's* eighteens. By the time Carden corrected his mistake by shortening the range, where his own guns would be more effective, *Macedonian's* mainmast had been shot away and many of her guns dismounted. "Grapeshot and canister were pouring through our portholes like leaden hail," wrote Sam Leech. "The large shot came against the ship's side, shaking her to the very keel, and passing through her timbers, and scattering terrific splinters, which did more appalling work than the shot itself."

"The whole scene grew indescribably confused and horrible," Leech continued. "It was like some awfully tremendous thunder-storm whose deafening roar is attended by incessant streaks of lightning, carrying death in every flash . . . the scene was rendered more horrible . . . by the presence of torrents of blood which dyed our decks."

Throughout the hour-long battle, the usually impetuous Decatur handled his ship with prudent calculation because he wished to bring in *Macedonian* as a prize rather than shoot her to pieces. The British vessel lost thirty-six men killed and sixty-eight wounded; *United States* had five killed and six wounded. Except for some damage to her sails and rigging, she emerged from the battle almost unscathed. *Macedonian* was escorted into New London and taken into the U.S. Navy.* Leech was among several British sailors who volunteered for service in the U.S. Navy.

On December 29, 1812, *Constitution,* which had now devolved on William Bainbridge, scored another victory. While cruising off the Brazilian coast in company with the sloop-of-war *Hornet,* she sighted a British frigate that proved to be *Java,* thirty-eight. As usual, the American vessel was considerably larger and more powerful than her adversary, Taking advantage of his vessel's superior speed, Captain Henry Lambert tried to rake *Constitution,* but she avoided the maneuver. The American opened the battle at 2:00 P.M. with a single ranging shot, and *Java* replied with a broadside. Forty minutes of complex maneuvering followed in which, as Bainbridge reported, "the enemy [was] keeping at a much greater distance than I wished."

A lucky shot carried away *Constitution's* wheel, but a substitute was quickly rigged and her superior sailing qualities and firepower began to

*The officers and crew of *United States* received two hundred thousand dollars in prize money for *Macedonian.* She remained on the rolls of the U.S. Navy for nearly twenty years.

The British frigate *Java* blowing up after an engagement with the U.S. frigate *Constitution* on December 29, 1812. (Beverley Robinson Collection, U.S Naval Academy Museum)

take their toll. Once again the British fired faster, but the Yankee gunners were more accurate, and within two hours the lightly built *Java* was a wreck. Twenty-two of her crew had been killed and another 102 wounded, including Captain Lambert, who later died. American casualties totaled 12 killed and 22 wounded. *Java* was so badly battered that she was scuttled. William Bainbridge had at last redeemed himself for the loss of *Philadelphia* during the Tripolitan War.

The last in the series of stunning American victories occurred about two months later, on February 24, 1813, when *Hornet*, commanded by James Lawrence, captured the brig *Peacock* off the coast of what is now Guyana. Both vessels were rated at eighteen guns, but *Hornet* had heavier carronades than *Peacock* and made short work of her opponent. Within fifteen minutes the British vessel's crew was decimated and she was sinking. The British naval historian William James attributed her loss to "neglect to exercise the ship's company at the guns." Similar conditions "prevailed ... over two thirds of the British navy," he added, "in which the Admiralty, by their sparing allowance of powder and shot for practice, were in some degree instrumental." As a result of these actions, the captains of British frigates cruising alone were ordered to avoid engaging the heavier American ships until the Royal Navy could produce its own large frigates.

During the opening months of the war at sea, the Americans had been successful far beyond their wildest expectations—giving rise to the legend that the United States won the War of 1812. Not only had three frigates and several smaller men-of-war been taken, but also Lloyd's of London reported that upward of five hundred British merchant vessels had been bagged by Yankee privateers and commerce raiders. The British were stunned by their losses. *The Pilot*, bible of Britain's maritime community, said that "any one who had predicted such a result of an American war this time last year would have been treated as a madman or traitor." Nevertheless, despite the alarm generated among Britain's commercial interests by the American victories at sea, they had little effect on the overall conduct of the war. And they reaped a wild wind.

AS THE WAR UNFOLDED in America, the roads of central Europe were thronged with men, horses, guns, and wagons headed eastward—toward Russia. Napoleon had decided to reach London by way of Moscow. To the emperor's fury, the Russians had continued to flout his Continental System. Even though Russia was a land of peasants, the ruling class depended on seaborne commerce for their luxuries, and Czar Alexander had thrown open the nation's ports to neutral ships—which meant disguised British vessels. In the summer of 1811 there were at least 150 British ships unloading in Russian harbors, most flying the American flag. Napoleon could not tolerate such defiance, but Alexander, having closely observed Wellington's campaign in the Iberian Peninsula, was no longer in awe of the emperor and the French Army. Worried about the French buildup on his frontier, in January 1812 Alexander demanded that all French troops be withdrawn to the west of the Oder River—an ultimatum completely unacceptable to Napoleon. So began the struggle later enshrined by Tolstoy and Tchaikovsky.

In the dark hours of June 24, 1812, the Grande Armée—five hundred thousand infantry, a hundred thousand cavalry, and twelve hundred guns—crossed the Niemen River into Russian territory. Some of these troops had been withdrawn from Spain, permitting Wellington to go on the offensive. Like Adolf Hitler a century and a quarter later, Napoleon committed numerous blunders in his invasion of Russia. By invading Russia, both would-be conquerors involved themselves in wars on two fronts, leaving an unbeaten Britain in their rear. And both started on the road to Moscow fatally late in the season. In 1941 Hitler was delayed by a spring sideshow in the Balkans. In 1812 the need to feed his army's two hundred thousand animals, including the eighty thousand horses of Joachim Murat's cavalry, forced Napoleon to delay his offensive until the grasses of the Russian steppes had reached their peak. Neither army was equipped for a winter campaign because both Hitler and Napoleon expected the war to be over in a few weeks, well before the onset of the bitter Russian winter.

For Napoleon, the campaign began with a bad omen. A hare got under his horse's hoofs, and he was thrown to the ground near the Niemen, although he was not injured. Every effort was made to defeat the Russians in a great decisive battle, but the Russians would not oblige. Trading space for time, they fought, fell back, and fought again—badly battered but never completely routed. By the end of July some hundred thousand French soldiers had fallen by the way in the dust and heat of the Russian summer. Napoleon's straggling legions, unprotected by cavalry after Murat's horses were enfeebled by the lack of grain—the result of the Russians' scorched-earth policy and the weather—suffered from slashing attacks by Cossacks who seemed to strike out of nowhere.

Most strategists are convinced that Napoleon should have gone into winter quarters after capturing Smolensk at the end of August and then renewed the campaign the following spring. But the Swedes had entered the war, and he was worried about attacks on his line of communications. With Moscow only 280 miles away, Napoleon pressed on, expecting that the capture of the city would end Russian resistance. Following a bloody battle at Borodino, the Russians abandoned Moscow to the French, who occupied it on September 14.

The rest of the story may be written in one word: ruin. Moscow was set ablaze, probably by accident, and three-quarters of the city was destroyed. What was left was plundered by French soldiers. Guerrillas attacked French communications, and the Czar would not come to terms. Unsettling news also came from Spain, where Wellington had captured Salamanca and was threatening Madrid itself. On October 19 the French abandoned Moscow, and what was left of the Grande Armée retreated over the same ground it had passed on the way to Moscow. Thousands of wounded, fearful of Russian vengeance, fought for places on the plunder-laden carts. Morale was further shaken by the sight of the battlefield of Borodino, with its half-buried mounds of dead. The ground was covered, said one officer, "with the debris of helmets, cuirasses, wheels, weapons, rags of uniforms—and thirty thousand corpses half eaten by wolves."

November brought the first snow. And as it fell, a terrible wind howled through the forests, piling the snow in immense drifts in the path of the retreating army. Hundreds of cannon, baggage wagons, and ammunition carts were abandoned. Famished and exhausted, men fell by the wayside to freeze to death or be slaughtered by guerrillas who moved rapidly through the forest even in winter. The French Army lost hope and cohesion and disintegrated. At the crossing of the Beresina in the last days of November, two Russian armies closed in, almost capturing Napoleon. The French broke through, but twelve thousand men drowned, another eighteen thousand were captured, and the Beresina was blocked with frozen corpses for weeks to come.

On December 5, 1812, Napoleon abandoned his army—as he had done in Egypt thirteen years before—and returned to Paris with the vainglorious promise to return to the Niemen in six months' time with three hundred thousand fresh troops. "His Majesty's health has never been better," proclaimed an imperial bulletin. Not long afterward, ten thousand typhus-stricken scarecrows, desperately looking over their shoulders with haunted eyes for the pursuing Cossacks, stumbled across the bridge at Königsberg into Prussia. They were all that remained of the Grande Armée of six hundred thousand men that had set out six months before on the invasion of Russia.

CHAPTER 22

Tattered Ensigns

AS 1813 BEGAN, Britain was revitalized by Napoleon's debacle in Russia. Sensing a historic turn in events, the British stripped their country of troops and reinforced Wellington's army, with the intention of not only driving the French from Spain but also of crossing the Pyrenees to invade France. The Baltic ports were reopened to British trade just in time to prevent economic collapse. And Britain had new partners in the struggle against the French. Paid by British gold, Sweden joined the war on Britain's side, and the Prussians, once again switching sides, allied themselves with the Russians. Revolt flared in Germany.

These developments were hardly good news for the Americans. The Yankees had banked on the bulk of the Royal Navy being tied up in European waters, but with Napoleon reeling, the British were able to reinforce their squadrons in North American waters. As a result, the frigates that had easily gotten to sea in the opening months of the struggle were bottled up in port on their return from their victorious cruises. Some did not get to sea again for the remainder of the war. *Constellation,* for example, was blockaded in Norfolk, and *United States* and the captured *Macedonian* were locked up in New London. Convoys also were established to protect merchantmen from the attacks of Yankee commerce-raiders. And the British soon got their chance to cheer a triumph at sea.

James Lawrence, as a reward for his victory over the British sloop *Peacock,* had been given command of *Chesapeake,* which was being fitted out in Boston. A few weeks before, John Rodgers had managed to evade a British blockading squadron with *President* and *Congress* and captured a dozen trading vessels, so Captain Philip Vere Broke, the British commander off Boston, resolved that *Chesapeake* would not be allowed to escape. He sent Lawrence a message saying he was sending away his supporting vessels and challenging him to an encounter between *Chesapeake* and his ship, the thirty-eight-gun *Shannon,* off Boston Light. Lawrence had put to sea on June 1, 1813, before he received this challenge, but he made no effort to elude Broke's vessel.

Lawrence had considerable difficulty in manning *Chesapeake* because she was considered an unlucky ship, and many sailors had already succumbed to the lure of privateering. A large number of those who did sign on were foreigners and green hands, and she was hardly in fighting trim. An officer of Lawrence's energy and experience would have improved the efficiency of his ship after a few weeks at sea, and rather than offering battle, he should have reined in his enthusiasm and slipped away to terrorize British commerce. In contrast, Broke was the Royal Navy's most efficient and innovative gunnery enthusiast and had been in command of *Shannon* for seven years. Unlike many British officers, he drilled his men at the guns every day and had personally sighted in each piece. "Don't try to dismast her," Broke told his crew as they put to sea to deal with *Chesapeake*. "Kill the men and the ship is yours."

Undoubtedly because his crew was inexperienced, Lawrence sailed *Chesapeake* to within fifty yards of *Shannon* without maneuvering for a raking position, and both ships unleashed broadsides at point-blank range. The intensive training that Broke had given his gun crews quickly paid off. The British fired far faster and more accurately than the Americans. British shot pounded *Chesapeake*'s hull and shrieked across her quarterdeck. Lawrence and several of his officers were mortally wounded. Taken below, he implored his remaining officers: "Don't give up the ship!"

Badly damaged, her headsails shot away and her stern swinging in the wind, *Chesapeake* fouled her opponent, and the two vessels were lashed together. "Boarders away!" cried Broke as he led fifty men onto the deck of the American frigate. With most of their officers shot down, the ship's polyglot crew fled below, and only her marine detachment made a stand. Gathered about the mainmast, they fought with bayonets and clubbed muskets until only a handful were still on their feet. "The enemy fought desperately, but in disorder," related Broke, who suffered a serious head wound in the melee but recovered. Within fifteen minutes of the firing of the first broadside, *Chesapeake* was in British hands. The "butcher's bill" was high—twenty-three British seamen killed and fifty-eight wounded, while forty-eight Americans were killed and ninety-nine wounded.

The sight of *Chesapeake* being shepherded into Halifax with the white ensign flying above the Stars and Stripes sent British spirits soaring, and the Royal Navy regained a portion of the luster lost in previous engagements with the Yankees. Broke was knighted, and his gunnery reforms were adopted by other officers.

Little more than two months later, the brig *Argus,* which had captured twenty British merchantmen in British waters, was brought to bay by the brig *Pelican,* off Cornwall. The night before, *Argus* had captured a wine-laden vessel out of Oporto. The ship was burned, but not before some of the American sailors got into the cargo, which probably influenced their performance in action. Although *Argus* could have shown her heels to the slower British vessel, Master Commandant William H. Allen chose to give battle. The two vessels were almost equal in force, but the British fire was brisk, and in short order *Argus* struck her flag. The action reflected little credit on Allen, who lost a leg and died of his wounds. Like James Lawrence, he displayed a romantic élan but showed no understanding of strategic reality. To have continued *Argus*'s successful career as a commerce raider would have been far more damaging to Britain than the capture of an insignificant brig—and even that was bungled.

In vivid contrast, early in 1813 David Porter took the stoutly built *Essex* around Cape Horn into the Pacific, on what became a classic raiding voyage. Porter's objective was to destroy Britain's Pacific whaling fleet off the Galapagos Islands, and at the same time to protect American vessels engaged in the trade. Within six months he captured a dozen whalers as well as several other ships with a total value of $2.5 million. Porter accomplished all this even though he had no base from which to operate and lived off captured supplies and gear. Prizes were so plentiful that twelve-year-old Midshipman David Glasgow Farragut, the captain's ward, was assigned to one of them. When *Essex* required a refit, Porter sailed her three thousand miles across the Pacific to the Marquesas, where his crew had a taste of life in the South Seas while they overhauled their ship.

Early in 1814 *Essex* put into Valparaiso, Chile, where two British vessels, the frigate *Phoebe* and the sloop-of-war *Cherub*, which had been searching for the raider, caught up with her. Although *Essex* was rated at thirty-two guns, she actually mounted forty-six. *Phoebe* was similarly armed, and *Cherub* mounted twenty-six. *Essex* could have dealt with either of the enemy vessels singly, but together they were more than a match for her. Moreover, the American ship's main battery consisted of short-range carronades, while *Phoebe* carried long eighteens, which meant she could stand off and demolish her opponent at long range without danger to herself. The ships lay in sight of each other for the better part of a month while waging a propaganda war. *Essex* hoisted a large white flag emblazoned "Free trade and sailors' rights"; the British countered with "God and country, British sailors' best rights."

On March 28, 1814, the wind blew up and *Essex* slipped her cable and headed for the open sea. Escape seemed possible until a sudden squall struck her, sending the frigate's main-topmast by the board. *Phoebe* and *Cherub* bore down on the disabled vessel as she lay in a small cove about three miles from Valparaiso. Porter made excellent use of his few long twelves and forced his opponents to draw off to make repairs. Taking up positions where *Essex*'s guns could not bear, they began systematically to shoot her to pieces. Midshipman Farragut later recalled that one gun was manned three times, one crew after another having been wiped out. As he helped work another gun, a single shot killed four of the gunners. Unable to close with the enemy, Porter tried to run *Essex* ashore and put the torch

Commodore David Porter. (U.S. Naval Academy Museum)

to her, but there was no escape. The spectacular odyssey of the Salem frigate
was over, and more than half her crew were either killed or wounded.

INCREASINGLY, AS THE British blockade of the U.S. Navy's warships tightened, the task of twisting the lion's tail fell to the privateers that had fanned
out across the sea lanes at the beginning of hostilities. It is estimated that
at least 515 privateers were commissioned, mostly from Massachusetts,
New York, and Maryland. They were credited with capturing 1,346 vessels, and probably took others that were not reported. Many of these vessels were bagged off the coast of Portugal and Spain, where the victims
were engaged in carrying supplies to Wellington's army. Navy ships captured another 165 prizes.

To meet the needs of the privateersman, as well as those of slavers and smugglers, ship designers had developed the swift-sailing Baltimore clipper, a topsail schooner with a slim hull crowned by two tall masts and an immense spread of canvas. Usually armed with one "Long Tom" and several smaller guns, they were among the most graceful ships ever built, leading even a landsman such as Henry Adams to rhapsodize:

> Beautiful beyond anything then known in naval construcion . . . the schooner was a wonderful invention. Not her battles, but her escapes won for her the open-mouthed admiration of the British captains who saw their prize double like a hare and slip through their fingers at the moment when capture was sure. Under any ordinary conditions of wind and weather, with an open sea, the schooner, if only she could get to windward, laughed at a frigate.

Privateer skippers often matched their ships in dash and daring. Captain Thomas Boyle of Baltimore raised havoc in the waters around Britain, first in the *Comet* and then in *Chasseur*. The profits from one cruise alone were $400,000. Taking a leaf from the British, Boyle, in the summer of 1814, published a mock proclamation putting the British Isles under blockade. Within two months he captured eighteen ships, burning them after removing their cargoes, which were valued at $100,000. The Baltimore schooner *Kemp* snatched five of the seven vessels in a convoy from under the nose of the escort and returned to port—all within eight days. The prizes were sold for $500,000, making this probably the war's shortest and most successful cruise.

ALTHOUGH PRIVATEERS WERE not supposed to engage British men of war, Captain Samuel Chester Reid of the seven-gun brig *General Armstrong* successfully violated this rule. Having captured twenty-four enemy prizes, Reid had taken shelter in the neutral port of Fayal in the Azores, where on September 26, 1814, the harbor was sealed by a squadron of British warships. Captain Robert Lloyd sent four boats carrying a hundred men rowing towards the *Armstrong*. Reid opened fire with his nine-pounders and the British withdrew.

The next night Lloyd launched another attack, this time with twelve boats carrying four hundred men. The attackers were badly cut up but kept coming. When the British boats bumped against the side of their ship, the Yankee privateersmen heaved cannonballs down into the craft, punching holes in the bottoms of several. Undeterred, the British swarmed on board the *Armstrong*. Reid and his ninety men met them with cutlass, pistol, and pike and the battle surged back and forth along the vessel's deck. The slaughter among the boarding party was appalling. In forty minutes, Reid estimated, nearly two-thirds of its members were casualties, and the survivors plunged into sea. Two Americans were killed, seven wounded.

Lloyd declared that he would have the privateer at all costs. At daybreak, he sent the 18-gun sloop-of-war *Carnation* to finish the *Armstrong*. Reid replied as best he could, but his ship was shot to pieces. He scuttled the vessel, and as she sank, the surviving Americans swam ashore and took refuge in a convent outside Fayal. Claiming that several of the privateer's crew were deserters from the Royal Navy, Lloyd had them rounded up. But he could not prove his claim, and the Portuguese authorities ordered the Americans released.

Yet, for all the enthusiasm with which Americans embraced privateering, it was not an effective weapon of war. Privateers damaged British commerce and sometimes captured valuable cargoes, but they were no substitute for a navy. They did nothing to weaken the stranglehold that the British had on the American coast, and possibly half the prizes captured by the privateers ended back in British hands when they were caught trying to make port. Throttled by the blockade and British privateers, which cost the Yankees some fourteen hundred vessels, American trade sank to disastrous levels. Exports dropped to only $6.9 million in 1814. A Boston newspaper presented a gloomy picture of conditions: "Our harbors blockaded, our shipping destroyed or rotting at the docks; silence and stillness in our cities; the grass growing upon the public wharves." The American merchant marine was paying a stiff price for the Jeffersonian theory that it was not necessary to have a seagoing navy to protect the nation's shipping.

⟿

WITH THE WAR AT SEA now going against the Americans, attention was increasingly focused on the Great Lakes. The defeat of General William Hull on the northern frontier in the opening months of hostilities convinced President Madison and his advisers that control of the lakes was essential to successful operations against Canada. Few roads existed in the wilderness, and the chain of lakes provided the only satisfactory means of moving large military forces. Captain Isaac Chauncey was given command of American naval forces on the lakes and the task of overcoming British naval supremacy there. He made his headquarters on Lake Ontario, where both sides' strongest forces were deployed.

Chauncey proved to be a conservative and methodical officer. Except for a few indecisive skirmishes, he and his British opposite number, Captain Sir James Yeo, conducted "a warfare of Dockyards and Arsenals" in which one side and then the other won temporary supremacy on Lake Ontario. By the time the war ended, the British had completed a 102-gun ship of the line and the Americans had two three-deckers of 120 guns each on the stocks.

Master Commandant Oliver Hazard Perry, who directed the American naval effort on Lake Erie, was more vigorous than Chauncey. The twenty-seven-year-old Perry had been in command of a gunboat flotilla at Newport and had sought more active service. When he realized the magnitude of the task given him, he may well have wondered at the wisdom of his request: his mission was nothing less than to build a fleet in the wilderness and use it to wrest control of the lake from a superior British force. Perry established his base at Presque Isle (now Erie, Pennsylvania), toward the northern end of the lake, early in 1813, and there, with the assistance of two remarkable craftsmen, Adam and Noah Brown, Perry set about building a fleet.

Originally the Browns were carpenters and house-builders rather than shipwrights, but they had opened a shipyard in New York a year before the war. With the outbreak of hostilities, they designed and built several privateers that were notable for their clean lines and speed. Using the green timber that grew beside the lake, Noah Brown, who was in charge of construction, built Perry two twenty-gun brigs—*Lawrence* and *Niagara*—and a flotilla of smaller craft. Iron, cordage, canvas, oakum, almost everything required for the building of the ships, as well as guns and munitions, had to be hauled overland from Pittsburgh or sailed from Buffalo. "The amount of work that Brown accomplished with about two hundred men, without power tools, and in a wilderness during the worst winter months, makes some of the modern wartime production feats something less than impressive," notes Howard Chapelle, a historian of the sailing navy. "The man was tireless and ingenious."

Although Perry had brought the nucleus of his crews with him from Newport, his ships were still shorthanded. Most seamen in the coastal ports avoided service on the lakes, even though a bonus of 25 percent was offered. There was little prospect of prize money in this frontier region, and Secretary of the Navy William Jones observed that such service was regarded as "one of peculiar privation, destitute of pecuniary stimulus." Perry pleaded for men from Chauncey's near-idle force, but Chauncey released only a handful. Relations between the two officers were so strained that Perry submitted his resignation, but the Navy Department refused it. To fill out his crews, Perry recruited untrained militiamen, Indians, and even one Russian who spoke no English. Fully one quarter of the men signed on and trained as sailors and marines were black.

While Perry was building his fleet, it was protected from British raids by a sandbar at the mouth of the harbor at Presque Isle. Now, he faced the problem of getting *Lawrence* and *Niagara* over the shoal in the face of a British blockade. Fortunately for the Americans, the British force, under the command of Commander Robert H. Barclay, a one-armed veteran of Trafalgar, left its station for a few days in August. Seizing the opportunity, Perry removed the guns from his heavier ships, and using "camels," or pontoons, floated them over the bar. Unexpectedly faced with this powerful force, Barclay wished to avoid battle until he had strengthened his own flotilla, but he was short of provisions and could not afford to delay very long.

The two fleets met about twenty miles north of Put-in-Bay at the western end of the lake on September 10, 1813. Perry's squadron consisted of nine vessels firing a total broadside of 896 pounds, to Barclay's six vessels and broadside of 459 pounds. The Americans also had more long guns than the British, even though *Lawrence* and *Niagara* were armed primarily with carronades. Flying a blue banner emblazoned with James Lawrence's dying words, "Don't give up the ship," in white letters, Perry led his fleet into battle in *Lawrence*. *Niagara* was commanded by Jesse D. Elliott, who had been senior officer on Lake Erie before Perry's arrival. Four years older than Perry, he was junior to him on the Navy List and was not happy with his subordinate position.

Perry bore down on the British line in a single column, and *Lawrence*, which was in the van, absorbed the bulk of the enemy fire. Shortly before noon, the band on *Detroit*, Barclay's flagship, struck up "Rule Britannia!" as her long twenty-fours pounded the slowly approaching Yankee flagship. Perry could not reply effectively because the range was too great for his guns. Shot thudded into *Lawrence's* hull, and lines and blocks trailed from aloft. Large splinters flew about like straw in a wind. Perry closed with *Detroit*, and the ships engaged at pistol range. Almost all the British fire was soon trained on *Lawrence*. Some of Perry's smaller ships and gunboats came to his aid, but Elliott, in *Niagara*, stood off, taking no part in the action.

The battle was fought at such close range that every shot struck home. Both *Detroit* and *Lawrence* suffered terribly. Barclay was badly wounded, as were many of his officers. *Lawrence* had gone into action with a crew of 103 men; all but 20 were killed or wounded. Many of the wounded were maimed again or killed while they were being treated, because the cockpit was above the waterline. Within two hours almost all her guns had been dismounted, and there were not enough unwounded men to fire those that were left. Perry summoned the surgeon's assistants to lend a hand at the guns and, when no one else was left, called down into the cockpit: "Can any of the wounded pull a rope?" Several pitiful figures limped up to the deck to help him aim and fire the few remaining cannon.

Finally, at about 2:30 P.M., when *Lawrence's* last gun had fallen silent, Perry decided to transfer to *Niagara*. Taking his twelve-year-old brother James, who was serving as a midshipman, four seamen, his broad pennant, and the flag bearing Lawrence's words, he had himself rowed a half mile through a hail of shot to Elliott's undamaged vessel. *Lawrence*, now an unmanageable wreck, surrendered, but the otherwise engaged British did not take possession of her.

Wasting no time in recriminations, Perry ordered Elliott to take the boat and bring up the remaining vessels of the squadron. *Niagara's* sails caught a sudden breeze, and Perry, to the cheers of the rest of his ships, signaled close action and drove the brig, her guns pouring smoke and flames, into the enemy line. The British were in no condition to resist this fresh onslaught, and one after another, the battered ships struck their colors. Perry's victory gave the Americans complete command of Lake Erie and allowed them to regain control of the Northwest. As soon as the surrendered ships had been secured, Perry penned on the back of an old letter a dispatch to General William Henry Harrison, the military commander in the Northwest:

> We have met the enemy; and they are ours. Two ships, two Brigs, one schooner, and one Sloop.

FROM THE HEIGHTS of the Pyrenees, Wellington's victorious Redcoats looked down on the fertile fields of France in the autumn of 1813. In the remote distance they could see the Bay of Biscay, where the warships of the Royal Navy were perpetually on the move, and the white sails of transports bearing the men and supplies that had made their triumphs possible. Had their eyes been able to penetrate the misty autumn horizon eastward to the Saxony plain, they would have seen the steely glint of marching armies. Scarcely a French family was not in mourning after the Russian debacle, but Napoleon had bled the nation for another half-million conscripts, many lads of only sixteen.

Near Leipzig in mid-October 1813, three hundred thousand Russians, Austrians, Swedes, and Prussians closed in on two-thirds as many Frenchmen. Some of the most savage fighting of the war followed, and the dead and wounded covered the surrounding fields. "The Battle of the Nations" ended with the utter rout of Napoleon's army and casualties five times those at Austerlitz. Yet the war was not over. Though his sword was broken in his hand, the emperor rejected the offer of the allied rulers to cease hostilities if France would withdraw to her "natural frontiers" of the Rhine, the Alps, and the Pyrenees. His sense of reality apparently having departed, Napoleon rejected the offer and told Prince Metternich that he might lose his throne, but he would bury Europe in ruins.

Like Hitler, Napoleon saw the hope of a reversal of fortune in the possibility that his enemies, all deeply suspicious of each other, would fall out. Several times before, European coalitions had dissolved before him. If he could persuade his father-in-law, the Austrian emperor, to make a separate peace, he was convinced he could crush the Russians and the Prussians, whose forces were dangerously overextended. On March 13, 1814, Napoleon made his last coup by defeating the Prussians near Rheims in a tactical stroke not unlike Hitler's Ardennes offensive of 1944. But Napoleon's success was only temporary. Wellington was advancing on Toulouse, Paris was betrayed to the invaders by a defecting marshal, and Cossacks soon clattered down the Champs-Élysées. The wily Talleyrand, who had already ingratiated himself with Czar Alexander, proclaimed a rump government that declared the emperor dethroned.

Awaiting the end at Fontainebleau, Napoleon attempted to save something from the debacle by vainly trying to pass the throne to his three-year-old son and then abdicated unconditionally. Not long afterward, he swallowed a vial of poison he had carried on his person in Russia in case of capture. It had lost its potency and only made him sick. The allies allowed him to retain his title but his domain was limited to the tiny island of Elba in the Mediterranean. On April 28, 1814, with his personal entourage and an imperial guard of six hundred soldiers, Napoleon sailed for his new realm in the British frigate *Undaunted*.* In Belgium, King Louis XVIII, gross, old, and almost forgotten, awaited the summons to the throne of France. "There is only one step," Napoleon noted wryly, "from the sublime to the ridiculous."

~

WHILE ALL THE CAPITALS of Europe were celebrating Napoleon's fall, some twenty thousand of Wellington's veterans were crossing the Atlantic to put an end to the annoying American war. With more troops and ships on hand, the British launched a three-pronged assault against the United States: an invasion from Canada, an escalation of the raids on the American coast, and an attack on New Orleans. The major objective of these offensives was to win pawns for use in the peace negotiations already under way in Ghent, Belgium.

Facing no opposition, the British put troops ashore at almost any point on the coast, disrupting trade and preventing American naval vessels and privateers from getting to sea. The Chesapeake Bay area was a major theater for such operations, which were climaxed by an amphibious assault on Washington and Baltimore in the summer of 1814. A flotilla of Yankee gunboats tried to intervene in the attack on Washington, but these craft were brushed aside and then destroyed by their crews to prevent them from failing into enemy hands. An attempt at a stand was made at Bladensburg, outside the capital, but the raw militiamen broke and ran. The only resistance was offered by the sailors and marines from the gunboat flotilla under the command of Joshua Barney, an old Revolutionary War hero. The British put the Capitol and other public buildings to the torch in revenge for the burning of York, the capital of Upper Canada. President Madison and most of the government fled.

*His wife, Marie Louise, had left him with their son and did not join him on Elba.

The invaders now turned their attention to Baltimore, which, as the home port of 126 privateers, was regarded as "a nest of pirates." Stalled by the city's hastily erected defenses, a British army of nearly five thousand men waited for a fleet of frigates and bomb vessels to silence Fort McHenry, at the entrance to the harbor. The night-long bombardment on September 12 inspired Francis Scott Key, a Georgetown lawyer who witnessed the bombardment from the British fleet, to write the words of "The Star-Spangled Banner." The fleet's guns outranged those of the fort, but the ships were prevented from running past it by a line of sunken hulks that blocked the channel, and the attack failed. A few days later, the troops were reembarked, neither side having suffered much damage.

The invasion from Canada began in the summer of 1814. Sir George Prevost, the governor-general, followed the route of General John Burgoyne forty years before. He halted at Plattsburgh, on the western shore of Lake Champlain, and waited for the naval commander, Captain George Downie, to deal with a small American squadron under Master Commandant Thomas Macdonough. Prevost, with twelve thousand men, could easily have brushed aside the fifteen hundred Americans led by General Alexander Macomb who were defending Plattsburgh, but he insisted that as long as the Americans controlled the lake, his flank and supply lines would be endangered.

With the aid of Noah Brown, the thirty-one-year-old Macdonough, who had been with Decatur at the burning of *Philadelphia,* built his fleet on the shores of the lake. They worked with such speed that the largest ship, the twenty-six-gun corvette *Saratoga,* was completed in little more than a month. She was joined by *Eagle,* a twenty-gun brig delivered just five days before the squadron went into action, two other sailing vessels, and ten oar-propelled gunboats manned mostly by soldiers and a handful of sailors. The British squadron consisted of the powerful frigate *Confiance,* of thirty-six guns, one brig, two sloops, and ten gunboats. The two squadrons were about equal in firepower.

Macdonough realized that to command Lake Champlain, he needed only to maintain what Mahan called "a fleet in being," while Downie, to gain control, had to win a decisive victory. Accordingly, Macdonough decided to anchor his vessels in Plattsburgh Bay, a deep inlet on the western side of the lake, and await a British attack, as Benedict Arnold had done at Valcour during the Revolution. Macdonough ordered his vessels drawn up in a line from Cumberland Head to the shallows off Crab Island, close to the shore, so it could not be turned. As an added precaution, he had springs run out of the sterns of his vessels and attached to their anchor cables, which allowed them to be swung so their guns could be brought to bear on the approaching British.

Downie had wanted to delay going into action until he had time to train his crews, which included a number of Canadian militiamen, but he was prodded along by Prevost. As a result, *Confiance* went into battle with the fitters still on board. The British sailed southward on September 11, propelled along the reed-lined shore by a light breeze. When they were sighted off Cumberland Head, Macdonough, a devout man, called *Saratoga*'s officers and crew to prayers—and then to quarters. Most of the ranging shots fired by the British fell short, but one splintered a coop that housed a pet gamecock. Unharmed, the bird flew to a nearby gun, where it flapped its wings and crowed defiantly. To Macdonough's crews, this seemed a good omen, and they cheered lustily. The commodore himself laid one of the first twenty-four-pounders that bore on the approaching British flagship, and the shot struck home.

Sailing into the bay in line abreast, the British came under heavy fire from the Americans. Downie tried to pass down the Yankee line, but in lee of Cumberland Head, the wind fell and he was forced to anchor *Confiance* only three hundred yards from Macdonough's flagship. A British broadside smashed into *Saratoga*, and her deck ran red with blood. Some forty men were killed or wounded. Nevertheless, she kept up a brisk fire. Fifteen minutes later, one of *Confiance*'s cannon was dismounted and crushed Downie. The death of their commander so early in the battle had a serious effect on British morale. Macdonough himself had several narrow escapes. As he was aiming a gun, he was knocked unconscious by a falling spar. Later, a round shot tore the head off one of the gun's crew and drove it into Macdonough's face with such force that he was knocked sprawling.

Fighting spread up and down the line, and two British sloops and a small American vessel were put out of action. *Saratoga* and *Confiance* suffered the most, and both were taking on water. *Saratoga* was hulled 55 times and *Confiance* 105, Macdonough reported. Within two hours of the start of the battle, every one of *Saratoga*'s starboard guns had been put out of action. Heaving in on his spring, Macdonough had his ship pulled around so her undamaged port battery faced *Confiance*. The British tried the same trick but failed—and were caught by *Saratoga*'s merciless fire. One by one, the British vessels surrendered. Both sides had suffered severely. American casualties totaled more than a hundred killed and wounded, and Macdonough estimated that the British lost double this number.

Macdonough's victory forced Prevost, whose simultaneous assault on Plattsburgh was repulsed by Macomb, to call off the invasion, and its effects reverberated far beyond the lake frontier. The peace talks at Ghent had stalled over British insistence on retaining all the territory she had conquered during the war, with a view to creating an Indian "buffer state" in the Northwest Territory between Canada and the United States. But the duke of Wellington, who had been offered command of British forces in America, said that unless Britain regained "a naval supremacy on the Lakes" peace should be made at once—and without territorial demands.

And Lord Castlereagh, the foreign secretary, regarded the war as a tiresome distraction while he was fully occupied with the much more pleasant task of reshaping the post-Napoleonic world at a conference in Vienna. On Christmas Eve 1814 Britain and the United States signed a peace treaty that made no mention of impressment, the Orders in Council, or Britain's violations of neutral rights, the reasons given by Madison for declaring war. The end of the conflict with Napoleon had rendered these issues moot.

⁓

ALTHOUGH THE WAR was officially over, the fighting was not. News traveled slowly in those days, so the British continued their preparation for the descent on New Orleans. The expedition appeared off the mouth of the Mississippi on December 8, 1814, but before the British could advance against the city, they had to deal with a scattering of small sailing vessels and gunboats commanded by Master Commandant Daniel T. Patterson. The shortest route to the city led though Lake Borgne, a shallow bayou that opened up to the sea. Patterson stationed five gunboats there under Lieutenant Thomas ap Catesby Jones. Forty-two British launches, each armed with a carronade and carrying a total of a thousand men, captured all of Jones's craft in a short, bloody battle on December 14, but at the cost of about a hundred men killed and wounded—and valuable time, which General Andrew Jackson put to good use in preparing his defense of New Orleans.

By December 23 the British had pushed to within nine miles of the city but were thrown into confusion when the fourteen-gun schooner *Carolina* bombarded their encampment and Jackson launched a supporting attack. The Americans were driven off, but the final assault on the city had to be delayed until heavy guns could be brought up from the fleet to deal with *Carolina*. Although the schooner was eventually destroyed, *Louisiana*, of sixteen guns and the sole survivor of Patterson's squadron, took part in repulsing the British attack on New Orleans on January 8, 1815. It was the worst British defeat in open battle for many years. Recognizing the important role the navy had played in the fight, a grateful Andrew Jackson told Patterson: "To your well-directed exertions must be ascribed in a great degree that embarrassment of the enemy which led to his ignominious flight."

⁓

THROUGHOUT THE CLOSING months of the war, American naval captains impatiently awaited opportunities to escape the vigilant British blockading squadrons that lay offshore. *Constitution* managed to escape from Boston in December 1814, and *President* slipped to sea from New York in January 1815 during a blinding snowstorm. Decatur's fabled luck soon ran out, however. *President* was severely damaged when the pilot ran her aground. Decatur managed to free the frigate and later said he would have returned to port had not the severity of the storm prevented him. The limping *President* was sighted by a British squadron consisting of *Majestic*, of fifty-six guns, and three frigates. Decatur tried to escape but was overhauled and forced to surrender. One of the pursuing vessels was knocked about by the Yankee frigate's guns, and *President* suffered in the exchange. "With about one-fifth of my crew killed and wounded, my ship crippled, and a more than four-fold force opposed to me, without a chance to escape left, I deemed it my duty to surrender," Decatur declared.

A month later, *Constitution*, sought by every ship of the Royal Navy since her escape from Boston, was cruising off Madeira when she encountered two British vessels, the light frigate *Cyane*, of twenty-two guns, and the sloop-of-war *Levant*, of twenty. The British captains gallantly if unwisely chose to fight. Within forty minutes, both ships were beaten into submission. Captain Charles Stewart put on one of the most brilliant demonstrations of shiphandling of the war. He attacked *Cyane*, backed down to engage *Levant*, then sailed ahead to reengage *Cyane*, and finally wore around to knock out *Levant*.

The Yankee sloops-of-war *Hornet* and *Peacock* also got to sea, and they took the last prizes of the war. *Hornet*, under Master Commandant James Biddle, captured the brig *Penguin*, of eighteen guns, after a twenty-minute fight in which the British vessel was transformed into little more than kindling. *Peacock* sailed into the Indian Ocean, where she captured four large Indiamen. On June 30, 1815, in Sunda Strait, she sighted a fourteen-gun brig belonging to the East India Company. The merchantman's skipper informed Master Commandant Lewis Warrington that the war was over. Believing this was a ruse designed to permit his prey to escape, Warrington ordered the brig to strike its flag and send a boat. When the Briton refused, Warrington poured a broadside into his vessel, causing fifteen casualties. The brig's name was *Nautilus*—the same as that of the first American vessel to be captured by the British at the beginning of the conflict three years before.

In years to come, Americans would forget the humiliations of the futile and inglorious War of 1812—the military defeats, the burning of the capital, the raids on the defenseless coast, and the blockade. With pride they recalled the exploits of Hull, Decatur, Perry, and Macdonough that had preserved the national honor and established a tradition of victory. By providing such a heritage, the U.S. Navy not only fostered a spirit of nationalism that at least temporarily put an end to narrow sectionalism that had threatened to tear the nation apart, it also gained popularity and acceptance for itself.

Epilogue

RIDING IN THE Basque Roads near Rochefort on the morning of July 15, 1815, the two-decker *Bellerophon* rocked comfortably in the long swells as a lookout sighted a boat coming out from shore. A familiar-looking figure—running to fat and wearing a cocked hat and a flowing olive overcoat over a green uniform—huddled in the stern sheets. A general's guard of honor snapped to attention and the boatswain's whistle wailed a salute as he came through the vessel's entry port. "At 7 received on board Napoleon Bonaparte, late Emperor of France," *Bellerophon's* log recorded laconically.

Napoleon had regained the empire he had lost in the mountains of Spain and the snows of Russia for a hundred days only to lose it again in the mud at Waterloo. Now, with every escape route closed, he had made arrangements to surrender to the most implacable of his enemies, the Royal Navy, in the person of Frederick Maitland, the "Billy Ruffian's" captain.

Restive in his exile on Elba, Napoleon had escaped from his Lilliputian domain little more than three months before to find the Napoleonic legend still vibrant in France. Troops sent by the Bourbons to arrest him as he made his way to Paris went over to his standard, and crowds of Frenchmen cheered him everywhere. Facing leveled muskets and bayonets at Grenoble, Napoleon stepped forward and threw open his coat to expose his chest. "Soldiers, if there is one among you who wishes to kill the Emperor he can do so," he declared. "Here I am!" Following a moment's hesitation, the muskets were lowered amid cheers and cries of *"Vive l'Empereur! Vive l'Empereur!"*

The European sovereigns, meeting in Vienna to make the world safe for autocracy, were attending a great ball given by Metternich. As the shocking news buzzed about the ballroom, the dancers abruptly broke off the waltz and stood uncertainly on the floor. Under the menace of the dreaded Bonapart's return, the monarchs set aside the internal quarrels that had delayed the making of peace to outlaw the Corsican ogre and to pledge themselves to his final destruction. The Continent's armies were mobilized and the duke of Wellington was appointed to command the advance guard in the Low Countries—the doorway to France—until the immense forces of Austria and Russia could be brought to bear.

Most of Wellington's Iberian Peninsula veterans were still in America, or on the high seas returning from that country, but every man available was sent in haste to Flanders. For the Royal Navy, the renewal of the war came after many of its ships had been paid off and were being dismantled. Ships that had just been laid up were hurriedly refitted and sent to sea to reimpose the blockade of the French coast. Lord Keith was appointed to command the Channel fleet, and Sir Edward Pellew was sent to the Mediterranean. "I am sending out all I have to look for Boney if he takes to the sea," Keith told his wife. By mid-June some two dozen men-of-war were on station between Ushant and Finisterre.

Napoleon mustered an army of 128,000 men and marched into Belgium to prevent the Prussians and the British from uniting against him. He was brought to bay at Waterloo on June 18, and fell victim to the steadfastness of the British soldier and the timely arrival on the field of the black-clad Prussians. In one final throw of the dice, Napoleon sent the elite Imperial Guard forward to attack Wellington's position on a plateau overlooking the battlefield. Undeterred by the pounding of enemy artillery, the guardsmen pressed forward like a rising tide. It crested the ridge, and for a moment the British line disappeared. And then, in a wild hail of bullets, the wave faltered and receded. By nightfall, Napoleon's last campaign was over, and 50,000 men—French, British and Prussian—had been killed or wounded.

For the third time, the Emperor abandoned an army in the field and hastened back to Paris. But there was no support for him there, and the empire slipped through his fingers. He toyed with the idea of trying to run the British blockade in a French frigate or a neutral American vessel and sailing to the United States, where anti-British sentiment was strong. No decision was made and in the confusion, Napoleon left Paris for Rochefort, riding past his unfinished Arch of Triumph with a few faithful followers. On the way he stopped at Malmaison, where he had lived with Josephine before their divorce. Briefly, he lingered alone in the room where she had died the previous year. Then he said his farewells to his mother and other relatives, including his two illegitimate sons.

From a window of the grim, gray house on the Gironde where he took shelter, the Emperor could see *Bellerophon* standing offshore like a sentinel blocking his escape. No ship better epitomized the British sea power that had always stood in the way of his conquests. The old ship had fought at the Glorious First of June, the very first fleet action of the war against France in 1794; at the Nile, where his dreams of oriental glory were dashed; and finally at Trafalgar, where his fleet had been annihilated. One morning, he heard *Bellerophon* firing her guns to celebrate the allied capture of Paris and the return of the Bourbons.

Always a master of the unexpected, Napoleon had one final surprise. Realizing at last that escape was impossible, he decided to throw himself on the mercy of the British. Writing directly to the prince regent, he asked permission to retire to the English countryside outside London and made arrangements to surrender to Captain Maitland. Like all other British naval officers who might capture Napoleon, Maitland had instructions to immediately return with the prisoner to the nearest English port. While the problem of what to do about him was debated, Napoleon remained on board *Bellerophon,* which went first to Tor Bay and then to Plymouth, where she remained offshore.

As she lay in the sound there, the ship became a tourist attraction. Hundred of small boats surrounded her, and Napoleon enjoyed the attention of his foes. Each day, no matter what his anxiety about his fate, he appeared on deck in plain view of the tourists, wearing the uniform of a colonel of the Imperial Guard. Sometimes he smiled and raised his hat to the ladies. He also expressed a keen interest in the operation of *Bellerophon,* questioning her officers and men about their duties. Language was no barrier; a number of the ship's complement spoke some French or Italian, his two languages. A midshipman would recall with delight many years later that when he gaped at the emperor, "the great Napoleon" smiled at him, cuffed his head lightly, and pinched his ear.

On July 31, Napoleon learned his fate. Much to his anger, he was told that he was to be banished to the remote South Atlantic island of St. Helena, from which it was thought he would be unable to escape and again upset the balance of Europe.* With a handful of oddly assorted followers, he sailed a week later in *Northumberland,* seventy-four, for his place of exile. Once at St. Helena, he entered into a strange half world between freedom and prison. There he spent the remaining six years of his life, gazing out to sea, rewriting history, and placing on others the blame for all that had gone wrong.

The navy that had played such a vital role in bringing about Napoleon's downfall did not long survive his reign. As soon as peace was assured, the ships were paid off, and the crews were mustered out. One by one, the twenty-seven ships of the line that had fought at Trafalgar met their fates: *Agamemnon,* "Nelson's favorite," had already broken her back in the River Plate; *Defence* was wrecked off Jutland and *Minotaur* at the mouth of the Texel; *Defiance* was degraded to a prison ship, and the same fate befell *Leviathan* as well as *Bellerophon* after her moment in the limelight; *Ajax* caught fire and blew up at Tenedos; Collingwood's *Royal Sovereign* was not even allowed to keep her name but finished her career as *Captain,* the

*Even today, St. Helena can only be reached by occasional freighter service.

receiving ship at Plymouth; *Téméraire*—"The Fighting *Téméraire*"—went to the shipbreakers, but not before being immortalized by J. W. Turner in a famous painting. Wreck, fire, convict hulk, target ship, the breaker's yard complete the roll. With the exception of *Victory* . . . Nelson's *Victory* . . . all vanished, leaving only a glorious memory.

In the end, Napoleon Bonaparte best summed it all up. While on board *Bellerophon,* the Emperor discussed with Captain Maitland the defense of Acre, in which the captain had taken part. Napoleon concluded by saying:

> If it had not been for you English, I should have been emperor of the East; but wherever there is water to float a ship, we are to find you in our way!

Appendix I: The Composition of the Royal Navy, 1793–1816*

on 1 Jan.	1st rates 100–120 guns	2nd rates 90–98 guns	3rd rates 64–80 guns	4th rates 50–60 guns	5th rates 32–44 guns	6th rates 20–28 guns	Sloops and other vessels	Total
1793	5	19	114	22	90	41	99	390
1794	6	19	117	22	94	42	120	420
1795	6	20	120	20	112	41	164	483
1796	6	19	117	30	118	44	200	534
1797	7	19	120	25	130	47	239	587
1798	8	20	130	25	135	49	293	660
1799	8	21	137	23	132	51	322	694
1800	9	19	136	26	132	47	360	729
1801	8	19	139	26	134	47	362	735
1802	8	19	138	26	141	44	370	746
1803	7	15	126	20	124	33	283	608
1804	7	15	129	20	128	33	291	623
1805	8	14	131	23	142	34	374	726
1806	8	15	139	22	153	36	416	789
1807	8	15	145	20	166	41	470	865
1808	8	14	165	19	175	46	494	921
1809	8	15	170	18	179	40	549	979
1810	8	15	177	17	185	40	534	976
1811	9	17	177	15	181	38	523	960
1812	9	15	181	14	173	30	476	898
1813	9	16	188	13	165	31	477	899
1814	9	12	183	19	180	40	493	936
1815	10	12	169	17	167	47	419	841
1816	9	14	150	17	147	42	364	743

*From William James, *Naval History of Great Britain.*

Appendix II: Nelson's Trafalgar Memorandum

NOTE: Subsequent insertions are shown within square brackets and deletions are given in italics.

Victory off Cádiz, 9 Octr. 1805

Mem[n.]

Thinking it almost impossible to bring a Fleet of forty Sail of the Line into a Line of Battle in variable winds thick weather and other circumstances which must occur, without such a loss of time that the opportunity would probably be lost of bringing the Enemy to Battle in such a manner as to make the business decisive.

I have [therefore] made up my mind to keep the fleet in that position of sailing (with the exception of the first and Second in Command) that the order of Sailing is to be the Order of Battle, placing the fleet in two Lines of Sixteen Ships each with an advanced Squadron of Eight of the fasting [*sic*] sailing Two decked ships [which] will always make if wanted a Line of Twenty four Sail, on which ever Line the Commander in Chief may direct.

The Second in Command will *in fact Command* [his line] *and* after my intentions are made known to him *will* have the entire direction of His Line to make the attack upon the Enemy and to follow up the Blow until they are Captured or destroy'd.

If the Enemy's fleet should be seen to Windward [in Line of Battle] *but* [and] *in that position that* the Two Lines and the Advanced Squadron can fetch them (I *shall suppose them forty Six Sail* [in] *of the Line of Battle*) they will probably be so extended that their Van could not succour their Rear.

I should therefore probably make *your* the 2nd in Commds signal to Lead through about their Twelfth Ship from their Rear (or wherever *you* [He] could fetch if not able to get so far advanced) My Line would lead through about their Centre and the Advanced Squadron to cut two or three or four Ships Ahead of their Centre, so as to ensure getting at their Commander In Chief on whom every effort must be made to Capture.

The whole impression of the British [fleet] must be, to overpower from two or three Ships ahead of their Commander In Chief, supposed to be in the centre, to the Rear of their fleet. [I will suppose] twenty Sail of the [Enemys] Line to be untouched, it must be some time before they could perform a Manoeuvre to bring their force compact to attack any part of the British fleet engaged, or to succour their own ships which indeed would be impossible, without mixing with the ships engaged.* Something must be left to chance, nothing is sure in a sea fight beyond all others, shot will carry away the masts and yards of friends as well as foes, but I look with confidence to a victory before the van of the Enemy could succour their *friends* [Rear] and then that the British Fleet would most of them be ready to receive their Twenty Sail of the Line or to pursue them should they endeavour to make off.

If the Van of the Enemy tacks the Captured Ships must run to Leeward of the British fleet, if the Enemy wears the British must place themselves between the Enemy and the captured & disabled British Ships and should the Enemy close I have no fear as to the result.

The Second in Command will in all possible things direct the Movements of his Line by keeping them as compact as the nature of their circumstances will admit *and* Captains are to look to their particular Line as their rallying point. But in case signals can neither be seen or perfectly understood no Captain can do very wrong if he places his Ship alongside that of an Enemy.

Of the intended attack from to Windward, the Enemy in Line of Battle ready to receive an attack:

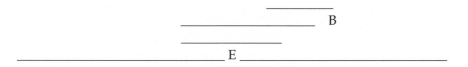

The Division of the British fleet will be brought nearly within Gun Shot of the Enemy's Centre. The signal will most probably [then] be made for the Lee Line to bear up together to set all their sails even steering sails† in order to get as quickly as possible to the Enemys Line and to cut through beginning from the 12 ship from the Enemies rear. Some ships may not get through their exact place, but they will always be at hand to assist their

*The Enemy's Fleet is supposed to consist of 46 Sail of the Line—British Fleet of 40—if either is less only a proportionate number of Enemy's ships are to be cut off; B to be 1/4 superior to E cut off.

†*Vide* instructions for Signal Yellow with Blue fly, page 17, eight Flat Signal Book, with reference to Appendix. [This and the above note were both written by Nelson in the margin.]

friends and if any are thrown round the Rear of the Enemy they will effectually compleat the business of Twelve Sail of the Enemy Should the Enemy wear together or bear up and sail Large still the Twelve Ships composing in the first position the Enemys rear are to be [the] Object of attack of the Lee Line unless otherwise directed from the Commander In Chief which is scarcely to be expected as the entire management of the Lee Line after the intentions of the Commander In Chief is [are] signified as intended to be left to the Judgement of the Admiral Commanding that Line.

The Remainder of the Enemys fleet 34 Sail are to be left to the Management of the Commander In Chief who will endeavour to take care that the Movements of the Second in Command are as little interrupted as is possible.

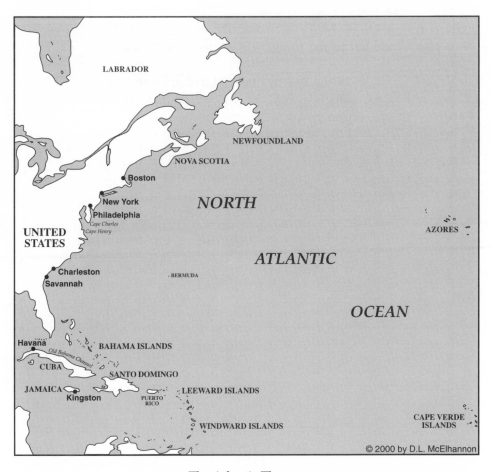

The Atlantic Theater

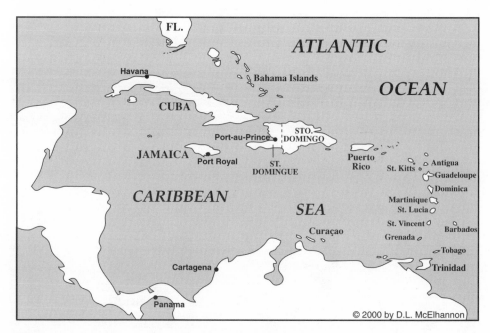

The Caribbean Theater

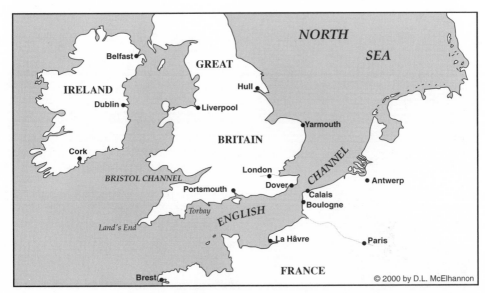

The English Channel and North Sea Theater

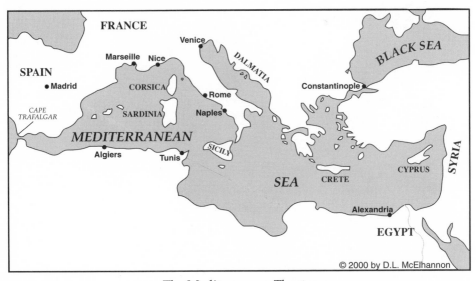

The Mediterranean Theater

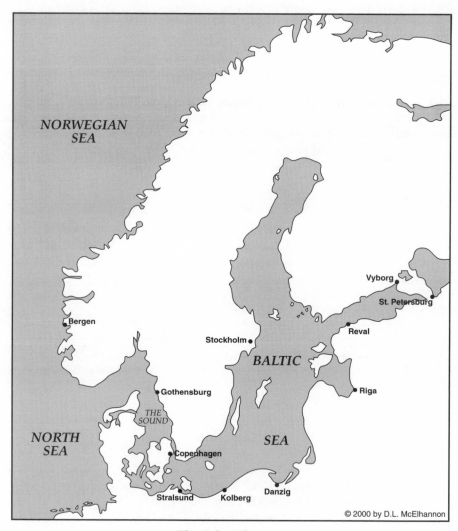

The Baltic Theater

Bibliography

Documents

American State Papers. Vol. 1, *Naval Affairs.* Washington, D.C.: Gales and Seaton, 1834.

The Despatches of Molyneux Shuldham, Vice-Admiral of the Blue and Commander-in-Chief of His Britannic Majesty's Ships in North America, January–July 1776. Edited by Robert W. Neeser. New York: Naval History Society, 1913.

Fighting Instructions, 1530–1816, vol. 19. Edited by Julian S. Corbett. London: Naval Records Society, 1905.

The Graves Papers and Other Documents Relating to the Naval Operations of the Yorktown Campaign. Edited by Francis E. Chadwick. New York: Naval History Society, 1916.

Journal of Rear Admiral Bartholomew James, vol. 6. Edited by John Knox Laughton. London: Naval Records Society, 1896.

The Keith Papers, vols. 62, 90, 96. Edited by Chistopher Lloyd. London: Naval Records Society, 1927–1955.

Letters of Admiral of the Fleet Lord St. Vincent, vols. 55, 61. Edited by David Boone Smith. London: Naval Records Society, 1927.

Letters and Papers of Admiral Thomas Byam Martin, vols. 14, 19, 24. Edited by Richard V. Hamilton. London: Naval Records Society, 1898–1903.

Letters and Papers of Charles, Lord Barham, vols. 32, 38. Edited by John Knox Laughton. London: Naval Records Society, 1906, 1910.

Letters Received by the Secretary of the Navy: Captains' Letters. National Archives, M-125.

Letters Received by the Secretary of the Navy: Commanders' Letters. National Archives, M-147.

Logs of the Great Sea Fights, 1794–1805, vols. 16, 18. Edited by T. Sturges Jackson. London: Naval Records Society, 1900–1901.

The Naval Chronicle, 40 vols. London: J. Gold, 1799–1818.

Nelson's Letters. Edited by Geoffrey Rawson. London: Everyman's Library, 1960.

Nelson's Letters to His Wife, vol. 100. Edited by George P. B. Naish. London: Naval Records Society, 1955.

Papers Relating to the Blockade of Brest, vols. 14, 21. Edited by John Leyland. London: Naval Records Society, 1899–1902.

The Private Correspondence of Admiral Lord Collingwood, vol. 98. Edited by Edward Hughes. London: Naval Records Society, 1956.

The Private Papers of John, Earl of Sandwich, vols. 69, 71, 75, 78. Edited by G. R. Barnes. London: Naval Records Society, 1932–1936.

Recollections of James Anthony Gardner, vol. 31. Edited by John Knox Laughton. London: Naval Records Society, 1907.

The Royal Navy in the River Plate, 1806–7, vol. 135. Edited by J. D. Grainger. London: Naval Records Society, 1996.

Ships' Logs. National Archives, RG 24.

U.S. Navy Department. *Naval Documents of the American Revolution.* Edited by William Bell Clark, William J. Morgan, and William S. Dudley. Ten vols. to date. Washington, D.C.: U.S. Government Printing Office, 1964–1996.

———. *Naval Documents Related to the United States War with the Barbary Pirates,* 6 vols. Edited by Dudley W. Knox. Washington, D.C.: U.S. Government Printing Office, 1939–1944.

———. *Naval Documents Relating to the Quasi-War with France,* 7 vols. Edited by Dudley W. Knox. Washington, D.C.: U.S. Government Printing Office, 1935–1938.

———. *The Naval War of 1812: A Documentary History,* 2 vols. Edited by William Dudley. Washington, D.C.: U.S. Government Printing Office, 1985–1992.

Bibliographies

Albion, Robert Greenhalgh. *Maritime and Naval History.* Rev. ed. Mystic, Conn.: Maritime Historical Association, 1955.

Coletta, Paolo. *A Bibliography of American Naval History.* Annapolis, Md.: Naval Institute Press, 1981.

Cowie, Leonard W. *Lord Nelson: 1758–1805.* Westport, Conn.: Meckler, 1990.

List of Admiralty Records Preserved in the Public Record Office. New York: Kraus, 1963.

Mainwaring, G. E. *A Bibliography of British Naval History.* London: Conway, 1970.

Smith, Myron J. *The American Sailing Navy, 1789–1860.* Metuchen, N.J.: Scarecrow Press, 1974.

Warner, Oliver. *Lord Nelson: A Guide to Reading.* London: Caravel Press, 1955.

Books and Articles

Adams, Henry. *A History of the United States During the Administrations of Jefferson and Madison,* 2 vols. New York: Library of America, 1995.

Albion, Robert Greenhalgh. *Forests and Sea Power.* Cambridge, Mass.: Harvard University Press, 1926.

———. *Makers of Naval Policy, 1798-1947.* Edited by Rowena Reed. Annapolis, Md.: Naval Institute Press, 1980.

Albion, Robert Greenhalgh, and Jennie B. Pope. *Sea Lanes in Wartime.* New York: W. W. Norton, 1942.

Allen, Gardner W. *A Naval History of the American Revolution,* 2 vols. Boston: Houghton Mifflin, 1913.

———. *Our Naval War with France.* Boston: Houghton Mifflin, 1909.

———. *Our Navy and the Barbary Corsairs.* Boston: Houghton Mifflin, 1905.

Archibald, E. H. *The Wooden Fighting Ship in the Royal Navy.* London: Blanford, 1968.

Arthur, Charles B. *The Remaking of the English Navy by Admiral St. Vincent.* Lanham, Md.: University Press of America, 1986.

Bass, William B. "Who Did Design the First U.S. Frigates?" *Naval History* (November 1991).

Baugh, Daniel A. "The Politics of British Naval Failure, 1775–1777." *American Neptune* (Fall, 1992).

Beirne, Francis F. *The War of 1812.* New York: E. P. Dutton, 1949.

Bennett, Geoffrey. *The Battle of Trafalgar.* Annapolis, Md.: Naval Institute Press, 1977.

———. *Nelson the Commander.* New York: Charles Scribner's Sons, 1972.

Berckman, Evelyn. *Nelson's Dear Lord: Earl St. Vincent.* London: Macmillan, 1962.

———. *The Unknown Navy.* London: Hamish Hamilton, 1973.

Bolster, W. Jeffrey. *Black Jacks: African-American Seamen in the Age of Sail.* Cambridge, Mass.: Harvard University Press, 1997.

Bonnett, Stanley. *The Price of Admiralty.* London: Robert Hale, 1968.

Bowen, A., ed. *The Naval Monument.* Boston: George Clark, 1840.

Brady, William. *The Kedge-Anchor; or Young Sailors' Assistant.* New York: Author, 1847.

Browne, Douglas C. *The Floating Bulwark.* New York: St. Martin's Press, 1963.

Bryant, Arthur. *The Age of Elegance.* New York: Harper & Brothers, 1950.

———. *Years of Endurance.* London: Collins, 1942.

———. *Years of Victory.* London: Collins, 1945.

Cecil, Henry. *A Matter of Speculation: The Case of Lord Cochrane.* London: Hutchison, 1965.

Chapelle, Howard I. *The History of the American Sailing Navy.* New York: W. W. Norton, 1949.

Clark, William Bell. *Lambert Wickes: Sea Raider and Diplomat.* New Haven, Conn.: Yale University Press, 1932.

———. *The Story of Nicholas Biddle of the Continental Navy.* Baton Rouge: Louisiana State University Press, 1949.

Clowes, William L. *The Royal Navy,* vols. iv, v. London: Sampson Low, 1899.

Coad, Jonathan. *The Royal Dockyards 1690–1850.* Aldershot, Eng.: Scolar, 1989.

Cooper, James Fenimore. *History of the Navy of the United States,* 2 vols. London: R. Bentley, 1839.

Corbett, J. S. *The Campaign of Trafalgar.* London: Longmans, Green, 1910.

Cormack, William S. *Revolution and Political Conflict in the French Navy.* Cambridge, Eng.: Cambridge University Press, 1995.

Cranwell, John Phillips and William Bowers Crane. *Men of Marque.* New York: W. W. Norton, 1940.

Creswell, John. *British Admirals of the Eighteenth Century.* London: Allen & Unwin, 1972.

Crowhurst, Patrick. *The French War on Trade: Privateering, 1793–1815.* Aldershot, Eng.: Scolar, 1989.

Dann, J. C., ed. *The Nagle Journal.* New York: Weidenfeld & Nicholson, 1988.

Davies, David. *Nelson's Navy.* Mechanicsburg, Pa.: Stackpole, 1997.

Deane, Anthony. *Nelson's Favourite: H.M.S. Agamemnon at War, 1781–1809.* Annapolis, Md.: Naval Institute Press, 1996.

de Kay, James Tertius. *Chronicles of the Frigate Macedonian.* New York: W. W. Norton, 1995.

Donovan, Frank. *The Tall Frigates.* New York: Dodd, Mead, 1962.

Duffy, Michael. *Soldiers, Sugar, and Sea Power.* Oxford, Eng.: Oxford University Press, 1987.

Dugan, James. *The Great Mutiny.* New York: G. P. Putnam's Sons, 1965.

Dundonald, Thomas, Tenth Earl. *Autobiography of a Seaman,* 2 vols. London: R. Bentley, 1860.

Dunne, W. M. P. "The *Constellation* and the *Hermione.*" *Mariner's Mirror* (August 1984).

Dye, Ira. "Early Merchant Seafarers." *Proceedings of the American Antiquarian Society, 120.*

Eckert, Edward K. *The Navy Department in the War of 1812.* Gainesville, Fla.: University of Florida Press, 1973.

Edwards, Samuel. *Barbary General: The Life of William H. Eaton.* Englewood Cliffs, N.J.: Prentice-Hall, 1968.

Estes, J. Worth. "Naval Medicine in the Age of Sail: The Voyage of the *New York,* 1802–1803." *Bulletin of the History of Medicine* 1982.

Ferguson, Eugene S. *Truxton of the Constellation.* Baltimore: Johns Hopkins University Press, 1956.

Field, James A., Jr. *Americans and the Mediterranean World.* Princeton, N.J.: Princeton University Press, 1969.

Forester, C. S. *The Age of Fighting Sail.* Garden City, N.Y.: Doubleday, 1956.

Fortescue, John W. *History of the British Army,* vols. III and IV. London: Macmillan, 1906.

Fowler, William M., Jr. *Jack Tars and Commodores: The American Navy, 1783–1815.* Boston: Houghton Mifflin, 1984.

———. *Rebels Under Sail.* New York: Charles Scribner's Sons, 1976.

Fraser, Edward. *The Sailors Whom Nelson Led.* London: Methuen, 1913.

Fremantle, Anne, ed. *The Wynne Diaries,* 3 vols. London: Oxford University Press, 1935.

French, David. *The British Way in Warfare, 1688–2000.* London: Unwin Hyman, 1990.

Fuller, J. F. C. *A Military History of the Western World,* vol. 2. New York: Funk & Wagnalls, 1955.

Gardiner, Leslie. *The British Admiralty.* London: Blackwood, 1968.

Gardiner, Richard, ed. *The Campaign of Trafalgar.* Annapolis, Md.: Naval Institute Press, 1997.

———. *Fleet Battles and Blockade.* Annapolis, Md.: Naval Institute Press, 1996.

———. *The Naval War of 1812.* Annapolis, Md.: Naval Institute Press, 1998.

———. *Navies and the American Revolution.* Annapolis, Md.: Naval Institute Press, 1996.

———. *Nelson Against Napoleon*. Annapolis, Md: Naval Institute Press, 1997.

Gates, David. *The Spanish Ulcer: A History of the Peninsular War*. New York: W. W. Norton, 1986.

Gilbert, Arthur N. "Buggery and the British Navy, 1700–1861." *Journal of Social History*, Fall 1976.

Gipson, Lawrence H. *The Coming of the American Revolution*. New York: Harper & Brothers, 1954.

Goldsborough, Charles W. *The American Naval Chronicle*. Washington, D.C.: James Wilson, 1824.

Graham, Gerald S. *The Empire of the Atlantic*. Toronto: University of Toronto Press, 1966.

———. *The Royal Navy in the War of American Independence*. London: H. M. Stationery Office, 1976.

Graves, Rodney. "When Courage Was Not Enough." *Naval History* (Spring 1989).

Grenfell, Russell. *Nelson the Sailor*. New York: Macmillan, 1950.

Gruber, Ira D. *The Howe Brothers and the American Revolution*. New York: Athenaeum, 1972.

Guttridge, Leonard F., and Jay D. Smith. *The Commodores*. New York: Harper & Row, 1969.

Hagan, Kenneth J. *This People's Navy: The Making of American Sea Power*. New York: Free Press, 1991.

Harbron, John. *Trafalgar and the Spanish Navy*. Annapolis, Md.: Naval Institute Press, 1988.

Henderson, James. *The Frigates*. New York: Dodd, Mead, 1971.

———. *Sloops and Brigs*. Annapolis, Md.: Naval Institute Press, 1972.

Henrich, Joseph G. "The Triumph of Ideology: The Jeffersonians and the Navy 1779–1807." Ph.D. diss., Duke University, 1971.

Herold, J. Christopher. *Bonaparte in Egypt*. New York: Harper & Row, 1962.

Hickey, Donald R. *The War of 1812*. Urbana, Ill.: University of Illinois Press, 1989.

Hood, Dorothy. *The Admirals Hood*. London: Hutchison, 1942.

Horne, Alistair. *How Far from Austerlitz?* New York: St. Martin's Press, 1996.

Howarth, David. *Trafalgar: The Nelson Touch*. New York: Athenaeum, 1969.

———. *Waterloo: Day of Battle*. New York: Athenaeum, 1968.

Hutchinson, J. R. *The Press-Gang Afloat and Ashore*. London: E. Nash, 1913.

James, C. L. R. *Black Jacobins*. New York: Vintage, 1963.

James, William. *The Naval History of Great Britain*, 6 vols. London: Macmillan, 1902.

James, M. William. *The British Navy in Adversity*. New York: Longmans, 1926.

———. *Old Oak: John Jervis, Earl St. Vincent*. London: Longmans, 1950.

Jenkins, H. J. K. "'The Colonial Robespierre': Victor Hugues on Guadeloupe, 1794–1798." *History Today* (November 1977).

Jenkins, John. *The Naval Achievements of Great Britain: From the Year 1793 to 1817*. London: Sim Comfort Associates, 1998. Facsimile of the 1817 edition.

Johnson, R. F. *The Royal George*. London: Charles Knight, 1971.

Jones, Robert F. "The Naval Thought and Policy of Benjamin Stoddert." *American Neptune* (January 1964).

Jordan, Gerald. "Nelson at the Nile." *Naval History* (December 1997).

Keegan, John. *The Price of Admiralty.* New York: Viking, 1989.

Kemp, Peter. *The British Sailor.* London: Dent, 1970.

———. *Prize Money.* Aldershot, Eng.: Gale & Polden, 1946.

Kennedy, Ludovic. *Nelson's Band of Brothers.* London: Oldham Press, 1951.

Kennedy, Paul M. *The Rise and Fall of British Naval Mastery.* London: Macmillan, 1976.

Kilby, John. "Kilby's Narrative as Seaman on the *Bonhomme Richard.*" Edited by Dunard T. Stokes. *Maryland Historical Magazine* (Spring 1972).

King, Dean, et al. *A Sea of Words.* New York: Henry Holt, 1995.

Knox, Dudley W. *A History of the United States Navy.* New York: G. P. Putnam's Sons, 1948.

Langley, Harold D. *A History of Medicine in the Early U.S. Navy.* Baltimore, Md.: Johns Hopkins University Press, 1995.

———. *Social Reform in the United States Navy, 1798–1862.* Urbana: University of Illinois Press, 1967.

Larrabee, Harold A. *Decision at the Chesapeake.* New York: Potter, 1964.

Lavery, Brian. *Building the Wooden Walls.* Annapolis, Md.: Naval Institute Press, 1991.

———. *Nelson and the Nile.* Annapolis, Md.: Naval Institute Press, 1998.

———. *Nelson's Navy: The Ships, Men, and Organization 1793–1815.* Annapolis, Md.: Naval Institute Press, 1989.

———. *The 74-Gun Ship of the Line,* vol. I. London: Conway Maritime Press, 1983; vol. II. Annapolis, Md.: Naval Institute Press, 1986.

Leech, Samuel. *Thirty Years from Home.* Boston: Charles Tappan, 1844.

Legg, Stuart. *Trafalgar: An Eye-Witness Account of a Great Battle.* New York: John Day, 1966.

Lemisch, Jesse. *Jack Tar vs. John Bull: The Role of New York's Seamen in Precipitating the American Revolution.* New York: Garland, 1997.

Lewis, Michael A. *England's Sea-Officers: The Story of the Naval Profession.* London: Allen & Unwin, 1939.

———. *The Navy of Britain.* London: Allen & Unwin, 1948.

———. *A Social History of the Navy, 1793–1815.* London: Allen & Unwin, 1960.

Lloyd, Christopher. *The British Seaman.* London: Collins, 1968.

———. *Captain Marryat and the Old Navy.* London: Longman's, 1939.

———. *Lord Cochrane.* New York: Owl, 1998.

———. *St. Vincent & Camperdown.* London: Batsford, 1963.

Lloyd, Christopher, and Jack S. Coulter. *Medicine and the Navy,* vol. III. Edinburgh: Livingstone, 1961.

Long, David F. *Nothing Too Daring: A Biography of Commodore David Porter.* Annapolis, Md.: Naval Institute Press, 1970.

Longridge, C. Nepean. *The Anatomy of Nelson's Ships.* Watford, Eng.: Model & Allied Publications, 1977.

Lord, Walter. *The Dawn's Early Light.* New York: W. W. Norton, 1972.

Lyon, David. *Sea Battles in Close-Up: The Age of Nelson.* Annapolis, Md.: Naval Institute Press, 1996.

Mackesy, Piers. *The War for America.* Cambridge, Mass.: Harvard University Press, 1965.

———. *The War in the Mediterranean.* London: Longmans, 1957.

Maclay, Edward S. *A History of American Privateers.* New York: Appleton, 1899.

Mahan, Alfred Thayer. *The Influence of Sea Power on the French Revolution and Empire,* 2 vols. Boston: Little, Brown, 1892.

———. *The Influence of Sea Power on History, 1660–1783.* Boston: Little, Brown, 1890.

———. *Major Operations of the Navies in the American War of Independence.* Boston: Little, Brown, 1913.

———. *Sea Power in Its Relation to the War of 1812,* 2 vols. Boston: Little, Brown, 1905.

McCusker, John J. *Alfred: The First Continental Flagship.* Washington, D.C.: Smithsonian Institution Press, 1973.

McKee, Christopher. *Edward Preble: A Naval Biography.* Annapolis, Md.: Naval Institute Press, 1972.

———. *A Gentlemanly and Honorable Profession: The Creation of the U.S. Naval Officer Corps.* Annapolis, Md.: Naval Institute Press, 1991.

Maine, René. *Trafalgar.* New York: Charles Scribner's Sons, 1957.

Mainwaring, G. E.. and Bonamy Dobre. *The Floating Republic.* New York: Harcourt, Brace, 1935.

Marcus, G. J. *The Age of Nelson.* New York: Viking, 1971.

———. *The Formative Centuries.* Boston: Atlantic, Little, Brown, 1961.

———. *Heart of Oak.* London: Oxford University Press, 1975.

Martin, Tyrone. "A Loved and Respected Machine." *Naval History* (August 1997).

Masefield, John. *Sea Life in Nelson's Time.* New York: Macmillan, 1937.

Melville, Herman. *Billy Budd, Sailor.* Baltimore, Md.: Penguin, 1967.

Meyers, Frank C. III. "Congress and the Navy: The Establishment and Administration of the American Revolutionary Navy by the Continental Congress." Ph.D. diss., University of North Carolina, 1972.

Miller, Nathan. *Sea of Glory: A Naval History of the American Revolution.* Annapolis, Md.: Naval Institute Press, 1992. Reprint of 1974 edition with minor changes.

———. *The U.S. Navy: A History.* 3rd ed. Annapolis, Md.: Naval Institute Press, 1997.

———. *War at Sea: A Naval History of World War II.* New York: Charles Scribner's Sons, 1995.

Millet, Allen R. *Semper Fidelis: A History of the United States Marine Corps.* New York: Macmillan, 1980.

Morison, Samuel Eliot. *John Paul Jones: A Sailor's Biography.* Boston: Little, Brown, 1959.

Morriss, Roger. *The Royal Dockyards During the Revolutionary and Napoleonic Wars.* Bath, Eng.: Leicester University Press, 1983.

Muir, Rory. *Britain and the Defeat of Napoleon.* New Haven, Conn.: Yale University Press, 1996.

O'Connor, Richard G. *Origins of the American Navy.* Lanham, Md.: University Press of America, 1994.

Oman, Carola. *Nelson.* London: Reprint Society, 1950.

Padfield, Peter. *Broke of the Shannon.* London: Hodder & Stoughton, 1968.

Palmer, Alan. *Metternich: A Biography.* New York: Harper & Row, 1972.

———. *Napoleon in Russia: The 1812 Campaign.* New York: Simon & Schuster, 1967.

Palmer, Michael A. *Stoddert's War: Naval Operations During the Quasi-War with France.* Columbia: University of South Carolina Press, 1987.

Parkinson, C. Northcote. *Britannia Rules.* London: Weidenfeld & Nicolson, 1977.

———. *Edward Pellew, Viscount Exmouth.* London: Methuen, 1934.

———. *War in the Eastern Seas, 1793–1815.* London: Allen & Uwin, 1954.

Paullin, Charles O. *The Navy of the American Revolution.* Cleveland: Burroughs, 1906.

———. *Paullin's History of Naval Administration, 1775–1911.* Annapolis, Md.: Naval Institute Press, 1968.

Pengelly, C. A. *The First Bellerophon.* London: John Baker, 1966.

Pocock, Tom. *Horatio Nelson.* New York: Alfred A. Knopf, 1988.

———. *Nelson and His World.* New York: Viking, 1968.

———. *The Young Nelson in the Americas.* London: Collins, 1980.

Pope, Dudley. *The Black Ship.* London: Weidenfeld & Nicolson, 1963.

———. *Decision at Trafalgar.* Philadelphia: J. B. Lippincott, 1960.

———. *The Great Gamble.* New York: Simon & Schuster, 1972.

———. *Life in Nelson's Navy.* Annapolis, Md.: Naval Institute Press, 1981.

Potter, E. B., and Chester W. Nimitz. *Sea Power.* Englewood Cliffs, N.J.: Prentice-Hall, 1960.

Pratt, Fletcher. *Empire and the Sea.* New York: Henry Holt, 1946.

———. *Preble's Boys: Commodore Preble and the Birth of American Sea Power.* New York: William Sloan, 1950.

Preston, D. L. "Why The Royal Navy Lost the American Revolution." *Naval History* (January 1996).

Price, Anthony. *Eyes of the Fleet.* New York: W. W. Norton, 1990.

Rasor, Eugene L. "The Problem of Discipline in the Mid-19th-Century Royal Navy." Ph.D. diss., University of Virginia, 1972.

Rediker, Marcus. *Between the Devil and the Deep Blue Sea.* Cambridge, Eng.: Cambridge University Press, 1987.

Richmond, Herbert. *Statesmen and Sea Power.* Oxford, Eng.: Clarenden Press, 1947.

Robinson, William. *Jack Nastyface: Memoirs of a Seaman.* London: Wayland Publishers, 1973.

Rodger, N. A. M. *Articles of War.* London: Kenneth Mason, 1982.

———. *The Insatiable Earl: A Life of John Montagu, Fourth Earl of Sandwich.* New York: W. W. Norton, 1994.

————. *The Wooden World: An Anatomy of the Georgian Navy.* Annapolis. Md.: Naval Institute Press, 1986.

Roosevelt, Theodore. *The Naval History of the War of 1812.* Annapolis, Md.: Naval Institute Press, 1987.

Russell, Jack. *Nelson and the Hamiltons,* New York: Simon & Schuster, 1969.

Schom, Alan. *Trafalgar: Countdown to Battle.* New York: Athenaeum, 1990.

Smelser, Martin. *The Congress Founds the Navy.* Notre Dame, Ind.: University of Notre Dame Press, 1959.

Spinney, David. *Rodney.* Annapolis, Md.: Naval Institute Press, 1969.

Sprout, Harold and Margaret. *The Rise of American Naval Power, 1776–1918.* Princeton, N.J.: Princeton University Press, 1939.

Stark, Suzanne J. *Female Tars: Women Aboard Ship in the Age of Sail.* Annapolis, Md.: Naval Institute Press, 1996.

Symonds, Craig L. *Navalists and Antinavalists: The Naval Policy Debate in the United States, 1785–1827.* Newark: University of Delaware Press, 1980.

Syrett, David. *The Royal Navy in American Waters.* Aldershot, Eng.: Scolar Press, 1989.

————. *The Royal Navy in European Waters During the American Revolutionary War.* Columbia: University of South Carolina Press, 1998.

————. *Shipping and the American War, 1775–1783.* London: Athlone Press, 1970.

Terraine, John. *Trafalgar.* New York: Mason/Charter, 1976.

Thomas, Donald. *Cochrane: Britain's Last Sea-King.* New York: Viking, 1978.

Tilley, John A. *The British Navy and the American Revolution.* Columbia: University of South Carolina Press, 1987.

Tours, Hugh. *The Life and Letters of Emma Hamilton.* London: Victor Gollancz, 1963.

Tracy, Nicholas. *Navies, Deterrence, and American Independence.* Vancouver, B.C.: University of British Columbia Press, 1988.

————. *Nelson's Battles: The Art of Victory in the Age of Sail.* Annapolis, Md.: Naval Institute Press, 1996.

Tucker, Glenn. *Dawn Like Thunder: The Barbary Wars and the Birth of the U.S. Navy.* Indianapolis, Ind.: Bobbs-Merrill, 1963.

Tucker, Spencer, and Frank T. Reuter. "The *Chesapeake-Leopard* Affair." *Naval History* (April 1996).

Tunstall, Brian. *Naval Warfare in the Age of Sail.* Annapolis, Md.: Naval Institute Press, 1990.

Tute, Warren. *Cochrane.* London: Cassell, 1965.

Uden, Grant. *The Fighting Téméraire.* Oxford, Eng: Blackwell, 1961.

U.S. Department of the Navy, Naval History Division. *Maritime Dimensions of the American Revolution.* Washington, D.C.: Author, 1977.

Valle, James E. *Rocks & Shoals: Order and Discipline in the Old Navy, 1800–1861.* Annapolis, Md.: Naval Institute Press, 1980.

von Pivka, Otto. *Navies of the Napoleonic Era.* London: David & Charles, 1980.

Walder, David. *Nelson.* New York: Dial Press, 1978.

Warner, Oliver. *The Glorious First of June.* New York: Macmillan, 1961.

————. *Life and Letters of Vice-Admiral Lord Collingwood.* London: Oxford University Press, 1968.

————. *Nelson's Battles.* New York: Macmillan, 1965.

Watts, Anthony J. *The Royal Navy: An Illustrated History.* Annapolis, Md.: Naval Institute Press, 1994.

Weigley, Russell F. *The American Way of War.* New York: Macmillan, 1973.

Whipple, A. B. C. *"To the Shores of Tripoli": The Birth of the U.S. Navy and Marines.* New York: William Morrow, 1991.

Whitehorne, Joseph A. *The Battle for Baltimore: 1814.* Baltimore: Nautical & Aviation, 1997.

Willcox, William B. "Why Did the British Lose the American Revolution?" *Michigan Alumnus Quarterly Review* (August 1956).

Wood, Virginia Steel. *Live Oak: Southern Timber for Tall Ships.* Boston: Northeastern University Press, 1981.

Woodman, Richard. *The Victory of Seapower.* Annapolis, Md.: Naval Institute Press, 1998.

Index

Abercromby, Sir Ralph, 222–23
Adams, Henry, 349
Adams, John, 35, 182, 239, 240, 334
  and Continental Navy, 20, 21
  presidential defeat of, 193
  and Quasi-War with France, 186–87
Addington, Henry, 226, 237, 259, 269
Admiralty Board, 15, 69, 161, 216
Agammemnon (Nelson's ship), 142, 361
  at Battle of Copenhagen, 229–31
  at Battle of Santo Domingo, 309
  at Battle of Trafalgar, 290
  sunk off Punta del Este, 311
Alexander I, czar of Russia, 234, 342, 354
  meeting with Napoleon, 313
Alfred (frigate), 11, 12, 20, 21, 74
Alliance (frigate), 34
American War of Independence, 9, 11–35, 42–51
  attack on New York, 25–28
  battle off Newport, 58–59
  Continental Navy losses, 74–76
  Cornwallis surrender at Yorktown, 13, 81, 86, 87
  formation of Continental Navy, 18–19
  as maritime war, 13–15
  occupation of Philadelphia, 45–46
  peace negotiations and treaty, 89–90, 97
  raids on enemy commerce, 37, 42–44
  Royal Navy blockade, 17
  success of French-American land/sea operations, 81–86
  See also Franco-American alliance
Amiens, Treaty of (1802), 238, 246, 259, 261
Andrew Doria (brigantine), 12, 13, 20, 21, 46

Armed Neutrality (Baltic coaltion), 224, 227
  collapse of, 233
Arnold, Benedict, 23–24, 355
Austerlitz, Battle of, 309, 353
Austria, 220, 353

Bainbridge, William, 255, 335
  as captain of *Constitution*, 340–41
  as captain of *George Washington*, 239
  as captain of *Philadelphia*, 246, 341
Baltic coalition, 224, 227, 233
Baltic expedition, 314–15
Baltimore clipper design, 349
Barbary War, 242–47
  attack on Tripoli, 252–56
  casualities, 254
Barham, Lord. *See* Middleton, Sir Charles
Barney, Joshua, 354
Barron, James, 301–2
Barron, Samuel, 255
Barry, John, 186
Basque Roads, 359
  battle of, 321–23
"Battle of the Nations" (1813), 353
battles. *See key word*
Bay of Biscay, 312–13, 353
Belgium, 324–26
Berkeley, George Cranfield, 301
Biddle, Nicholas, 13, 21, 74–75
Billy Budd (Melville), 162
Bligh, William, 102, 168, 178
Bonaparte, Napoleon. *See* Napoleon
Bonhomme Richard (Jones' ship), 65–68, 242
Borodino, Battle of, 343
Boston (frigate), 34
Bounty mutiny, 102, 168
Brandywine, Battle of, 45

Brest, 270
 blockade of, 221–22, 235, 261, 266–67
 French fleet at, 307
Bristol (Parker's flagship), 25
Britain. *See* Great Britain
British East India Company, 9
British Navy. *See* Royal Navy
Broke, Philip Vere, 345
Broughton, Nicholson, 19
Brown, Adam and Noah, 351, 355
Brueys d'Aigallieri, François-Paul, 197
 and Battle of the Nile, 202–10
Bruix, Eustache, 215
Bucentaure (Villeneuve's flagship), 296
Buenos Aires surrender, 311
Bunker Hill, Battle of, 17, 22
Burgoyne, John, 31, 44, 46, 355
Burke, Edmund, 16
Byron, John, 49, 58, 69

Cabot (brigantine), 12, 20
Cabot, George, 187n
Calder, Sir Robert, 279
 and "Calder's Action," 280–81
Cape Trafalgar, 289
captains, ship, 6–7
Caribbean area. *See* West Indies
Carleton (schooner), 30
Carleton, Sir Guy, 29, 30
carronade, 89
casualties. *See individual battles*
Charleston, S.C.
 failed land-sea assault, 24–25
 siege and American loss of, 75–76
Chesapeake (frigate), 301, 329, 331
 taken by British, 345–46
Chesapeake Capes, Battle of the, 80–86, 93
Christian, Fletcher, 102
Churchill, Winston, 40, 319
Cintra, Convention of, 318, 323
Cleopatre (frigate), 99, 100, 149
Clinton, Sir Henry, 24, 48
Cochrane, Lord Thomas, 304–7, 323
 and Bay of Biscay patrol, 312–13
 created knight of the Bath, 322
 criticism of Admiralty, 319
 and Peninsula War, 319–21
Collier, Sir George, 75

Collingwood, Cuthbert Lord, 267, 277, 283–85
 at Battle of Trafalgar, 32, 289–99
 on Cochrane, 320–21
 created baron, 300
 death of, 310
 on Glorious First of June battle, 130
 at Lake Nicaragua, 88
 Mediterranean fleet command, 310
 in Spanish war, 157–58
Columbus (frigate), 12, 21, 33, 74
Combined Fleet (France and Spain), 273–87, 308
 at Battle of Trafalgar, 289–99
 and Nelson's strategy, 285–86
 surrender and annihilation of, 298–99
Confiance (ship), 356
Congress (galley), 30, 31
Constantinople, 311
Constellation (frigate), 184, 186, 345
Constitution (frigate), 246, 286
 in War of 1812, 336–38, 340–41, 357, 358
Continental Army, 11, 12
Continental Congress, 18, 20–21, 25
Continental Navy, 18
 elimination at Charleston, 75–76
 founding of, 20, 21
 shipboard life, 37–42
Continental System, 313, 316, 342
Conyngham, Gustavus, 43–44
Cook, James, 4, 15
Copenhagen, Battle of, 226–34, 311
 casualties, 231, 233–34
coppering, 61
Cornwallis, Earl, 76
 and Graves mission to rescue, 85
 surrender of, 81, 86, 87
Cornwallis, Sir William, 136–37, 275, 279, 323
 and blockade of Brest, 261, 266, 270
Correglia, Adelaide, 140
Corsica, 147
 British evacuation of, 147
 British retaking of, 139–41
 casualties in retaking of, 141
 siege of, 114–18
Craig, Sir James, 269, 274, 287, 310
Culloden, 156, 158, 200, 205
 mutiny on, 166

Dale, Richard, 242
Decatur, Stephen, 247, 302, 335, 357–58
  and attack on Tripoli, 253
  as captain of *United States*, 339
  and retaking and destroying of
    Philadelphia, 251–52, 355
Decatur, Stephen, Sr., 189
Declaration of Independence, 25, 27
Department of Navy, 187
  Stoddert as first secretary, 187–94,
    241
Douglas, Sir Charles, 89
Downie, George, 355–56
Droits de l'Homme, 150–52, 152
Duckworth, Sir John, 308, 311, 323
Duguay Trouin (later *Implacable*), 299
Dumanoir le Pelley, Pierre, 295, 298
Duncan, Adam Viscount, 168–69, 175,
  176, 180
Dundas, Henry, 105, 118, 276
Dunsmore, Lord, 21

Eaton, William, 256, 257
Egyptian campaign, 196–208, 219–20,
  222–24, 234–35
El Gamo (frigate), 305, 306
Elgin, Lord, 218
Elphinstone, Sir George Keith, 147
England. *See* Great Britain
Essex (frigate), 347–48
Estaing, Comte d,' 48, 57–59, 109

Falkland Islands, 1
Farragut, David Glasgow, 347
Ferdinand, king of the Two Sicilies,
  211–13
firepower, 4–5, 7
First Coalition, 106, 115, 134
Fly (schooner), 11, 12
Forester, C. S., xi, 320
Fort McHenry, 355
Fort Ticonderoga, 44
Foudroyant (Nelson's flagship), 217,
  218, 223
Fox, Charles James, 309, 310
France
  attack on Malta, 200
  challenge to British naval supremacy
    (1795), 137
  defeat by "Battle of Nations," 353–56

Egyptian campaign, 196–208,
  222–24, 234–35
  Mediterranean sea war, 143, 210
  naval defeat off Santo Domingo,
    308–9
  occupation of Rome by, 213
  Quasi-War with United States,
    186–87, 192, 243
  surrender of Egypt to Britain, 236
  territorial gains from Versailles
    treaty (1783), 97
  threatened invasion of England by,
    195–96, 300
  trade war with Britain, 301, 303, 313,
    331–32
  and U.S. grain convoy, 123–24
  war with Britain, 53, 134, 300
  war with Britain in Caribbean,
    57–58, 72–74, 90–95, 118–22
  See also French Navy; French Revo-
    lution; Grande Armée; Napoleon
Franco-American alliance, 51, 185
  abrogation of, 185, 193
  and failure at Newport, 51, 58–59
  Franklin's negotiations, 42
  and success in Chesapeake, 80–86
Franco-Spanish alliance, 59–60, 62, 88
  in Caribbean, 73–74
Franklin, Benjamin, 37, 42, 43, 65, 89–90
French Navy, 101, 108–9, 261
  attempted invasion of Ireland,
    147–53, 198
  deficiencies of, 262–63, 303, 333
  demoralization of, 136, 139, 307
  last major action in Napoleonic
    wars, 308–9
  rejuvenation of, 47–48, 148–49
  See also specific battles and ships
French Revolution, 100, 104, 105, 185

Gallatin, Albert, 240, 246, 333
Gambier, Sir James, 314–15, 321, 323
Genêt, Edmond, 185
George III, king of Great Britain, 72, 87,
  88, 268–69, 309
George Washington (frigate), 239
Germain, Lord George, 15, 23, 48–49, 87
Ghent, Treaty of, 356–57
Gibraltar, 71–72, 97
Glasgow (frigate), 13, 21

Glorious First of June, 129–37, 148, 180, 280, 360
causalties, 132, 133
Goldsborough, Charles W., 187–188
Grand Design (Bonaparte plan), 271, 275
Grande Armée, 263, 266, 281, 285
defeated in Russia, 300, 342–44, 345, 353
overextension of, 300
See also Napoleon
Grasse, Comte de, 78–87, 83–86, 90–96, 197
Graves, Samuel, 17–18
Graves, Thomas, 82, 83–86
Great Britain
attack on Belgium, 324–26
attack on French forces in Egypt, 222–24
crumbling of empire, 88
grief over Nelson's death, 299–300
regained naval supremacy, 137
trade war with France, 301, 303, 313, 331–32
war with France, 53, 100, 112, 261, 300
war with France in Caribbean, 57–58, 72–74, 90–95, 118–22
war with Holland, 78, 175–80
war with Spain, 1, 59, 146, 153–59, 270
See also American War of Independence; Royal Navy; War of 1812
Great Lakes, 350–53, 356
Grenville, Lord, 309
Guerrière (frigate), 329, 337–39
Guichin, Comte de, 72, 89

Hamilton, Lady Emma, 113–14, 146, 234, 282, 283
life with Nelson and Hamilton, 260
meeting with Lady Nelson, 225
and Nelson in Sicily, 211–19
on Nelson's death, 300
Nelson's failed pension attempt for, 282, 290, 300
pregnancy by Nelson, 218–19. See also Thompson, Horatia Nelson
rejoined by Nelson, 234
Hamilton, Paul, 335, 339

Hamilton, Sir William, 113–14, 200, 209, 211–19, 260
Hancock (frigate), 34
Hannah (schooner), 19
Hardy, Sir Charles, 61, 69
Hazard, John, 33
Hermione mutiny, 170–71
Hitler, Adolph, strategy compared with Napoleon's, 342–43, 353–54
Holker (brig), 35
Holland, England, 78, 134, 175–80
Hood, Sir Samuel, 77–81, 82
and Battle of the Saintes, 90–95
command of Mediterranean fleet, 109–18
as Nelson's mentor, 78
Hopkins, Esek, 11, 12, 13, 21, 33, 75
Hopkins, Stephen, 11
Hornet (sloop), 11, 12, 46
Hotham, Sir William, 139–41
Howe, Richard Lord, 97, 102
and American Revolution, 26, 27, 28, 45, 50
as commander of Channel fleet in French war, 109–10
and Glorious First of June, 123–37, 180
and mutinies, 162–63, 167
Howe, William, 26, 27, 28, 44–45
Hugues, Victor, 121–22, 188
Hull, Isaac, 336–38

Imperiuse (frigate), 319–20
impressment
of American sailors, 329–33, 357
press gang tactics, 82, 107–8, 135, 262
Indefatigable (Pellew's ship), 149–52
Inflexible (sloop), 30
Insurgente (frigate), 190–92
Ireland, 147–53, 198, 209, 215

Jackson, Andrew, 357
James, William, 341
Java (frigate), 340–41
Jay, John, 185–86
Jay's Treaty, 186
Jefferson, Thomas, 182, 185, 240, 303, 333
defeat of Adams for presidency, 193
trade embargo, 333

Jervis, Sir John, 180, 198, 234, 306, 310,
    313, 323
    and blockade at Cádiz, 171–72
    in Caribbean, 119–20
    commands, 143–44, 221
    created Earl St. Vincent, 159, 171
    death of, 310
    removed from command, 275–76
    and war with Spain, 153–59
Johnson, Samuel, 14
Jones, John Paul, 21, 22, 46, 242
    and Bonhomme Richard-Serapis battle,
        65–68
    career of, 63–68
Jones, William, 339
Josephine, 220n
Junot, Androche, 315, 317

Keith, Lord, 215, 216, 222–24, 261, 266,
    275, 360
Kempenfelt, Richard, 61, 89
Keppel, Augustus, 53, 56, 69
Key, Francis Scott, 355
Kléber, Jean-Baptiste, 219, 224

Lafayette, Marquis de, 74, 76, 81
Lake Champlain, 24, 355
Latouché-Tréville, Louis de, 268
Lawrence (brig), 351–52
Lawrence, James, 345, 352
Lee (schooner), 19
Leopard, 302, 329
Lewis, Michael A., 40
Little Lucy (schooner), 35
L'Orient (Brueys' flagship), 203, 205,
    207, 233
Louis XVIII, king of France, 354
Louisiana, 261, 263
Lowestoft (frigate), 35

Macdonough, Thomas, 355
Macedonian (frigate), 339–40, 345
Macomb, Alexander, 355
Madison, James, 333, 335, 354
Mahan, Alfred Thayer, 14, 241, 266, 331
Malta, 200–201, 209
Manley, John, 19, 34
Marengo, Battle of, 220, 221
Margaretta (schooner), 18
Marine Corps, U.S., founding of, 188

Marryat, Frederick, 319, 320, 321–22
Martin, Pierre, 139–42
Massena, André, 327
Melville, Herman, 162
Menou, Abdullah Jacques, 224
merchant marine, 182, 333, 350
Metternich, Prince, 123, 353, 359
Middleton, Sir Charles, 276, 279, 323
    created Lord Barham, 276
Montgomery, Richard, 23
Moore, Sir John, 223–24, 318–19
Morris, Richard V., 244–45
Moultrie, William, 25
Murat, Joachim, 343
mutinies, 161–72, 175

Nancy (ordnance brig), 19
Naples, 211–14
Napoleon, 100, 139, 359, 360
    on British sea supremacy, 362
    as Consul for Life, 219–20, 238
    coup against Directory, 219–20
    defeats (1813–1814), 353–54
    Egyptian campaign, 196–208, 219,
        234–35
    embargo on British trade, 303, 313–14
    as emperor, 268, 270
    exile at Elba, 354
    exile at St. Helena, 361
    failed attack on Acre, 214–15
    final defeat at Waterloo, 359–61
    first defeat, 208
    Grand Design, 271, 275
    invasion of Russia, 342–44, 345
    Malta campaign, 200–201, 209
    Marengo victory, 220, 221
    military commands, 145, 195, 196
    in negotiation with British, 237–38
    Peninsula War, 315–24, 326–28
    planned invasion of Britain, 259–72,
        279–81, 300, 303, 315
    at Toulon, 114, 115
    in Vienna, 324–25
    See also Grande Armée
Napoleonic wars. See France;
    Napoleon; specific battles, countries,
    and personalites
Nautilus (brig), 358
navies. See French Navy; Royal Navy;
    U.S. Navy

Navy Board, 8–9, 15
Nelson, Fanny Nisbet, 103, 113, 141,
    159, 300
Nelson, Horatia (daughter). *See*
    Thompson, Horatia Nelson
Nelson, Horatio, 35, 144, 281–82, 303,
    323
    affair with Hamilton. *See* Hamilton,
        Lady Emma
    and amputation of arm, 174–75
    in Baltic, 225–34
    at Battle of the Nile, 202–10
    and blockade at Cádiz, 171–72
    and blockade of Corsica, 115–18
    boyhood of, 1, 2, 103
    and Combined Fleet pursuit, 273–87
    death and funeral of, 298–300, 309
    on Decatur, 252
    defiance of British tactics code, 159,
        208, 275
    evacuation of Corsica, 147
    eye injury, 117
    on Hotham, 139, 141–42
    on Howe's victory, 134
    in Italy, 112–14, 210, 211
    marriage, 103, 225
    naval career, 1–9, 11, 35, 75, 88, 105
    retirement at Merton Place, 260
    return to active duty, 198
    return to Mediterranean, 261–62,
        267–68, 283–87
    tactics of, 141
    and Tenerife attack, 172–75
    titles, 210, 218, 234, 259
    at Trafalgar, 32, 98, 177, 289–99
    Trafalgar strategy, 294–95
    Trafalgar wounding, 297–98
    and war with Spain, 153–59
New Orleans, Battle of, 357
Newport, siege of, 51, 58–59
New York, British attack on, 25–28
Niagara (*brig*), 351–52
Nicholson, James, 75, 83
Nicholson, Samuel, 186
Nielly, Joseph Marie, 124
Nile, Battle of the, 202–10, 229, 360
Nonintercourse Act, 333
Nore mutiny, 167–70
North, Lord, 16, 26, 47, 87
Nymphe (frigate), 99, 100

O'Brian, Patrick, xi, 305
Orvilliers, Comte d,' 48, 56, 60–63

Paine, Thomas, 135
Pallas (frigate), 312
Parker, Richard, 168, 170
Parker, Sir Hyde, 225, 234
Parker, Sir Peter, 24
Patterson, Daniel T., 357
Paul, czar of Russia, 224, 233
Pearson, Richard, 65–68
Pellew, Sir Edward, 99–101, 263, 323,
    360
    and French invasion of Ireland, 149–52
    and raid on Dutch East Indies, 310
Peninsula War, 315–24, 326–28
Permanent Fighting Instructions (British
    code), 55, 56, 72
    Nelson defiance of, 159, 208, 275
Perry, Oliver Hazard, 350–53
Philadelphia (frigate), 242
    captured off Tripoli, 248, 249, 252,
        255, 341
    ransom of crew, 257
    retaken and destroyed by Decatur,
        251–52, 355
Philadelphia, British occupation, 45–46
Pinckney, Charles C., 187
piracy, 242
Pitt, William, 102, 112, 159, 224–25,
    268–70
    death of, 309
    and Ireland, 148
    reluctance to go to war, 104
    and Second Coalition, 210
Popham, Sir Home, 311
Porter, David, 347
Portugal, 315, 316
Preble, Edward, 245–57
President (frigate), 242, 329, 336, 357–58
press gangs. *See* impressment
Prevost, Sir George, 355, 356
privateering, 34–35, 43, 44, 259, 313
    American, 346, 348, 349
    French, 333
    as weapon of war, 350
Providence (sloop), 12, 21, 33, 75

Quasi-War (French-U.S.), 185–87, 192,
    243

Québec, siege of, 23

Raisonnable (man-of-war), 1–2, 5, 75
Reprisal (sloop-of-war), 37, 42
Rights of Man (Paine), 135
Rochambeau, Comte de, 74, 80
Rockingham, Marquis of, 89
Rodgers, John, 329–31, 335–37, 339
Rodgers, N. A. M., 14
Rodney, Sir George Bridges, 69–71, 72, 74
    in Caribbean, 76–81
    Nelson on, 98
    and Saintes battle, 89–95
Rose (frigate), 18
Rosily, François, 285, 286, 317
Royal Navy, 14, 16, 98, 101, 353
    achievements of, 15
    Admiralty Board, 15, 69, 161, 216
    attack on U.S. Navy, 301–2
    and Battle of the Nile, 202–10
    crew assignments, 6
    crew recruitment, 33–34, 55, 60, 107
    discipline, 3, 40, 40–41, 135, 143–44, 162, 221
    disrepair of, 49–50, 60
    mobilized for French war, 105–8
    Nelson's early experiences with, 1–9
    reduced under Addington, 259–60
    reopening of Mediterranean by, 159
    seamen's wages, 163–64
    shipboard conditions, 7–8, 37–42, 102, 165
    social structure, 4
    in South America, 311
    warship classification, 4
    See also specific battles and ships
Royal Sovereign (Collingwood's flagship), 289, 290, 361
Russia, 342–44, 345

Saintes, Battle of the, 90–95
    casualties, 96–97
St. George (Nelson's flagship), 225
St. Helena Island, 361
St. Vincent, Earl. *See* Jervis, Sir John
Saltonstall, Dudley, 21, 75
Sandwich, John Montagu, fourth earl of, 15–16, 43, 47, 49, 53, 69

Santa Cruz de Tenerife, attack on, 172–75
    casualities, 175, 199
Santo Domingo, Battle of, 308–9
Saratoga (corvette), 355–56
Saratoga, Battle of, 46
Saumarez, Sir James, 315
Savannah, siege of, 59
sea fighting, 53–55, 65–68
Second Coalition, collapse of, 219
Secret Expedition, 269–70, 274–77
Serapis (frigate), 65–68
Shannon (Broke's ship), 345
shipbuilding, 16, 31–33
    British corruption, 262, 276, 312
    coppering of bottoms, 71, 107
    design, 5, 8, 184, 349
    in Republican France, 136
    rigging, 5–6
    in United States, 183–84, 351
Sicily, 211–19, 310
Sick and Hurt Board, 15
smuggling, 314, 315, 333, 349
Social History of the Navy, 1793–1815, A (Lewis), 40
Soult, Nicholas Jean, 318
Spain
    French alliance, 59–60, 62, 73–74, 88
    and Versailles treaty provisions, 97
    war with England, 1, 59, 146, 153–59, 270
    war with France, 315–17, 324–28
Speedy (brig), 305, 306
Spencer, George Earl, 136, 162, 164, 198, 209, 219
Spithead mutiny, 161–67
Stewart, Charles, 358
Stoddert, Benjamin, 187–94, 241
Stuart, John, 310
Suckling, Maurice, 1–2, 8–9

Talavera, Battle of, 326
Talleyrand-Périgord, Charles Maurice de, 187, 354
Téméraine (ship), 362
Tenerife. *See* Santa Cruz de Tenerife
Third Coalition, 269, 309
Thompson, Horatia Nelson, 260, 262, 282, 283, 291, 300
Thunder (bomb ketch), 25
Tone, Wolfe, 148–50, 164, 175, 210

Toulon, siege of, 114–15
Toussaint L'Ouverture, 119, 193, 261
trade war, 301, 303, 313, 331–32
Trafalgar, Battle of, 4, 32, 98, 177, 272,
    289–99, 360
  casualties, 293, 294, 296
  Combined Fleet surrender at, 298–99
  fates of participant ships, 361–62
  Nelson's death at, 298–99
  Nelson's strategy, 294–95
treaties. See key word
Tripoli, 335, 352–57
Troubridge, Thomas, 156, 200, 205, 226,
    262
  at Tenerife, 173–74
Truxtun, Thomas, 186, 189–91, 242, 244
Turner, J. W., 362

United Irishmen, 148, 164, 209
United States, 97, 240, 243
  British impressment of sailors,
    329–33, 357
  Quasi-War with France, 186–87, 192,
    243
  and trade wars, 301, 303
  See also American War of Indepen-
    dence; privateering; U.S. Navy;
    War of 1812
United States (frigate), 186, 189, 339–40,
    345
U.S. Navy, 181–94, 238
  achievements of, 15, 358
  and Barbary war, 242–47, 252–57
  Decatur as youngest captain, 252
  expansion of, 339
  founding of, 20, 182–83, 187–88
  government expenditures on, 240
  and Great Lakes, 350–53
  and Jefferson presidency, 239–42
  seamen and wages, 188, 246
  War of 1812, heritage of, 358
  See also specific battles and ships

Valcour Island, Battle of, 30–31, 355
Vanguard (Nelson's flagship), 198, 211
Vergennes, Comte de, 42, 44, 46
Versailles, Treaty of (1783), 97
Victory (Nelson's flagship), 4, 5, 17, 273,
    283, 362

Victualing Board, 15
Vienna, Congress of 357 (1814), 359
Villaret-Joyeuse, Louis Thomas, 124,
    136, 148
  at Glorious First of June battle,
    129–34
Ville de Paris (flagship of Grasse), 78,
    83, 92
  captured at Battle of the Saintes, 96
Villeneuve, Pierre de, 271, 277, 285, 287
  at Battle of Trafalgar, 291–300
Vrijheid (Dutch flagship), 178

Wallace, James, 18
War at Sea: A Naval History of World
    War II (Miller), 28
War of 1812, 331–42, 345–58
  casualties, 338, 340, 341, 349, 356
Warren, Sir John Borlase, 335
Warrington, Lewis, 358
Washington, George, 11, 12, 87, 181,
    185
  on naval power, 13, 19, 22, 87
  warning of British attack on New
    York, 25–26
Wasp (schooner), 12, 13, 46
Waterloo, Battle of, 359–60
Wellesley, Arthur (Duke of
    Wellington), 323, 342, 345, 353, 356
  on control of Great Lakes, 356
  created viscount, 326
  on Nelson, 282–83
  and Peninsula War, 317–18, 326–28
  and Waterloo, 359–60
West Indies
  British-French war in, 57–58, 72–74,
    90–95, 118–22
  strategic significance of, 57
Whipple, Abraham, 18, 21
Wickes, Lambert, 37, 42, 43, 44
Winter, Jan Williem de, 175, 176
Wooden World, The (Rodgers), 14

XYZ affair, 187

Yarmouth mutiny, 167
Yorktown, Battle of, 13, 81, 86, 87